Societal Impact on Aging Series

Series Editor

K. Warner Schaie, PhD
Director, Gerontology Center
College of Health and Human Development
The Pennsylvania State University
University Park, PA

2003   **Impact of Technology on Successful Aging**
Neil Charness and K. Warner Schaie, Editors

2002   **Personal Control in Social and Life Course Contexts**
Steve H. Zarit, Leonard I. Pearlin, and K. Warner Schaie, Editors

2002   **Effective Health Behavior in Older Adults**
K. Warner Schaie, Howard Leventhal, and Sherry L. Willis, Editors

2000   **The Evolution of the Aging Self:**
The Societal Impact on the Aging Process
K. Warner Schaie and Jon Hendricks, Editors

2000   **Mobility and Transportation in the Elderly**
K. Warner Schaie and Martin Pietrucha, Editors

1998   **Impact of Work on Older Adults**
K. Warner Schaie and Carmi Schooler, Editors

1997   **Societal Mechanisms for Maintaining Competence**
in Old Age
Sherry L. Willis, K. Warner Schaie, and Mark Hayward, Editors

1996   **Older Adults' Decision-Making and the Law**
Michael Smyer, K. Warner Schaie, and Marshall Kapp, Editors

1995   **Adult Intergenerational Relations: Effects of Societal Change**
Vern L. Bengtson, K. Warner Schaie, and Linda K. Burton, Editors

1993   **Societal Impact on Aging: Historical Perspectives**
K. Warner Schaie and W. Andrew Achenbaum, Editors

Neil Charness, PhD, is a Professor in the Psychology Department at Florida State University and an Associate in the Pepper Institute on Aging and Public Policy at Florida State. He received his undergraduate honors BA degree at McGill University in 1965, and his MSc (1971) and PhD (1974) at Carnegie Mellon University. He was an Assistant Professor at Wilfrid Laurier University, Ontario, Canada, from 1974 to 1977, and then an Assistant, Associate, and Full Professor at the University of Waterloo, Ontario, Canada, from 1977 to 1994. He spent one sabbatical (1984–1985) at the Mental Performance and Aging lab at the VA Outpatient Clinic in Boston and another at the University of Victoria, British Columbia (1990–1991). He also spent a summer as a Visiting Scientist at the Max Planck Institute for Human Development and Education, Berlin (1993). His research interests concern aging and technology use, particularly the role of input devices and computer hardware and software interfaces, as well as age and expert performance across the life span. He is a Fellow of the American Psychological Association's Division 20, the American Psychological Society, the Canadian Psychological Association, and the Gerontological Society of America.

K. Warner Schaie, PhD, is the Evan Pugh Professor of Human Development and Psychology and director of the Gerontology Center at Pennsylvania State University. He also holds an appointment as Affiliate Professor of Psychiatry and Behavioral Science at the University of Washington. He has previously held professorial appointments at the University of Nebraska, West Virginia University, and the University of Southern California. Dr. Schaie received his BA from the University of California at Berkeley and his MS and PhD from the University of Washington, all in psychology. He also holds an honorary Dr. phil. degree from the Friedrich Schiller University of Jena, Germany and an honorary Doctor of Science degree from West Virginia University. He is author or editor of 35 books, including the textbook *Adult Development and Aging* (with S. L. Willis) and the *Handbook of the Psychology of Aging* (with J. E. Birren), both of which are now in their fifth edition. He has directed the Seattle Longitudinal Study of cognitive aging since 1956 and is the author of more than 250 journal articles and chapters on the psychology of aging. Dr. Schaie is the recipient of the Robert W. Kleemeier Award for Distinguished Research Contributions from the Gerontological Society of America, the Distinguished Scientific Contributions award from the American Psychological Association, and the Lifetime Research Career award from the Mensa Research Foundation.

Impact of Technology on Successful Aging

Neil Charness, PhD
K. Warner Schaie, PhD

Editors

 Springer Publishing Company

Springer Publishing Company, Inc.
536 Broadway
New York, NY 10012-3955

Acquisitions Editor: Helvi Gold
Production Editor: J. Hurkin-Torres
Cover design by Joanne Honigman

03 04 05 06 07 / 5 4 3 2 1

Library of Congress Cataloging-in-Publication Data

Impact of technology on successful aging / [editors] Neil Charness,
  K. Warner Schaie.
     p. cm. — (Societal impact on aging)
  Edited proceedings of a conference held at the Pennsylvania State
University, October 8–9, 2001.
  Includes bibliographical references and indexes.
  ISBN 0-8261-2403-8
  1. Aging—Social aspects—Congresses. 2. Aged–Social conditions—
Congresses. 3. Technology and the aged—Congresses. 4. Technological
innovations—Social aspects—Congresses. 5. Cognition in old age.
I. Charness, Neil. II. Schaie, K. Warner (Klaus Warner), 1928–
III. Series.

HQ1061.I39 2003
305.26—dc21

                 2003054207

Printed in the United States of America by Maple-Vail Book
Manufacturing Group.

Contents

Contributors

Chardie L. Baird
Florida State University
Pepper Institute on Aging and
    Public Policy
Tallahassee, FL

Sara Czaja, PhD
University of Miami School
    of Medicine
Department of Psychiatry and
    Behavioral Sciences
Miami, FL

Stephanie R. Dailey, MA
National Institute on Aging
Office of Communications
    and Public Liaison
Bethesda, MD

Arthur D. Fisk
Georgia Institute of Technology
School of Psychology
Atlanta, GA

James Fozard, PhD
Florida Gerontological Research
    and Training Services
Palm Harbor, FL

Laura N. Gitlin, PhD
Thomas Jefferson University
Jefferson College of Health
    Professions
Department of Occupational
    Therapy
Community and HomeCare
    Research Division
Philadelphia, PA

Sarah H. Gueldner, DSN, FAAN
The Decker School of Nursing
State University of New York
Binghamton, NY

Gloria M. Gutman, PhD
Simon Fraser University
Gerontology Center
Vancouver, Canada

Melissa Hardy, PhD
Florida State University
Pepper Institute on Aging and
    Public Policy
Tallahassee, FL

Donald W. Kline, PhD
The University of Calgary
Department of Psychology and
Department of Surgery
Calgary, Alberta
Canada

Chin Chin Lee
University of Miami School
  of Medicine
Department of Psychiatry and
  Behavioral Sciences
Miami, FL

Linda L. Liu
University of Michigan
Institute for Social Research
Ann Arbor, MI

Susan J. Loeb, PhD, RN
University of Delaware
School of Nursing
Newark, DE

William Mann, PhD
University of Florida
Occupational Therapy
Gainesville, FL

Heidrun Mollenkopf, Dr. phil.
The German Center for
  Research on Aging
University of Heidelberg
Heidelberg, Germany

Roger W. Morrell, PhD
Director of Research
GeroTech Corporation
Reston, VA

Daniel G. Morrow, PhD
University of Illinois at
  Urbana-Champaign
Aviation Human Factors Division
Savoy, IL

Denise C. Park, PhD
University of Michigan
Institute for Social Research
Ann Arbor, MI

Wendy Rogers, PhD
Georgia Institute of Technology
School of Psychology
Atlanta, GA

Gabriel K. Rousseau, PhD
Scientific Applications
  International Corporation
McLean, VA

Rick Scheidt, PhD
Kansas State University
Department of Human
  Development and Family
  Studies
Manhattan, KS

Frank Schieber, PhD
University of South Dakota
Department of Psychology
Vermillion, SD

John C. Thomas, PhD
Manager, Knowledge
  Socialization
IBM Research Hawthorne
Yorktown Heights, NY

Hans-Werner Wahl, Dr. phil.
The German Center for
  Research on Aging
University of Heidelberg
Heidelberg, Germany

Preface

This is the fifteenth volume in a series on the broad topic of "Societal Impact on Aging." The first five volumes of this series were published by Erlbaum Associates under the series title "Social Structure and Aging." The present volume is the tenth published under the Springer Publishing Company imprint. It is the edited proceedings of a conference held at Pennsylvania State University, October 8–9, 2001.

The series of Penn State Gerontology Center conferences originated from the deliberations of a subcommittee of the Committee on Life Course Perspectives of the Social Science Research Council chaired by Matilda White Riley in the early 1980s. That subcommittee was charged with developing an agenda and mechanisms that would serve to encourage communication between scientists who study societal structures that might affect the aging of individuals and those scientists who are concerned with the possible effects of contextual influences on individual aging. The committee proposed a series of conferences that would systematically explore the interfaces between social structures and behavior, and in particular, would identify mechanisms through which society influences adult development. When the second editor was named director of the Penn State Gerontology Center, he was able to implement this conference program as one of the center's major activities.

The previous fourteen volumes in this series have dealt with the societal impact on aging in psychological processes (Schaie & Schooler, 1989); age structuring in comparative perspective (Kertzer & Schaie, 1989); self-directedness and efficacy over the life span (Rodin, Schooler, & Schaie, 1990); aging, health behaviors, and health outcomes (Schaie, Blazer, & House, 1992); caregiving in families (Zarit, Pearlin, & Schaie, 1993); aging in historical perspective (Schaie & Achenbaum, 1993); adult intergenerational relations (Bengtson, Schaie, & Burton, 1995); older adults' decision making and the law (Smyer, Schaie, & Kapp, 1996); the impact of social structures on decision making in the elderly (Willis,

Schaie, & Hayward, 1997); the impact of the workplace on aging (Schaie & Schooler, 1998); mobility and transportation (Schaie & Pietrucha, 2000); the evolution of the aging self (Schaie & Hendricks, 2000); societal impact on health behavior (Schaie, Leventhal, & Willis, 2002); and mastery and control in the elderly (Zarit, Pearlin, & Schaie, 2002).

The strategy for each of these volumes has been to commission six reviews on three major topics by established subject matter specialists who have credibility in aging research. We then invited two formal discussants for each chapter—usually one drawn from the writer's discipline and one from a neighboring discipline. This format seems to provide a suitable antidote against the perpetuation of parochial orthodoxies as well as to make certain that questions are raised with respect to the validity of iconoclastic departures in new directions.

To focus each conference, the organizers chose three topics of broad interest to gerontologists. Social and behavioral scientists with a demonstrated track record were then selected and asked to interact with those interested in theory building within a multidisciplinary context.

The present volume focuses on the impact of technology on successful aging. There have been marked changes in technology over the adult life span of today's elderly that have many beneficial effects but also leave older cohorts at some disadvantage to the extent that their education and life experience provided inadequate preparation for the full utilization of modern technology. Changes with age in sensory capacities and cognitive abilities may also disadvantage the elderly in making full use of technological advances, or may even introduce new difficulties due to the shift from personally provided services to ever increasing use of automated, computerized information and service processes.

In this volume the reader will find a detailed examination of changes in technology that impact individuals as they age, with particular emphasis upon cultural contexts and person-environment fit from human factors, and psychological and sociological perspectives. We consider the role of macroinfluences upon shaping technological changes in industrialized societies that affect successful aging in terms of quality of life. For our purposes such quality is measured by the availability and access to resources of importance to independent functioning of the elderly. This includes a major focus on changing technology in the fields of communication, transportation, and housing.

The volume begins by reviewing the human factor issues that must be considered when assessing the impact of technology on an aging population. The first chapter in this section reviews age changes in sensory capacities and other physiological factors that may either be ameliorated by suitable advances in technology or may actually disadvantage the older user. The second chapter elaborates on the cognitive, motivational, and other psychological factors that must be considered in understanding the impact of technology changes.

The second topic in this volume is concerned with communication technology and other assistive devices that might compensate for the sensory and cognitive losses associated with normal aging. Probably the greatest impact of technology upon the elderly has been the increasing emphasis on computers and computer technology in providing information and access to a variety of services. This process has, however, diminished opportunities for social interaction with service providers, even as the cheaper access to telecommunication services and the Internet has expanded virtual contacts with family and specialized interest groups. Internet shopping may also reduce transportation needs even though opportunities for fraud may increase. The first chapter in this section focuses therefore on the impact of computers and the Internet on the elderly, while the second chapter addresses the use of assistive devices in rehabilitating and supporting the needs of physically disabled and cognitively impaired older persons.

The third topic is concerned with technology and the quality of living environments as well as the provision of services for older persons living in the community. The first paper describes how changing technology may make it possible for our elders to extend their time of independent living in the community by reducing physical hazards and enhancing the supportive quality of their living environment. Hence, assisted living facilities may become more efficient, individualized, and homelike. Smart homes may become both easier and less expensive to maintain, thus facilitating aging in place. The final paper examines how technological change can enhance independent functioning through the provision of services for the elderly. Included here are discussions of medication management, transportation, shopping, and support for other activities of daily living.

We are grateful for the financial support of the conference that led to this volume, which was provided by conference grant AG 09787 from the National Institute on Aging, and by additional support from the Vice-president for Research and Dean of the Graduate School of the Pennsylvania State University. We are also grateful to Judy Hall and Lindsey Estright for handling the conference logistics, to Anna Shuey for coordinating the manuscript preparation, and to Pamela Davis for help in preparing the indexes.

K. WARNER SCHAIE

REFERENCES

Bengtson, V. L., Schaie, K. W., & Burton, L. (Eds.). (1995). *Adult intergenerational relations: Effects of societal changes.* New York: Springer.

Kertzer, D., & Schaie, K. W. (Eds.). (1989). *Age structuring in comparative perspective.* Hillsdale, NJ: Erlbaum.

Rodin, J., Schooler, C., & Schaie, K. W. (Eds.). (1990). *Self-directedness and efficacy: Causes and effects throughout the life course.* Hillsdale, NJ: Erlbaum.

Schaie, K. W., & Achenbaum, W. A. (Eds.). (1993). *Societal impact on aging: Historical perspectives.* New York: Springer.

Schaie, K. W., Blazer, D., & House, J. (Eds.). (1992). *Aging, health behaviors, and health outcomes.* Hillsdale, NJ: Erlbaum.

Schaie, K. W., & Hendricks, J. (Eds.). (2000). *The evolution of the aging self: The societal impact on the aging process.* New York: Springer.

Schaie, K. W., Leventhal, H., & Willis, S. L. (Eds.). (2002). *Effective health behavior in older adults.* New York: Springer.

Schaie, K. W., & Pietrucha, M. (Eds.). (2000). *Mobility and transportation in the elderly.* New York: Springer.

Schaie, K. W., & Schooler, C. E. (Eds.). (1989). *Social structure and aging: Psychological processes.* Hillsdale, NJ: Erlbaum.

Schaie, K. W., & Schooler, C. E. (Eds.). (1998). *Impact of work on older adults.* New York: Springer.

Smyer, M., Schaie, K. W., & Kapp, M. B (Eds.). (1996). *Older adults' decision-making and the law.* New York: Springer.

Willis, S. L., Schaie, K. W., & Hayward, M. (Eds.). (1997). *Societal mechanisms for maintaining competence in old age.* New York: Springer.

Zarit, S. H., Pearlin, L., & Schaie, K. W. (Eds.). (1993). *Social structure and caregiving: Family and cross-national perspectives.* Hillsdale, NJ: Erlbaum.

Zarit, S. H., Pearlin, L., & Schaie, K. W. (Eds.). (2002). *Personal control in social and life course contexts.* New York: Springer.

CHAPTER 1

Technology Design, Usability, and Aging: Human Factors Techniques and Considerations

Wendy A. Rogers and Arthur D. Fisk

Technology has the potential to change lives—generally for better, but sometimes for worse. Obviously, technological developments in the past century have made fundamental improvements in many areas of our lives: transportation, work, communication, health care, and leisure activities. However, with such improvements has come a reliance on technology, and technological failures can have dire consequences. In addition, rapid changes in technology may leave segments of the population ill prepared to interact with some of these complex systems due to inexperience, lack of training, or poor system design.

There are currently over 30 million Americans over the age of 65 (U.S. Government Census, 2000). Imagine the technology changes those individuals have observed in their lifetime. Since the 1930s, mass marketing of major technological developments include television, microwave ovens, videocassette recorders, compact disk players, electric cars, answering machines, cellular telephones, and, of course, desktop, laptop, and hand-held computers. For older adults to benefit from the advances that technology brings, but not be harmed by the potential for technological failures, we must ensure that systems are designed with the capabilities and limitations of the older user in mind, proper training is provided, and the needs of older users are considered in the development of future technologies. Our goal in this chapter is to illustrate these points by providing some case studies from our laboratory.

1

A HUMAN FACTORS APPROACH

The discipline of human factors examines "the role of humans in complex systems, the design of equipment and facilities for human use, and the development of environments for comfort and safety" (Salvendy, 1997, p. xvii). The application of human factors principles to technology development is essential to ensure that new systems are usable and useful for their intended user group.

Human factors researchers aim to match the demands of a system to the capabilities of the user, as illustrated in Figure 1.1. This figure represents the approach adopted by the Center for Research on Aging and Technology Enhancement (CREATE; Czaja, Sharit, Charness, Fisk, & Rogers, 2001). The system imposes certain demands on the user as a function of the characteristics of the hardware, software, and instructional support that is provided for it. The operator of the system has certain sensory/perceptual, cognitive, and psychomotor capabilities. The degree of fit between the demands of the system and the capabilities of the user will determine performance on the system as well as attitudes, acceptance, usage of the system, and self-efficacy beliefs about one's own capabilities to use that system. Understanding each of the components of this graph is the mission of CREATE.

In the present chapter, we focus primarily on issues related to the technological system side, rather than the user side. We are, however, concerned with older adults as the user population, which entails recognizing the characteristics of this population. Rather than review this information here, the reader is referred to other contributors to this volume (e.g., Schieber) as well as the following sources for detailed reviews of age-related changes in perceptual, cognitive, and psychomotor abilities: Craik and Salthouse (2000), Fisk and Rogers (1997), and Park and Schwarz (2000).

Before we delve into specifics, we must first address a general question: Will future cohorts of older adults more easily adapt to new technologies? In other words, will the unique needs of older adults diminish when current young adults age because they will have had so much experience with technologies? The answer to this question is twofold. First, new technologies will always be new—when today's 30-year-olds reach the age of 70 there will be technologies in the world that are now beyond our imagination. Design and usability of those systems will remain an important concern. Second, the age-related changes in perceptual, cognitive, and psychomotor abilities contribute

Human Factors Approach to Studying Problems of Aging and Technology

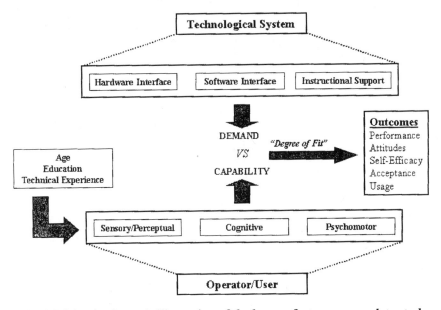

FIGURE 1.1 A schematic illustration of the human factors approach to studying aging and technology that is espoused by the Center for Research and Education on Aging and Technology Enhancement (**CREATE**).

to age-related differences in technology interactions. Such changes will likely continue to be evident in future cohorts, and ability-performance relationships will thus remain essential areas of scientific inquiry.

Understanding Interface Characteristics: Task-Analytic Approach

Every artifact with which we interact imposes some demands on us as users. The pen we are using may require very little pressure for the ink to flow or it may require more pressure than is comfortable over a long period of time. The computer software system we are using may be intuitive and seem to almost know what we wish to do, or be infuriatingly difficult to use. In a recent study of household products, Hancock, Fisk, and Rogers (2001) found that 72% of the adults they surveyed (aged 18 to 91) reported having usability problems with products such as cleaners, over-the-counter medications, toiletries, and health care products. The types of difficulties reported ranged from difficulty comprehending or seeing the text or symbols on the product label, to difficulty manipulating the product, or remembering how to use the product. Perhaps surprisingly, the patterns of difficulties reported differed little across age groups. The crux of the Hancock and colleagues survey was that even common, everyday products pose usability problems.

Understanding the source of usability problems is the first step toward resolving them. The human factors technique of task analysis, which is a science-based procedure to determine the elements of a task and how these elements are arranged in time and space (Luczak, 1997), affords a method to take that step. Task-analytic procedures may be used to understand aspects of functional limitations, why these limitations exist, and ways to address them. In fact, such detailed analyses date to early human factors studies conducted during the early 1900s by Frederick Taylor and Frank and Lillian Gilbreth (see Meister, 1999, for a historical review).

Applied to technological systems used by older adults, a task analysis can be *predictive* in helping to anticipate errors, as well as *prescriptive* in terms of motivating design and instructional development. To illustrate, Rogers, Mykityshyn, Campbell, and Fisk (2001) analyzed a blood glucose meter that had been advertised by the manufacturer as being as "easy to use as 1, 2, 3." They methodically defined the information required by a user to complete each task (i.e., task/knowledge requirements), the feedback provided by the system, and the potential problems that might arise if the task were not carried out properly. What they found was that this seemingly easy-to-use system required a total of 52 substeps. Moreover, the system provided minimal feedback to the user about the (in)correctness of an action. Thus, there were many opportunities for design-induced errors, and the consequences of such errors could be serious for an individual making dietary and medicinal decisions based on the reading obtained from the blood glucose meter.

Understanding Interface Characteristics:
User Observations

The difficulty users encounter and the errors they make when using a device should be examined through usability testing of the device. Usability testing involves systematic observations of people using products and evaluating the difficulties they encounter and the errors they make. Individuals who are representative of the ultimate user population should be recruited to test the range of things that a user might do with the device. The tasks presented during the usability testing should be representative of the range of tasks that would actually be performed on the system, and the evaluation should be conducted in a context that simulates the actual operator environment (see Nielsen, 1997, for an overview of usability testing). The performance metrics may be both quantitative (e.g., number of times particular errors are made) and qualitative (e.g., types of errors).

The observation of users interacting with an existing system provides valuable information about how to improve (i.e., redesign) that system and how to develop future systems. In addition, such observations may provide insights into the knowledge and techniques of experienced users; these methods may be incorporated into training programs and even designed into the system as user supports (Enkawa & Umemuro, 1997). This approach to "knowledge engineering" can be illustrated by a study we are conducting investigating the search strategies used by younger and older adults when searching for information on the World Wide Web (Rogers, Stronge, & Pak, 2001; Stronge, 2002).

We examined the search strategies of younger and older experienced adult Web users by observing them perform search tasks varying in complexity. The preliminary results suggest that both age groups are able to adjust their search strategy in accordance with the complexity of the task. In addition, the number of strategies used was fairly similar for both age groups. However, younger adults conducted advanced searches more often than older adults whereas older adults relied more on system tools such as an online encyclopedia. In addition, the older adults were less likely to understand and take advantage of Boolean operators (e.g., using "or" to broaden a search, "and" to constrain a search; see also Mead, Sit, Rogers, Rousseau, & Jamieson, 2000). These data have implications for training older adults to use the Web and recommendations for Web designers. For example, older adults seem to be more influenced by system tools, even when the tools are not optimal for the search task they are trying to complete. This tendency should be considered when designing the interface of search tools to ensure that they are presented in a manner so that users understand how they work and when they should be implemented. The finding that older adults were unfamiliar with Boolean searching techniques speaks directly to the development of instructional materials to illustrate these tools.

Understanding Interface Characteristics: Design Manipulations

Another technique for better understanding the demands imposed by a system interface is to directly compare performance for different interface designs. We used this approach to attempt to discover if the spatial demands of a computer system interface may differentially influence the performance of younger and older adults (Pak, 2001; Rogers, Stronge, & Pak, 2001). Younger and older participants were asked to perform search tasks on a simulated Web-searching system. They were provided with one of two navigational aids: (1) step-by-step: a verbally based aid that told participants which links to select, one at a time or (2) map: a tree structure that indicated graphically the links that the participants were to follow. The latter aid was presumed to be more spatially demanding and hence possibly more difficult to use by individuals with lower spatial abilities. For younger adults in this study, the specific navigation aid did influence performance. Participants were able to perform the task more quickly with the step-by-step aid. However, the ability to successfully use the map aid was correlated with spatial ability such that participants who scored higher on a test of basic spatial relations ability were better able to perform with the more spatially demanding map aid. For the older adults, the specific navigational aid did not differentially influence performance. However, spatial ability was predictive of performance such that performance on a measure of spatial visualization predicted performance on the search tasks, regardless of navigational aid. These data point to the potential complexity of understanding the interrelationships of the factors displayed in Figure 1.1. That is, a specific software interface characteristic can interact with the age and specific capabilities of a user. Consequently, we need to conduct more research to better understand these relationships and to translate that understanding into both design and training recommendations.

Instructional Support

Even the best-designed system will likely require some training for novice users (consider automobiles and personal computers). The aging process may also result in the need for age-specific instructional designs that enable older individuals to safely and effectively interact with systems. We advocate a systems approach to training older adults to use technologies (Rogers, Campbell, & Pak, 2001). This approach is standard practice in the field of human factors (see Helander, 1997). However, it is unfortunately not standard practice in environments wherein older adults are being trained. Typically, training is either not provided for common technologies or it is not empirically and theoretically based training.

Inherent in the systems approach is the consideration of the user within the context of the tasks that will be performed. Detailed analyses of the tasks and users must precede the development and selection of training programs. Too often trainers skip the analysis phases of the process and proceed directly to selection of training programs without a solid basis for their selection (see Salas, Cannon-Bowers, & Blickensderfer, 1997, for a review of this issue). In addition, it is not sufficient to design a training program for young adults and use it for older adults as well. Training programs may be differentially effective for different age groups (see Jamieson & Rogers, 2000; Mead & Fisk, 1998). Understanding of age-related changes in cognition is crucial for the development of age-appropriate training programs.

Older adults exhibit decline in abilities shown to be important for learning and skill acquisition. Such abilities include fluid intelligence, working memory, perceptual speed, and spatial ability (Hertzog, Cooper, & Fisk, 1996; Rogers, Fisk, & Hertzog, 1994). Older adults learn new skills; yet, proper instructional design that capitalizes on intact abilities and compensates for declining abilities holds much promise for proficient novice-level performance, substantive proficiency gains with training (Mead & Fisk, 1998; Rogers et al., 1994), and retention of proficient levels of system usage (Fisk, Cooper, Hertzog, & Anderson-Garlach, 1995; Fisk, Hertzog, Lee, Rogers, & Anderson-Garlach, 1994). Research has shown that proper training coupled with adequate system design can lead to dramatic increases in complex system usage accuracy for older adults (see Mead & Fisk, 1998; Rogers, Fisk, Mead, Walker, & Cabrera, 1996). Moreover, the combination of design and appropriate training seems to promote maintenance of trained performance levels over extended retention intervals.

Proper training has the potential to compensate for inadequate design. Recall the blood glucose meter discussed earlier that was analyzed by Rogers, Mykityshyn, Campbell, and Fisk (2001) and found to have a rather complex and potentially error-inducing design. They also analyzed the instructional support that accompanied the system and found that it was woefully inadequate for training either young adults or older adults to use the meter. Following a viewing of the manufacturer-provided video, young adults were only about 75% accurate in completing calibration tasks on the meter whereas older adults were even worse at approximately 25% accurate. However, an improved video training system that was based on a fundamental understanding of the task requirements, and an adherence to cognitive instructional principles, improved the performance of both younger and older adults to 90% accurate for the same subset of tasks (Mykityshyn, Fisk, & Rogers, 2002).

DEVELOPMENT OF FUTURE TECHNOLOGIES

The human factors approach to the development of technologies in general must be integrated into the design process for systems that are developed for all users, but perhaps especially for those to be used by older adults. The goal is to develop a cycle that increases motivation to use technologies: Initial Use → Success → More Use → More Success (King, 1999). To accomplish this goal, the initial use must lead to initial success. An approach to design based on user needs assessment and a commitment to training users to effectively interact with systems will result in older users willing to embrace and use the systems developed to meet their needs.

Designers must move away from the idea of technological determinism (that technology itself should be the impetus for change) and move toward the viewpoint of the social construction of technology (that technology instead should be influenced by societal norms and needs) (E. Rogers, 1995).

Needs analysis research must be conducted both to refine our understanding of the needs of users and to identify potential solutions. "Needs assessment and requirements analysis are the most important activities for initiating system improvement because, done well, they are the foundation upon which all other activities build" (Beith, 2001, p. 14). We should capitalize on well-developed human factors techniques such as task analysis, surveys, interviews, focus groups, and systematic observation in our needs analysis studies. The major goals of needs analysis research are to develop training protocols, interface design solutions, general system design improvements, and directions for technology development, *based on the needs and requirements of the target user population.*

We will illustrate the potential for needs analysis research with two examples from our laboratory that used focus group techniques. In the first instance, our goal was to understand better the difficulties that older adults encountered in their daily activities (Rogers, Meyer, Walker, & Fisk, 1998). Individuals aged 65 to 80 were interviewed in group settings and asked to discuss general difficulties they encountered in various categories of activities such as transportation, entertainment, home maintenance, cooking/eating, and use of new technologies. The qualitative data obtained from these interviews were coded to represent the types of difficulties encountered by older adults, what activity was involved, the source of the problem, and the response of the individual to dealing with the problem. We discovered that older adults engage in a variety of activities that include activities of daily living (ADLs such as bathing) and instrumental activities of daily living (IADLs such as food preparation) (Lawton, 1990). However, the older adults reported numerous activities that were not captured by the categories of ADLs and IADLs. We thus identified another activity category that we labeled enhanced activities of daily living (EADLs). These were the higher-level activities older adults engaged in involving adaptation, flexibility, and new learning to adapt to changing environments. Many of the EADLs revolved around technology use, either by necessity or by choice. That is, libraries no longer have card catalogs so users are forced to use the computerized search tools. At the same time, contrary to stereotypical views, many older adults sought out new technologies to learn, such as computers and fax machines. A clear theme in the Rogers and colleagues data was the desire of older adults that training be provided to assist them in learning to use novel systems.

In sum, the Rogers and colleagues (1998) focus group data provide direction for designers. These data illustrate where older adults encounter difficulties and what the difficulties are—clearly areas for designers to target for improved designs. In addition, understanding how older adults respond to problems and limitations may provide ideas for the development of augmenting or assistive technologies to support performance. Rogers and colleagues estimated that over 50% of the difficulties reported by their older participants had the potential to be remedied through human factors efforts in redesign, improved training, or a combination of redesign and training.

A focus group approach may also be informative for delving into a particular task domain in more depth. To understand the needs, preferences, and concerns of older adults in communication (with family, friends, health care providers, etc.), Melenhorst, Rogers, and Caylor (2001) conducted a series of focus groups wherein the entire discussion was about communication. Participants were given scenarios such as "You have good news that you wish to share with a large number of people" or "You wish to schedule an appointment with your dentist." They were then asked to discuss how they would most prefer to communicate in this situation, what the pros and cons were of that communication method, and how might such communication be improved. Preliminary analyses of the data centered on the communication methods that the older adults preferred and their reasons for preferring such methods. Comparisons were also made between individuals who used email and those who did not. The results suggested that people make their decisions about communication methods based on the benefits of that method, rather than on the costs or disadvantages of another method. For example, a preference for email might be due to the ability to bridge long distances, the flexibility, and the nonintrusiveness of the method. Even the non-email users did not focus so much on the costs of email (e.g., time to learn) but instead seemed not to realize the potential benefits of the medium for their communication needs. Melenhorst and colleagues concluded that one reason older adults may choose not to adopt a new technology such as email to meet their communication needs is a lack of perceived benefit. It is thus incumbent on technology designers to better understand the communication needs of older adults and develop systems that will provide benefits for them, and that the benefits be clearly conveyed to the user population.

These two focus group examples are intended to illustrate just one method for understanding the technology needs of older adults. The needs and preferences of older adults may or may not be the same as younger adults: researchers must answer this question. Most important, however, is to recognize that older adults must be actively engaged in the process of development of future technologies.

Interviewing users to gauge their preferences is a good starting point for any design, but designers must be aware of the fact that what users say they want is not necessarily what will enable them to best use the system. Reported user preferences should always be empirically tested by observing the performance of users (Ellis & Kurniawan, 2000). Formative evaluation (during the design phase) and summative evaluation (evaluation of prototypes) are both critically important for ensuring that the final product is usable and useful for its intended user population (Landauer, 1997).

The basic guidelines for designing usable systems are early and continual focus on users, empirical measurement and user testing, iterative design, and integrated design that incorporates all aspects of usability (Gould, Boies, & Ukelson, 1997). The older adult user population has unique needs, capabilities, and limitations that must be considered throughout the design process.

SUPPORTING FUNCTIONAL INDEPENDENCE

We conclude by providing an example of future technology development that has the potential to substantially benefit the lives of older adults: namely, a home that has built-in computer technology designed to support the functional independence of older adults. What could such an "aware" home do? It might recognize a crisis such as an accident, or a fire, or a potential crisis such as a pan left on the stove too long. It might provide supports for everyday cognition such as medication monitoring or meal preparation. It might provide clinicians with information about daily and long-term trends that presage illness or indicate rehabilitation improvements. It might even support improved communication with family and friends.

Efforts to develop such computer technologies are currently under-way. The potential is great, as is the need for thorough research to understand how best to harness the power of computer technology to truly support the needs of older individuals in their homes (Mynatt & Rogers, 2002). At Georgia Tech, for example, there is a house on campus that is referred to as the Aware Home. This house is built with all the functional and design requirements of a normal home, as well as facilities for instrumenting every room with sensors and displays to support ubiquitous interactions between the residents and the house. As part of a multidisciplinary group of researchers, we are installing a wide range of sensing equipment (cameras, microphones, infrared, radio frequency, sonar, tactile), including general metering on utilities, as well as specific instrumentation on appliances. The goal is to auto-matically and unobtrusively measure activities of the residents and pro-vide support for their daily needs and activities. Of critical importance is understanding how to accomplish this goal without intruding on the privacy of the individual.

Technology designs should be adaptable to the individual needs of the user. It is a well-known fact that older adults vary tremendously in terms of their sensory, motor, and cognitive capabilities. As such, for homes to support the needs of users, the technology within the home will have to be able to adapt to users' needs. In addition, interactive interfaces should be developed that provide information to the users and not merely respond to commands. Current technological sophis-tication can provide the opportunity to "construct technology that can augment greatly the adaptivity and functionality of the older adult user" (National Research Council, 2000, p. 166). Success in the devel-opment of adaptive and interactive interfaces is going to depend on a solid understanding of the underlying behavior of an individual with-in the context of that behavior. The human factors approach illustrat-ed in Figure 1.1 will have to be applied to the systems developed in the aware home if the computing technology in that home is to be useful to and usable by the older inhabitants of the home.

ACKNOWLEDGMENTS

The authors were supported in part by grants from the National Institutes of Health (National Institute on Aging): Grant No. PO1

AG17211-01 under the auspices of the Center for Research and Education on Aging and Technology Enhancement (CREATE) and Grant No. R01 AG18177.

Support for the Aware Home is provided in part by the National Science Foundation (ITR grant #0121661) and the Aware Home Research Initiative (http://www.cc.gatech.edu/fce/ahri/).

REFERENCES

Beith, B. H. (2001). Needs and requirements in health care for the older adult: Challenges and opportunities for the new millennium. In W. A. Rogers & A. D. Fisk (Eds.), *Human factors interventions for the health care of older adults* (pp. 13–30). Mahwah, NJ: Erlbaum.

Craik, F. I. M., & Salthouse, T. A. (2000). *The handbook of aging and cognition* (2nd ed.). Mahwah, NJ: Erlbaum.

Czaja, S. J., Sharit, J., Charness, N., Fisk, A. D., & Rogers, W. A. (2001). The Center for Research and Education on Aging and Technology Enhancement (CREATE): A program to enhance technology for older adults. *Gerontechnology, 1,* 50–59.

Ellis, R. D., & Kurniawan, S. H. (2000). Increasing the usability of online information for older adults: A case study in participatory design. *International Journal of Human-Computer Interaction, 12*(2), 263–276.

Enkawa, T., & Umemuro, H. (1997). Transferring experts' jobs to novices and computers by information sharing in office work. In M. J. Smith, G. Salvendy, & T. F. Koubek (Eds.), *Design of computing systems: Social and ergonomic considerations* (Proceedings of the 7th International Conference on Human-Computer Interaction, 21B, 291–294). Amsterdam: Elsevier.

Fisk, A. D., Cooper, B. P., Hertzog, C., & Anderson-Garlach, M. M. (1995). Age-related retention of skilled memory search: Examination of associative learning, interference, and task-specific skills. *Journal of Gerontology: Psychological Sciences, 50B,* P150–P161.

Fisk, A. D., Hertzog, C., Lee, M. D., Rogers, W. A., & Anderson-Garlach, M. M. (1994). Long-term retention of skilled visual search: Do young adults retain more than old adults? *Psychology and Aging, 9,* 206–215.

Fisk, A. D., & Rogers, W. A. (1997). *Handbook of human factors and the older adult.* San Diego, CA: Academic Press.

Gould, J. D., Boies, S. J., & Ukelson, J. (1997). How to design usable systems. In M. G. Helander, T. K. Landauer, & P. V Prabhu (Eds.), *Handbook of human computer interaction* (2nd ed., pp. 231–254). Amsterdam: North-Holland.

Hancock, H. E., Fisk, A. D., & Rogers, W. A. (2001). Everyday products: Easy to use . . . or not? *Ergonomics in Design, 9,* 12–18.

Helander, M. (1997). The human factors profession. In G. Salvendy (Ed.), *Handbook of human factors and ergonomics* (2nd ed., pp. 3–16). New York: Wiley.

Hertzog, C., Cooper, B. P., & Fisk, A. D. (1996). Aging and individual differences in the development of skilled memory search performance. *Psychology and Aging,* 11, 497–520.

Jamieson, B. A., & Rogers, W. A. (2000). Age-related effects of blocked and random practice schedules on learning a new technology. *Journals of Gerontology: Psychological Sciences, 55B,* P343–P353.

King, T. W. (1999). *Assistive technology: Essential human factors.* Boston, MA: Allyn & Bacon.

Landauer, T. K. (1997). Behavioral research methods in human-computer interaction. In M. G. Helander, T. K. Landauer, & P. V. Prabhu (Eds.), *Handbook of human computer interaction* (2nd ed., pp. 203–227). Amsterdam: North-Holland.

Lawton, M. P. (1990). Aging and performance on home tasks. *Human Factors, 32,* 527–536.

Luczak, H. (1997). Task analysis. In G. Salvendy (Ed.), *Handbook of human factors and ergonomics* (2nd ed., pp. 340–416). New York: Wiley.

Mead, S. E., & Fisk, A. D. (1998). Measuring skill acquisition and retention with an ATM simulator: The need for age-specific training. *Human Factors, 40,* 516–523.

Mead, S. E., Sit, R. A., Rogers, W. A., Rousseau, G. K., & Jamieson, B. A. (2000). Influences of general computer experience and age on library database search performance. *Behaviour and Information Technology, 19,* 107–123.

Meister, D. (1999). *The history of human factors and ergonomics.* Mahwah, NJ: Erlbaum.

Melenhorst, A. S., Rogers, W. A., & Caylor, E. C. (2001). The use of communication technologies by older adults: Exploring the benefits from the user's perspective. *Proceedings of the Human Factors and Ergonomics Society 46th Annual Meeting* (pp. 221–225). Santa Monica, CA: Human Factors and Ergonomics Society.

Mykityshyn, A., L., Fisk, A. D., & Rogers, W. A. (2002). Learning to use a home medical device: Mediating age-related differences with training. *Human Factors, 44,* 354–364.

Mynatt, E. D., & Rogers, W. A. (2002). Developing technology to support the functional independence of older adults. *Ageing International, 27,* 24–41.

National Research Council. (2000). *The aging mind: Opportunities in cognitive research.* Washington, DC: National Academy Press.

Nielsen, J. (1997). Usability testing. In G. Salvendy (Ed.), *Handbook of human factors and ergonomics* (2nd ed., pp. 1543–1568). New York: Wiley.

Pak, R. (2001). *A further examination of the influence of spatial abilities on computer task performance in younger and older adults.* Unpublished master's thesis, Georgia Institute of Technology, Atlanta, GA.

Park, D. C., & Schwarz, N. (2000). *Cognitive aging: A primer.* Philadelphia: Psychology Press.

Rogers, E. M. (1995). *Diffusion of innovations* (4th ed.). New York: Free Press.

Rogers, W. A., Campbell, R. H., & Pak, R. (2001). A systems approach for training older adults to use technology. In N. Charness, D. C. Park, & B. A.

Sabel (Eds.), *Communication, technology, and aging: Opportunities and challenges for the future* (pp. 187–208). New York: Springer.

Rogers, W. A., Fisk, A. D., & Hertzog, C. (1994). Do ability-performance relationships differentiate age and practice effects in visual search? *Journal of Experimental Psychology: Learning, Memory, and Cognition, 20,* 710–738.

Rogers, W. A., Fisk, A. D., Mead, S. E., Walker, N., & Cabrera, E. F. (1996). Training older adults to use automatic teller machines. *Human Factors, 38,* 425–433.

Rogers, W. A., Meyer, B., Walker, N., & Fisk, A. D. (1998). Functional limitations to daily living tasks in the aged: A focus group analysis. *Human Factors, 40,* 111–125.

Rogers, W. A., Mykityshyn, A. L., Campbell, R. H., & Fisk, A. D. (2001). Only 3 easy steps? User-centered analysis of a "simple" medical device. *Ergonomics in Design, 9,* 6–14.

Rogers, W. A., Stronge, A. J., & Pak, R. (2001). Enabling older adults to successfully use the World Wide Web. *International Journal of Experimental, Clinical, and Behavioural Gerontology, 47* (Suppl. 1), 216. Basel: Karger Medical and Scientific Publishers.

Salas, E., Cannon-Bowers, J., & Blickensderfer, E. L. (1997). Enhancing reciprocity between training theory and practice: Principles, guidelines, and specifications. In J. K. Ford, S. W. J. Kozlowski, K. Kraiger, E. Salas, & M. S. Teachout (Eds.), *Improving training effectiveness in work organizations* (pp. 291–322). Mahwah, NJ: Erlbaum.

Salvendy, G. (1997). *Handbook of human factors and ergonomics* (2nd ed.). New York: Wiley.

Stronge, A. J. (2002). *Age-related differences in strategies: Investigating problem solving in a complex real-world task.* Unpublished master's thesis, Georgia Institute of Technology. Atlanta, GA.

U.S. Government Census. (2000). Age and sex of the population aged 65 and over by citizenship status: March 2000. Online: http://www.census.gov/population/www/socdemo/age.html

Commentary

Access, Motivation, Ability, Design, and Training: Necessary Conditions for Older Adult Success with Technology

Neil Charness

T
he objective of this chapter, as one anonymous commentator once put it, is to place the work presented by Rogers and Fisk (this volume) into the broader context of my own research. In this case, I plan to depart a bit from that tradition to concentrate on enabling conditions for success with technology. I will describe the categories of access, motivation, ability, training and design.

Rogers and Fisk have provided an informative and expansive tour of technology design, usability, and aging from the perspective of the discipline of human factors. Their research represents cutting edge efforts to apply basic human factors principles for training and design to alleviate potential difficulties with technology arising from normative age differences in human abilities. Drawing on survey data from focus groups, Rogers and Fisk point out that everyday consumer products (OTC medications, cleaners, toiletries) pose somewhat greater difficulties for older than younger adults, though differences were not consistent and it is clear that younger adults report design flaws too. As one speaker at a recent conference put it so colorfully: "the world is not a well-designed place."

This characterization puts Darwin's evolutionary shoe on the other foot. The discipline of human factors is revolutionary by being anti-evolutionary. Rather than waiting for natural selection to adapt humans to their environmental surroundings by evolving appropriate genotypes and phenotypes, a strategy that has worked successfully over the eons, we humans would prefer to modify the environment to fit our current capabilities. To be fair, human factors practitioners also use the strategy of changing the human to fit the tool via training interventions.

I would also broaden the issue of "the world being poorly designed" to the question of "not well-designed for whom?" It is clear that the "whom" for the purpose of this volume is older adults, but as we well know, "older adults" turn out to be a pretty diverse group of individuals, even from the elementary but difficult to define perspective of the chronological age range for who is considered old.

Design decisions always involve trade-offs. The World Trade Center in New York City was apparently designed nearly 40 years ago so that its prominent towers could withstand the impact of an errant 727 jetliner. It actually stood up to a much larger impact. What was not envisioned well enough was the aftermath of an impact with a jetliner: namely, the ensuing fire that would weaken the steel cabling and result in the building's implosion (e.g., *New York Times,* 2001).

Exhortations to use "good, better, best" design (Fisher, 1993) beg the very difficult question of how to select appropriate criteria for what should be optimized. More to the point, except when supplied with artificial computational power and having the explicit goal of optimization, human problem solvers usually "satisfice" (Simon, 1981), that is, find "good enough" rather than optimal solutions to life's multifaceted problems. Design falls into the category of problem solving by satisficing.

When we discuss designing products for typical older adults, we also need to consider some of their living environments. In their wide-ranging review, Rogers and Fisk also emphasize this point when they mention the need to perform task analyses of how older adults use technology. Careful analysis of living environment constraints is an important theme in Schaie, Wahl, Mollenkopf, and Oswald (2003). Let me try to address this in a minimalist way with an example. If we are thinking of design or training for a 75-year-old male, the odds are 5:1 that he lives with someone, most likely his spouse. If we are thinking about design or training for a 75-year-old female, the odds are about even that she lives alone, as can be seen in Figure 1.2 from U.S. census data from 1998.

There is also a strong trend in the general population for an increase in one-person households, now at about 25% of all households (Simmons & O'Neill, 2001). Such findings speak eloquently to the issue of whether older adults will be able to use collaborative problem solving (see Gould & Dixon, 1993) or will be solo problem solvers when dealing with technology.

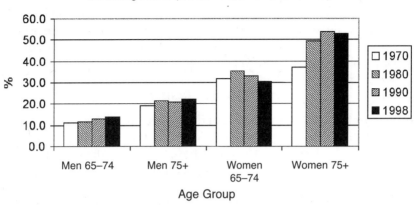

FIGURE 1.2 Percent of males and females living alone by age and year.

Data obtained from U.S. Census Bureau, Current Population Survey Reports, "Marital Status and Living Arrangements: March 1994" (P20-484) and March 1998 (Update) (P20-514).

Similarly, when we think of training and design, even for basic issues such as warning labels, we need to consider that one of the fastest growing segments in our society is the Latino/Hispanic community. Although they are younger on average than the majority white population, older Spanish-speaking adults may not speak or read English fluently. One of the "design wins" I noted many years ago on trips to Europe was putting instruction sets for ATMs in a number of languages using familiar symbols (for Europeans) such as the British flag for English, French flag for French, German flag for German, and so on. It is quite common to see ATMs in North America offering English and Spanish instruction sets in the southern U.S. or English and French in Canada. Technology can be harnessed to provide language-sensitive instructional support more easily now than ever before. There are even free web page translation tools to convert the predominantly English language Web to other languages, though the quality of translation is often not good enough for conveying other than the gist.

ENABLING CONDITIONS FOR TECHNOLOGY TO IMPROVE THE LIVES OF OLDER ADULTS

I am assuming that technology has the potential to improve the quality of life of older adults, something that is a basic tenet of the field of gerontechnology (Harrington & Harrington, 2000). What are the societal conditions and social structures that would enable technology to improve the quality of life of older adults and their families (the usual caregivers)? The enabling conditions that I would like to discuss seem to fall under the categories of access, motivation, ability, training, and design.

Access to Technology

Doing careful usability studies and designing and redesigning health information pages for the World Wide Web are not going to be helpful to older adults unless they also have access to those pages. The current picture, circa the year 2000, is not encouraging, as seen in Figure 1.3.

Fewer than 30% of households headed by people 65+ have a computer, and fewer than 15% of such households have Internet access. Put differently, 85% of those 65+ are not likely to be browsing the Web from their home. Given mobility limitations that are associated with increased age, it seems unreasonable to expect those without home access to trudge off to their local library to access the Web every time they want to look up information.

On the positive side, however, older adults are one of the fastest growing segments in the computer/Internet market, if only because other age groups are nearly saturated for access. Table 1.1 provides statistics from the Pew Foundation study of growth in access to the Internet (Rainie & Packel, 2001).

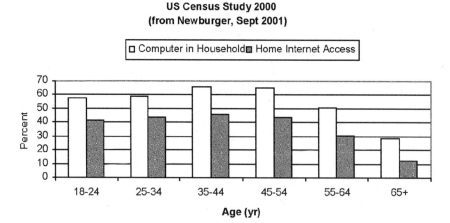

FIGURE 1.3   U.S. Bureau of Commerce data on percent of households in the year 2000 with a computer and with Internet access by age.

TABLE 1.1   Pew Foundation Statistics About Access to the Internet by Age Group and by Middle and End of the Year 2000

Age Group (yr)	Access to Internet May–June 2000 (%)	Access to Internet Nov.–Dec. 2000 (%)
18–29	61	75
30–49	57	65
50–64	41	51
65+	12	15

Produced from data in Rainie and Packel, 2001.

As can be seen, older adults 65+ show 25% growth from the first to the second half of 2000 and could easily keep up this rate for some years to come. The rest of the population will saturate out pretty quickly at this growth rate.

However, there are a number of reasons to be optimistic about improved access. First, prices for computer systems have declined steadily in the past few years, though cost of Internet access, particularly broadband access, has risen recently. One of the barriers to computer access is income, and lower prices make computers more affordable to lower income adults. There is a well-documented "digital divide" on income level (U.S. Department of Commerce, 1998). We need to keep in mind that older adult cohorts are highly variable in income and that low income is associated with non-use of computers and the Internet. Second, future cohorts of older adults (today's young adults) are already avid users and are likely to remain so. Third, modern operating systems for computers are finally becoming more reliable (less prone to system crashes). Also, graphic user interfaces are easier to learn to use than older command line interfaces (Charness et al., 2001). In summary, accessibility problems may be lessening as barriers to technology adoption by older adults.

Motivation to Use Technology

"You can lead a senior to technology, but you can't make her a user." This is a reminder that the older population is predominantly female, with nearly a 2:1 ratio of women to men by the time this population reaches age 80 (Smith & Spraggins, 2001).

A great deal of research and theorizing (e.g., Azjen & Fishbein, 1977) has shown the importance of attitudes in bridging the intention to overt behavior pathway. Further, large-scale belief structures, such as perceived self-efficacy (Bandura, 1982) may also mediate technology adoption. It was not that long ago when companies introduced email into their organizations. They often found that senior executives had their secretaries manage email and schedules for them. They were simply too time- and/or interest-constrained to learn to use computer technology.

A similar problem exists for today's retired older cohorts. They may not see sufficient utility for technology such as computers and the Internet. Most will admit to being curious about such technology but will not expend the resources (time, money) to acquire it or use it. Researchers have shown time-mediated selectivity for investment in social relationships (Carstensen, Isaacowitz, & Charles, 1999) with older adults more willing to expend resources to maintain and regulate old relationships and less willing to pursue new ones. Carstensen and colleagues also argue that motivation for knowledge acquisition may wane in older adults facing a constrained time-to-live horizon. If so, that might explain the low participation rates of older adults in computer ownership.

It is useful to raise the issue of *whether* older adults should be encouraged to use computer technology. Although the effects are weak, there is some evidence that increased Internet use is associated with decreases in socializing and well-being (Kraut, Patterson, Lundmark, Kiesler, Mukopadhyay, & Scherlis, 1998). It might be wise to assume that as intendedly rational decision makers, older adults have not yet found the benefits of such technology to outweigh the costs of acquiring and learning how to use it. There has been less of a problem with the adoption of microwave ovens, judging by the estimate of 90% penetration into U.S. households by 1995 (Cox & Alm, 1997). Australian estimates give 89% household penetration in 2001 (Australian Greenhouse Office, 2001). Statistics Canada (2003) shows 89% penetration by 1999, higher than that for washing machines or clothes dryers. Part of the difference may be in both the cost and the ease of use of these products. However, if older adults can get other family members (e.g., their children or grandchildren) to help out with technology, they will. Let me provide a personal anecdote:

> My 82-year-old mother-in-law, living alone in Pittsburgh, encountered a series of medical emergencies a year ago that had her bouncing back and forth between hospitals, skilled nursing care facilities, assisted living, and her home. When she was suddenly admitted to a new facility, phone contact was not immediately available, increasing the stress level for both her and my wife, who had not yet made the journey from Tallahassee to

Pittsburgh. My son, who lived in Pittsburgh, offered his grandmother his cell phone. The problem was that it was not intuitive to use. For one, it was very different than a normal phone wherein when you dial a legitimate number it immediately connects, compared to the extra step of hitting the send button after entering digits. The cell phone also needed to be activated when a call came in, unlike picking up a wired phone from the cradle. Finally, unlike a normal phone, it needed to be recharged frequently. Given that she was in serious pain, overmedicated, and suffering from normative age-related changes in cognition, vision, hearing, and psychomotor ability, such "just-in-time" learning did not take place very effectively. Nonetheless, there were differences in her success rate in sending and receiving with a more modern cell phone and an older one that her son had given her.

More recently, my mother-in-law was unable to visit her new great-grandchild (our grandson, living in Kitchener, Canada) so my son brought his notebook computer to her house and arranged a desktop videoconference session with his sister in Canada, though with the low bandwidth connection of a phone line, the quality of the image was probably not adequate for her to see much. When my mother-in-law visited her son at a much later date, she also got to see a CD with pictures of the great-grandchild that I had sent to relatives (but not to her because she didn't have a computer).

Making use of other people is a reasonable strategy for older adults who are not strongly enough motivated to acquire the tools and the skills to do things by themselves. Incidentally, using other people as support resources is a common strategy even in the workplace. When things are poorly designed, getting someone more knowledgeable to help you seems to be a fairly typical problem-solving strategy with balky technology.

Are older adults less favorably inclined toward technology? That seems to be a complicated question to answer. Overall attitudes may not differ much between young and old volunteer groups who come in for an experiment using computers, though specific dimensions may indeed differ and prior experience with computers is moderately ($r = .3$) positively associated with attitudes toward computers (Czaja & Sharit, 1998). Further, the type of interaction with computers during an experiment may change attitudes differentially, depending on the quality of the interaction. These findings are particularly salient for those who design technological systems. You may get only one chance to design well because a bad experience may change attitudes for the worse and alienate a potential consumer.

A problem with interpreting this literature is that most of the studies that measured attitudes toward computers used volunteers in laboratory experiments, and those fearful of using computers are unlikely to have volunteered to participate. There is clear evidence that older adults are less likely to use technology (Brickfield, 1984), though how much this trend is mediated by age-related income disparities and how much by age-related attitude differences is unknown.

The one piece of good news on attitudes is that they seem to be unrelated to success in using technology once people are induced to interact with computer systems. As the review by Kelley and Charness (1995) indicated, there is virtually no relation between attitudes and degree of success in training to use software. Again, it is worth remembering that these findings are for the most part restricted to volunteer populations.

Ability

"Honor thy user" is one of the tenets of human factors science. Within the traditional framework of studying individuals, we often have trouble addressing the question: Who is the user set for a product or environment? Human factors specialists may need to broaden their focus to sets of individuals in order to better approach the goal of generating "best designs." This entails considering individual difference variables, something that Rogers and Fisk (this volume) have done particularly well when they investigated the role of spatial ability in web search tasks.

The lay public often makes individual difference attributions with respect to technology use. For instance, a bank representative was reputed to have commented that "people who can't use an ATM are the same people who can't set their own alarm clocks."

Is it the case that those with ATM problems also have problems with other (simpler) technology? The answer is likely to be yes. Experience with technology can be a powerful individual difference predictor. In a study of word processing training and retraining in adulthood, my lab showed that one of the best predictors of performance during and after training was breadth of prior software experience (Charness et al., 2001; see Table 1.2). As a bivariate predictor of factor scores for performance accuracy and performance time it had a magnitude of $r = .55$, a value that rivaled even the strong negative relationship between chronological age and performance. (Caveat: this data included a set of novices with zero experience as well as those with varying amounts of experience, so the correlation is somewhat inflated.)

In more recent work in the CREATE project, we do not show significant correlations ($N = 72$) between computer experience and the time to do a simple computer menu item selection task with a lightpen or a

TABLE 1.2   Relationship Between Software Experience and Word Processing Performance

	Software Experience	Time Factor Score	Performance Factor Score
Software Experience	1.000		
Time Factor Score	−0.562	1.000	
Performance Factor Score	0.545	−0.778	1.000

Note: $N = 119$
Produced from data given in Charness, Kelley, Bosman, and Mottram, 2001.

mouse using preferred or non-preferred hands. Simple tasks might not make strong demands on cognitive abilities that wane normatively with age. One lesson that can be taken from these conflicting findings is that one way to succeed in design or training is to make tasks simpler, thereby eliminating the (current) age-related disadvantage of lack of familiarity with technology. As Rogers and Fisk showed with the redesigned instructional videotape for the glucose monitor, better instruction can work wonders.

Design

As mentioned earlier, a major tool of the human factors trade is redesign. When flaws are found in existing designs, they need to be corrected. A generally recognized but not well articulated tenet in the age and human factors field is that older adults will show you design flaws sooner than will younger adults, given that they have lessened capabilities (see above). This viewpoint is generally confirmed in the focus group usability percentages reported by Rogers and Fisk, with older adults generally showing the highest complaint levels, though there is often a lower complaint level for the old compared to the middle-aged. This decline in complaint may represent a cohort effect (stiff upper lip) or a case of survival of the fittest, given that similar trends have been observed for self-reports of arthritis prevalence (Verbrugge, Lepkowski, & Konkol, 1991).

A worrisome issue raised by the Rogers and Fisk intervention with the blood glucose monitor videotape and the different navigation aids for the Web search task is that even with redesign that can move younger adults to near perfect performance, older adults may still lag behind. Best design for older adults may not equal best design for younger adults for a given product. Rogers and Fisk raise the important issue of aptitude by treatment interaction when discussing the influence of spatial ability in Web navigation. Even if such effects are found (and even if they are more than modest in size) there is the practical question of whether specialized design for older adults with different ability profiles will be commercially viable. Will software engineers develop elder-specific interfaces that vary for low versus high spatial ability seniors? Here demographics are likely to play a critical role. I suspect that as the market grows (aging of the baby boomers) so will interest in tailoring interfaces to older user capabilities, and, perhaps, to subgroups with the older adult population.

Training

Fisk and Rogers have also provided wonderful examples from their long-standing research program of how to design training interventions that work. The revised glucose monitoring videotape just about eliminated age differences in performance between young and old, a notable achievement that contrasts with their earlier work on action training with ATMs (Mead & Fisk, 1998). That study demonstrated that despite showing improvements for older adults with action training (procedural training) they still lagged behind action-trained younger adults rather badly. There is a growing tradition of intervening with training for older adults who show deficits in basic abilities (Willis, 2001; Willis & Schaie, 1986). The Willis and Schaie work showed fairly narrow transfer of training, suggesting that tailored interventions such as those tried by Rogers and Fisk are the only viable approach to improving older adult performance on complex problem-solving tasks. Because many human skills are quite knowledge-dependent (Charness & Schultetus, 1999), interventions may have to be quite focused to succeed with young and old alike. Training older adults on one medical device should not be expected to promote much positive transfer to the next device. However, if device interfaces can be kept similar, the learning curve need not be overly steep.

Not stressed in their chapter was the very important theoretical work that Rogers and colleagues have contributed to the issue of the role of consistency for training success in search tasks (Fisk & Rogers, 1991). They and their colleagues have been doing some very interesting work on environmental support issues such as the role of task-irrelevant consistency. Having desktop icons always show up in the same location makes accessing relevant operations quite a bit easier than if they change locations over time.

CONCLUSIONS

I have suggested that there is a relatively constrained set of conditions necessary for success in adopting technology. Access to technology is the first step. Although the majority of today's older adults lack access to computer technology we have reason to be optimistic that accessibility will become less of a barrier over time. Motivation is a critical piece of the puzzle, particularly the role of attitudes as mediators of adoption and use. We need much more research on paths from attitudes to adoption to long-term use. Ability (e.g., spatial ability) has been shown to be an important mediator of success in using technology. Age has long been believed to be a surrogate variable and hence distal mediator of performance. Specific abilities may be the more important proximal determinants of successful technology use. However, Rogers and Fisk have made a powerful case that design and training are the key elements in successful use of technology. Indeed, this is where our research efforts are probably best deployed. What would be helpful, however, is to have better design and training principles to guide development efforts. It is here that modest societal investments such as the Center for Research and Education on Aging and Technology Enhancement (CREATE) may bear significant fruit (Czaja, Sharit, Charness, Fisk, & Rogers, 2001).

REFERENCES

Australian Greenhouse Office. (2001). Quantification of residential standby power consumption in Australia: Results of recent survey work. Available online: http://www.greenhouse.gov.au/energyefficiency/appliances/naeeec/standby/report/pubs/report.pdf.

Azjen, I., & Fishbein, M. (1977). Attitude-behavior relations: A theoretical analysis and review of empirical research. *Psychological Bulletin, 84,* 888–918.

Bandura, A. (1982). Self-efficacy mechanisms in human agency. *American Psychologist, 37,* 122–147.

Brickfield, C. F. (1984). Attitudes and perceptions of older people toward technology. In P. K. Robinson & J. E. Birren (Eds.), *Aging and technological advances* (pp. 31–38). New York: Plenum.

Carstensen, L. L., Isaacowitz, D. M., & Charles, S. T. (1999). Taking time seriously: A theory of socioemotional selectivity. *American Psychologist, 54,* 165–181.

Charness, N., Kelley, C. L., Bosman, E. A., & Mottram, M. (2001). Word processing training and retraining: Effects of adult age, experience, and interface. *Psychology and Aging, 16,* 110–127.

Charness, N., & Schultetus, R. S. (1999). Knowledge and expertise. In F. T. Durso, R. S. Nickerson, R. W. Schvaneveldt, S. T. Dumais, D. S. Lindsay, & M. T. H. Chi (Eds.), *Handbook of applied cognition* (pp. 57–81). Chichester, UK: Wiley.

Cox, W. M., & Alm, R. (1997). Time well spent: The declining real cost of living in America, Federal Reserve Bank of Dallas—1997 Annual Report. Available online: http://www.dallasfed.org/htm/pubs/pdfs/anreport/arpt97.pdf (accessed 9/21/01).

Czaja, S. J., & Sharit, J. (1998). Age differences in attitudes toward computers. *Journal of Gerontology: Psychological Sciences, 53B,* P329–P340.

Czaja, S. J., Sharit, J., Charness, N., Fisk, A. D., & Rogers, W. (2001). The Center for Research and Education on Aging and Technology Enhancement (CREATE): A program to enhance technology for older adults. *Gerontechnology, 1,* 50–59.

Fisher, R. L. (1993). Optimal performance engineering: Good, better, best. *Human Factors, 35,* 115–139.

Fisk, A. D., & Rogers, W. (1991). Toward an understanding of age-related memory and visual search effects. *Journal of Experimental Psychology: General, 120,* 131–149.

Gould, O., & Dixon, R. A. (1993). How we spent our vacation: Collaborative storytelling by young and old adults. *Psychology and Aging, 8,* 10–17.

Harrington, T. L., & Harrington, M. K. (2000). *Gerontechnology: Why and how.* Maastricht, The Netherlands: Shaker.

Kelley, C. L., & Charness, N. (1995). Issues in training older adults to use computers. *Behaviour and Information Technology, 14,* 107–120.

Kraut, R., Patterson, M., Lundmark, V., Kiesler, S., Mukopadhyay, T., & Scherlis, W. (1998). Internet paradox. A social technology that reduces social involvement and psychological well-being? *American Psychologist, 53,* 1017–1031.

Mead, S., & Fisk, A. D. (1998). Measuring skill acquisition and retention with an ATM simulator: The need for age-specific training. *Human Factors, 40,* 516–523.

New York Times. (2001). Compressed air and gravity: Physics finished what terror began. Available online: http://www.nytimes.com/2001/09/25/science/physical/25TOWE.html.

Newburger, E. (2001). Home computers and Internet use in the United States: August 2000. Available online: http://www.census.gov/prod/2001pubs/p23-207.pdf.

Rainie, L., & Packel, D. (2001). More online, doing more. 16 million newcomers gain Internet access in the last half of 2000 as women, minorities, and families with modest incomes continue to surge online. Available from: http://www.pewinternet.org/reports/pdfs/PIP_Changing_Population.pdf (accessed 9/25/2001).

Schaie, K. W., Wahl, H-W., Mollenkopf, H., & Oswald, F. (2003). *Independent aging: Living arrangements and mobility.* New York: Springer.

Simmons, T., & O'Neill, G. (2001). Households and families 2000: Census 2000 brief. September 20001. Available online: http://www.census.gov/prod/2001pubs/c2kbr01-8.pdf (accessed 9/26/01).

Simon, H. A. (1981). *The sciences of the artificial* (2nd ed.). Cambridge, MA: MIT Press.

Smith, D. I., & Spraggins, R. E. (2001). Gender 2000: Census 2000 Brief. Available online: http://www.census.gov/prod/2001pubs/c2kbr01-9.pdf (accessed 9/26/2001).

Statistics Canada. (2003). Selected dwelling characteristics and household equipment. Available online: http://www.statcan.ca/english/Pgdb/People/Families/famil09.htm.

U.S. Department of Commerce. (1998). National Telecommunications and Information Administration. Falling through the Net II: New data on the digital divide. Available online: http://www.ntia.doc.gov/ntiahome/net2/falling.html.

Verbrugge, L. M., Lepkowski, J. M., & Konkol, L. L. (1991). Levels of disability among U.S. adults with arthritis. *Journal of Gerontology: Social Sciences, 46,* S71–S83.

Willis, S. L. (2001). Methodological issues in behavioral intervention research with the elderly. In J. Birren & K. W. Schaie (Eds.), *Handbook of the psychology of aging* (5th ed., pp. 78–108). San Diego: Academic Press.

Willis, S. L., & Schaie, K. W. (1986). Training the elderly on the ability factors of spatial orientation and inductive reasoning. *Psychology and Aging, 1,* 239–247.

Commentary

Is It all About Aging?
Technology and Aging in
Social Context

Melissa A. Hardy and Chardie L. Baird

Anthropologists have long considered the ability to make tools one of the pivotal developments in the evolution of man. Since that first spark of creativity, we have moved from making simple machines that enhance our ability to move, assemble, and manufacture large objects to making much more complex machines to transmit, connect, and compose information. We have shifted from an emphasis on the mechanics of force and motion to the development of technology that improves the productivity of machines (and that of the people using them) by eliminating manual operations. These changes in the labor processes on which "new" industries rely have also led to changes in the worker skills required to use these new technologies. Fundamental social changes such as these rarely affect all groups of people uniformly. Instead, the human costs of a transition from "old" industries to "new" industries fall more heavily on those groups already operating at a disadvantage. Historically, those groups have been the less educated and the older aged.

As Rogers and Fisk report, the research literature that addresses aging and technology has expanded our understanding of the age differences in how quickly people learn new technologies, how likely they are to purchase new technologies, and how directly they incorporate new technologies into their everyday lives. But these are not necessarily all

28

issues of aging and technology. As is commonly acknowledged, when researchers discuss age differences estimated from cross-sectional designs, these differences are at once age *and* cohort differences. Clearly, cohort differences are important. A telling anecdote makes the point. George Abbott was a well-known Broadway entrepreneur. Not long before his death in 1995 at the age of 107, he was asked what he thought was the most important change to affect Broadway during his lifetime. His answer? "Electricity."

Many people may find that surprising, since electricity is such a taken-for-granted part of our everyday lives. To be without it, as we are occasionally during storms, blackouts, or catastrophic events, is to be surrounded by objects that don't work. That is the process of modernization. As we shift from one technology to the next, our "new" products presume the "new" technology. "Old-fashioned" products—oil lamps, treadle sewing machines, hand mixers, manual typewriters—become collectibles. People currently aged 70 or older were born in or before 1930. Those born after 1960 include the next generation of elders. The age groups studied by Rogers and Fisk include these two cohorts. Do these two cohorts differ in ways that are likely to affect their relationships with new technologies of the twentieth and twenty-first centuries?

THE COHORT OF 1930

A relatively small cohort born during the depression year of 1930, they were still children when the United States was yanked into World War II in response to the bombing of Pearl Harbor. Seven in ten had high school diplomas in hand when the post-war United States economy began a prolonged period of growth. With the exception of those called to fight in Korea, workers in this cohort stepped early onto the economic escalator and were able to stay on this upward path for the next 30 years. But not all gained equal advantage from this economic boom. African Americans and Hispanics remained hampered by resource-starved school programs, narrowed opportunities for employment, and relatively rare opportunities for advancement. "Separate but equal" schooling was certainly separate, but far from equal. Those who did fight in Korea could take advantage of the GI Bill for Korean War veterans, which translated into college degrees for one in five men. During this period, real national output per person increased 107 percent. United States households, spurred by unprecedented increases in home ownership, began the transformation from home production to home consumption. Labor-saving devices for the home transformed the role of homemaker, and an increasing number of women took on the additional role of paid employee (Hardy, 2002).

Higher incomes, financed by a growing economy that provided higher real wages to workers, improved the general standard of living. Advances in medicine resulted in generally improved health, increased survivorship, and longer lives. Two thirds of men and more than three in four women lived to age 65, and could expect to live at least another 10 years.

THE COHORT OF 1960

Born at the beginning of a turbulent decade, this cohort's educational opportunities were considerably improved over those of earlier cohorts. Attending college after high school was becoming the normative path, as one in two made their way onto college campuses, and one in four earned degrees. Race/ethnic gaps remained, but were not as wide as in previous years. This cohort faced no major wars, no peacetime draft. But many would try to enter the labor force during recession periods, and although their starting wages would be higher than those of previous cohorts, the impressive wage growth of previous decades would not be repeated.

For many, the experience on the job meant dealing with new technologies. Beginning in the 1980s, desktop computers were becoming normal feature of the typical office. Once offices became computerized, worker skills were necessarily linked to the steady succession of upgrades and innovations. Office machinery was now office "equipment," which required a technical support staff. Office workers were becoming office "technicians" who needed regular training on their new "equipment" so they could operate "efficiently."

The children of this cohort were learning in computer classrooms. Research, which had been done almost exclusively in libraries, was now routinely accomplished "on the Web," which meant that the kids needed "access" in their homes as well as their schools. Computer chips were showing up everywhere—in cars, in toys, on "smart" cards, even in your pet's ear. Computer technology was both ubiquitous and invisible in many of its applications. But anyone interested in taking advantage of the new wave of consumer products had to be willing to learn how to use them. It was no longer a question of simply hitting a power button. New toys had to be programmed. "Some assembly required" had become more complex.

THE RELATIONSHIP BETWEEN TECHNOLOGY
AND OLDER WORKERS

The cohort of 1930 was less educated, defined by greater gender and race/ethnic disparities, and more likely to be moved into retirement than trained in new workplace technology than its 1960 counterpart. But at the same time, members of the older cohort have been healthier, living longer, and maintaining a better standard of living than they had anticipated.

The introduction to "new" technology through workplace innovations began around the turn of the century, as part of the industrial revolution. Workers were demanding a shorter work week. In manufacturing industries, typical work schedules were 10 hours a day and 6 days a week. Unions were faced with the dilemma of assuring the same pay for fewer hours of work. Of course, employers found a reduction in work schedule without a reduction in pay acceptable only if output remained constant. The solution involved increasing productivity, which translated into increasing the speed of the labor process. Increasing speed was, in part, made possible by new workplace machinery. But an essential element of this equation was the ability to use this new machinery at a relatively rapid pace.

The historical evidence supports the notion that, rather than the machinery itself posing a problem for older workers, it was instead the speed of its operation that was problematic. But then, increasing the speed of operations was the major goal of the new technology. Employers could justify the expense of the new equipment only if the speed of its operation increased worker productivity (Graebner, 1980). Therefore, for the cohort of working Americans during the early part of the 20th century, the shift to "new technologies" coincided with a loss of control over the labor process, a loss of discretion in how tasks were performed, and a loss of alternative organizations of their workdays. By the 1920s, "technology" was a common explanation for the "problem" of older workers. However, the emphasis shifted to a construction of the older workers' inability to adapt to new technology—their stubbornness and inflexibility—rather than on the rigidity and unforgiving pace of the new technological regimes (Beveridge, 1908). Frederick Taylor's principles of scientific management turned the factory into an experimenter's laboratory, dissecting the components of each task and reconstructing the work habits of the employees. There was one right way to perform the task, and each step was choreographed into a timed sequence of micromovements that could be performed mechanically, automatically.

This type of training discourages experimentation in the use of new tools and tends to link a successful performance not only to outcomes, but also to a specific labor process.

The amount of variability in modes of performance that tools can tolerate depends on how the connections between users and tools are designed. Work tools and home appliances "interact" with users in terms of an interface, which reflects recent technological advances. Use of the "tool" is therefore facilitated by knowledge of and experience with the relevant type of user interface. Early in the 1980s, the electro-mechanical style of user interface, which was typical of electronic consumer devices during earlier decades, shifted to a software style of user interface. This shift had different consequences for different generations of potential users. Recently reported research indicates that cohorts who, in their formative years, learned to use tools with electro-mechanical user interfaces made more errors then younger cohorts (who had early experiences with software) when using devices based on a software style of user interface (Rama et al., 2001). One proposed reason for this difference in performance involved differences in user strategies that could be located in their earlier experiences. Whereas electro-mechanical interfaces tended to be intolerant of mistakes, software-based interfaces lend themselves to trial-and-error approaches. Knowing that learning to use a device through a trial-and-error strategy is unlikely to break it allows users to be more experimental and less informed in their approaches.

THE SIGNIFICANCE OF SPEED

In tests of differences in performance between older and younger users, speed is often an outcome variable of interest. Not surprisingly, age-related differences in speed are frequently identified. Is it reasonable to expect that younger and older users will be able to complete most tasks at the same pace, especially those tasks that involve a manual component? One age-related difference on which most scientists agree is the difference in processing speed. The older you are, the longer (on average) it takes.

Why is speed important? If the goal is simply to design a technology that is *accessible* to older users, then the speed at which they perform individual tasks may not be important so long as the task can be completed in a reasonable amount of time. What is reasonable? A time frame that does not erode the view that the technology is useful may be all that is necessary. If, however, the goal is to design a technology that will not put older workers at a disadvantage because of their age, then speed may be of central concern, since the emphasis will be on worker productivity, which is inextricably linked to speed. In this latter case, aspects of design might compensate for age-related declines in processing speed, but can such features erase the age *differences* in processing speed? If the issue in the workplace remains one of *relative* performance rather than *reasonable* performance, then speed will remain a fundamental issue. But not all workplace applications require speed. Then the question becomes one of better matching these "new" tools to their users.

Even if we are concerned with speed and its reflection in productivity, existing research has demonstrated that skill plays an important intermediary role by modifying the relationships among age, speed, and productivity. Age is not the only individual trait correlated with speed, nor it is the only time-dependent trait. Skill is also a strong predictor of speed, and it may well serve to buffer the declines ordinarily associated with aging. Research on the performance of tasks for which skill plays an important role has demonstrated that older practitioners' skill may allow them to compensate for memory deficits (Charness, 1981; Charness & Bosman, 1990) and develop compensatory strategies for a slowing in perceptual-motor efficiency (Salthouse, 1984).

Studies suggest that, in the performance of manual tasks for which speed is one indicator of performance quality, skill effects arise from an increased efficiency of component processes. In assessments of age effects in typing, for example, older typists seemed to compensate for a slowing in the efficiency of perceptual-motor translation, in part through expanded anticipation of subsequent text (Salthouse, 1984). Older highly skilled typists also performed as well as comparably skilled younger typists without the availability of advance preparation, suggesting the use of additional strategies of compensation (Bosman, 1993).

Finally, meta-analyses of research investigating the relationship between age and productivity report that age and performance appear to be generally unrelated (Hunter et al., 1982; Walsman & Avolio; McEvoy & Cascio, 1989). This correlational absence was unperturbed by type of job, and only among very young employees was a consistent and positive, although relatively weak, relationship between age and performance found. Whether these results reflect the selective retention of older workers in the labor force; the presence of more complex curvilinear relationships; differences in experience, education, or work values; or a sparse (age 50 and older) and somewhat truncated (age 60 and older) age distribution is unclear. What is suggested, however, is that the measure of productivity versus job performance be carefully chosen (McEvoy & Cascio, 1989), since the latter often reflects a subjective assessment of "potential for promotion" or other perceptions that could be influenced by the time horizon differences applied to older compared to younger workers.

THE CONNECTION BETWEEN THE OLDER PERSON AND NEW TECHNOLOGY

One of the problems with the early workplace technology was that it treated technological tools as separate from their users and users as secondary to their tools. The technology was designed to perform some function, and then the use patterns were established to maximize the speed at which the function could be repeated. But for many people, and for older cohorts in particular, tools and their users are not entirely separate entities. Tools are an extension of human capability; they "fit" an individual user such that a kind of melding takes place between person and tool. "Tools of the trade" provided an important part of the definition of a particular trade *and* the tradesman. An important part of the rites of passage into the membership of a trade involved securing one's own set of tools. More than a source of pride in ownership, they were symbols of skill and of identity.

One way to illustrate this relationship between people and their tools is to use the work of a young sculptor whose series on men and their tools incorporates this theme. This piece, *Builder Boy as a #2 Pencil* (Figure 1.4) illustrates the dialectical relationship between the writer and the simplest of writing implements—the pencil. The utility of the pencil is linked to the creativity of the writer, such that what flows from lead to paper is not simply the pencil, but the expressiveness of the author through the pencil. Though the pencil is clearly a simple technology, the connectedness of tool and user is not limited to simple tools. Anthropomorphizing tools is an ancient practice made more difficult by the miniaturization of complex circuitry that is incomprehensible to the average user. As a consequence, what could be conceived as a relationship of mastery—the author using the pencil—becomes a more complicated relationship once the pencil is transformed into desktop computer. To regain the utility of a worn-down pencil, one need only sharpen it. To regain the utility of a cranky computer, one needs technical support staff. The pencil can break, but what is lost is the mechanism for transcribing thoughts to paper; the thoughts remain with the author or are collected on paper. With computer technology, a vast quantity of collected thoughts can be lost on crashed disks or through corrupted software. (So, too, can some of the basic skills of

FIGURE 1.4   Builder Boy as a #2 Pencil, a sculpture in plywood, epoxy, and papier-mache, by Greg Gilbertson, 1998.

composition, such as spelling, syntax, and grammar.) Working with the newer technology can so influence the creative process that we find we can only be creative when we use the new technology.

LEARNING AND THE NEW TECHNOLOGIES

Whenever technology shifts to a new paradigm rather than developing along an established pathway, the approach to learning the new technology must be carefully considered. We tend to learn through analogy, an approach that works quite well so long as there is a consistency in the sequence of ever newer tools. But once that sequence is broken, this practice can create problems, since the tendency will be for people to want to operate the new tool in a similar fashion to an older tool with which they are familiar. For many older people, the issue is not simply teaching one new tool, but convincing them to invest in learning to operate an entirely new category of tool that seems to be prone to ever quicker obsolescence.

So what do we know about how older people learn? A rapidly accumulating body of research on memory functions in older adults has provided us with important insights. An earlier emphasis on learning-about-learning was focused on children, infants and toddlers in particular. Part of the mythology of aging was a kind of wear-and-tear theory of aging, which argued a steady pace of decline.* In contrast to current recommendations for maintaining activity and involvement, this approach suggested that less activity was preferable. Consistent with early capitalism's view of consumption versus saving, this theory argued judicious spending of one's energy so that one might enjoy a longer life.

Among the more recent neurological findings about the aging brain are those that indicate a continuing capacity for productive activity. More recent research indicates that changes in the aging brain are not uniformly downhill (Schaie, 1996). In particular, research has emphasized the benefits of experience, the cognitive strategies of compensation, and the possibility of the growth and elaboration of neural synapses. But age-related declines in process cognition and in the efficiency of cognitive processes, which are manifested in age-related differences in learning, memory, reasoning, and spatial abilities, are well documented (Baltes & Lindenberger, 1997a, 1997b).

COHORT DIFFERENCES IN LEARNING

Although cohort differences in educational attainment have been well documented, there have been fewer studies of cohort differences in

---

* For example, late in the 1800s a physician named George Beard argued that aging was an exercise in the steady depletion of nervous force. This condition, which he named *neurasthenia*, held that any given individual was born with some initial endowment of nervous energy and, once born, simply used up, more or less quickly, whatever stock was available.

learning. A major exception is work by Schaie and others (Schaie, 1996), which demonstrates considerable cohort variation in cognition manifested by sizeable positive cohort trends in intellectual performance. Schaie's work supports the idea that individual-level cognitive performance may be linked to the cognitive character of the era in which individuals are born and those in which we live our everyday lives. This cohort-specific cognitive experience can shape the kinds of cognitive tasks we become adept at performing, the kind of learning by analogy of which we are capable.

Other recently reported research may also shed some light on older learners. One of the features of learning that has been identified but not well understood is that of neural efficiency. The brain appears to exert less effort as individuals learn to perform tasks or are able to recognize relationships. How does this apparent neural efficiency arise? And how does it facilitate learning?

When people first try to discern locations of objects or identify them, separate brain areas that participate in this display are jolted into activity. As people learn, these regions toil less, but the regions themselves form a working relationship; they work as a *system* of associative learning (see, e.g., Buchel, Coull, & Eriston, 1999; Buchel & Eriston, 1997).

We also know that the brain compensates for age-related declines by recruiting brain areas that had not previously been involved in the performance of specific tasks. In young adults, verbal and spatial learning occur in specialized regions of the brain. In older adults, additional regions participate in the learning process. Positron emission tomography, which is used to compare brain activity in young and old adults engaged in particular tasks, indicate that both right and left frontal lobes are active for both verbal and spatial tasks in older people (Reuter-Lorenz, Stanczak, & Miller, 1999; Reuter-Lorenz et al., 2000). In addition, older people respond faster when they use both sides of the brain, so long as they are working on a single task rather than on competing tasks (Kray & Lindenberger, 2000; Li, Lindenberger, Freund, & Baltes, 2001; Li, Lindenberger, Runger, & Frensch, 2000; Lindenberger, Mariske, & Baltes, 2000; Lindenberger, Scherer, & Baltes, 2001).

Finally, research on the learning strategies of children (e.g., Siegler & Chen, 2000) suggest that children who learn best tend to express a variety of problem-solving strategies using both words and gestures. Some of the research conclusions are that after discovering more effective strategies, children resort to older ways of thinking about a task, at least for a while; that children discover new thinking strategies while succeeding *or* while failing; that children who devise several problem-solving strategies, even incorrect ones, often learn more than those who generate only one or two strategies, even if both those strategies are correct; and that children draw on intuitive knowledge to solve problems.

SINGLE-MINDEDNESS OR PERFORMANCE STYLES

One of the central themes of Rogers and Fisk's argument is that, in approaching issues of aging and technology—issues of design, training, or performance—we may need to be more flexible in our thinking. For example, measures of success depend on the context in which the technology will be used. If our purpose is to help integrate older people into the world of computer technology, then an emphasis on speed may be misplaced. Whether they can use search engines, locate the information they seek, and distinguish between sites that report valid information versus misinformation are useful indicators of success. In addition, perhaps more emphasis should be placed on assessing the logic of the process as well as the success of the outcome. Here the question of variability is particularly salient. One of the consequences of new technologies is often a new set of limitations on the types of tasks that are possible as well as limitations on the order of operations and the extent to which the system can tolerate even minor variants in process. If, for example, older users are more prone to mistakes in process at a particular juncture, then perhaps we should rethink the relationship between process and user. The tendency in addressing age differences in performance is to assign the errors to the user, to some deficiency in the user, which detracts from the user's competence in performing the tasks. Instead, we must consider the *relationship* between user and design, consider the dialectic between ease of use and design options. Both sides of this relationship are constrained, but it is essential that the process of adaptation in new technologies not be singularly located in the user.

In addition to variability in design approaches, Rogers and Fisk also emphasize the importance of variability in training. Perhaps our emphasis should shift toward producing training regimens that combine verbal and spatial dimensions, as well as those that integrate the subject into the strategizing process and allow individualization of techniques to the extent that these individual expressions do not compromise the task itself. The kind of research being produced through the CREATE project, in general, and by researchers such as Rogers and Fisk will enhance our understanding of how technology design and training can be better suited to heterogeneous users. Age is an important dimension of this heterogeneity, but the insights gained by studying the relationship between aging and technology may be generalizable to other groups who find the demands of technological innovations somewhat daunting.

CONCLUSIONS

One of the ironies of modern times lies in the manifestation of the friction between standardized (or collective) approaches versus individualized (variant) approaches to key problems. In the arena of public policy, for example, collective approaches to income security have been criticized because they do not allow sufficient choice, nor do they allocate key decisions to the discretion of the individual. In contrast, standardized sentencing for criminals has removed judicial discretion and severely limited the justice system's ability to consider the individual merits of any particular case.

In revolutionizing the process of production, the "new" industrial technology of the early 20th century took worker control of pacing, task order, and labor process and placed them inside the machinery. And by constraining the discretion of workers to make judgments about how the tasks would be performed and how the work would be shared, the "new" technology imposed skill requirements, primarily in terms of speed and strength, that older workers found more difficult to meet.

The "new" technology of the late twentieth and early twenty-first centuries requires less physical strength, but speed remains a central issue because speed is generally viewed as being at the heart of productivity. If part of our concern with older people and technology is to provide new avenues for older workers to remain in the labor force rather than curtail the limited avenues currently available, then this issue of speed must be addressed. For older workers to have a chance, variation in speed must be viewed not simply as a deficit of the user, but as a failure of the technology to creatively compensate for individual variations in processing. Only when we stop assigning the root cause of performance failures to the user, and instead view them as a challenge for better designs, will be able to overcome the tendency of "new" technologies to exclude older people.

REFERENCES

Baltes, P. B., & Lindenberger, U. (1997a). Emergence of a powerful connection between sensory and cognitive functions across the adult life span: A new window to the study of cognitive aging. *Psychology and Aging, 12*(1), 12–22.

Baltes, P. B., & Lindenberger, U. (1997b). Intellectual functioning in old and very old age: Cross-sectional results from the Berlin Aging Study. *Psychology and Aging, 12*(3), 410–433.

Beveridge, W. I. B. (1908). *The art of scientific investigation.* New York: Norton.

Bosman, E. A. (1993). Age-related difference in the motoric aspects of transcription typing skill. *Psychology and Aging, 8,* 87–102.

Buchel, C., Coull, J. T., & Friston, K. J. (1999). The predictive value of changes in effective connectivity for human learning. *Science, 283,* 1538–1541.

Buchel, C., & Friston, K. J. (1997, December 7). Modulations of connectivity in visual pathways by attention: Cortical interactions evaluated with structural equation modeling and MRI. *Cerebral Cortex, 8,* 768–778.

Charness, N. (1981). Aging and skilled problem solving. *Journal of Experimental Psychology: General, 110,* 21–38.

Charness, N., & Bosman, E. A. (1990). Expertise and aging: Life in the lab. In T. M. Hess (Ed.), *Aging and cognition: Knowledge organization and utilization* (pp. 343–385). Amsterdam: Elsevier/North-Holland.

Graebner, W. (1980). *A History of retirement: The meaning and function of an American institution.* New Haven, CT: Yale University Press.

Hardy, M. A. (2002). The transformation of retirement in 20th century America. *Generations, 26*(2), 9–16.

Hunter, J. E., Schmidt, F. L., & Jackson, G. B. (1982). *Meta-analysis: Cumulating research findings across studies.* Beverly Hills, CA: Sage.

Kray, J., & Lindenberger, U. (2000). Adult age differences in task switching. *Psychology and Aging, 15*(1), 126–147.

Li, K. Z. H., Lindenberger, U., Freund, A. M., & Baltes, P. B. (2001). Walking while memorizing: Age-related differences in compensatory behavior. *Psychological Science, 12*(3), 230–237.

Li, K. Z. H., Lindenberger, U., Runger, D., & Frensch, P. A. (2000). The role of inhibition in the regulation of sequential action. *Psychological Science, 11*(4), 343–347.

Lindenberger, U., Mariske, M., & Baltes, P. B. (2000). Memorizing while walking: Increase in dual-task costs from young adulthood to old age. *Psychology and Aging, 5*(3), 417–436.

Lindenberger, U., Scherer, H., & Baltes, P. B. (2001). The strong connection between sensory and cognitive performance in old age: Not due to sensory acuity reductions operating during cognitive assessment. *Psychology and Aging, 16*(2), 196–205.

McEvoy, G. M., & Cascio, W. F. (1989). Cumulative evidence of the relationship between employee age and job performance. *Journal of Applied Psychology, 74,* 11–17.

Rama, M. D., de Ridder, H., & Bouma, H. (2001). Technology generation and age in using layered user interfaces. *Journal of Gerontechnology, 1,* 25–40.

Reuter-Lorenz, P. A., Jonides, J., Smith, E. E., Hartley, A., Miller, A., Marshuetz, C., & Koeppe, R. A. (2000). Age difference in the frontal lateralization of verbal and spatial working memory revealed by PET. *Journal of Cognitive Neuroscience, 12*(1), 174–187.

Reuter-Lorenz, P. A., Stanczak, L., & Miller, A. C. (1999). Neural recruitment and cognitive aging: Two hemispheres are better than one, especially as you age. *Psychological Science, 10*(6), 494–500.

Salthouse, T. A. (1984). Effects of age and skill in typing. *Journal of Experimental Pyschology: General, 113*, 345–371.

Schaie, K. W. (1996). *Intellectual development in adulthood: The Seattle longitudinal study.* Cambridge,UK: Cambridge University Press.

Siegler, R. S., & Chen, Z. (2000). *Across the great divide.* London: Blackwell Publishing.

Waldman, D. A., & Avolio, B. J. (1986). A meta-analysis of age difference in job performance. *Journal of Applied Psychology, 71*, 33–38.

CHAPTER 2

Human Factors and Aging: Identifying and Compensating for Age-related Deficits in Sensory and Cognitive Function

Frank Schieber

INTRODUCTION

Human factors is an interdisciplinary field organized around the central endeavor of fitting the designed environment to the individual. The process of achieving optimal person-environment interaction requires knowledge about the broad range of human functional capacity, including—but not limited to—anthropometry, biomechanics, sensory processes, and cognitive psychology.

This chapter attempts to provide the reader with an introduction to the major empirical findings and principles of experimental psychology as they relate to the more specific domain of aging and technology. This survey is limited in its scope insofar as it pertains only to the area of cognitive psychology. As such, it explores the age-related changes in sensory processes, attention, and memory that present challenges to an older person's ability to interact with his or her environment. Some opportunities for applying this knowledge toward the optimization of the person-environment interface are presented. It is hoped that the basic research findings and principles reviewed herein, and the accompanying examples and recommendations for improving functional capacity, will inspire the reader to generate innovative approaches toward designing a better fit between the designed environment and persons of all ages.

VISION

Anatomical Changes

The maximum diameter of the pupil declines with advancing adult age (a condition known as *senile miosis*). Under low light conditions, the resting diameter of the pupil falls from 7 mm at age 20 to approximately 4 mm at age 80 (Lowenfeld, 1979). Although senile miosis reduces the amount of light reaching the retina, there is reason to suspect that smaller pupil diameters may actually benefit visual performance in older adults in many situations by increasing the contrast of the retinal image (see Sloane, Owlsey, & Alvarez, 1988).

The crystalline lens of the eye becomes increasingly opaque as individuals grow older. This loss of transparency appears to be particularly pronounced at short wavelengths, that is, for blue light (Said & Weale, 1959). This opacification appears to be nearly universal. For example, a large-scale epidemiological study reported that more than 90% of those 75–85 years of age demonstrated significant opacification of the lens (Kahn et al., 1977). The combined effects of lenticular opacity and diminished pupil size contribute to diminished retinal illumination. Weale (1961) has estimated that only one third of the light reaching the retina of a 20-year-old will reach that of a 70-year-old. Half of those over 65 years of age suffer from lenticular opacity that is severe enough to be classified as cataract. Approximately 1.5 million cataract surgery procedures are performed each year in the United States. Ninety percent of these procedures result in a measurable improvement in visual function (Desai, Pratt, Lentzner, & Robinson, 2001).

At the level of the retina, there is some evidence of photoreceptor and ganglion cell loss with advancing age (e.g., Curcio & Drucker, 1993; Yuodelis & Hendrickson, 1986). Curcio, Millican, Allen, and Kalina (1993) reported that nearly 30% of the rods in the central 30 degrees of vision are lost by 90 years of age. The prevalence of retinal diseases that impair visual function increases remarkably with advancing age. Noticeable degrees of macular degeneration afflict 18% of persons 70–74 years of age and upwards of 47% among those over 85 years of age. Nearly 8% of those over 65 years of age suffer from glaucoma. Unlike age-related macular degeneration, however, glaucoma often responds well to treatment. Unfortunately, nearly half of those with glaucoma remain unaware of their condition (Desai et al., 2001).

Dark Adaptation

The sudden transition from a high level of ambient illumination to a very low one is accompanied by a significant reduction in visual sensitivity. Some portion of this loss in light sensitivity is typically recovered once the visual system has had a chance to adapt to the lower level of illumination. Such dark adaptation processes occur in two phases: a *photopic* phase (cone vision) lasting 6–8 minutes and a concomitant *scotopic* phase (rod vision) extending approximately 30 minutes (Geldard, 1972). There is evidence of an age-related slowing in the rate of the photopic dark adaptation (Herse, 1995). However, the rate at which full scotopic dark adaptation develops probably does not change as a function of advancing adult age. What is certain, however, is that light sensitivity of older adults is significantly worse than their young counterparts at all phases of the dark adaptation cycle. Eisner, Fleming, Klein, and Maudlin (1987) demonstrated that light sensitivity in the fully dark adapted eye declined at a rate of nearly 19% per decade of age. This rate of loss would be even greater for short wavelength light (i.e., blue, green) due to the age-related "yellowing" of the lens. These findings indicate that emergency lighting and guidance systems should use broadband or long wavelength illuminaires and specify intensity levels that meet the needs of the older eye. Other generalizations of these dark adaptation findings to human factors applications are limited as very few engineered environments for civilian populations approach such low illumination levels.

Visual Acuity

Visual acuity is a measure of the visual system's ability to resolve fine spatial detail. The ability to resolve well-illuminated, high-contrast spatial features that subtend a visual angle of 1 minute of arc (minarc) represents normal (i.e., 20/20 Snellen) acuity. Since the crystalline lens of the eye must accommodate, or change shape, in order to focus on near targets, separate visual acuities for near (16 inches) versus far (20 feet) targets are often measured. Since small amounts of refractive error in the eye yield reliable decrements in acuity, the acuity test has been widely adopted as the basis for correcting optical aberrations of the eye with eyeglasses or contact lenses (Schieber, 1992).

Near Acuity

The human eye is "designed" to focus upon objects that are 20 feet (or farther) away. In order to clearly focus light coming from objects closer than 20 feet, the crystalline lens within each eye needs to increase its light refracting power by bending itself into a more convex shape. As noted above, the crystalline lens becomes less capable of bending as we grow older (i.e., presbyopia). Consequently, by the mid-forties people begin to have difficulty focusing upon printed text that is closer than arm's length in distance (Atchison, Capper, & McCabe, 1994). By 60 years of age, the ability to focus upon objects within a range of 3 feet has all but vanished, a finding first quantified by Donders (1864). Although presbyopia can interfere significantly with the ability to accurately and comfortably perform near work, it can be easily corrected with reading glasses or by adding an additional lens (bifocals) to existing optical corrections.

Far Acuity

Until around 70 years of age, the vast majority of problems leading to diminished (far) visual acuity are due to refractive errors that can be corrected using eyeglasses or contact lenses (Pitts, 1982). For example, the *Framingham Eye Study* reported that 98.4% of those 52–64 years of age could be refracted to a far acuity of 20/25 or better. However, this proportion falls to 69.1% for those 75–85 years of age (Kahn et al., 1977). Recent survey and epidemiological studies reveal that nearly all (92%) of those over 70 years of age wore eyeglasses. Difficulty seeing even when wearing eyeglasses increased from 14% among persons 70–79 years of age to 32% for those 85 years of age or older. Eighteen percent also relied upon hand-held magnifiers for reading and related visually guided activities (Desai et al., 2001). The impaired visual acuity observed among those in the 70+ age group is primarily the result of the increased prevalence of diseases of the retina. Even the best available eyeglasses cannot compensate for pathological deterioration of the retina and related neural structures. However, improved design of products and environments can enhance visual functioning for most of this population (Schieber, Fozard, Gordon-Salant, & Weiffenbach, 1991).

Age deficits in visual acuity, in both healthy and pathological eyes, are exacerbated under challenging viewing conditions. Haegerstrom-Portnoy, Schneck, and Braybyn (1999) have demonstrated that acuity among healthy older adults (but not younger adults) drops precipitously for low luminance and/or low contrast stimuli. Vola, Cornu, Carrvel, Gastaud, and Leid (1983) found that age differences in low luminance acuity emerged as early as 50 years of age. Sturr, Kline, and Taub (1990) also observed a disproportionate drop in acuity among those over 65 years of age as target luminance fell from 107 to 0.1 cd/m^2. Owsley and Sloane (1990) found that reductions in target letter contrast from 96% to 4% had no demonstrable effects upon young observers, but that older observers exhibited as much as a 25% decline in visual acuity. Similar results have been reported by other investigators (e.g., Adams, Wong, Wong, & Gould, 1988).

Disability Glare

Glare is another challenging condition in which disproportionate age-related decrements in visual function are observed. The senescent lens scatters significant amounts of "off-axis" light across the retina. This results in a *veiling luminance* across the back of the eye that decreases the contrast of the retinal image (Ijspeert, de Waard, van den Berg, & de Jong, 1990). Hence, acuity (and related visual functions) is significantly impaired in the presence of peripheral glare sources (Haegerstrom-Portnoy et al., 1999; Olson & Sivak, 1989; Schieber & Kline, 1994). These visual disabilities in the presence of glare are especially problematic for low contrast stimuli (Schieber, 1988). The time required to recover lost visual sensitivity in response to a bright transient glare source also increases appreciably with age (Burg, 1967; Elliott & Whitaker, 1990; Schieber, 1994).

Contrast Sensitivity

The capacity to visually detect and identify spatial forms varies as a function of target size, orientation, and contrast (Olzak & Thomas, 1985). As a consequence, visual acuity reveals limited information about an individual's ability to detect objects of large to intermediate size or targets of diminished contrast. A more complete assessment of spatial vision is provided by the contrast sensitivity function—a measurement of the minimum contrast needed to detect targets ranging in size from very small to very large. Studies of age differences in the contrast sensitivity function reveal that older adults demonstrate weakened visual sensitivity for stimulus objects much larger than those they can recognize on a standard acuity test (Owsley, Sekuler, & Siemsen, 1983). Age-related declines in contrast sensitivity begin to emerge for critical spatial details as large as 2 cycles per degree of visual angle or 15 minarc (see Schieber & Baldwin, 1996). The additional information provided by the contrast sensitivity function—relative to simple measures of acuity—has extended and improved the ability to predict and explain age differences in real-world visual performance (e.g., Dewar, Kline, Schieber, & Swanson, 1994; Evans & Ginsburg, 1985; Owsley & Sloane, 1987). These findings have been leveraged to develop computer-based image processing techniques to develop highway signs optimized to the visual needs of older drivers (Kline & Fuchs, 1993; Schieber, 1998). Such techniques hold great potential for optimizing the visual interface between older adults and the engineered environment.

Peripheral Vision

The spatial resolving powers of the visual system decline markedly as targets move away from central vision into the peripheral visual field. Letter size must be increased by a factor of 0.046 (i.e., 2.7 minarc must be added to the height of a letter) for every degree of eccentricity away from the point of fixation (Anstis, 1974). This loss in visual acuity associated with increased eccentricity appears to be more dramatic among older observers. Collins, Brown, and Bowman (1989) examined peripheral visual acuity in young and old observers with good central acuity (20/20 or better). A 2.4 minarc (20/40) target was moved into the periphery until it could no longer be resolved. Young observers could identify the target at eccentricities up to 30.8 degrees while older observers failed to accurately identify it beyond 22.8 degrees—a 23% reduction in the "useful field of acuity." The magnitude of this effect was reduced when a larger (4.8 minarc) target was employed. Similar age-related decrements in peripheral visual sensitivity have been observed for contrast sensitivity assessments (Crassini, Brown, & Bowman, 1988; Jaffe, Alvarado, & Juster, 1986). Binocular reductions in the extent of peripheral vision are associated with an increased risk of being involved in an automobile driving accident (Johnson & Keltner, 1986). Age-related losses in extrafoveal perception have also been observed in more complex visual tasks. These results are best understood as limitations in mechanisms of attention and are reviewed in another section presented below.

Motion Perception

Numerous studies have demonstrated age-related decrements in motion sensitivity and/or the accuracy of speed perception. Yet, the nature and the magnitude of these effects vary tremendously across investigations (see Schieber & Baldwin, 1996). Buckingham, Whitaker, and Banford (1987) measured thresholds for the detection of oscillatory motion with a large visual object. Older adults demonstrated dramatic reductions in motion sensitivity across a wide range of oscillatory frequencies. Similar results have been reported by other investigators (e.g., Schieber, Hiris, Brannan, & Williams, 1990; Whitaker & Elliot, 1989). The careful experimental controls implemented in these studies clearly suggest that such age-related losses are mediated by neural rather than optical mechanisms.

Age differences in thresholds for the detection of motion in depth, or "looming," have also been reported (e.g., Hills, 1975; Shinar, 1977). Several studies have also reported evidence of age differences in the ability to judge the apparent speed of automobiles (Hills, 1980; Scialfa, Kline, & Lyman, 1987). Older females, in particular, appear to exhibit pronounced errors in estimating the "time to arrival" of approaching automobiles in a part-task driving simulator (Schiff, Oldak, & Shah, 1992).

Color Vision

Normal observers are capable of distinguishing among more than 100,000 hues in side-by-side comparisons (Geldard, 1972). Small but systematic age-related declines in this ability to distinguish between similar hues have been demonstrated in numerous studies. Dalderup and Fredricks (1969) reported notable age-related deficiencies in color discrimination ability among those over 70 years of age. Gilbert (1957) conducted a large-scale study of color discrimination ability in observers ranging from 10 to 93 years of age. Although all observers demonstrated more discrimination errors among blues and greens (shorter wavelengths) than among yellows and reds on a hue sequential ordering task, this increased tendency to "confuse" related shades within the blue-green range was especially pronounced among older observers. Numerous other studies have reported that age-related declines in color discrimination are more pronounced for hues in the short wavelength region of the spectrum (e.g., Eisner et al., 1987; Knoblauch et al., 1987). Early studies attributed this "red shift" in color discrimination to the selective absorption of short wavelength light by the senescent lens (e.g., Weale, 1986). However, more recent investigations suggest this phenomenon may result from a differential loss of sensitivity in short-wavelength photoreceptors and/or their opponent neural projections to the brain (Haegerstrom-Portnoy, 1988; Johnson & Marshall, 1995). As with other visual functions, age-related deficits in color discrimination are exacerbated under low light conditions (Kraft & Werner, 1999a). Perhaps of greater significance, Knoblauch and colleagues found that age differences in blue-green color discrimination were substantially reduced at high levels of target illumination.

Although the magnitude of the age-related decrements in blue-green color discrimination noted above is small, Cody, Hurd, and Bootman (1990) demonstrated that a significant proportion of older adults made errors when trying to distinguish between medicine capsules with similar color-coded markings. Findings like those reported by Knoblauch and colleagues (1987) suggest that such errors can probably be minimized when more optimal lighting conditions are employed. Finally, a recent investigation by Kraft and Werner (1999b) demonstrated that *color constancy* mechanisms remain relatively intact among older observers. This suggests that dynamic color adaptation processes may serve to compensate for low-level inefficiencies in short-wavelength mechanisms, thus, normalizing phenomenal color experience and minimizing performance decrements on real-world tasks.

Compensating for Age-Related Visual Deficits

The age differences in the structure and function of the visual system outlined above suggest numerous opportunities for enhancing performance via optimized design. Some guidelines for achieving these ends are listed below. Additional details regarding the optimization of visual environments for older persons can be found in Kline and Scialfa (1997) and Schieber and colleagues (1991).

1. In general, increased levels of ambient and task illumination are required to optimized visual performance for older adults. There are many opportunities to improve performance via increased illumination as ambient light levels in the built environment are often found to be well below recommended minimums (see Charness & Dijkstra, 1999). Increased illumination helps overcome the opacity of the ocular media and is known to mitigate age differences in text legibility, object recognition, and color discrimination. However, the expected benefits of improved illumination are minimal when performance is limited by cognitive rather than sensory deficits.

2. Increased levels of luminance contrast are required to meet the visual needs of older persons. Blackwell and Blackwell (1971, 1980) have demonstrated that older persons require 2–6 times more luminance contrast to achieve equivalent levels of object detection and recognition performance.

3. Minimize the need to perform "near" work. When *close-up* work cannot be avoided, older persons should be fitted with eyeglasses optimized for the specific working distance required by the task.

4. Choose text font sizes of at least 12 points in character height to accommodate the needs of those 60–75 years of age. Font heights of

18 points are required to accommodate the needs of the 85th percentile 80-year-old (Schieber et al., 1991; Steenbekkers, 1998).

5. Deploy lighting strategies that minimize the opportunity for disability glare effects. Avoid narrow angles of incidence and/or use indirect lighting schemes where possible. Special text fonts have been developed that mitigate age-related reductions in legibility due to a form of disability glare known as irradiation effects (i.e., the *Clearview*™ highway sign font; see Garvey, Pietrucha, & Meeker, 1998).

6. Minimize dependence upon peripheral vision.

7. Adopt marking strategies that enhance motion perception and/or speed estimation capabilities. For example, the use of vehicle *daytime running lights* may provide disproportionate performance and safety benefits for older drivers (see Koornstra, Bijleveld, & Hagenzieker, 1997).

8. Use larger color contrast steps when discrimination between short wavelength (blue, green) colors is required.

9. Explore the use of computer-based image processing techniques for optimizing the legibility of spatial form (e.g., the *recursive-blur* optimization technique; see Schieber, 1998).

HEARING

Anatomical Changes

Age-related changes in the outer ear that might potentially impair hearing function include excess accumulations of earwax, which could block the auditory canal (Corso, 1963), as well as a tendency for the auditory canal to narrow or collapse (Schow, Christensen, Hutchinson, & Nerbonne, 1978). In the middle ear, the joints connecting the ossicular bones (malleus, incus, and stapes) tend to become arthritic and less elastic with advancing age (Belal, 1975). However, Corso (1981) has concluded that such changes rarely affect sound transmission to the cochlea. The inner ear and its ascending nervous system connections are the site of several dramatic age-related changes. There is a significant age-related loss in the number of inner and outer hair cells along the *organ of Corti* (Schuknecht, 1974). The loss of inner hair cells occurs disproportionately among those responsible for the sensory transduction of high-frequency acoustic stimuli, and, hence, contribute to the development of *sensorineural presbycusis* (see below). Finally, there appears to be a large age-related reduction in the number of neurons comprising the auditory nerve (Schuknecht, 1974; Spoendlin & Schrott, 1989, 1990), brainstem auditory nuclei, and the auditory cortex (see Willott, 1991).

Absolute Sensitivity

Adult aging is associated with a significant increase in the stimulus intensity required to detect a sound. This age-related loss of sensitivity (known as *presbycusis*) is especially pronounced for high-frequency sounds (Fozard, 1990). This loss of sensitivity proceeds at a rate of approximately 1 dB per year for those beyond 60 years of age; increasing to as high as 1.5 dB per year among those 80–95 years of age (Brant & Fozard, 1990; Davis, Ostri, & Parving, 1991). Many studies have also indicated that hearing loss is accelerated among men during middle age and early old age. This phenomenon has often been attributed to sex differences in noise exposure at the workplace (Corso, 1981; Kryter, 1983; Moscicki, Elkins, Baum, & McNamara, 1985). This pattern of results clearly suggests that hearing in the later years of life might be better preserved given lifelong protection against noise exposure.

Frequency and Intensity Discrimination

The ability to discriminate small changes in the frequency or intensity of sounds is an important subcomponent of complex auditory processing tasks such as speech recognition and sound localization (Corso, 1981). Numerous studies have reported age-related decrements in these abilities (e.g., Cranford & Stream, 1991; Konig, 1957; Lutman, Gatehouse, & Worthington, 1991). More recently, studies by He, Dubno, and Mills (1998) and Humes (1996) have demonstrated that older adults were less able to discriminate between similar sounds that differed in intensity and/or frequency. Abel, Krever, and Alberti (1990) demonstrated particular age-related difficulties for frequency discrimination tasks with very brief tones (20 msec) relative to longer tones (200 msec), suggesting that older adults may have greater difficulty processing phonemes (20 msec) than syllables (200 msec) during speech discourse.

Sound Localization

Localization of a sound source is heavily dependent upon the auditory system's ability to process and interpret small differences in intensity and/or time-of-arrival between the two ears (Geldard, 1972). Laboratory studies in which interaural intensity and time-of-arrival have been manipulated reveal significant age-related decrements in the accuracy of sound localization performance (e.g., Hausler, Colburn, & Marr, 1983; Herman, Warren, & Wagener, 1977; Tillman, Carhardt, & Nichols, 1973). Herman and colleagues (1977) reported that age differences in sound localization ability appeared to be due to problems discriminating interaural time-of-arrival rather than interaural intensity differences. Since the localization of low-frequency sound sources is primarily dependent upon discrimination of interaural time-of-arrival cues, Olsho, Harkins, and Lenhardt (1985) have suggested that older adults may exhibit particular problems localizing events or objects that emit low-frequency sounds. This possibility has important implications for real-world performance domains such as negotiating busy roadway traffic as either a pedestrian or a driver (Schieber, 1992).

Speech Recognition

Many studies have reported age-related decrements in speech perception. Particularly dramatic effects have been reported in the classic study by Jerger (1973), who found that speech recognition for monosyllabic words decreased from just below 100% at 20 years of age to less than 60% correct for those 80–89 years of age. Age-related decrements in speech intelligibility are exacerbated under challenging listening conditions such as background noise (Jokinen, 1973; Plomp & Mimpen, 1979), architectural echo or reverberation (Bergman, 1971, 1980; Helfer & Wilber, 1990; Nabelek & Robinson, 1987) and time compression (Letowski & Poch, 1996; Sticht & Gray, 1969). Recent research in this area has focused upon determining the relative contribution of *peripheral* versus *central* mechanisms to age-related performance decrements. This distinction between peripheral (sensory) and central (cognitive) mechanisms is important. If age-related decrements in speech perception are primarily due to sensory factors, rehabilitation and compensation would involve some sort of signal processing intervention. If decrements are primarily cognitive in nature, rehabilitation might best be accomplished through a comprehensive training approach (Schieber & Baldwin, 1996).

Age-related decrements in the ability to understand speech can be mitigated somewhat when stimulus intensity levels are increased substantially, suggesting that much of the age-related decrement is mediated by peripheral rather than central mechanisms (Gordon-Salant, 1987). However, age-related decrements in the perception of "speeded speech," which are remarkably robust, appear to be mediated by central mechanisms as they are not mitigated by increased stimulus intensity level (Gordon-Salant & Fitzgibbons, 1999). Most of the classic literature on age differences in speech perception employed single-word stimuli that were not embedded within a semantic context. However, when speech stimuli are presented within sentence or paragraph contexts, age-related deficits in speech intelligibility are reduced (Gordon-Salant & Fitzgibbons, 1997; Holtzman, Familant, Deptula, & Hoyer, 1986; Wingfield, Poon, Lombardi, & Lowe, 1985). These findings clearly suggest that old adults can successfully employ higher-order cognitive mechanisms to compensate for age-related losses in sensory function. What remains to be established is the "attentional costs" of such compensatory processes.

Compensating for Age-Related Hearing Deficits

The age differences in the structure and function of the auditory system outlined above suggest several opportunities for enhancing performance via optimized design. Some guidelines for achieving these ends are listed below. Additional information regarding the optimization of auditory environments for older persons can be found in Kline and Scialfa (1997) and Schieber and colleagues (1991).

1. Increase stimulus intensity. Age-related declines in auditory perception and speech recognition are often mitigated by increasing stimulus volume.

2. Control background noise. Age differences in auditory perception are exacerbated in the presence of background noise. Background noise can be reduced at the source (e.g., replacing noisy heating/air-conditioning equipment with quieter models) and through the careful selection of architectural elements that reduce reverberation or absorb stray acoustic energy, and so forth.

3. Avoid the need to detect and/or recognize high-frequency acoustic information.

4. Long-term exposure to high levels of noise (i.e., 88 dB or greater) should be avoided across the life span in order to minimize the cumulative effects of *presbycusis*.

5. Do not signal location with low frequency sound sources. When this cannot be avoided, provide redundant localization cues such as warning signs or flashing lights. Kline and Scialfa (1997) also suggest that sound localization performance in older adults can be improved by increasing the duration of the signal.

6. Speech recognition can be significantly enhanced through the use of semantically well-structured prose that is rich in context and redundant. Hence, designers of voiced-based output systems must be concerned with message content in addition to physical design characteristics such as frequency and intensity.

7. Speech recognition among older adults is improved when presented at a reasonable and consistent pace (maximum rate of 140–200 words per minute (see Charness & Bosman, 1992).

8. Technological advances in hearing aid development need to be complemented by proper training of users and compensatory adjustments based upon user feedback. Without such a *systems approach,* 25–50% of persons fitted with hearing aids refuse to wear them due to various complaints related to comfort and/or function (see Fozard & Gordon-Salant, 2001).

9. Embedded computer systems with real-time signal processing capabilities should be combined with the increasingly ubiquitous Internet infrastructure to provide anytime/anywhere assistive listening support to older adults and other hearing-impaired individuals. For example, speech information (from public speakers, media presentations, broadcast TV, etc.) could be digitized and distributed in real time to personal assistive listening devices using the Internet backbone and protocols. This "direct approach" to speech signal enhancement would provide heretofore rarely attained signal/noise ratios and enhance end-user performance and satisfaction.

ATTENTION

Attention is a nebulous yet central construct for modern cognitive science. It at once encompasses both the capacity and component operations of human information processing. That is, attention is comprised of both resources and processes. An essential characteristic of attention is that it is highly limited. As such, its functional capacity (i.e., efficiency) can benefit greatly from the application of top-down management or "executive control." These interacting aspects of attention can be organized into four functional categories: (1) attention span, (2) selective attention, (3) divided attention, and (4) sustained attention. Important age-related developments in each of these areas will be introduced in the sections that follow.

Attention Span
(or Useful Field of View)

Binocular light sensitivity extends across the full (150–180 degree) field of peripheral vision. However, the ability to accurately identify and discriminate visual stimuli (without making an eye movement) is restricted to a much smaller region of the visual field. The size of this region, often called the *useful field of view* (UFOV), varies with display characteristics and task demands. For example, UFOV size decreases when attentional demands are increased through the addition of a secondary discrimination task in central vision (Ball, Beard, Roenker, Miller, & Griggs, 1988) or when the number of background stimuli is increased (Sekuler & Ball, 1986; Scialfa, Kline, & Lyman, 1987).

Sekuler and Ball (1986) reported that the spatial extent of the useful field of view was restricted in many older adults. These results were soon replicated and extended in additional studies (e.g., Ball et al., 1988; Scialfa, Kline, & Lyman, 1987). Ball, Roenker, and Bruni (1990) reported that UFOV spatial extent decreased under dual-task and brief exposure conditions and that the size of these effects was magnified among their older observers. Although the exact cause of age-related restrictions in the useful field of view remains unclear, it is apparent that much of the age-related variation in its spatial extent can be attributed to cognitive and attentional mechanisms rather than to sensory limitations.

Significant age-related reductions in the area over which visual attention can effectively operate have obvious implications for real-world performance. For example, in a noteworthy series of studies, Ball and her colleagues (Ball & Owsley, 1991; Owsley et al., 1998) have demonstrated that significant reductions in UFOV (assessed under conditions where processing time was greatly restricted) were highly predictive of past and/or future involvement in "at-fault" automobile driving accidents. In what may prove to be a remarkable development, Ball and colleagues (1988) also demonstrated that age-related UFOV deficits could be reversed following extended practice using a perceptual training protocol. Maintenance of these beneficial training results was still observed at a 6-month follow-up assessment. If age-related UFOV restriction is associated with widely observed deficits in visual information processing (see below), then it follows that perceptual training holds great potential for remediation of a wide variety of performance deficits. These and related possibilities are currently being investigated by cognitive scientists around the world.

Selective Attention

At any given moment the human senses generate a massive amount of information about the environment. It is self-evident that conscious awareness is limited to a select subset of this information as organized by interacting perceptual and cognitive mechanisms. Selective attention is a mechanism whereby incoming sensory-perceptual information is routed to higher-order cognitive mechanisms for additional processing. Selective attention is a "gatekeeper" that assigns priority based upon a complex interaction between the perceptual features of incoming information and the current goals and intentions of the observer.

The classic study of age-related changes in selective attention was reported by Rabbitt (1965). Rabbitt found that older observers became disproportionately disadvantaged in their ability to discern target stimuli from non-target (distracter) stimuli as the number of distracters increased. He concluded that older observers had "difficulty ignoring irrelevant information." Recent reviews of the selective attention literature (e.g., McDowd & Shaw, 2000; Plude, Schwartz, & Murphy, 1996) point out that such age-related deficits in selective attention are ubiquitous but not universal. Contemporary research appears to be focused upon (1) delineating the boundary conditions within which age-related deficits occur and (2) isolating the mechanisms of age-related deficits in selective attention. While the boundary conditions have yet to be established, many mechanisms have been proposed to account for such age differences in performance. Among the most likely general mechanisms are slowing in the rate of information processing (see Salthouse, 1985), diminished availability and/or executive control of attentional resources (Madden, 1986; Salthouse, Rogan, & Prill, 1984), and inhibition insufficiency (Hasher & Zachs, 1988). Unfortunately, these mechanisms are not mutually exclusive and are difficult to distinguish from one another experimentally (see Hartley, 1992).

The vast majority of research on age-related changes in selective attention has been conducted using some variant of the visual search paradigm. Plude and Doussard-Roosevelt (1989) investigated age differences in visual search within the context of Treisman and Gelade's (1980) influential *Feature Integration Theory* of attention. This theory holds that the objects of visual cognition are constructed via a two-stage process of encoding: namely, *feature extraction* and *feature integration.* The feature extraction process selects information based upon primitive perceptual characteristics (such as color, orientation, luminance, contrast, etc.). Since these properties are automatically segregated by perceptual systems, feature extraction is fast, efficient, conducted in parallel with other feature extraction operations, and consumes very few cognitive resources. Feature integration processes, however, cannot take advantage of perceptual automaticity and are therefore slow, sequential operations that consume significant cognitive resources. Plude and Doussard-Roosevelt compared young and older observers on visual search under conditions where target discrimination was limited by the feature extraction process (i.e., feature search) or feature integration (i.e., conjunction search). No age differences in performance were observed in the feature search condition where there was no overlap between the target color and the color of the background distracters. Search time was independent of the variation in the number of distracters across trials indicating that fast, efficient, automatic feature extraction processes appeared to be intact in the older observers. However, sizable age differences in performance were observed in the conjunction search condition. As is typically the case for a conjunction search, where multiple perceptual features must be combined by attentional processes to distinguish targets from distracters, search time increased as the number of background distracter stimuli grew. However, the search costs for older observers increased at a rate of 50 msec/distracter compared to only 25 msec/distracter for their younger counterparts. These results indicate that feature integration processes deteriorate with increasing adult age and suggest that age differences in visual search are mediated by encoding inefficiency rather than a selection deficit, per se.

Other studies have provided evidence for more specific mechanisms of age-related failure of selective attention in visual search tasks. Posner, Inhoff, Friedrich, and Cohen (1987) depict the deployment of attention in visual search tasks as three sequential operations: engagement, disengagement, and movement of the locus of attention. Employing this conceptualization, D'Aloisio and Klein (1990) have presented evidence that age-related declines in visual search performance result from a difficulty in the disengagement of attention from previously inspected targets. McDowd, Filion, and Oseas-Kreger (1991; cited in Cavanaugh, 1997) showed that when task relevant and irrelevant stimuli were presented in the same sense modality (e.g., both in the visual or both in the auditory domain), older persons failed to demonstrate good selectivity and attended equally to both relevant and irrelevant information alike. However, when relevant and irrelevant information were presented in *separate sense modalities* (e.g., visual versus auditory) older observers demonstrated improved selective performance. This finding is consistent with *multiple resource theories* of attention (e.g., Wickens, 1984) and may have important implications for the design of complex human-computer interfaces such as those being developed for advanced technology automobile instrument panels.

Scialfa, Thomas, and Joffe (1994) examined age differences in visual search while simultaneously monitoring gaze location using a corneal reflectance eye tracker. Age differences in visual search for targets requiring feature integration comparable to those demonstrated by Plude and Doussard-Roosevelt (1989) were obtained. These same differences were also reflected in the eye movement data. Older observers required a greater number of saccadic eye movements in order to find the target. This finding clearly suggests that older persons process smaller "chunks" of visual information at any given moment, a trend that is exacerbated as the width of the visual search area increases from 3.82 to 13.94 degrees (Scialfa & Joffe, 1997). Scialfa and his colleagues propose that reductions in the spatial extent of the useful field of view (UFOV) may be an important contributing factor to age-related declines in the efficiency of visual information processing. If this conclusion is correct, then training programs that increase the effective size of the UFOV may generalize to improved performance upon a variety of visual search tasks both inside and outside of the laboratory.

In domains where individuals have developed high levels of expertise through many years of practice, such as the interpretation of medical x-ray images, older experts outperform younger novices despite exhibiting normative search decrements on laboratory visual search tasks (Clancey & Hoyer, 1994). A likely explanation for this phenomenon is that prolonged and repeated practice eventually results in a qualitative shift in the manner in which skill-based tasks are processed. According to Shiffrin and Schneider (1977), highly practiced skills develop as slow, sequential, and resource-consuming *effortful* processes used to accomplish a task are gradually replaced by fast, parallel, and resource-efficient *automatic* processes. Hence, the automatization of skill-based behaviors results in a reduction in the demand for scarce attentional resources and may explain why expertise developed during one's young and middle-aged years appears to be particularly resistant to the deleterious effects of aging (see Salthouse, 1990a, 1990b). What remains to be seen is whether attentional automaticity can be developed after one has reached the later years of the life span.

Fisk and his colleagues (Fisk, McGee, & Giambra, 1988; Fisk & Rogers, 1991) have conducted several studies exploring the development of automaticity in the domain of visual information processing. This work has employed extensive training protocols previously shown to lead to the development of automaticity in young observers (i.e., a "consistent stimulus mapping" strategy in which target and distracter feature sets remain mutually exclusive throughout the acquisition phase of skill development). Unfortunately, however, these researchers have consistently demonstrated a failure to achieve automaticity of visual search skills among older adults, even when the training regimen exceeded 5,000 trials. Fisk and colleagues have concluded that attentional skills are resistant to the development of automaticity in old age. It is interesting to note that Ball and colleagues (1988) were highly successful in applying perceptual training to expand and maintain the spatial extent of the useful field of view among older research participants.

Additional research is needed to ascertain the mechanisms mediating these different patterns of results across such similar visual information-processing domains.

Divided Attention

Divided attention refers to processes by which attention is allocated and controlled to successfully perform two or more tasks simultaneously. Laboratory measures of divided attention typically employ the dual-task paradigm in which two tasks are performed both separately as well as concomitantly. The cost of dividing attention is typically quantified by measuring the difference in performance upon a given task when performed under dual task conditions relative to performance on the same component task assessed under single task (baseline) conditions. Laboratory measures of divided attention are of particular significance in the field of human factors since they have been shown to be predictive of complex performance in real-world domains such as aviation (Damos, 1978; Gopher, 1982) and automobile driving (Avolio, Kroeck, & Panek, 1985; Ball & Owsley, 1991).

According to several major reviews of the literature, large and robust age-related declines have been consistently observed in studies of dual-task performance (Craik, 1977; Hartley, 1992; Kramer & Larish, 1996). Some investigators have attributed these deficits to insufficient, inefficient, and/or mismanaged cognitive resources (e.g., Korteling, 1991; McDowd & Craik, 1988; Park, Smith, Dudley, & Lafronza, 1989). Consistent with this view, the magnitude of the age-related increase in multitasking "costs" grows as the complexity or information-processing demands of the component tasks increase (e.g., Salthouse et al., 1984; Somberg & Salthouse, 1982). Other investigators have suggested that age-related declines in dual-task performance are mediated by a difficulty with switching attention between task domains (e.g., D'Aloisio & Klein, 1990; Hawkins, Kramer, & Capaldi, 1992; McDowd, Vercruyssen, & Birren, 1991).

Brouwer and his colleagues (Brouwer, Ickenroth, Ponds, & van Wolffelaar, 1990; Ponds, Brouwer, & van Wolffelaar, 1988) have performed a series of studies that have focused upon age-related problems in divided attention during simulated driving. Older subjects (mean age: 66.2) demonstrated declines in steering performance in the dual-task condition (employing a visual scanning subsidiary task). The performance of their younger subjects (mean age: 30.2) did not vary across the single- versus dual-task conditions. Remarkably, the size of the age-related reduction in steering accuracy under divided attention conditions was cut in half when a vocal response was required on the secondary task (as opposed to a manual response). Similar findings have been reported by van Wolffelaar, Rotthengatter, and Brouwer (1991). This pattern of results suggests that both cognitive (i.e., supervisory task control) and motor (i.e., dual response coordination) deficits mediated the age-related performance problems, and that age-related deficits in driving performance may be offset somewhat by reducing the programming load of the motor channel. These findings appear to have great significance for the design of in-vehicle interfaces that will meet the needs of older drivers without overloading their attentional reserve capacity.

Korteling (1994) has also performed a series of simulator-based studies exploring age differences in the dynamics of divided attention during driving. Young (mean age: 27) and older (mean age: 70) subjects performed a steering and car-following task in an advanced driving simulator. During some driving sessions, pressing the gas pedal increased acceleration (normal condition) but in other sessions, its function was reversed—pressing down on the gas pedal caused deceleration (inverted condition). No age-group differences in performance were observed for the "normal" condition, but a fascinating pattern of age differences emerged for the inverted condition. The age-related deficit in performance was found only for the steering task—not for the car-following task that required the difficult compensation due to the reversal of a previously overlearned skill. The older drivers clearly tended to focus their attentional resources upon the compensatory activities required to meet the challenges imposed by the "impaired" operational subtask, but at the expense of another important subtask—steering. This result is somewhat surprising since contemporary attention theory would suggest that well-learned skills (such as steering a car) have become automatized and, hence, are usually immune to performance deficits during competition for attentional resources. Korteling's (1994) study suggests that there may be complex and unexpected "costs" associated with compensatory behaviors among older adults.

Gopher and his colleagues (Gopher, Weil, & Bareket, 1994; Gopher, Weil, & Siegel, 1989) have presented evidence that the development of performance in multitask situations is improved when *variable priority* strategies are implemented. In a variable priority training schedule, the trainee is instructed to progressively increase and then decrease the priority given to one of the component tasks in a multitask scenario. This continuous variation in task prioritization appears to provide trainees with the opportunity to develop improved skills in the management of cognitive resources. Kramer, Larish, and Strayer (1995) recently reported that compared to fixed priority schedules, older adults demonstrated improved development of dual-task skills as well as increased transfer of training following the adoption of a variable priority strategy.

Sustained Attention

Sustained attention, or vigilance, refers to those processes that enable an observer to continuously monitor, detect, and correctly respond to rare environmental events over a prolonged duration. The few studies that are available, when considered together, suggest that (1) older subjects are more likely to "miss" the detection of rare events (rare being defined as 0.01–0.25 Hz) and (2) this age-related reduction in sensitivity for rare events is relatively independent of time-on-task (Giambra & Quilter, 1988; Parasuraman, Nestor, & Greenwood, 1989; Surwillo & Quilter, 1964); that is, little or no "vigilance decrement" has been observed among healthy persons less than 75 years of age.

Compensating for Age-Related Deficits in Attention

The age differences in attention that were outlined above can be used to generate guidelines for improving the design of products and environments for older persons. Several such guidelines are listed below for consideration. Some are speculative and await verification via "hands-on" cognitive engineering and field validation tests. *Caveat emptor!*

1. Stimulus "clutter" should be minimized. Task-irrelevant information may be especially distracting to older observers.
2. Present visual information in smaller "chunks." This applies to both the amount of information as well as its spatial distribution. Reductions in the useful field of view (UFOV) suggest that older persons sample complex visual scenes using spatial windows of restricted size/area (e.g., 10–15 degrees of visual angle). It may follow, therefore, that presenting fewer stimuli, distributed within a smaller spatial frame, may support improved visual performance. In applying this strategy, however, one must be careful not to pack the stimuli so closely together as to cause crowding effects.
3. Minimize the need to search for "conjunctions" of stimulus features. Use well-established perceptual features when developing schemes to highlight text or graphical stimulus materials. Feature integration processes are impaired in older persons while simple feature search appears to remain robust across age.

4. Remove information from dynamic displays (such as computer monitors) as soon as its usefulness has expired. This practice will not only help control visual clutter but may serve to mitigate age-related decrements in the ability to disengage attention from sampled displays.

5. Explore the use of multimedia (guided by *Multiple Resource Theory*) to segregate competing information streams across separate sensory modalities in multitasking situations.

6. Minimize the need to develop new perceptual skills. The development of automatized perceptual grouping appears to be significantly impaired in old age (but note the exception in the case of UFOV training).

7. Use cognitive task analysis to design multitasking operations so that they reduce overall component complexity and distribute task load over multiple resource pools. Age-related decrements in multitasking performance are particularly acute when component task complexity is high and/or when resource demands are great. *Multiple resource theory* (Wickens, 1984) holds particular promise for engineering workstation solutions optimized to the cognitive/attentional capacities of older users.

8. The deployment of voice recognition technology appears to hold some promise for mitigating age-related attentional difficulties in complex multitasking environments (e.g., high technology automobile instrument clusters complete with Internet access). However, the operational success of such applications may be greatly limited by their high demands upon *recall memory*, which is significantly impaired in old age (see below).

9. Leverage sustained attention capabilities, which remain robust in old age, to redesign multitasking procedures when possible.

MEMORY

Most research in the area of aging and memory has been designed and interpreted within the context of an information-processing model such as the one schematically represented in Figure 2.1. The module labeled STM represents short-term memory processes that serve to mediate awareness and manipulation of sensory input. Primary memory subsumes the static representation of information whereas working memory and executive control processes represent active transformation and manipulation of cognitive objects derived from immediate sensory stimulation or previously acquired knowledge. The box labeled LTM represents long-term memory which, is subdivided into three

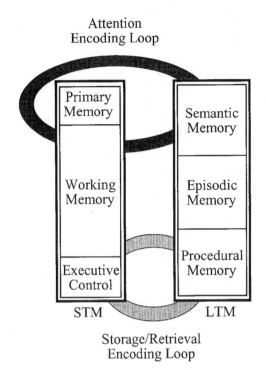

FIGURE 2.1 An information processing model of memory.

separate memory systems: Semantic memory represents linguistically categorized knowledge. Episodic memory represents the coding of events. Procedural memory represents highly automatized or skilled behaviors. The transformation, or encoding, of incoming sensory information into short-term memory is constrained by previously acquired knowledge and skills as well as current goals and intentions. This influence is represented by the attention loop depicting both upstream and downstream encoding processes. Similarly, the processes driving memory storage and retrieval are represented via the storage/retrieval encoding loop (see Figure 2.1).

Primary Memory

The static capacity of primary memory can be assessed using devices such as the digit span or word span test. Individuals are given a list of single digit numerals or unrelated words and then required to immediately repeat the list (usually in the same order in which it was presented). Static memory capacity is given by the length of the longest list that can be remembered without error. Extensive studies of young individuals reveal that the average capacity of primary memory is seven items, with the entire normal population being encompassed by plus or minus two items about this mean value (Miller, 1956). Studies examining age differences in the static capacity of primary memory reveal systematic but very small age-related declines. For example, Parkinson (1982) reported mean digit span scores of 6.6 and 5.8 for his younger and older subjects, respectively. Similar findings have been confirmed in numerous studies (e.g., Johansson & Berg, 1989; Salthouse & Babcock 1991).

Another important dimension of primary memory function is the rate at which its contents decay over time. Such measures are usually obtained using some variant of the Brown-Peterson technique. Individuals are presented with a short list of stimuli to be remembered. However, the recall of the stimulus items is delayed by the imposition of a distraction task that prevents active rehearsal of the to-be-remembered material (e.g., counting backwards by threes). Recall is then measured after various delay intervals. The contents of primary memory usually fade away completely within 20–30 seconds, depending upon the initial memory load (Brown, 1958; Peterson & Peterson, 1959). Research comparing young and older participants shows that the persistence of primary memory contents remains unchanged as a function of old age (e.g., Craik, 1977; Puckett & Stockberger, 1988).

Working Memory

Working memory is the *dynamic* extension of primary memory. It is the "system that performs the task of temporarily manipulating information" (Baddeley, 1989, p. 36). An important aspect of the working memory construct is the "executive control" process that coordinates the allocation of cognitive/attentional resources required to mediate goal-directed transformations of short-term memory contents. There is overwhelming evidence that normal adult aging is accompanied by a working memory deficit. That is, when the contents of primary memory must be manipulated, significant age differences in memory capacity become evident. Craik (1986), for example, had young and older participants perform a modified version of the word span test of primary memory capacity. Participants were required to recall short lists of stimulus words in alphabetical order rather than the random order in which the stimuli had been presented (requiring an in-memory manipulation of stimulus information that is *not* required on a simple test of primary memory capacity). The addition of this simple information-processing requirement resulted in the occurrence of large age-related declines in the capacity of dynamic or "working" memory. Similar results have been reported in numerous studies (e.g., Dobbs & Rule, 1987; Wingfield, Stine, Lahar, & Aberdeen, 1988).

The magnitude of the age-related deficit in working memory capacity increases with the complexity of the cognitive processing or in-memory transformation requirements (Craik, Morris, & Glick, 1990; Salthouse, Mitchell, Skovronek, & Babcock, 1989). Salthouse (1990a) has argued that such age-related differences in working memory can be attributed to reductions in the ability to monitor and/or coordinate concurrent processing demands rather than a structural limitation in memory capacity, per se. A similar but more specific mechanism has been proposed by Hasher and Zacks (1988). Their *inhibition insufficiency hypothesis* holds that older adults have weakened inhibitory control processes. As a result, task irrelevant recollections can accumulate in short-term memory and lead to a functional decline in the ability to perform cognitive work. The resulting "cluttered" memory space yields what appears to be a decline in working memory capacity. This mechanism is also compatible with the age-related declines in selective attention outlined above.

Long-Term Memory

Long-term memory, like any complex system, can be partitioned into several functional parts. Tulving (1972) has proposed an influential repartitioning of memory into several complementary subsystems: namely, the episodic, semantic, and procedural memory systems. The *episodic memory system* mediates the "storage and retrieval of temporally dated, spatially located and personally experienced events or episodes" while the *semantic memory system* mediates the "storage and utilization of knowledge about words and concepts, their properties and interrelations" (Tulving & Thompson, 1973, p. 354; Benjafield, 1992). One's understanding of the phrase "Internet browser" is rooted in semantic memory, whereas the recollection of having used an Internet browser while at work yesterday morning to look-up a stock quote would be the stuff of episodic memory. *Procedural memory* refers to the implicit (i.e., unconscious) representation of the rules for various domains of skilled performance. One's ability to ride a bicycle or "touch type" would be housed within the procedural memory system. There is general agreement that episodic memory performance declines with age while procedural and semantic memory performance remains relatively intact

(Kausler, 1991; Salthouse, 1982; Smith & Earles, 1996). As such, the remainder of this section will provide a survey of research findings regarding aging of episodic memory performance.

Recall versus Recognition

Schonfield and Robertson (1966) presented a list of to-be-remembered words to participants in five groups ranging in age from 20 to 70 years old. Memory for these words was then immediately assessed using either free recall or a multiple choice recognition procedure. Sizable age-related decrements in memory were observed with the free recall procedure. However, no significant age differences in performance were observed with the recognition memory task. Numerous studies have replicated this classic study of aging (e.g., Craik & McDowd, 1987; Smith, 1975). Clearly, age differences in episodic memory are reduced and sometimes eliminated when recognition procedures are used rather than free recall.

Encoding Insufficiency

It is commonly presumed that sensory-perceptual input to higher cognitive systems must first be transformed into a complex hierarchical and ultimately meaningful representational network. This process of transforming a signal from a proximal sensory code into a representation contextualized by an individual's accumulated world knowledge is known as *encoding*. The breadth and depth of the encoding processes can vary greatly, depending upon the individual's goal, available cognitive resources and effort, and environmental context/constraints. It is generally assumed that memory retrieval must recapitulate encoding processes during acquisition (i.e., storage). This notion, known as the *encoding specificity principle* (Tulving & Thompson, 1973), suggests that the level and richness of encoding during memory acquisition sets the limits upon its subsequent accessibility.

Under conditions where cognitive resources are restricted (e.g., multitasking, divided attention situations) individuals tend to encode events in a more stimulus-driven, automatic fashion and are less likely to mentally elaborate events in rich or contextually meaningful ways. As a result, subsequent memory performance is often impaired for information acquired during these conditions. Normal adult aging, with its apparent reduction in available cognitive resources, may result in a similar bias toward more shallow encoding processes (Craik & Simon, 1980; Hasher & Zacks, 1979; Rabinowitz, Craik, & Ackerman, 1982). In fact, there is a large body of evidence that suggests that many age-related decrements in memory performance can be attributed to inefficient encoding during storage and/or retrieval—the so-called *encoding insufficiency hypothesis* (Craik & Jennings, 1992). Hence, any manipulation or technology that could support systematic encoding of stimulus information would provide potential opportunities for improving memory-based performance among older adults.

Memory Source Monitoring

Older people appear much more likely to demonstrate *source monitoring* errors. That is, although they may recognize or recall a given object or event, they are much more likely to forget the source or context in which that information was originally acquired (Hashtroudi, Johnson, & Chrosniak, 1989; McIntyre & Craik, 1987). A similar age-related decrement has been reported by Cohen and Faulkner (1989), who studied memory for actions that had been actually performed by subjects as opposed to those that had merely been vicariously observed or imagined. When source monitoring errors did occur, young subjects reported high confidence in their erroneous source attributions about 9% of the time. However, older participants reported high confidence for 37% of their misattribution or source monitoring errors. This result stands in stark contrast to research reporting that metamemorial processes involving the accuracy of semantic memory (e.g., world knowledge) remain relatively intact among healthy older adults (Lachman & Lachman, 1980). Hence, older folks may "know what they know and what they do not know" with regard to semantic memory but may not be so accurate in knowing "from whence" their episodic memories have originated. This so-called "source amnesia" may have important implications for the reliability of eyewitness testimonials from older observers (see Craik & Jennings, 1992; Howard, 1996) and/or predispose older persons to *action slips,* a type of error in which one emits an unintended action (Craik & Jacoby, 1996).

Prospective Memory

Prospective memory involves remembering to carry out an action that is scheduled for some time in the future (i.e., remembering to remember). Several studies have demonstrated significant age-related increases in the rate of prospective memory errors (e.g., Cockburn & Smith, 1991; Dobbs & Rule, 1987). However, Maylor (1990) reported that many older persons charged with remembering to perform a future action spontaneously adopted the use of some form of external memory aid (such as notes, calendar entries, etc.). In fact, older persons who did employ such external memory aids actually tended to outperform their younger counterparts on prospective memory tasks. Other studies have also found that age differences in prospective memory can be mitigated through the use of environmental supports (e.g., Einstein, Smith, McDaniel, & Shaw, 1997; Loewen, Shaw, & Craik, 1990).

Automatic versus Volitional Memory Processes

Memory can be conceptualized as consisting of both *automatic* and *volitional* component processes. Automatic memory processes activate a web of preexisting associations between stimulus features and long-term memory representations and occur rapidly, effortlessly, and below the level of conscious awareness. These "implicit" memory processes are essential for perceiving and understanding any stimulus. Volitional or "explicit" memory, on the contrary, involves slow, effortful, consciously controlled strategic processes such as those that guide the study of materials to be remembered and when later retrieved. Most of the accumulated literature on aging and memory has focused upon volitional (i.e., explicit) memory. Recently, however, significant resources have been invested to investigate age differences in automatic (i.e., implicit) memory using stimulus priming procedures and assessing their subsequent impact upon critical dependent measures such as lexical decision making and work stem completion. Currently, the emerging consensus among the cognitive aging research community appears to be that automatic memory processes (e.g., spreading activation) remain relatively intact with advancing adult age (see reviews by Craik & Jacoby, 1996; Light & LaVoie, 1993). This consensus opinion is well represented in a quote taken from a recent review of the implicit memory literature by Howard (1996):

> There appears to be no decline with normal aging in the extent to which processing a stimulus automatically results in some alteration of preexisting perceptual pathways and conceptual representations; one way in which this alteration can be viewed is as a continuing activation of the relevant pathways and representations (though it is not yet clear how long any such activation continues). This hypothesis follows from the finding that, when perceptual and conceptual priming of facilitation materials are examined, age differences in priming are either nonexistent or minimal. (pp. 241–242)

Howard goes on to describe how this maintenance of implicit or automatic memory function has potentially great implications for everyday functioning, including cognitive training and intervention programs, differentiation of normal versus pathological aging, susceptibility to unconscious repetition and/or plagiarism, and social cognition (e.g., impression formation and persuasion). Craik and Jacoby (1996) note that expanding our knowledge about the conditions that allow for the establishment and maintenance of automatic memory processes will allow for the design of environments and products that improve everyday functioning in older people. Indeed, research has already shown how computer-based technology can be used to leverage implicit memory processes in the service of improved cognitive performance (e.g., Glisky, Schacter, & Tulving, 1986; Jennings & Jacoby, 1993; Schacter, 1996).

Environmental Support

The findings reviewed above make a strong case for the notion that age differences in memory performance can be ameliorated by providing environmental supports that (1) enhance or elaborate the encoding process and/or (2) minimize the demand for diminished cognitive resources. A select survey of a few studies yielding results consistent with this view are summarized below.

Backman (1986) presented a series of short sentences for immediate recall to young and older participants. The presentation rate (slow, fast) and sensory modality (visual, auditory, both visual and auditory) of the stimuli were varied. Age differences in memory performance were reduced when the presentation rate was slowed and when the text passages were redundantly presented in both the visual and auditory modalities simultaneously. Arenberg (1968) reported a similar "auditory augmentation" of recall among older adults. In a now classic study, Canestrari (1963) demonstrated that memory performance of older adults was significantly enhanced by removing stimulus time constraints during the encoding (acquisition) phase of attending to the to-be-remembered verbal stimuli. Hence, it would appear that *stimulus self-pacing* and *multimedia augmentation* may be valuable opportunities for enhancing memory encoding among older persons via environmental support.

Puglisi, Park, Smith, and Dudley (1988) found that memory performance among older adults was improved under certain conditions where stimuli were presented pictorially instead of verbally. A likely explanation for this effect was that the use of pictorial stimuli caused the older participants to switch from a shallow to a more elaborate encoding scheme. However, it should be noted that merely providing pictorial representations of to-be-remembered concepts is no panacea for comprehension or memory problems among the aged (see Morrell, Park, & Poon, 1990; Puglisi & Park, 1987). A follow-up study by Park, Smith, Morrell, Puglisi, and Dudley (1990) revealed that the encoding benefit of pictorial stimulus presentations was especially helpful for older adults when it served to automatically provide an integrative context linking to-be-remembered content—a dramatic demonstration of improved memory encoding and performance through environmental support.

Finally, it is well known that systematic sociohistoric, or cohort, differences exist between young and older groups of adults. The existence of these differences suggests that conceptual information may be biased in such a way that it becomes more meaningful (and, hence, easier to encode) for one (age) generation than another. Barrett and Wright (1981) demonstrated the potential influence of such cohort-mediated effects upon memory performance. Two cohort-specific word lists were constructed. The young-cohort list contained words that were more familiar to young college students than to their older counterparts (e.g., tweeter, gig, synthesizer). The old-cohort list contained words that were more familiar to old than young participants (e.g., poultice, fedora, vamp). Tests performed using these two word lists revealed that each age group demonstrated superior memory acquisition performance for the list of words that was optimized for their particular cohort. Remarkably, the performance of the old group was superior to that of the young group when the old-cohort stimuli were used. This finding suggests yet another means of using environmental supports to enhance learning and memory performance among older populations. The development of cohort-specific lexicons and knowledge bases might provide important new tools for the application of cognitive engineering to implement technology-based interventions designed to optimize high-level performance among people of all ages.

Compensating for Age-Related Deficits in Memory

Some of the key age-related differences in memory performance outlined above have been translated into the list of design guidelines that follow. Again, several of these guidelines must be considered as speculative until validated by field application data. Nonetheless, they provide a starting point for considering ways in which technological developments may provide design opportunities for enhancing higher-order cognitive function for those entering the later years of life.

1. Minimize the need to manipulate or transform information in short-term memory. Age-related decrements in the capacity of *working*

memory increase dramatically when "in-line" transformations are required. Tasks can be redesigned or augmented via technology interfaces to off-load such demands.

2. Apply guidelines for mitigating selective attention problems (outlined above) in the service of optimizing working memory capacity. Attentional capture of irrelevant stimuli may inefficiently tie up working memory capacity as well as interfere with "in-line" memory operations (see Hasher & Zacks, 1988).

3. Leverage recognition memory, which is relatively robust in old age, to redesign tasks that rely upon recall memory.

4. Design environmental supports to guide and/or enhance memory encoding processes. This can be accomplished via:

   a. Systematic cueing.
   b. Enriching perceptual and/or semantic contexts.
   c. Leveraging cohort-specific stimulus representational networks.
   d. Using pictorial formats to aid integration of multiple stimulus items into a predictable and unitary concept.

5. Avoid reliance upon *source memory*.

6. Provide environmental structural supports and prompts to aid *prospective memory*. Park (1992) provides a comprehensive set of guidelines for implementing such supports to augment adherence to medication schedules among older adults.

7. Leverage intact *automatic* memory processes (such as semantic priming) to support or off-load *volitional* memory processes. Of course, this is much easier said than done. However, several encouraging prototype applications of this cognitive engineering approach can be seen in the "method of vanishing cues" (Schacter, 1996) and "method of gradual shaping" (Jennings & Jacoby, 1993). The growing pervasiveness of *embedded computer systems* will contribute greatly to the opportunity to develop and deploy such subtle, yet potentially powerful, cognitive enhancement strategies based upon *intelligent* interaction and determination of end-user cognitive style and/or capactity.

8. Avoid (or control) stimulus "pacing" effects, which can interfere with encoding and response selection during both the acquisition and retrieval phases of memory operations. Technological interfaces need to be carefully designed to algorithmically optimize the rate of stimulus presentation or implement user-paced input/output strategies.

9. Explore the potential of multisensory/multimedia presentation formats for improving the encoding and retention of to-be-remembered information.

CONCLUDING COMMENTARY

This chapter has presented an overview of the major age-related changes in information-processing capacity that may constrain the ability of older people to interact with a technological environment that is becoming increasingly complex. There are significant structural and conceptual challenges facing those who will attempt to translate the theoretical knowledge of scientific gerontology into products and designs that will optimize behavioral functioning among our growing cohort of older adults. Yet, these difficulties are tempered by the great potential that the fusion of scientific theory and practice holds for enhancing the quality of life in our later years.

REFERENCES

Abel, S. M., Krever, E. M., & Alberti, P. W. (1990). Auditory detection, discrimination and speech processing in ageing, noise-sensitive and hearing-impaired listeners. *Scandinavian Audiology, 19,* 43–54.

Adams, A. J., Wong, L. S., Wong, L., & Gould, B. (1988). Visual acuity changes with age: Some new perspectives. *American Journal of Optometry and Physiological Optics, 65,* 403–406.

Anstis, S. M. (1974). A chart demonstrating variations in acuity with retinal position. *Vision Research, 14,* 589–592.

Arenberg, D. (1968). Input modality in short-term retention. *Journal of Gerontology, 23,* 462–465.

Atchison, D. A., Capper, E. J., & McCabe, K. L. (1994). Critical subjective measurement of amplitude of accommodation. *Optometry and Visual Science, 71,* 699–706.

Avolio, B., Kroeck, K., & Panek, P. (1985). Individual differences in information processing ability as a predictor of motor vehicle accidents. *Human Factors, 27,* 577–587.

Backman, L. (1986). Adult age differences in cross-modal recoding and mental tempo, and older adults' utilization of compensatory task conditions. *Experimental Aging Research, 12,* 135–140.

Baddeley, A. D. (1989). The psychology of remembering and forgetting. In T. Butler (Ed.), *Memory: History, culture and mind* (pp. 36–60). Oxford, UK: Basil Blackwell.

Ball, K. K., Beard, B. L., Roenker, D. L., Miller, R. L., & Griggs, D. S. (1988). Age and visual search: Expanding the useful field of view. *Journal of the Optical Society of America-A, 5,* 2210–2219.

Ball, K., & Owsley, C. (1991). Identifying correlates of accident involvement for the older driver. *Human Factors, 33,* 583–595.

Ball, K. K., Roenker, D. L., & Bruni, J. R. (1990) In J. T. Enns (Ed.), *The development of attention: Research and theory* (pp. 489–508). Amsterdam: North-Holland.

Barrett, T. R., & Wright, M. (1981). Age-related facilitation in recall following semantic processing. *Journal of Gerontology, 36,* 194–199.

Belal, A. (1975). Presbycusis: Physiological or pathological? *Journal of Laryngology, 89,* 1011–1025.

Benjafield, J. G. (1992). *Cognition.* Englewood Cliffs, NJ: Prentice-Hall.

Bergman, M. (1971). Hearing and aging. *Audiology, 10,* 164–171.

Bergman, M. (1980). *Aging and the perception of speech.* Baltimore: University Park Press.

Blackwell, O. M., & Blackwell, H. R. (1971). Visual performance data for 156 normal observers of various ages. *Journal of the Illuminating Engineering Society, 1,* 3–13.

Blackwell, O., & Blackwell, H. (1980). Individual responses to lighting parameters for a population of 235 observers of various ages. *Journal of the Illuminating Engineering Society, 10,* 205–232.

Brant, L. J., & Fozard, J. L. (1990). Age changes in pure-tone hearing thresholds in a longitudinal study of normal aging. *Journal of the Acoustical Society of America, 88,* 813–820.

Brouwer, W., Ickenroth, J., Ponds, R., & van Wolffelaar, P. (1990). Divided attention in old age: Difficulty integrating skills. In P. J. D. Drenth et al. (Eds.), *European perspectives in psychology, Volume 2* (pp. 335–348). New York: Wiley.

Brown, J. (1958). Some tests of the decay theory of immediate memory. *Quarterly Journal of Experimental Psychology, 10,* 12–21.

Buckingham, T., Whitaker, D., & Banford, D. (1987). Movement in decline? Oscillatory movement displacement thresholds decline with age. *Ophthalmic and Physiological Optics, 7,* 411–413.

Burg, A. (1967). *The relationship between vision test scores and driving record: General findings.* Los Angeles: Institute of Transportation and Traffic Engineering, University of California.

Canestrari, R. E., Jr. (1963). Paced and self-paced learning in young and elderly adults. *Journal of Gerontology, 18,* 165–168.

Cavanaugh, J. C. (1997). *Adult development and aging* (3rd ed.). Pacific Grove, CA: Brooks/Cole.

Charness, N., & Bosman, E. A. (1992). Human factors and age. In F. I. M. Craik & T. A. Salthouse (Eds.), *The handbook of aging and cognition* (pp. 495–551). Hillsdale, NJ: Erlbaum.

Charness, N., & Dijkstra, K. (1999). Age, luminance and print legibility in homes, offices, and public places. *Human Factors, 41,* 173–193.

Clancey, S., & Hoyer, W. J. (1994). Age and skilled differences in the processing demands of visual recognition performance. *Developmental Psychology, 30,* 545–552.

Cockburn, J., & Smith, P. T. (1991). The relative influence of intelligence and age on everyday memory. *Journals of Gerontology: Psychological Sciences, 46,* P31–P36.

Cody, P. S., Hurd, P. D., & Bootman, J. L. (1990). The effects of aging and diabetes on the perception of medication color. *Journal of Geriatric Drug Therapy, 4,* 113–121.

Cohen, G., & Faulkner, D. (1989). Age differences in source forgetting: Effects on reality monitoring and on eyewitness testimony. *Psychology and Aging, 4,* 10–17.

Collins, M. J., Brown, B., & Bowman, K. J. (1989). Peripheral visual acuity and age. *Ophthalmic and Physiological Optics, 9,* 314–316.

Corso, J. F. (1963). Age and sex differences in pure tone thresholds. *Archives of Otolaryngology, 77,* 385–405.

Corso, J. F. (1981). *Aging, sensory systems and perception.* New York: Praeger.

Craik, F. I. M. (1977). Age differences in human memory. In J. E. Birren & K. W. Schaie (Eds.), *Handbook of the psychology of aging* (pp. 384–420). New York: VanNostrand-Reinhold.

Craik, F. I. M. (1986). A functional account of age differences in memory. In F. Klix & H. Hagendorf (Eds.), *Human memory and cognitive capabilities, mechanisms and performances* (pp. 409–422). Amsterdam: North-Holland.

Craik, F. I. M., & Jacoby, L. L. (1996). Aging and memory: Implications for skilled performance. In W. A. Rogers, A. D. Fisk, & N. Walker (Eds.), *Aging and skilled performance: Advances in theory and applications* (pp. 113–137). Mahwah, NJ: Erlbaum.

Craik, F. I. M., & Jennings, J. M. (1992). Human memory. In F. I. M. Craik & T. A. Salthouse (Eds.), *The handbook of aging and cognition* (pp. 51–110). Hillsdale, NJ: Erlbaum.

Craik, F. I. M., & McDowd, J. M. (1987). Age differences in recall and recognition. *Journal of Experimental Psychology: Learning, Memory and Cognition, 13,* 474–479.

Craik, F. I. M., Morris, R. G., & Glick, M. L. (1990). Adult age differences in working memory. In G. Vallar & T. Schallice (Eds.), *Neuropsychological impairment of short-term memory* (pp. 247–267). Cambridge, UK: Cambridge University Press.

Craik, F. I. M., & Simon, E. (1980). Age differences in memory: The roles of attention and depth of processing. In L. W. Poon, J. L. Fozard, L. Cermak, D. Arenberg, & L. W. Thompson (Eds.), *New directions in memory and aging: Proceedings of the George Talland memorial conference* (pp. 95–112). Hillsdale, NJ: Erlbaum.

Cranford, J. L., & Stream, R. W. (1991). Discrimination of short duration tones by elderly subjects. *Journal of Gerontology, 46,* 37–41.

Crassini, B., Brown, B., & Bowman, K. (1988). Age related changes in contrast sensitivity in central and peripheral retina. *Perception, 17,* 315–332.

Curcio, C. A., & Drucker, D. N. (1993). Retinal ganglion cells in Alzheimer's disease and aging. *Annals of Neurology, 33,* 248–257.

Curcio, C. A., Millican, C. L., Allen, K. A., & Kalina, R. E. (1993). Aging of the human photoreceptor mosaic: Evidence for selective vulnerability of rods in central vision. *Investigative Ophthalmology and Visual Science, 34,* 3278–3296.

Dalderup, L. M., & Fredricks, M. L. C. (1969). Color sensitivity in old age. *Journal of the American Geriatrics Society, 17,* 388–390.

D'Aloisio, A., & Klein, R. M. (1990). Aging and the deployment of visual attention. In J. T. Enns (Ed.), *The development of attention: Research and theory* (pp. 447–466). Amsterdam: North-Holland.

Damos, D. (1978). Residual attention as a predictor of pilot performance. *Human Factors, 20,* 435–440.

Davis, A. C., Ostri, B., & Parving, A. (1991). Longitudinal study of hearing. *Acta Otolarygologica Supplement, 476,* 12–22.

Desai, M., Pratt, L. A., Lentzner, H., & Robinson, K. N. (2001). Trends in vision and hearing among older Americans. *Aging Trends: No. 2.* Hyattsville, MD: National Center for Health Statistics.

Dewar, R., Kline, D., Schieber, F., & Swanson, A. (1994). *Symbol signing design for older drivers [Report No. FHWA-RD-94-069].* McLean, VA: Federal Highway Administration.

Dobbs, A. R., & Rule, B. G. (1987). Prospective memory and self-reports of memory abilities in older adults. *Canadian Journal of Psychology, 41,* 209–222.

Donders, F. C. (1864). *On the anomalies and accommodation and refraction of the eye.* London: The New Sydenham Society.

Einstein, G. O., Smith, R. E., McDaniel, M. A., & Shaw, P. (1997). Aging and prospective memory: The influence of increased task demands at encoding and retrieval. *Psychology and Aging, 12,* 479–488.

Eisner, A., Fleming, S. A., Klein, M. L., & Maudlin, M. (1987). Sensitivities in older eyes with good acuity: Eyes whose fellow eye has exudative AMD. *Investigative Ophthalmology and Visual Science, 28,* 1832–1837.

Elliott, D. B., & Whitaker, D. (1990). Decline in retinal function with age. *Investigative Ophthalmology and Visual Science (Supplement), 31*(4), 357.

Evans, D. W., & Ginsburg, A. P. (1985). Contrast sensitivity predicts age differences in highway sign discriminability. *Human Factors, 27,* 637–642.

Fisk, A. D., McGee, N. D., & Giambra, L. M. (1988). The influence of age on consistent and varied semantic category search performance. *Psychology and Aging, 3,* 323–333.

Fisk, A. D., & Rogers, W. A. (1991). Development of skilled performance: An age-related perspective. In D. Damos (Ed.), *Multiple task performance* (pp. 415–433). London: Wiley.

Fozard, J. L. (1990). Vision and hearing in aging. In J. E. Birren & K. W. Schaie (Eds.), *Handbook of the psychology of aging* (3rd ed., pp. 150–170). New York: Academic Press.

Fozard, J. L., & Gordon-Salant, S. (2001). Changes in vision and hearing with age. In J. E. Birren & K. W. Schaie (Eds.), *Handbook of the psychology of aging* (5th ed., pp. 241–266). New York: Academic Press.

Garvey, P. M., Pietrucha, M. T., & Meeker, D. T. (1998). Clearer road signs ahead. *Ergonomics in Design, 6,* 7–11.

Geldard, F. (1972). *The human senses* (2nd ed.). New York: Wiley.

Giambra, L. M., & Quilter, R. E. (1988). Sustained attention in adulthood: A unique, large sample, longitudinal and multi-cohort analysis using the Macworth Clock test. *Psychology and Aging, 3,* 75–83.

Gilbert, J. G. (1957). Age changes in color matching. *Journal of Gerontology, 12,* 210–215.

Glisky, E. L., Schacter, D. L., & Tulving, E. (1986). Computer-learning by memory impaired patients: Acquisition and retention of complex knowledge. *Neuropsychologia, 24,* 313–328.

Gopher, D. (1982). A selective attention test as a predictor of success in flight training. *Human Factors, 24,* 173–184.

Gopher, D., Weil, M., & Bareket, T. (1994). Transfer of skill from a computer game trainer to flight. *Human Factors, 36,* 387–405.

Gopher, D., Weil, M., & Siegel, D. (1989). Practice under changing properties: An approach to training of complex skills. *Acta Psychologica, 71,* 147–179.

Gordon-Salant, S. (1987). Age-related differences in speech recognition performance as a function of test format and paradigm. *Ear and Hearing, 8,* 277–282.

Gordon-Salant, S., & Fizgibbons, P. J. (1997). Selected cognitive factors and speech recognition performance among young and elderly listeners. *Journal of Speech, Language, and Hearing Research, 40,* 423–431.

Gordon-Salant, S., & Fitzgibbons, P. J. (1999). Profile of auditory temporal processing in older listeners. *Journal of Speech, Language and Hearing Research, 42,* 300–311.

Haegerstrom-Portnoy, G. (1988). Short-wavelength cone sensitivity loss with aging: A protective role for macular pigment. *Journal of the Optical Society of America A, 5,* 2140–2144.

Haegerstrom-Portnoy, G., Schneck, M. E., & Braybyn, J. A. (1999). Seeing into old age: Vision function beyond acuity. *Optometry and Visual Science, 76,* 141–158.

Hartley, A. A. (1992). Attention. In F. I. M. Craik & T. A. Salthouse (Eds.), *The handbook of aging and cognition* (pp. 3–49). Hillsdale, NJ: Erlbaum.

Hasher, L., & Zacks, R. T. (1979). Automatic and effortful processes in memory. *Journal of Experimental Psychology: General, 108,* 356–388.

Hasher, L., & Zacks, R. T. (1988). Working memory, comprehension and aging: A review and a new view. In G. H. Bower (Ed.), *The psychology of learning and motivation, Volume 22* (pp. 193–225). New York: Academic Press.

Hashtroudi, S., Johnson, M. K., & Chrosniak, L. D. (1989). Aging and source monitoring. *Psychology and Aging, 4,* 106–112.

Hausler, R., Colburn, S., & Marr, E. (1983). Sound localization in subjects with impaired hearing: Spatial discrimination and discrimination tests. *Acta Otolaryngologica Supplement, 40C,* 6–62.

Hawkins, H. L., Kramer, A. F., & Capaldi, D. (1992). Aging, exercise and attention. *Psychology and Aging, 7,* 643–653.

He, N., Dubno, J. R., & Mills, J. H. (1998). Frequency and intensity discrimination measured in a maximum-likelihood procedure from young and aged normal-hearing subjects. *Journal of the Acoustical Society of America, 103,* 553–565.

Helfer, K. S., & Wilber, L. A. (1990). Hearing loss, aging, and speech perception in reverberation and noise. *Journal of Speech and Hearing Research, 33,* 149–155.

Herman, G. E., Warren, L. R., & Wagener, J. W. (1977). Auditory lateralization: Age differences in sensitivity to dichotic time and amplitude cues. *Journal of Gerontology, 32,* 187–191.

Herse, P. (1995). A new method for quantification of the dynamics of dark adaptation. *Optometry and Vision Science, 72,* 907–910.

Hills, B. (1975). *Some studies of movement perception, age and accidents (Report 137).* Crowethorne, UK: Transport Road Research Laboratory.

Hills, B. (1980). Vision, visibility and perception in driving. *Perception, 9,* 183–216.

Holtzman, R. E., Familant, M. E., Deptula, P., & Hoyer, W. (1986). Aging and the use of sentential structure to facilitate word recognition. *Experimental Aging Research, 12,* 85–88.

Howard, D. V. (1996). The aging of implicit and explicit memory. In F. Blanchard-Fields & T. M. Hess (Eds.), *Perspectives on cognitive change in adulthood and old age* (pp. 221–254). New York: McGraw-Hill.

Humes, L. E. (1996). Speech understanding in the elderly. *Journal of the American Academy of Audiology, 7,* 161–167.

Ijspeert, J. K., de Waard, P. W., van den Berg, T. J., & de Jong, P. T. (1990). The intraocular straylight function in 129 healthy volunteers: Dependence on angle, age and pigmentation. *Vision Research, 30,* 699–707.

Jaffe, G. J., Alvarado, J. A., & Juster, R. P. (1986). Age-related changes in the normal visual field. *Archives of Ophthalmology, 104,* 1021–1025.

Jennings, J., & Jacoby, L. L. (1993). Automatic versus intentional uses of memory: Aging, attention and control. *Psychology and Aging, 8,* 283–293.

Jerger, J. (1973). Audiological findings in aging. *Advances in Otorhinolaryngology, 20,* 115–124.

Johansson, B., & Berg, S. (1989). The robustness of the terminal decline phenomenon: Longitudinal data from the digit-span memory test. *Journals of Gerontology: Psychological Sciences, 44,* P184–P186.

Johnson, C., & Keltner, J. (1986). Incidence of visual field loss in 20,000 eyes and its relationship to driving performance. *Archives of Ophthalmology, 101,* 371–375.

Johnson, C. A., & Marshall, D. (1995). Aging effects for opponent mechanisms in the central visual field. *Optometry and Vision Sciences, 72,* 75–82.

Jokinen, J. (1973). Presbycusis. VI: Masking of speech. *Acta Otolaryngologica, 76,* 426–430.

Kahn, H. A., Leibowitz, H. W., Ganley, S. P., Kini, M. M., Colton, J., Nickerson, R. S., & Dawber, T. R. (1977). Framingham eye study. I. Outlines and major prevalence findings. *American Journal of Epidemiology, 106*, 17–32.

Kausler, D. H. (1991). *Experimental psychology, cognition and human aging* (2nd ed.). New York: Springer.

Kline, D. W., & Fuchs, P. (1993). The visibility of symbolic highway signs can be increased among drivers of all ages. *Human Factors, 35*, 25–34.

Kline, D. W., & Scialfa, C. T. (1997). Sensory and perceptual functioning: Basic research and human factors implications. In A. D. Fisk & W. A. Rogers (Eds.), *Handbook of human factors and the older adult* (pp. 27–54). New York: Academic Press.

Knoblauch, K., Sanders, F., Kusuda, M., Hynes, R., Podgor, M., Higgins, K. E., & de Monasterio, F. M. (1987). Age and illuminance effects in Farnsworth-Munsell 100 hue test. *Applied Optics, 26*, 1441–1448.

Konig, E. (1957). Pitch discrimination and age. *Acta Otolaryngologica, 48*, 475–489.

Koornstra, M., Bijleveld, F., & Hagenzieker, M. (1997). *The safety effects of daytime running lights.* Leidschendam, The Netherlands: SWOV Institute for Safety Research.

Korteling, J. E. (1991). Effects of skill integration and perceptual completion on age-related differences in dual-task performance. *Human Factors, 33*, 35–44.

Korteling, J. E. (1994). Effects of aging, skill modification and demand alternation on multiple-task performance. *Human Factors, 36*, 27–43.

Kraft, J. M., & Werner, J. S. (1999a). Aging and the saturation of colors. 1. Colorimetric purity discrimination. *Journal of the Optical Society of America A, 16*, 223–230.

Kraft, J. M., & Werner, J. S. (1999b). Aging and the saturation of colors. 2. Scaling of color appearance. *Journal of the Optical Society of America A, 16*, 231–234.

Kramer, A. F., & Larish, J. L. (1996). Aging and dual-task performance. In W. A. Rogers, A. D. Fisk, & N. Walker (Eds.), *Aging and skilled performance: Advances in theory and applications* (pp. 83–112). Mahwah, NJ: Erlbaum.

Kramer, A. F., Larish, J. L., & Strayer, D. L. (1995). Training for attentional control in dual-task settings: Beyond a unitary view of inhibitory processing in attention. *Journal of Experimental Psychology: Applied, 1*, 50–76.

Kryter, K. D. (1983). Presbycusis, sociocusis and nosocusis. *Journal of the Acoustical Society of America, 73*, 1897–1917.

Lachman, J. L., & Lachman, R. (1980). Age and the actualization of world knowledge. In L. W. Poon, J. L. Fozard, L. S. Cermak, D. Arenberg, & L. W. Thompson (Eds.), *New directions in memory and aging* (pp. 285–311). Hillsdale, NJ: Erlbaum.

Letowski, T., & Poch, N. (1996). Comprehension of time-compressed speech: Effects of age and speech complexity. *Journal of the American Academy of Audiology, 7*, 447–457.

Light, L. L., & LaVoie, D. (1993). Direct and indirect measures of memory in old age. In P. Graf & M. E. J. Masson (Eds.), *Implicit memory: New directions in cognition, development and neuropsychology* (pp. 207–230). Hillsdale, NJ: Erlbaum.

Loewen, E. R., Shaw, R. J., & Craik, F. I. M. (1990). Age differences in components of metamemory. *Experimental Aging Research, 16,* 43–48.

Lowenfeld, L. E. (1979). Pupillary changes related to age. In H. S. Thompson (Ed.), *Topics in neuro-ophthalmology* (pp. 124–150). Baltimore: Williams & Wilkins.

Lutman, M. E., Gatehouse, S., & Worthington, A. G. (1991). Frequency resolution as a function of hearing threshold level and age. *Journal of the Acoustical Society of America, 89,* 320–328.

Madden, D. J. (1986). Adult age differences in the attentional capacity demands of visual search. *Cognitive Development, 1,* 335–363.

Maylor, E. A. (1990). Age and prospective memory. *Quarterly Journal of Experimental Psychology: Human Experimental Psychology, 42,* 471–493.

McDowd, J. M., & Craik, F. I. M. (1988). Effects of aging and task difficulty on divided attention performance. *Journal of Experimental Psychology: Human Perception and Performance, 14,* 267–280.

McDowd, J. M., Filion, D. L., & Oseas-Kreger, D. M. (1991, August). *Inhibitory deficits in selective attention and aging.* Paper presented at the annual meeting of the American Psychological Society, Washington, DC (cited in Cavanaugh, 1997, p. 16).

McDowd, J. M., & Shaw, R. J. (2000). Attention and aging: A functional perspective. In F. I. M Craik & T. A. Salthouse (Eds.), *The handbook of aging and cognition* (2nd ed., pp. 221–292). Mahwah, NJ: Erlbaum.

McDowd, J. M., Vercruyssen, M., & Birren, J. E. (1991). Aging, divided attention and dual-task performance. In D. Damos (Ed.), *Multiple task performance* (pp. 387–414). Bristol, PA: Taylor & Francis.

McIntyre, J. S., & Craik, F. I. M. (1987). Age differences in memory for item and source information. *Canadian Journal of Psychology, 41,* 175–192.

Miller, G. A. (1956). The magical number seven, plus or minus two: Some limits on our capacity for processing information. *Psychological Review, 63,* 81–97.

Morrell, R. W., Park, D. C., & Poon, L. W. (1990). Effects of labelling techniques on memory and comprehension of prescription information in young and old adults. *Journal of Gerontology, 45,* 345–354.

Moscicki, E. K., Elkins, E. F., Baum, H. F., & McNamara, P. M. (1985). Hearing loss in the elderly: An epidemiological study of the Framingham Heart Study cohort. *Ear and Hearing, 6,* 184–190.

Nabelek, A. K., & Robinson, P. K. (1987). Monaural and binaural speech perception in reverberation in listeners of various ages. *Journal of the Acoustical Society of America, 71,* 1242–1248.

Olsho, L. W., Harkins, S. W., & Lenhardt, M. L. (1985). Aging and the auditory system. In J. E. Birren & K. W. Schaie (Eds.), *Handbook of the psychology of aging* (2nd ed., pp. 332–377). New York: VanNostrand-Reinhold.

Olson, P. L., & Sivak, M. (1989). Glare from automobile rear-vision mirrors. *Human Factors, 26,* 269–282.

Olzak, L. A., & Thomas, J. P. (1985). Seeing spatial patterns. In K. R. Boff, L. Kaufman, & J. P. Thomas (Eds.), *Handbook of perception and human performance* (pp. 7:1–7:56). New York: Wiley.

Owsley, C., Ball, K., McGwin, G. Jr., Sloane, M. E., Roenker, D. L., White, M., & Overley, T. (1998). Visual processing impairment and risk of motor vehicle crash among older adults. *Journal of the American Medical Association, 279,* 1083–1088.

Owsley, C., Sekuler, R., & Siemsen, D. (1983). Contrast sensitivity throughout adulthood. *Vision Research, 23,* 689–699.

Owsley, C., & Sloane, M. E. (1987). Contrast sensitivity, acuity and the perception of real-world targets. *British Journal of Ophthalmology, 71,* 791–796.

Owsley, C, & Sloane, M. E. (1990). Vision and aging. In F. Boller & J. Grafman (Eds.), *Handbook of neuropsychology,. Volume 4* (pp. 229–249). Amsterdam: Elsevier.

Parasuraman, R., Nestor, P., & Greenwood, P. (1989). Sustained attention capacity in young and older adults. *Psychology and Aging, 4,* 339–345.

Park, D. (1992). Applied cognitive aging research. In F. I. M. Craik & T. A. Salthouse (Eds.), *The handbook of aging and cognition* (pp. 440–493). Hillsdale, NJ: Erlbaum.

Park, D., Smith, A., Dudley, W., & Lafronza, V. (1989). Effects of age and a divided attention task presented during encoding and retrieval on memory. *Journal of Experimental Psychology: Learning, Memory and Cognition, 15,* 1185–1191.

Park, D. C., Smith, A. D., Morrell, R. W., Puglisi, J. T., & Dudley, W. N. (1990). Effects of contextual integration on recall of pictures by older adults. *Journal of Gerontology: Psychological Sciences, 45,* P52–P57.

Parkinson, S. R. (1982). Performance deficits in short-term memory tasks: A comparison of amnesic Korsakoff patients and the aged. In L. S. Cermak (Ed.), *Human memory and amnesia* (pp. 77–96). Hillsdale, NJ: Erlbaum.

Peterson, L. R., & Peterson, M. J. (1959). Short-term retention of individual items. *Journal of Experimental Psychology, 58,* 193–198.

Pitts, D. G. (1982). The effects of aging upon selected visual functions: Dark adaptation, visual acuity, stereopsis and brightness contrast. In R. Sekuler, D. Kline, & K. Dismukes (Eds.), *Aging and human visual function* (pp. 131–160). New York: Alan R. Liss.

Plomp, R., & Mimpen, A. M. (1979). Speech recognition threshold for sentences as a function of age and noise level. *Journal of the Acoustical Society of America, 66,* 1333–1342.

Plude, D. A., & Doussard-Roosevelt, J. A. (1989). Aging, selective attention and feature integration. *Psychology and Aging, 4,* 98–105.

Plude, D. A., Schwartz, L. K., & Murphy, L. J. (1996). Active selection and inhibition in the aging of attention. In F. Blanchard-Fields & T. M. Hess

(Eds.), *Perspectives on cognitive change in adulthood and aging* (pp. 165–191). New York: McGraw-Hill.

Ponds, R. W. H. M., Brouwer, W. H., & van Wolffelaar, P. C. (1988). Age differences in divided attention in a simulated driving task. *Journal of Gerontology: Psychological Sciences, 43,* P151–P156.

Posner, M. I., Inhoff, A. W., Friedrich, F. J., & Cohen, A. (1987). Isolating attentional systems: A cognitive-anatomical analysis. *Psychobiology, 15,* 107–121.

Puckett, J. M., & Stockberger, D. W. (1988). Absence of age-related proneness to short-term retroactive interference in the absence of rehearsal. *Psychology and Aging, 3,* 342–347.

Puglisi, J. T., & Park, D. C. (1987). Perceptual elaboration and memory in older adults. *Journal of Gerontology, 42,* 160–162.

Puglisi, J. T., Park, D. C., Smith, A. D., & Dudley, W. N. (1988). Age differences in encoding specificity. *Journal of Gerontology: Psychological Sciences, 43,* P145–P150.

Rabbitt, P. (1965). An age decrement in the ability to ignore irrelevant information. *Journal of Gerontology, 20,* 233–238.

Rabinowitz, J. C., Craik, F. I. M., & Ackerman, B. P. (1982). A processing resource account of age differences in recall. *Canadian Journal of Psychology, 36,* 325–344.

Said, F. S., & Weale, R. A. (1959). The variations with age of the spectral transmissivity of the living human crystalline lens. *Gerontologia, 3,* 213–231.

Salthouse, T. A. (1982). *Adult cognition: An experimental psychology of human aging.* New York: Springer.

Salthouse, T. A. (1985). Speed of behavior and its implications for cognition. In J. E. Birren & K. W. Schaie (Eds.), *Handbook of the psychology of aging* (2nd ed., pp. 400–426). New York: VanNostrand-Reinhold.

Salthouse, T. A. (1990a). Working memory as a processing resource in cognitive aging. *Developmental Review, 10,* 101–124.

Salthouse, T. A. (1990b). The influence of experience on age differences in cognitive function. *Human Factors, 32,* 551–569.

Salthouse, T. A., & Babcock, R. L. (1991). Decomposing adult age differences in working memory. *Developmental Psychology, 27,* 763–776.

Salthouse, T. A., Mitchell, D. R., Skovronek, E., & Babcock, R. L. (1989). Effects of adult age and working memory on reasoning and spatial abilities. *Journal of Experimental Psychology: Learning, Memory and Cognition, 15,* 507–516.

Salthouse, T. A., Rogan, J. D., & Prill, K. (1984). Division of attention: Age differences on a visually presented memory task. *Memory and Cognition, 12,* 613–620.

Schacter, D. L. (1996). *Searching for memory.* New York: Basic Books.

Schieber, F. (1988). Vision assessment technology and screening of older drivers: Past practices and emerging techniques. In National Research Councils, *Transportation in an aging society: Improving mobility and safety of older persons, Special Report 218, Vol. 2* (pp. 325–378). Washington, DC: Transportation Research Board.

Schieber, F. (1992). Aging and the senses. In J. E. Birren, R. B. Sloane, & G. Cohen (Eds.), *Handbook of mental health and aging* (pp. 251–306). New York: Academic Press.

Schieber, F. (1994). Age and glare recovery time for low-contrast stimuli. *Proceedings of the Human Factors and Ergonomics Society, Volume 1* (pp. 496–499). Santa Monica, CA: Human Factors and Ergonomics Society.

Schieber, F. (1998). Optimizing the legibility of symbol highway signs. In A. Gale (Ed.), *Vision in vehicles, VI* (pp. 163–170). Amsterdam: Elsevier.

Schieber, F., & Baldwin, C. L. (1996). Vision, audition and aging research. In F. Blanchard-Fields & T. M. Hess (Eds.), *Perspectives on cognitive change in adulthood and old age* (pp. 122–162). New York: McGraw-Hill.

Schieber, F., Fozard, J. L., Gordon-Salant, S., & Weiffenbach, J. (1991). Optimizing the sensory-perceptual environment for older adults. *International Journal of Industrial Ergonomics, 7*, 133–162.

Schieber, F., Hiris, E., Brannan, J., & Williams, M. J. (1990). Assessing age differences in motion perception using simple oscillatory displacement versus random dot cinematography. *Investigative Ophthalmology and Visual Science, 31*, 355.

Schieber, F., & Kline, D. W. (1994). Age differences in the legibility of symbol highway signs as a function of luminance and glare level. *Proceedings of the Human Factors and Ergonomics Society. Volume 1* (pp. 133–136). Santa Monica, CA: Human Factors and Ergonomics Society.

Schiff, W., Oldak, R., & Shah, V. (1992). Aging persons' estimates of vehicular motion. *Psychology and Aging, 7*, 518–525.

Schonfield, D., & Robertson, B. A. (1966). Memory storage and aging. *Canadian Journal of Psychology, 20*, 228–236.

Schow, R., Christensen, J., Hutchinson, J., & Nerbonne, M. (1978). *Communication disorders of the aged: A guide for health professions.* Baltimore: University Park Press.

Schuknecht, H. (1974). *Pathology of the ear.* Cambridge, MA: Harvard University Press.

Scialfa, C. T., & Joffe, K. M. (1997). Age differences in feature and conjunction search: Implications for theories of visual search and generalized slowing. *Aging, Neuropsychology and Cognition, 4*, 1–21.

Scialfa, C. T., Kline, D. W., & Lyman, B. J. (1987). Age differences in target identification as a function of retinal location and noise level: Examination of the useful field of view. *Psychology and Aging, 2*, 14–19.

Scialfa, C. T., Thomas, D. M., & Joffe, K. M. (1994). Age differences in the useful field of view: An eye movement analysis. *Optometry and Visual Science, 71*, 1–7.

Sekuler, R., & Ball, K. (1986). Visual localization: Age and practice. *Journal of the Optical Society of America-A, 3*, 864–867.

Shiffrin, R. M., & Schneider, W. (1977). Controlled and automatic human information processing: 2. Perceptual learning, automatic attending and a general theory. *Psychological Review, 84,* 127–190.

Shinar, D. (1977). *Driver visual limitations: Diagnosis and treatment.* (Department of Transportation Contract DOT-HS-5-1275). Bloomington, IN: Institute for Research in Public Safety, Indiana University.

Sloane, M. E., Owsley, C., & Alvarez, S. L. (1988). Aging, senile miosis, and spatial contrast sensitivity at low luminances. *Vision Research, 28,* 1235–1246.

Smith, A. D. (1975). Partial learning and recognition memory in the aged. *International Journal of Aging and Human Development, 6,* 359–365.

Smith, A. D., & Earles, J. L. K. (1996). Memory changes in normal aging. In F. Blanchard-Fields & T. M. Hess (Eds.), *Perspectives on cognitive change in adulthood and old age* (pp. 192–220). New York: McGraw-Hill.

Somberg, B. L., & Salthouse, T. A. (1982). Divided attention abilities in young and old adults. *Journal of Experimental Psychology: Human Perception and Performance, 8,* 651–663.

Spoendlin, H., & Schrott, A. (1989). Analysis of the human auditory nerve. *Hearing Research, 43,* 25–38.

Spoendlin, H., & Schrott, A. (1990). Quantitative evaluation of the human cochlear nerve. *Acta Otolaryngologica Supplement, 470,* 61–70.

Steenbekkers, L. P. A. (1998). Visual contrast sensitivity. In L. P. A. Steenbekkers & C. E. M. van Beijsterveldt (Eds.), *Design-relevant characteristics of aging users* (pp. 131–136). Delft, The Netherlands: Delft University of Technology Press.

Sticht, R., & Gray, B. (1969). The intelligibility of time compressed words as a function of age and hearing loss. *Journal of Speech and Hearing Loss, 12,* 443–448.

Sturr, J. F., Kline, G. E., & Taub, H. A. (1990). Performance of young and older drivers on a static acuity test under photopic and mesopic luminance conditions. *Human Factors, 32,* 1–8.

Surwillo, W. W., & Quilter, R. E. (1964). Vigilance, age and response time. *American Journal of Psychology, 77,* 540–620.

Tillman, T. W., Carhardt, R., & Nichols, S. (1973). Release from multiple maskers in elderly persons. *Journal of Speech and Hearing Research, 16,* 152–160.

Treisman, A., & Gelade, G. (1980). A feature-integration theory of attention. *Cognitive Psychology, 12,* 97–136.

Tulving, E. (1972). Episodic and semantic memory. In E. Tulving & W. Donaldson (Eds.), *Organization of memory* (pp. 382–403). New York: Academic Press.

Tulving, E., & Thompson, D. M. (1973). Encoding specificity and retrieval processes in episodic memory. *Psychological Review, 80,* 352–373.

van Wolffelaar, P. C., Rotthengatter, J. A., & Brouwer, W. H. (1991). Elderly drivers' traffic merging decisions. In A. Gale et al. (Eds.), *Vision in vehicles III* (pp. 247–255). Amsterdam: Elsevier Science.

Vola, J. L., Cornu, C., Carrvel, P., Gastaud, P., & Leid, J. (1983). L'age et les acuities visuelles photopiques et mesopiques. [Age and photopic versus mesopic visual acuity]. *Journale Français Ophthalmologie, 6,* 473–479.

Weale, R. A. (1961). Retinal illumination and age. *Transactions of the Illuminating Engineering Society, 26,* 95–100.

Weale, R. A. (1986). Aging and vision. *Vision Research, 26,* 1507–1512.

Whitaker, D., & Elliott, D. (1989). Toward establishing a clinical displacement threshold technique to evaluate visual function behind cataract. *Clinical Vision Science, 4,* 61–69.

Wickens, C. D. (1984). Processing resources in attention. In R. Parasuraman & R. Davies (Eds.), *Varieties of attention* (pp. 63–102). New York: Academic Press.

Willott, J. F. (1991). *Aging and the auditory system: Anatomy, physiology and psychophysics.* San Diego, CA: Singular.

Wingfield, A., Poon, L. W., Lombardi, L., & Lowe, D. (1985). Speed of processing in normal aging: Effects of speech rate, linguistic structure and processing time. *Journal of Gerontology, 40,* 579–585.

Wingfield, A., Stine, A. L., Lahar, C. J., & Aberdeen, J. S. (1988). Does the capacity of working memory change with age? *Experimental Aging Research, 14,* 103–107.

Yuodelis, C., & Hendrickson, A. (1986). A qualitative and quantitative analysis of the human fovea during development. *Vision Research, 26,* 847–855.

Commentary

Aging Effects on Vision: Impairment, Variability, Self-Report, and Compensatory Change

Donald W. Kline

The chapter by Schieber (this volume), "Human Factors and Aging: Identifying and Compensating for Age-related Deficits in Sensory and Cognitive Function," is a systematic, well-organized, and comprehensive review of the fundamental visual, auditory, and cognitive challenges that confront human factors research and practice directed to technological solutions to the real-world problems of aging persons. Consistent with the principle of "the greatest good for the greatest number," the chapter appropriately emphasizes findings regarding normal age-related changes that come from well-controlled, small-group experimental studies. Fozard's follow-up commentary in this volume provides an insightful and well-integrated scholarly perspective on the historical and prospective issues associated with "Using Technology to Lower the Perceptual and Cognitive Hurdles of Aging." The present commentary uses these outstanding reviews as the embarkation point from which (1) to explore some recent research regarding aging effects on the eye, (2) to evaluate the extent of the challenge facing technological innovation directed to the alleviation of older persons' visual problems through a brief review of epidemiological research on age-related visual impairment, (3) to assess the impact of visual loss on the lives of older persons as well as their efforts to compensate for them as revealed by their self-reported visual problems, and finally, (4) to offer a few additional guidelines for the design of "age-friendly" visual tasks and displays.

As both the Schieber and the Fozard reviews in this volume make clear, aging effects on visual function adversely affect the ability of older persons to detect, interpret, and respond to the visual information needed for safe, comfortable, and effective performance of everyday tasks. Typically, these deficits develop gradually and are moderate in degree (Kline & Scialfa, 1997; Owsley & Sloane, 1990; Schieber, 1992; Spear, 1993). Even these "normal" age-related visual deficits, however, can compromise performance on a wide range of daily tasks (Kline & Scialfa, 1997; West et al., 1997), including driving (Kline et al., 1992; Owsley, McGwin, & Ball, 1998; Yee, 1985). Aging is also associated with an increased prevalence of severe visual impairments (e.g., Hirvela & Laatikainen, 1995; Klein, Klein & Lee, 1996; Rubin et al., 1997; Salive et al., 1992; West et al., 1997) that can profoundly alter a person's ability to carry out critical everyday tasks (e.g., Elliott et al., 1997; Hakkinen, 1984; Marsiske, Klumb, & Baltes, 1997; Owsley et al., 1998b; Wahl, Oswald, & Zimprich, 1999; Yee, 1985).

THE AGING EYE

Pupil and Lens Effects on Retinal Illuminance

By adjusting the pupil to its smallest size for ambient light levels, the circular (constriction) and radial (dilation) muscles of the iris minimize optical aberration and maximize the eye's depth of field (i.e., range of focus). As Schieber (this volume) notes, there is an age-related decline in the pupil's resting diameter *(senile miosis)* that contributes to an estimated threefold (.5 log unit) reduction in retinal illuminance from age 20 to 60 (Weale, 1961). Elliott, Whitaker, and MacVeigh (1990) have estimated that about .3 log units of this loss is due to the smaller pupil and .2 log units to the increased opacity of the lens. Whereas the .2 log unit lost to increased lens opacity can be regained through lens replacement (i.e., cataract surgery), the loss due to pupillary miosis cannot. Since the reduction in retinal illuminance is proportionate to the square of the pupillary change, older observers are most disadvantaged relative to their younger counterparts in low illumination conditions (Winn, Whitaker, Elliott, & Phillips, 1994).

Optical Aberration and Iris Pupil Effects on Image Quality

Schieber's review (this volume) notes that age-related changes in the optical properties of the eye contribute to a progressive degradation of retinal image quality. Recent research has elucidated some of the specific mechanisms that underlie these changes; it also clarifies the role of pupillary miosis in compensating for them.

Guiaro and colleagues (1999) found that even after equating for differences in optical correction, pupil dilation, and retinal luminance, a progressive decline in the eye's ability to transfer light differences (i.e., contrast) to the retina remained. Some of this loss is explained by changes in the cornea (Oshika, Klyce, Applegate, & Howland, 1999), but aberrations in the lens, as well as possible changes in the balance between corneal and lens transmission, may also be involved (Guiaro, Redondo, & Artal, 2000).

In considering the impact of such visual changes on the performance of the tasks of daily life, it is worth noting that some of the older eye's optical aberrations are significantly compensated for by senile miosis. When Calver, Cox, and Elliott (1999) measured the modulation transfer function (MTF) and the extent of monochromatic wave-front aberrations with the pupil's diameter fixed at the same size, they found that older eyes were worse than young eyes. When natural pupil diameters were used, however, the MTFs of the two age groups were very similar and wave-front aberrations were actually smaller in the older eye. So, while the older eye is disadvantaged by a small pupil under low illumination conditions, the retinal image is improved by reduced light scatter, less refractive aberration, and an increased depth-of-focus (Winn et al., 1994).

Because of age-related reductions in contrast image and luminance, older observers are disadvantaged by displays that are low in contrast and/or luminance to a greater degree than are their younger counterparts. But it is also important to recognize that individual needs for contrast and luminance vary widely with age, lighting conditions, the observer's optical correction, and the design legibility of target elements. Thus, older observers can benefit from displays that allow them to adjust contrast and light levels to their needs for the prevailing viewing conditions (Cambell, Carney, & Kantowitz, 1998). Given that older observers may be less likely to explore or modify such user-adjustable controls, it is critical that such an option be readily apparent and accessible. Another approach to this problem would be the provision of one or more age-appropriate settings that default to lighting levels appropriate for the observer's age and visual abilities.

Aging Effects on Refractive Error

In reviewing the effects of aging on visual acuity, Schieber (this volume) discusses how optically correctable refractive errors become increasingly common with advancing age and contribute to older observers' prevalent use of corrective lenses. Most often this takes the specific form of increased far-sightedness *(hyperopia)*. Aging also appears to affect astigmatism, both as to degree and axis of orientation. Technologies intended for use by older persons and that use a visual display or interface can be effective only to the extent that both types of refractive error are corrected.

Based on a study of 4,926 adults aged 43 to 84 years in Beaver Dam, Wisconsin, Wang, Klein, Klein, and Moss (1994) reported that far-sightedness *(hyperopia)* in the right eye in excess of .5 diopters rose from 22.1% in those 43 to 54 years of age to 68.5% among those 75 and older. The prevalence of nearsightedness *(myopia)* in excess of 0.5 diopters declined from 42.9% to 14.4% in the same age groups. Attebo, Ivers, and Mitchell (1999) reported similar age-related differences in the prevalence of hyperopia and myopia in the Blue Mountains Eye Study in Australia, a population-based study of 3,654 Australians age 49 years and older. As shown in Table 2.1, which summarizes some of their findings with respect to age and gender effects on refractive error, the age-related increase past age 64 in the prevalence of hyperopia was more marked among women than men. Conversely, myopia rates were somewhat higher among males in all age groups except for the one aged 55 to 64. The degree to which a similar relative prevalence of myopia and hyperopia will be observed in future cohorts, however, is unclear. It is known that genetic factors as well as experiential ones such as extensive near-work experience cause myopia during development and early adulthood. The prevalence of myopia, for example, increases with education and is much higher in cultures where intensive school work is the norm (Schwartz, 1999). Future cohorts of older observers may show higher prevalence rates for myopia due to greater near-display experience in reading, office work, and in the use of computers and electronic entertainment devices. It is also possible that this trend could be offset or even reversed toward higher prevalence rates for hyperopia by the rapid ongoing proliferation of treatments for refractive error. These include the regular intermittent use of hard gas-permeable contact lenses to shape the cornea (i.e., orthokeratology), intraocular "contact" lens implants, and refractive surgeries such photorefractive keratotomy (PRK) and laser assisted in situ keratomileusis (LASIK) to reshape the cornea. In the near term, however, the age-related progression to a fixed focus state means that the majority of older observers, even with optimal bifocal correction for near and far, will encounter difficulty bringing stimuli at intermediate viewing distances (e.g., 60 to 100 cm) to focus. Where visual displays must be accessed by older

TABLE 2.1   Prevalence (%) of Myopia and Hyperopia by Sex and Age Group

Refractive Problem	Sex	Age Group (Years)				
		45–54	55–64	65–74	75–84	85+
Myopia	Women (%)	21.3	16.4	10.3	10.2	9.1
	Men (%)	30.4	11.9	11.8	13.2	11.8
Hyperopia	Women (%)	30.6	54.7	72.0	72.6	81.8
	Men (%)	22.2	52.0	62.6	63.5	64.7

(Attebo, Ivers, and Mitchell, 1999).

observers at intermediate distances (e.g., automobile instrument panels), a trifocal or progressive-lens prescription and/or careful consideration of display legibility parameters (i.e., contrast, luminance, stroke width, character size, and stimulus spacing) should be considered.

Astigmatism

Astigmatism is a common refractive error in which the focus of the eye is irregular due to greater refractive power for some line orientations than others. Usually due to irregular curvature of the cornea, astigmatism is labeled as to type depending on the orientation along which the eye has its greatest refractive power and thus offers its clearest vision. If the eye has greater power around the vertical axis (i.e., 90°) it is termed *with-the-rule astigmatism;* if it is close to the horizontal axis (0°), it is termed *against-the-rule astigmatism.* Eyes with greater focusing power along the axes between the vertical and horizontal are said to manifest *oblique astigmatism.*

Astigmatism appears to be more prevalent in the later years. There also appears to be a fairly consistent change in the axis along which the eye has more refractive power and for which vision is best in the absence of an appropriate cylinder lens correction. Gudmundsdottir and colleagues (2000) found that the prevalence of right eyes requiring (± .75 D or more of cylindrical lens correction among their 1,045 study participants increased markedly with age for men and women (see Table 2.2). And as shown in Table 2.3, the same study also reported an age-related decline in the prevalence of with-the-rule astigmatism (± 15° of the vertical axis), and a marked elevation in both against-the-rule (± 15° of the horizontal axis) and oblique astigmatism in the remaining orientations. No differences were seen between men and

TABLE 2.2 Prevalence (%) of Astigmatism of ± .75 D or Greater by Sex and Age Group

Refractive Problem	Sex	Age Group (Years)						
		50–54	55–59	60–64	65–60	70–74	75–70	80+
Astigmatism	Men (%)	36	42	62	56	67	72	88
	Women (%)	38	42	42	53	64	74	90

(Gudmundsdottir et al., 2000).

women on either measure. Very similar results were observed for left eyes. Attebo and colleagues (1999) found that the mean severity of astigmatism increased with age in the Blue Mountains Eye Study: –0.6 D for the group aged 49–59, –0.7 D for 60–69, –1.0 D for 70–79, and –1.2 D for 80–97. Although they also found that the prevalence of against-the-rule astigmatism exceeded with-the-rule astigmatism, the difference did not vary significantly with observer age or sex.

Given the high rates of against-the-rule and oblique astigmatism in old age, in the absence of cylinder lenses of the appropriate power and axis, many older observers are likely to have difficulty seeing vertically and obliquely oriented target elements clearly. Since the prevalence and axis of astigmatism both appear to change progressively with aging, it is important that this correction be updated on a regular basis.

AGING AND SEVERE VISION LOSS

Schieber's review (this volume) provides a well-balanced explanation of the "normal" age-related sensory/perceptual/cognitive context for technology aimed at enhancing the everyday lives of older persons. Technology designed to foster the well-being of older observers confronted by severe sensory loss (although they comprise a very much smaller group) may be particularly important in that their lives are even more likely to benefit from or be challenged by technological change.

The incidence of disorders causing blindness increases in the later years, as does the prevalence of lesser degrees of visual impairment (Attebo, Mitchell, & Smith, 1996; Klein et al., 1996; Klein, Klein, Lee, Cruickshanks, & Chappell, 2001). The increase in blindness, defined as a best-corrected acuity of 20/200 or worse in the better eye and/or a visual field, smaller than 20 degrees, becomes marked after age 85.

TABLE 2.3   Prevalence (%) of With-the-Rule, Oblique, and Against-the-Rule Astigmatism of ± .75 D or Greater in the Right Eye by Age Group (Years)

Age Group (Years)	With-the-Rule Astigmatism (%)	Oblique Astigmatism (%)	Against-the-Rule Astigmatism (%)
50–54	15	14	8.5
55–59	12.5	17	11.5
60–64	11.8	23.7	12.8
65–69	8.7	22	23
70–74	9.9	32.2	23
75–79	3.8	32.6	31
80+	10	35.8	42

(Gudmundsdottir et al., 2000).

In the U.S., the prevalence of blindness among those aged 70 to 74 is about 1%; among those 85 years of age and older, it is 2.4% (Desai, Pratt, Lentzner, & Robinson, 2001).

Visual impairment, defined generally as a vision loss that cannot be corrected with lenses, increases sharply in the 70s and beyond. When Klein and colleagues (1996) measured the acuity of 3684 persons aged 43 to 86 years over a ten-year period in the Beaver Dam (Wisconsin) Eye Study, they found that people over 75 were 15 times more likely to develop impaired vision (20/40 or worse in the better eye) and 19.8 times as likely to develop severe visual impairment (20/200 or worse in the better eye) than those younger than 75 at the time of baseline measurement. Those over 75 at baseline, living in nursing or group homes, were 2.6 times more likely to have impaired vision, and 1.6 times more likely to have severely impaired vision than those not residing in such a group setting.

Four disorders account for most of the elevated prevalence of visual impairment and blindness in old age: age-related macular degeneration (ARMD), cataracts, diabetic retinopathy, and glaucoma (Desai et al., 2001). Because all of these diseases are progressive, the incidence of severe loss is highest among the oldest groups.

Attebo and colleagues (1996) studied the prevalence of mild, moderate, and severe acuity impairment in the Blue Mountains Eye Study (BMES). Mild impairment was defined as acuity of 20/40 to 20/63 in the worse eye and 20/40 or better in the better eye, moderate as 20/80 to 20/160 acuity in the worse eye and better than 20/80 in the better eye, and severe as 20/200 or worse in the worse eye and better than 20/200 in the better eye. As can be seen in Table 2.4, prevalence rates were higher for mild than moderate or severe impairment, especially so for the two oldest groups. Marked elevations for all three impairment types were seen from about age 65 onward. Severe acuity impairment was higher among men than women in all age groups.

THE SELF-REPORTED VISUAL PROBLEMS OF OLDER OBSERVERS

Objective clinical and laboratory measures of vision are often inadequate predictors of the difficulties that older persons face in carrying out visual tasks in the natural environment. Several factors appear to contribute to differences across individuals in the extent of experienced visual disability for any given level of visual loss. These include variation in the type of tasks characteristically performed, differences in health and socioeconomic status, and available environmental and social support systems. For these reasons, the self-reported visual problems of aging individuals can provide valuable insights into the range of effects of visual loss on everyday tasks, as well as the factors that might ameliorate their impact.

As an outstanding vision researcher, clinician, and dean emeritus of optometry at the University of California, Meredith Morgan (1988) has been a particularly insightful and unusually well-informed observer of his own visual aging. The changes in his eyes that he has reported are consistent with those documented in the scientific and clinical literature, including decreased sensitivity to blur, increased hyperopia, against-the-rule-astigmatism and depth of field. He has also described a number of significant changes in the performance of everyday visual tasks. These include a significant decline in visual search as when attempting to locate signs and house numbers, a decrease in the size of his "working fields," and increased difficulty seeing and thus driving at twilight. He has reported problems seeing in shadowed areas of high contrast and where there are rapid changes in roadway luminance, such as occur when driving through a forested area. He has also described his increased difficulty in seeing effectively when entering dark areas from well-illuminated ones, such as when entering a theater during daytime, as well as under conditions of glare. He also finds that reading difficulty is increased when print is low in contrast, crowded, set in a

TABLE 2.4   Prevalence (%) of Mild, Moderate, and Severe Visual Impairment by Sex and Age Group

Age Group (Years)	Mild Visual Impairment		Moderate Visual Impairment		Severe Visual Impairment	
	Men (%)	Women (%)	Men (%)	Women (%)	Men (%)	Women (%)
49–54	0.9	2.2	0.0	0.0	1.9	0.7
55–64	1.9	2.9	0.2	0.6	1.9	0.9
65–74	5.7	5.1	2.1	1.5	3.8	1.2
75–84	15.5	14.5	2.9	3.5	4.7	2.9
85+	14.9	17.6	6.4	4.7	10.6	5.9

(Attebo et al., 1996).

wide typeface, or printed in long lines. His overall impression is that the most troublesome aspect of his changed vision is that it doesn't operate as effortlessly as it once did, particularly when attempting to perceive complex or quickly changing scenes. Morgan has described a number of strategies he has used to reduce the age-related visual problems that he has experienced. For example, when forced to read low-contrast or crowded print, he has found a card held under the line being read to be helpful. He maximizes available luminance while avoiding glare. To reduce glare from oncoming headlights, he deviates his gaze to the right side of the roadway and closes his left eye until the vehicle is past.

Hakkinen (1984) employed visual testing in combination with personal interviews to assess the visual difficulties of older persons in their own environment. The relationships between clinical measures and independent functioning were generally positive, although there also were some notable inconsistencies. For example, many elderly persons appeared to cope effectively even with acuity as poor as 20/120, and many did not use their prescribed visual correction. Presumably, these individuals found ways to compensate for their loss so as to carry out their daily activities.

Yee (1985) surveyed 446 drivers over 55 regarding the problems they encountered when driving. Older drivers reported significantly more visual difficulty resulting from night blindness, highway design, and highway signs and signals. They also more frequently reported that they dealt with declining performance skills by avoiding more hazardous driving conditions such as at night or during rush hour. When Kosnik, Winslow, Kline, Rasinski, and Sekuler (1988) surveyed healthy adults about their everyday visual problems, they found five dimensions that declined with age: visual processing speed, light sensitivity, dynamic vision, near vision, and visual search. Such self-reported losses seem to go beyond the tasks that were directly evaluated. Kosnik, Sekuler, and Kline (1990) reported that those who experienced such difficulty on everyday visual tasks were also more likely than their like-age cohorts to stop driving. Kline and colleagues (1992) surveyed several hundred drivers in the Baltimore Longitudinal Study on Aging regarding the visual problems they experienced on a wide range of everyday tasks as well as those encountered during driving. Their findings confirmed the five problem dimensions observed by Kosnik and colleagues (1988) for everyday visual tasks. They also found that several of the visual problems encountered while driving were age-related. These included difficulties with unexpected vehicles, judging vehicle speed, seeing dim displays, seeing in the presence of windshield glare or haze, and reading street signs in time to respond. Consistent with Yee's (1985) survey findings, older drivers appeared to compensate to some degree for driving-related problems by driving significantly fewer miles and by avoiding driving in adverse conditions such as at night, in poor weather, or during rush-hour. It is also clear, however, that older persons' self-insights into sensory and cognitive losses that affect such tasks as driving are often less than complete. Holland and Rabbitt (1992) found that many older drivers were aware of their sensory deficits and tried to compensate for them by using strategies such as reducing night driving, updating their optical prescription, and avoiding complex intersections. Many of these drivers, however, appeared to be unaware of their sensory losses; even fewer of them appeared to recognize cognitive deficits that could affect safe driving.

Research on the relationships between self-reported visual problems and objectively measured visual functioning have yielded somewhat inconsistent results. Schieber, Kline, Kline, and Fozard (1992) found that the five visual problem dimensions of older drivers reported by Kline and colleagues (1992) were significantly related to contrast sensitivity losses at intermediate and high spatial frequencies. Rumsey (1993) found that visual complaints and decrements on acuity, contrast sensitivity, stereopsis, glare sensitivity, and color vision increased with age. Only the global complaint of decreased vision, however, was directly related to objective performance. Rubin, Roche, Prasada-Rao, and Fried (1994), however, observed quite specific relationships between spatial vision loss and self-reported disability on everyday tasks. Acuity deficits were associated with problems requiring good resolution and adjustment to changing light conditions, whereas declines in contrast sensitivity were related to distance judgment, night driving, and mobility. Reasons for inconsistent vision/disability relationships between different studies can include variability in individual environmental factors and tasks factors, variation in the type and degree of visual loss, interindividual differences in insight regarding visual loss, and differences in the degree to which the self-report measures utilized are anchored to specific everyday tasks. For example, self-reports appear to underestimate the prevalence of cataract and age-related macular degeneration (Linton, Klein, & Klein, 1991) as well as binocular field loss (Johnson & Keltner, 1983).

FURTHER RECOMMENDATIONS FOR COMPENSATING FOR AGING-RELATED VISUAL LOSS

The reviews by Schieber and Fozard in this volume each offer an evidence-based series of recommendations for enhancing the performance of older observers through optimized visual task design. Some additional related suggestions that complement their guidelines follow:

1. Technological design or selection should be guided by the abilities of the least visually able end-users. This effort should be accompanied by the recognition that inter- and intraindividual variability are usually higher among older persons, as well as a careful determination of any possible age-related sex differences on visual impairments relevant to the task(s) under consideration.

2. Given the older observer's inability to adjust focus, performance and comfort can often be enhanced by optical correction for the task viewing distance. For visual tasks based on extended or frequent inspection of displays at intermediate viewing distances (e.g., car instrument panels or computer screens), trifocal or progressive lens prescriptions can be considered. Some user experience or practice, however, is critical to the adjustment to and effective use of such multifocal lenses. New wearers need to learn which "add" region or segment to use for different viewing distances, and bifocal and trifocal lenses can induce prism effect "image jump" between the adjacent bifocal or trifocal lower lens add segments (Rubin, 1971). In addition, new wearers of multifocal lenses frequently complain of the difficulty of walking without stumbling due to image blur caused by the lower near correction. This is

particularly likely to occur when the near correction segment is a large one. Finally, when hyperopes view objects through the lower add component, the objects will appear closer and larger than they are (Milder & Rubin, 1991). Such problems can adversely affect the lens wearer's mobility, and is of particular concern for the safe descent of stairways. A determination of how the adjustment to new multifocal lenses could be facilitated by a well-designed perceptual training regimen would a worthwhile goal of future research.

3. Visual screening tests should be matched carefully to the task of concern by a systematic analysis of the type and variability of all of its visual demands.

4. Given that there are prominent individual differences in the strength of the relationship between visual change and experienced visual disability, self-report and observational measures should be viewed as valuable supplements to objective testing when assessing technology designed to assist end-users meet the visual demands of their environment.

5. Although coping mechanisms are highly variable from one person to another, older observers employ a variety of strategies to enhance their adjustment to age-related sensory and cognitive loss. A systematic research effort is needed to catalog these compensatory strategies, to determine the circumstances under which they are effective, and, finally, to evaluate the extent to which older observers more generally can be trained in their use.

REFERENCES

Attebo, K., Ivers, R. Q., & Mitchell, P. (1999). Refractive errors in an older population. *Ophthalmology, 106,* 1066–1072.

Attebo, K., Mitchell, P., & Smith, W. (1996). Visual acuity and the causes of visual loss in Australia. *Ophthalmology, 103,* 357–364.

Calver, R. I., Cox, M. J., & Elliott, D. B. (1999). Effect of aging on the monochromatic aberrations of the human eye. *Journal of the Optical Society of America A—Optics, Image Science and Vision, 16,* 2069–2078.

Cambell, J. L., Carney, C., & Kantowitz, B. H. (1998). *Human factors guidelines for advanced traveler information systems (ATIS) and commercial vehicle operations (CVO).* McLean, VA: U.S. Department of Transportation, Federal Highway Administration.

Desai, M., Pratt, L. A., Lentzner, H., & Robinson, K. N. (2001). Trends in vision and hearing among older Americans. *Aging Trends, No. 2.* Hyattsville, MD: National Center for Health Statistics.

Elliott, D. B., Trukolo-Ilic, M., Strong, G., Pace, R., Plotkin, A., & Bevers, P.

(1997). Demographic characteristics of the vision-disabled elderly. *Investigative Ophthalmology & Visual Science, 38,* 2566–2575.

Elliot, D. B., Whitaker, D., & MacVeigh, D. (1990). Neural contribution to spatiotemporal contrast sensitivity decline in healthy ageing eyes. *Vision Research, 30,* 541–547.

Gudmundsdottir, E., Jonasson, F., Jonsson, V., Stefansson, E., Sasaki, H., Sasaki, K., & the Iceland-Japan Co-Working Study Groups. (2000). "With the rule" astigmatism is not the rule in the elderly Reykjavik Eye Study: A population based study of refraction and visual acuity in citizens of Reykjavik 50 years and older. *Acta Ophthalmologica Scandinavica, 78,* 642–646.

Guiaro, A., Gonzale, G., Redondo, M., Geraghty, E., Norrby, S., & Artal, P. (1999). Average optical performance of the human eye as a function of age in a normal population. *Investigative Ophthalmology & Visual Science, 40,* 203–213.

Guiaro, A. Redondo, M., & Artal, P. (2000). Optical aberrations of the human cornea as a function of age. *Journal of the Optical Society of America A—Optics, Image Science and Vision, 17,* 1697–1702.

Hakkinen, L. (1984). Vision in the elderly and its use in the social environment. *Scandinavian Journal of Social Medicine, 35,* 5–60.

Hirvela, H., & Laatikainen, L. (1995). Visual acuity in a population 70 years or older: Prevalence and causes of visual impairment. *Acta Ophthalmologica Scandinavica, 73,* 99–104.

Holland, C. A., & Rabbitt, P. M. A. (1992). People's awareness of their age-related sensory and cognitive deficits and the implications for road safety. *Applied Cognitive Psychology, 6,* 217–231.

Johnson, C., & Keltner, J. (1983). Incidence of visual field loss in 20,000 eyes and its relationship to driving performance. *Archives of Ophthalmology, 101,* 371–375.

Klein, R., Klein, B. E. K., & Lee, K. E. (1996). Changes in visual acuity in a population. *Ophthalmology, 103,* 1169–1178.

Klein, R., Klein, B. E. K., Lee, K. E., Cruickshanks, K. J., & Chappell, R. J. (2001). Changes in visual acuity in a population over a 10-year period. *Ophthalmology, 108,* 1757–1766.

Kline, D. W., Kline, T. J. B., Fozard, J. L., Kosnik, W., Schieber, F., & Sekuler, R. (1992). Vision, aging and driving: The problems of older drivers. *Journal of Gerontology: Psychological Sciences, 47,* 27–34.

Kline, D. W., & Scialfa, C. T. (1997). Sensory and perceptual functioning: Basic research and human factors implications. In A. D. Fisk & W. A. Rogers (Eds.), *Handbook of human factors and the older adult* (pp. 27–54). New York: Academic Press.

Kosnik, W. D., Sekuler, R., & Kline, D. W. (1990). Self-reported problems of older drivers. *Human Factors, 32,* 597–608.

Kosnik, W., Winslow, L., Kline, D., Rasinski, K., & Sekuler, R. (1988). Visual changes in daily life throughout adulthood. *Journal of Gerontology: Psychological Sciences, 43,* 63–70.

Linton, K. L. P., Klein, B. E. K., & Klein, R. (1991). The validity of self-reported and surrogate-reported cataract and age-related macular degeneration in the Beaver Dam Eye Study. *American Journal of Epidemiology, 143,* 1438–1446.

Marsiske, M., Klumb, P., & Baltes, M. M. (1997). Everyday activity patterns and sensory functioning in old age. *Psychology and Aging, 12,* 444–457.

Milder, B., & Rubin, M. L. (1991). *The fine art of prescribing glasses (without making a spectacle of yourself).* Gainesville, FL: Triad.

Morgan, M. W. (1988). Vision through my aging eyes. *Journal of the American Optometric Association, 59,* 278–280.

Oshika, T., Klyce, S. D., Applegate, R. A., & Howland, H. C. (1999). Changes in corneal wavefront aberrations with aging. *Investigative Ophthalmology & Visual Science, 40,* 1351–1355.

Owsley, C., Ball, K., McGwin, G. Jr., Sloane, M. E., Roenker, D. L., White, M., & Overley, T. (1998a). Visual processing impairment and risk of motor vehicle crash among older adults. *Journal of the American Medical Association, 279,* 1083–1088.

Owsley, C., McGwin, G. Jr., & Ball, K., (1998b). Vision impairment, eye disease, and injurious motor vehicle crashes in the elderly. *Ophthalmic Epidemiology, 5,* 101–113.

Owsley, C., & Sloane, M. E. (1990). Vision and aging. In F. Boller & J. Grafman (Eds.), *Handbook of neuropsychology, Volume 4* (pp. 229–249). Amsterdam: Elsevier.

Rubin, G. S., West, S., Munoz, B., Bandeen-Roche, K., Zeger, S., Schein, O., & Fried, L. P. (1997). A comprehensive assessment of visual impairment in a population of older Americans. *Investigative Ophthalmology & Visual Science, 38,* 557–568.

Rubin, G. S., Roche, K. B., Prasada-Rao, P., & Fried, L. P. (1994). Visual impairment and disability in older adults. *Optometry and Vision Science, 71,* 750–760.

Rubin, M. L. (1971). *Optics for clinicians* (2nd ed.). Gainesville, FL: Triad.

Rumsey, K. E. (1993). Redefining the optometric examination: Addressing the vision needs of older adults. *Optometry and Visual Science, 70,* 587–591.

Salive, M. E., Guralnik, J., Christen, W., Glynn, R. J., Colsher, P., & Ostfeld, A. M. (1992). Functional blindness and visual impairment in older adults from three communities. *Ophthalmology, 99,* 1840–1847.

Schieber, F. (1992). Aging and the senses. In J. E. Birren, R. B. Sloane, & G. Cohen (Eds.), *Handbook of mental health and aging* (pp. 251–306). New York: Academic Press.

Schieber, F., Kline, D. W., Kline, T. J. B., & Fozard, J. L. (1992). The relationship between contrast sensitivity and the visual problems of older drivers. *SAE Technical Paper, No. 920613.* Warrendale, PA: Society of Automotive Engineers.

Schwartz, S. H. (1999). *Visual perception: A clinical orientation.* New York: McGraw Hill.

Spear, P. D. (1993). Neural bases of visual deficits during aging. *Vision Research, 33,* 2589–2609.

Wahl, H. W., Oswald, F., & Zimprich, D. (1999). Everyday competence in visually impaired older adults: A case for person-environment perspectives. *The Gerontologist, 39,* 140–149.

Wang, Q., Klein, B. E. K., Klein, R., & Moss, S. E. (1994). Refractive status in the Beaver Dam eye study. *Investigative Ophthalmology & Visual Science, 35,* 4344–4347.

Weale, R. A. (1961). Retinal illumination and age. *Transactions of the Illuminating Engineering Society, 26,* 95–100.

West, S. K., Munoz, B., Rubin, G. S, Schein, O. D., Bandeen-Roche, K., Zeger, S., German, P. S., Fried, L. P., & SEE Project Team. (1997). Function and visual impairment in a population-based study of older adults. *Investigative Ophthalmology & Visual Science, 38,* 72–82.

Winn, B., Whitaker, D., Elliott, D. B., & Phillips, N. J. (1994). Factors affecting light-adapted pupil size in normal human subjects. *Investigative Ophthalmology & Visual Science, 35,* 1132–1137.

Yee, D. (1985). A survey of the traffic safety needs and problems of drivers age 55 and over. In J. L. Malfetti (Ed.), *Drivers 55+: Needs and problems of older drivers: Survey results and recommendations* (pp. 96–128). Falls Church, VA: AAA Foundation for Traffic Safety.

Commentary

Using Technology to Lower the Perceptual and Cognitive Hurdles of Aging

James L. Fozard

INTRODUCTION

Schieber (this volume) proposed 36 human factors-based compensations for age-related declines in vision, hearing, attention, and memory processes. The present paper reviews these recommendations. In addition to specific comments, it makes three general points about the recommendations. First, many of the recommendations have been made repeatedly by a number of experts over the past 35 years; for these, some specific approaches to implementing them are made. The second is that more attention should be given to applied research approaches that specifically identify the sufficient conditions for reducing the age-related limitations in perceptual and memory processes. Much published research in these areas identifies significant interactions between age differences and quality of perceptual and memory processes but often does not help identify the conditions that would minimize or eliminate them. The third is that relatively more attention should be paid to developing and evaluating interventions that can delay or prevent some age-related perceptual and attention deficits in addition to interventions that compensate for them.

Using a classical ergonomics approach, Schieber developed nine proposals each for human factors compensations related to age-associated declines in vision, hearing, attention, and memory. In each area, some of his proposals fall into what I term the "known but neglected category," especially for vision and hearing. They are similar or identical to many made earlier for over a quarter of century by a variety of scientists in gerontology, many of whom are contributors to the present volume. The main commentary to be made with respect to this class of recommendations concerns how to turn these recommendations into practice. The remaining recommendations fall into what I characterize as a "new and needed" category; most of them require some further applied research to determine their usefulness.

VISION

Five of Schieber's recommendations, summarized in Table 2.5, apply to both static and dynamic visual environments. Two others—minimize dependence on peripheral vision and adopt marking strategies that enhance motion perception and distance estimation—are particularly relevant to dynamic visual environments, such as driving. Schieber recommends the further use of computer-generated image processing techniques for optimizing the legibility of spatial forms (see Kline, 1994).

Current but Neglected Recommendations

The first four recommendations in Table 2.5 have been made in approximately 20 references found in my personal professional library. Going into various levels of detail and covering about 30 years, they were written by various experts including the organizers and some participants in the present conference, including Charness (Charness & Bosman, 1990), Fozard (Fozard, 2000; Fozard & Gordon-Salant, 2001), Kline (Kline & Scialfa, 1995), Schieber (Schieber, Fozard, Gordon-Salant, & Weiffenbach, 1991) and Wahl (Wahl, Oswald, & Zimprich, 1999). Some recommendations in these references related to illumination, glare, and contrast are based in part on research performed initially in the 1950s and 1960s. The recommendations have been largely ignored in practice by designers (e.g., Coleman, 1998), and elderly persons both in home and work situations (e.g., Charness & Dijkstra, 1999; Wahl, Oswald, & Zimprich, 1999).

One reason offered for the lack of application of the available knowledge is that much of the information comes from laboratory research. However, over the past decade much of the laboratory-based information—particularly that related to contrast, illumination levels, and size of visual target—has been confirmed and extended to population-based

TABLE 2.5   Compensations for Age-Related Difficulties in Vision

- Increase luminance and contrast
- Reduce disability glare—use indirect lighting, glare-resistant type, avoid narrow incident angles from light sources
- 12 point font for 65 years +
- 18 point font for 85 years +
- Minimize tasks requiring changes in accommodation, use spectacles specifically for close viewing distances
- Larger contrast steps for visual targets in short wave lengths

assessments of age differences and changes in visual function (Fozard & Gordon-Salant, 2001). Another reason offered is that the visual limitations of elderly people usually do not meet the statutory criteria for legal blindness or severe visual impairment and therefore do not receive professional assistance with low vision aids. However, some low vision organizations such as the Lighthouse now include age in its visual remediation programs and the Society for Illuminating Engineers has considered changes in its lighting recommendations for older persons (see Charness & Dijkstra, 1999).

The recommendations on dynamic vision, particularly as it relates to driving, have received a significant amount of applied research and development attention (aee Ball & Owsley, 2000; Fozard, 2000; Owens, 2000; Staplin, 2000, for recent discussions). For many years, the United States Department of Transportation has sponsored research and development efforts related to the older driver. Dr. Schieber has been involved in much of that work.

Actions for the Known and Neglected Recommendations

Although more applied research is needed that addresses the complex interactions among the effects of illumination, contrast, and target size on visibility, there has been significant recent progress made relative to specifying the proper type size for reading by older persons under varying conditions of illumination, contrast, and glare (see Akizuki & Inoue, 2001; Steenbekkers, 1998).

Direct action steps are needed to educate and interest older persons in the possibilities for manipulating their visual environments. To this end I (Fozard, 2001) have proposed changes in the marketing of lighting products, such as providing mockup displays of kitchens, and hobby, work, and reading areas in lighting stores and optician offices that allow persons to alter lighting and contrast to meet their needs. A simple example of this approach was provided in a participatory visual exhibit related to human development and aging hosted by the Boston (Massachusetts) Museum of Science in the summer of 2001. The viewer could vary the intensity of the light source that illuminated a cookbook in a mockup of a kitchen. Comments by other museum goers overheard by me in a two-minute period included statements such as "Wow, you don't have to be old to need more light," and "I want this in my kitchen before I'm 70."

In principle, this approach could be extended to educational Web sites to provide approximate information on functionally equivalent visual environments that can be achieved under various combinations of lighting, contrast, and target size. The phrase "in principle" is used because there are many variations in viewing conditions and contrast capabilities for computer displays that could limit the effectiveness of using computer-driven displays. However, some existing software can be used to illustrate some of the effects of varying contrast and characteristics of type, such as the various combinations of background color, shading and fonts available in the Powerpoint software for preparing slide shows.

Action for the New and Needed Compensations

The remaining two recommendations related to avoiding tasks requiring changes in accommodation and the use of relatively larger contrast steps for targets in the short wavelengths address important visual problems of older persons. Neither one has received much applied research. Possibly the automatic devices for changing focal length in cameras could be adapted to compensate for the inability of older persons to change accommodation, at least in some restricted settings.

HEARING

As seen in Table 2.6, the first four of Schieber's recommendations for hearing are conceptually similar to those for vision. Implementation of the recommendations is somewhat different because the portability of wearable hearing aids that amplify the signal is not present in as wide a range of situations in the visual analog, for example, flashlights and candles.

TABLE 2.6   Compensations for Age-Related Difficulties in Hearing

- Increase volume, decrease background noise
- Avoid high-frequency signals
- Combine fitting of hearing aids with user training
- Improve speech recognition through better structure, pacing, and redundancy
- Avoid providing auditory signals requiring localization of low frequencies
- Use modern technology to provide listening support in public spaces
- Avoid long-term exposure to noise (88dB+)

Known but Neglected Recommendations

As in the case with vision, the first four recommendations relative to signal strength—volume, noise suppression, speech speed, and acoustics—have been made repeatedly by many persons, including several at this conference as mentioned above.

Action for the Known and Neglected Recommendations

Despite continuing advances in the quality and sophistication of hearing aids, their use by persons who could benefit from them is low (Fozard & Gordon-Salant, 2001). One reason is lack of consumer education. Another concerns the marketing and dispensing of particular brands of hearing aids. There is a potential conflict of interest for persons who both provide professional evaluations of hearing and market particular brands. Moreover, advertising in magazines and other media targeted toward older persons is often exaggerated and uninformative. One practical solution is to find and use audiologists whose evaluation and advice are not linked to certain brands or types of hearing aids. Such professionals are often located in university-run speech and hearing departments that operate clinical settings for educational purposes. Independent evaluation of hearing aids, such as those provided by the Consumers Union in the United States, is also needed.

As in the case of vision, a significant research effort should be made to identify equal audibility or equal recognition functions across different levels of background noise, signal distortion, and signal sources, including male and female speakers of different ages. The efforts of Gordon-Salant and Fitzgibbons (1995) provides a good effort in this area. The essentials of their approach and its significance are reviewed by Fozard (2001).

The recommendation about noise suppression in Table 2.6 is based on the National Institutes of Health Consensus Conference (1990). The data supporting the recommendations are weak and may underestimate the contribution to hearing loss by long-term exposure to moderate levels of noise. For these reasons, I proposed a full-scale clinical evaluation of long-term exposure to noise and cardiovascular disease in relation to the development of presbycusis. The trial would employ modern hearing aid technology both to assess and if appropriate, control exposure to noise (Fozard, 2001; pp. 7–9).

Action for the New and Needed Recommendations

Schieber's proposal to take advantage of a growing computer infrastructure to provide assistive hearing possibilities in public spaces is certainly worth investigation. The delivery system for the information is of particular importance, as is the number of potential sources of information. Along these lines, technology for the use of miniature portable microphones, receivers, and broadcasting systems to improve audibility is developing quite rapidly; the resulting products will require human factors evaluation.

ATTENTION

Schieber's analysis of four types of attention tasks—span, selective, divided, and sustained—is a very useful way of combining aspects of a complex literature that is usually reviewed in terms of specific perceptual channels. By their nature, studies on attention usually challenge the research participant in order to determine limiting conditions with respect to capacity and speed. Therefore any analysis of the research literature must be quite task specific.

Known and Neglected Research

As in the cases of hearing and vision, some of the nine recommendations have been made over a period of years, such as reducing the number of stimuli to be attended to, especially in conjunctive search tasks or others where the distracters compete significantly for processing time needed for the targeted items. Another is to present information in smaller units or chunks. Both of these recommendations are especially relevant to the temporal aspects of attention tasks. A variety of research shows that the time required to process a stimulus at all stages from sensory memory to working memory are longer in old age.

Action on Known but Neglected Research

Despite the impressive array of published studies on attention demonstrating interactions between task difficulty and age, there is a lack of specific research needed to implement many of Schieber's recommendations. Studies that identify interactions between age differences and task difficulty are usually better suited for problem identification than problem solution. An alternative is to focus on applied research that identifies the sufficient conditions that yield equivalent or at least equally satisfactory task performance by young and old adults. The "sufficient conditions" in this type of research are operationally defined as the various combinations of task demands, such as various requirements related to speed, and number and complexity of targets that yield similar levels of performance by older and younger adults. Discussions and examples of this approach include Welford's (1981) discussion of signal strength, Fozard's (1981) discussion of paced inspection, and Madden's (2001) discussion of selective and divided attention tasks. Because age differences in the time required for responses are of central importance in attention tasks, research paradigms that investigate input and central attention processes by using cueing and stimulus onset asynchrony (SOA) in the same studies can provide useful information (see Johnston, McCann, & Remington, 1995).

Novel and Needed Research

Although common in general human factors applications, Schieber's suggestions to use auxiliary perceptual and response channels to better distribute attentional task requirements deserves applied research with respect to age. At present, little is known about the conditions under which vibration, sound, or other auxiliary input channels would reduce age differences in performance, particularly in divided and selective attention tasks.

MEMORY

Schieber's nine recommendations are the result of sifting through a vast literature covering topics ranging from primary, working, secondary, long-term semantic and episodic memory to procedural and prospective memory processes. Because age differences are most evident in secondary and working memory, many of his recommendations and my comments about them are similar to those made for attention and will not be repeated here. In the remainder of this section, two of Schieber's recommendations will be discussed.

The fourth recommendation is "Design environmental supports to guide and/or enhance memory encoding processes . . . via systematic cueing, enriching . . . contexts, leveraging cohort-specific stimulus representational networks, [and] using pictorial formats to aid integration of multiple stimulus items into a predictable and unitary concept" (this volume, pp. 71). Two kinds of research provide possible leads for evaluating and implementing Schieber's recommendation relative to cohort-specific stimulus representation. Poon and colleagues (Poon & Fozard, 1978; Poon, Fozard, Paulshock, & Thomas, 1979) demonstrated that, not surprisingly, older persons recognized popular sayings and dated visual representations of common household items that were used when they were young adults better than young adults representing later cohorts. Younger adults and older adults were more similar in recognizing dated information that was shared by the different cohorts. Perhaps such information could be used to design age-specific aids to encoding processes. The recent research on technology generations by Docampo Rama, deRidder, and Bouma (2001) shows that age differences in mastering and utilizing user interfaces in communication technology are fewer when the interfaces are designed to match the early experience with technical devices available to different cohorts of users. Specifically they showed that older users of communication technology had more difficulty using menu-driven interfaces than younger generations of users whose early encounters with technology involved such devices.

Schieber's eighth recommendation is to "avoid (or control) stimulus 'pacing' effects, which can interfere with encoding and response selection during . . . acquisition . . . and retrieval . . ." (p. 71, this volume). This recommendation speaks directly to the age deficits in working memory that have been identified repeatedly in studies of cognitive aging. The available research indicates that the amount and complexity of the material to be remembered and the amount of time that the information must be retained all contribute to the age differences in working memory. This particular recommendation most directly involves the temporal aspects of short-term memory.

The usual reference tasks for memorization of verbal materials involve some variation of the study test procedure, such as paired associate learning. There are two components of stimulus pacing that affect age differences in performance in such memorization tasks. One is the amount of time provided for study of the items to be learned. The other—less well understood—is the number of other items being learned that occur between successive presentations of the same item. Because of the age-related increases in the rate of forgetting in short-term memory, the benefits of studying a particular item in a list diminish relatively more rapidly for older adults. Some evidence for this was provided by Fozard (1981) in a study of age differences in memorization of twelve paired associates, for example, ace–boy, eel–fox, . . . yam–zoo. The sequence of presentations of items in the list was manipulated so that successive presentations of a particular pair were separated by up to five other pairs. The main finding was that particular items in the list were mastered more rapidly as the number of intervening pairs was smaller. A related finding was that the time required to recall specific pairs in the list that had already been memorized was much longer for persons who had not mastered all the pairs than for those who had completely memorized the list.

The rapid loss of information from short-term memory experienced by older persons is particularly vexing when the person is trying to perform a sequence of operations that require retaining an arbitrary instruction or piece of information for short periods of time. The complexity or difficulty of the tasks such as using computer-driven displays to get travel information or perform business transactions is often linked to the requirement to retain information about one operation in a sequence while a couple of other operations are being performed. When needed a second time, the required information may have been lost from short-term memory.

Two types of studies illustrate the age differences in the rate of loss of information from memory. The first is the continuous memory task in which a word, picture, or other stimulus is presented twice and the participant judges whether the target item is new, that is, presented for the first time, or old, presented for the second time. Poon and Fozard (1980) demonstrated that errors and the time required to correctly identify the second presentation of an item increased systematically as the number of other intervening items increased, more so for the older participants. The age differences in performance were greatest when the number of intervening items was small, that is, within the range of primary memory,

A second type of study comes from research on age differences in keeping track of many things at once (Yntema, 1962). In such studies, the participant is required to remember the current state of an arbitrary category such as the direction of the compass or the name of a particular card in a suit of cards. Over the course of the study messages are presented about changes in the current state, such as a change from "north" to "west." In a later question about the current state of the directions category, the participant attempts to recall the current state (e.g., "west") in the example. With respect to age differences, a major finding in such research is that the accuracy of knowing the current state of a category declines much more rapidly in older participants as the total number of intervening messages and questions increase (Fozard, 1981). By comparing memory performance in a recall and a recognition version of the task, Baker (1985) confirmed and extended this finding by showing that the locus of the age difficulty in memory was in encoding the information rather than in retrieval.

The implications of these studies for Schieber's recommendations are straightforward: Do not require retention of arbitrary information in tasks that require a sequence of operations. If possible, redesign the task to eliminate the need to hold information in short-term memory or somehow provide cues that help a person keep the information available over a short sequence of operations. The idea of cohort-specific cueing discussed above might be an example.

Schieber recommends taking a systems approach to task redesign with memory as well as attention. This excellent suggestion is relevant to memory training as well as to restructuring of tasks. His suggestions remind us that age differences in memory are very task specific, a fact often overlooked in the stream of research that emphasizes the importance of a generalized slowing of behavioral processes with aging.

The main focus of the recommendations discussed in the present paper is on compensation for age-related differences in perception, attention, and memory. Future human factors efforts in these areas should also focus on primary prevention as well as compensation—a new opportunity made possible by recent research developments (Fozard, 2001).

SUMMARY

Schieber's 36 recommendations for human factors interventions targeted toward compensating for age-related declines in vision, hearing, attention, and memory were divided into two categories for purposes of the present discussion: "known but neglected" and "new and needed." With respect to the known but neglected recommendations, the present discussion emphasizes the need to take actions involving consumer education through demonstrations in businesses, interactive websites, and other approaches. With respect to the new but needed recommendations, it is proposed that applied research and demonstration efforts focus on identifying the sufficient conditions that will reduce the age differences in performance that have been demonstrating in studies interactions between task difficulty and age differences. Finally, a general recommendation was made to broaden the application of human factors research and intervention to preventing as well as compensating for age-related differences in perception, attention, and memory.

ACKNOWLEDGMENTS

The author wishes to thank the volume editors for their constructive suggestions.

REFERENCES

Akizuki, Y., & Inoue, Y. (2001). The evaluation method for visibility by introducing the maximum level of individual visual acuity. In K. Sagawa & H. Bouma (Eds.), *Proceedings of the International Workshop on Gerontechnology* (pp. 79–80). Tsukubu, Japan: National Institute for Bioscience and Human Technology.

Baker, J. D. (1985). *The relationship of aging to retrieval processes in short term memory*. Unpublished doctoral dissertation, Catholic University of America, Washington, DC.

Ball, K., & Owsley, C. (2000). Increasing mobility and reducing accidents of older drivers. In K. W. Schaie & M. Petrucha (Eds.), *Mobility and transportation in the elderly* (pp. 213–250). New York: Springer.

Charness, N., & Bosman, E. A. (1990). Human factors and design for older adults. In J. E. Birren & K. W. Schaie (Eds.), *Handbook of the psychology of aging* (3rd ed., pp. 446–464). San Diego: Academic Press.

Charness, N. S., & Dijkstra, K. (1999). Age, luminance, and print legibility in homes, offices and public places. *Human Factors, 41,* 173–193.

Coleman, R. (1998). Improving the quality of life for older people by design. In J. A. M. Graafmans, V. Taipele, & N. Charness (Eds.), *Gerontechnology: A sustainable investment in the future* (pp. 74–83). Amsterdam: IOS.

Docampo Rama, M., deRidder, H., & Bouma, H. (2001). Technology generation and age in using layered user interfaces. *Gerontechnology, 1,* 25–40.

Fozard, J. L. (1981). Person-environment relations in adulthood: Implications for human factors engineering. *Human Factors, 23*(1), 7–27.

Fozard, J. L. (2000). Sensory and cognitive changes with age. In K. W. Schaie & M. Pietrucha (Eds.), *Mobility and transportation in the elderly* (pp. 1–44). New York: Springer.

Fozard, J. L. (2001). Gerontechnology and perceptual motor function: New opportunities for prevention, compensation, and enhancement. *Gerontechnology, 1,* 5–24.

Fozard, J. L., & Gordon-Salant, S. (2001). Changes in vision and hearing with aging. In J. E. Birren & K. W. Schaie (Eds.), *Handbook of the psychology of aging* (5th ed., pp. 241–266). San Diego: Academic Press.

Gordon-Salant, S., & Fitzgibbons, P. J. (1995). Comparing recognition of distorted speech using an equivalent signal-to-noise ratio index. *Journal of Speech and Hearing Research, 38,* 706–713.

Johnston, J. C., McCann, R. S., & Remington, R. W. (1995). Chronometric evidence for two types of attention. *Psychological Science, 6,* 365–369.

Kline, D. W. (1994). Optimizing the visibility of older displays for older observers. *Experimental Aging Research, 20,* 11–23.

Kline, D. W., & Scialfa, C. T. (1995). Visual and auditory aging. In J. E. Birren & K. W. Schaie (Eds.), *Handbook of the psychology of aging* (4th ed., pp. 181–203). San Diego: Academic Press.

Madden, D. J. (2001). Speed and timing of behavioral processes. In J. E. Birren & K. W. Schaie (Eds.), *Handbook of the psychology of aging* (5th ed., pp. 288–312). San Diego: Academic Press.

National Institutes of Health. (1990). Consensus conference on noise and hearing loss. *Journal of the American Medical Association, 263,* 3185–3190.

Owens, D. F. (2000). The place of ambient vision in understanding problems of mobility and aging. In K. W. Schaie & M. Pietrucha (Eds.), *Mobility and transportation in the elderly* (pp. 45–62). New York: Springer.

Poon, L. W., & Fozard, J. L. (1978). Speed of retrieval from long term memory in relation to age, familiarity and datedness of information. *Journal of Gerontology, 33,* 711–717.

Poon, L. W., & Fozard, J. L. (1980). Age and word frequency effects in continuous recognition memory. *Journal of Gerontology, 33,* 77–86.

Poon, L. W., Fozard, J. L., Paulshock, D. R., & Thomas, J. C. (1979). A questionnaire assessment of age differences in retention of recent and remote events. *Experimental Aging Research, 5,* 401–411.

Schieber, F., Fozard, J. L., Gordon-Salant, S., & Weiffenbach, J. (1991). Optimizing the sensory-perceptual environments of older adults. *International Journal of Industrial Ergonomics, 7,* 133–162.

Staplin, L. (2000). Countering mobility losses due to functional impairments in normally aging individuals: Applying Fozard's framework to everyday driving situations. In K. W. Schaie & M. Pietrucha (Eds.), *Mobility and transportation in the elderly* (pp. 63–70). New York: Springer.

Steenbekkers, L. P. A. (1998). Visual contrast sensitivity. In L. P. A. Steenbekkers & C. E. M. van Beijsterveldt (Eds.), *Design relevant characteristics of ageing users* (pp. 131–136). Delft, The Netherlands: Delft University of Technology Press.

Wahl, H. W., Oswald, F., & Zimprich, D. (1999). Everyday competence in visually impaired older adults: A case for person-environment perspectives. *Gerontologist, 39,* 140–149.

Welford, A. T. (1981). Signal, noise, performance, and age. *Human Factors, 23*(1), 97–109.

Yntema, D. B. (1962). Keeping track of several things at once. *Human Factors, 5,* 7–17.

CHAPTER 3

The Impact of the Internet
on Older Adults

Sara J. Czaja and Chin Chin Lee

INTRODUCTION

The recent growth of the Internet and the expanding power of computers have made it possible for large numbers of people to have direct access to an increasingly wide array of information sources and services. Time that users are spending online is increasing and new interfaces, search engines, and features are becoming available at an unprecedented rate. Now, commercial access providers such as America Online, Netscape, Microsoft Internet Explorer, and other phone companies that provide Internet connections, are serving as gateways for home users and small businesses. Originally designed to transmit text and numeric data, the Internet now carries different types of information (e.g., travel, health, business, politics, financial) through graphic, video, and audio representations. Furthermore, technical advances such as high-speed transmission of information and affordable computer systems and modems have made Internet access possible to large numbers of people.

In September 2001, 66% of the population in the United States had used computers and about 54% were using the Internet, an increase of about 26 million people since 2000 (U.S. Department of Commerce, 2002). The number of users worldwide is about 600 million (Nua Internet Service). Today's computer users, unlike those in the past, include a wide variety of people, many of whom are not technically trained and not interested in technology per se. Rather, most of today's users consider technology as a tool to be used as a means of accomplishing a task. For example, the most common reasons adults use the Internet at home include e-mail, finding information, checking the news or weather, work-related tasks, or shopping and bill paying. Nearly half (45%) of the U.S. population now uses e-mail and approximately one third use the Internet for product and service information. In addition, 39% of Americans use it to make online purchases and about 35% use the Internet for health information (U.S. Department of Commerce, 2002).

Although access to such information is generally desirable, effective use of the Internet may be a challenge for many people, especially those who have had limited exposure to technology. In fact, the National Research Council (1997) issued a report suggesting that although the usability of systems has improved substantially, current interfaces still exclude many people, such as those who are older or who have disabilities, from effective Internet access.

Although design issues related to the Internet have received attention within the human-computer interaction literature, available data on this topic regarding older people is limited. The topic of the Internet and older adults is important and needs attention within the research and design communities, given the aging of the population and the increased reliance on network technologies such as the Internet for information dissemination and communication. By the year 2030 people aged 65+ will represent 20% of the United States population, an increase of about 8% since 2000 (see Figure 3.1) (U.S. Department of Health and Human Services, 2001). Paralleling this demographic shift is the continued explosion of information technology. In the near future television, the telephone, and other communication media will become integrated with computer network resources, and more and more functions are likely to depend on computer technology. Thus not being able to successfully interact with information technology will have increasingly negative ramifications for individuals and place them at a disadvantage in most environments.

OLDER ADULTS AND THE INTERNET

Although the number of people over the age of 65 who use the Internet is increasing, Internet usage among this age group is low compared to other age groups. In fact, seniors are among the least likely people to go online. Only about 15% of Americans aged 65+ access the Internet

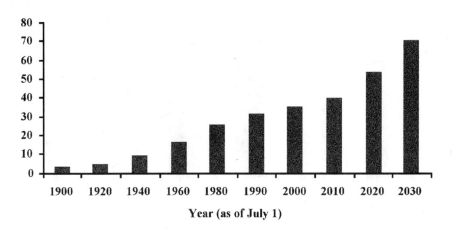

FIGURE 3.1 Number of persons 65+, 1900–2030 (number in millions).
Source: U.S. Department of Health and Human Services, 2001.

as compared to about 56% for the general population (see Figure 3.2) (U.S. Bureau of Census, 2001). Furthermore, even among older adults there is a digital divide. Seniors who access the Internet tend to be males (~60%), highly educated, married, and relatively affluent (Pew Internet & American Life, 2002). Furthermore, people with a disability such as impaired vision or problems with manual dexterity such as arthritis are only half as likely to access the Internet as those without a disability (U.S. Department of Commerce, 2002). Most older people have at least one chronic condition, and arthritis is one of the most frequently occurring conditions among older adults (U.S. Department of Health and Human Services, 2001).

There are a number of ways that the Internet may be beneficial to older people, especially those who live alone, in rural environments, or have some type of mobility restriction. For example, the Internet can facilitate linkages between older adults and health care providers and communication with family members and friends, especially those who are far away. It is quite common within the United States for family members to be dispersed among different geographic regions. Also, about 30% of noninstitutionalized older people live alone, with the number of older people who live alone increasing with age. Several studies (e.g., Czaja, Guerrier, Nair, & Laudauer, 1993; Furlong, 1989) have shown that older adults are receptive to using e-mail as a form of communication and that e-mail is effective in increasing social interactions among the elderly.

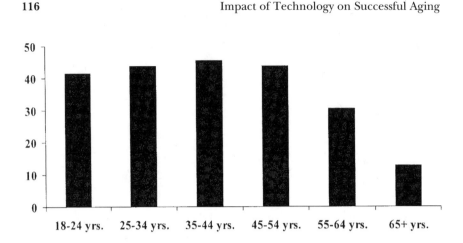

FIGURE 3.2   Use of Internet at home by adults 18 years and over.
Source: U.S. Census Bureau, 2001.

A number of studies have also shown that computer networks may prove to be beneficial for family caregivers of older relatives. Currently about 15% of U.S. adults are providing care for a seriously ill or disabled relative (Otten, 1991). Galliene, Moore, and Brennan (1993) found that access to a computer network "ComputerLink," increased the amount of psychological support provided by nurses to a group of homebound caregivers of Alzheimer's patients. ComputerLink also enabled the caregivers to access a caregiver support network that allowed them to share experiences and fostered the development of new friendships. Recent data from the Miami site of the Resources for Enhancing Alzheimer's Caregiver Health (REACH) program also demonstrate that computer network technology may prove to be beneficial for family caregivers of persons with dementia. Specifically, a computer-integrated telephone (CTIS) system was used to facilitate the ability of caregivers to communicate with health care professionals, family members, and other caregivers. The system also enabled caregivers to access information databases such as the Alzheimer's resource guide and to participate in online support groups. Caregivers reported that they liked using the system and that access to the system increased their knowledge about caregiving. They also found participation in the online support groups to be valuable (Czaja and Rubert, 2002). Computer links may also facilitate communication between caregivers and long-distance relatives. Currently, nearly 7 million Americans are long-distance caregivers for older relatives (Family Caregiver

Alliance, 1997). Clearly, network linkages can make it easier for family members to communicate, especially for those who live in different time zones. In the Miami REACH project, the CTIS system was also used to conduct family therapy sessions with long-distance relatives.

The Internet may also help older people communicate with health care providers or other older people and may help older people become involved in continuing education. For example, telemedicine applications allow direct communication between health care providers and patients. These opportunities will be enhanced with future developments in technology such as video conferencing. The Internet can also be used by older people to access information about health care, community services and resources, and for continuing education. A recent survey of 550 adults aged 40+ years (Morrell, Mayhorn, & Bennett, 2000) who were selected to fit the profile of older Web users found that older adults are particularly interested in learning how to use the World Wide Web to locate information on health-related topics.

The Internet may also be used to facilitate the performance of routine tasks such as financial management or shopping. Access to these resources and services may be particularly beneficial for older people who have mobility restrictions or lack of transportation. According to a study conducted by *SeniorNet* and Charles Schwab & Co. (1998), the top Internet activities performed by older adults are (1) exchanging e-mail with family and friends (72%), (2) researching a particular issue or subject (59%), (3) accessing news or current events (53%), (4) researching vacation or travel destination plans (47%), and (5) accessing local or regional weather information (43%). The study also indicates that the Web sites visited regularly among older adults are search engine Web sites (55%), news or current event-related sites (52%), hobby specific sites (41%), health-related sites (39%), and investment sites (38%).

Finally, access to computers and the Internet may expand employment opportunities for older people. The number of workers over the age of 55 is expected to grow significantly over the next few decades. In fact, the Bureau of Labor Statistics projects that by 2025 there will be approximately 33.3 million older people in the labor force. Most of these workers will be employed in white collar and service occupations where they are likely to use computers as a routine part of their jobs (U.S. Government Accounting Office, 2001). By 2001, more than half (57%) of workers in the U.S. used a computer at work and of these, 66% used the Internet. Use of computers and the Internet in the workplace varies somewhat by occupation and is more likely for people in managerial, professional specialty occupations, and technical, sales, and administrative support occupations. These are occupations where older people are likely to be employed. Computers and the Internet may help older people continue working, as computer-based work is more amenable to part-time work, flexible work scheduling, or telecommuting. In 1995 at least three million Americans were telecommuting for purposes of work (Nickerson & Landauer, 1997) and this number increased to 28 million in 2001 (International Telework Association and Council, 2001).

Web pages are also increasingly being developed for seniors. For example Seniors.gov (http://www.seniors.gov) is a comprehensive collection of links to government resources geared toward the needs of seniors such as social security and retirement planning. The administration on aging has also developed a web directory for seniors (http://www.aoa.gov/aoa/webres/craig.htm), and the National Institutes on Aging (NIA) has an online resource directory available for seniors. NIA has also recently published a compendium of scientific research and design guidelines related to the Internet and older adults (Morrell, Dailey, Feldman, Mayhorn, & Echt, 2001).

Clearly, the Internet has great potential value for older people who are receptive to using Internet technology. However, available data (e.g., Czaja & Sharit, 1998; Mead, Spaulding, Sit, Meyer, & Walker, 1997) also indicate that although older people are generally willing and able to use computers and the Internet, they typically have more problems learning to use this technology than younger adults. They have less knowledge about uses and how to access computers and other forms of technology. Morrell, Mayhorn, and Bennett (2000) found that the two primary predictors for not using the Web among people aged 60+ years were lack of access to a computer and lack of knowledge about the Web. The intent of this chapter is to highlight the potential implications of age-related changes in functional abilities for interface and training design. Before the full benefits of these types of technology can be realized for older people it is important to understand how to maximize their usefulness and usability for this population.

USING THE INTERNET

Overview

As discussed, the Internet refers to a vast interconnected system of networks that span the globe. The term *Internet* is not synonymous with the World Wide Web. The Internet is the physical medium used to transport information, whereas the World Wide Web (WWW) is a collection of protocols used to access the information. Current Web applications include communication, information databases, online shopping, online banking, and online travel services. Basically, documents on the Web (Web pages) reside on a server and are accessed by programs such as Web browsers. In turn, Web browsers are either text-based or graphical. In text-based browsers, users interact with a keyboard to select information, whereas in graphic-based browsers information selection is accomplished with a pointing device such as a mouse. Most graphic-based browsers have multimedia capabilities and can include graphics, sound, and video (see Vora and Helander, 1997, for a more complete discussion of these issues). These types of browsers are more common and generally easier to use.

One critical issue confronting users of the Internet/WWW is finding desired information without spending large amounts of time. A survey of Internet users (Georgia Tech Graphic, Visualization and Usability Center, 1996) found the most common user problems included slow response speed, finding information, and difficulty finding Web pages already visited. Currently, with the explosive growth of the WWW there are no guidelines that are systematically applied to the design of most Web interfaces. In this regard, Vora and Helander (1997) outlined several usability problems with current Web interfaces including outdated and incomplete information content, poor use of graphics, slow response time, overcrowding of screen information, and poor navigation support. Although indexes and search engines are helpful with respect to Web navigation, finding information on the Web is often difficult. These problems are likely to become exacerbated with the continued expansion of information on the Web and the increased number of Internet users. Without effective tools to help people deal with the information glut the new information technologies such as the Internet could hinder rather than help people access information.

Electronic Information Seeking

Essentially, use of the Internet involves information seeking, a fundamental process people engage in to acquire knowledge or solve problems. It generally represents a higher-level cognitive activity and as such involves memory, reasoning, attention, learning, and problem solving. Generally, people develop strategies and skills for information seeking according to their abilities, experiences, and available physical resources such as information systems. In this regard, information seeking involves the interaction among six factors: the information seeker, task, search system, domain, setting, and search outcomes. The process is both opportunistic and systematic and involves a number of inter-dependent subprocesses or phases including defining and under-standing the problem, choosing a search system, formulating a query, executing a search, examining results, extracting and integrating infor-mation, and, finally, stopping the search. An information search is sel-dom complete with only a single query and retrieval. Deciding when and how to stop requires an assessment of the information-seeking process. Monitoring progress is crucial to the development of infor-mation-seeking strategies (Marchionini, 1995).

Generally, through practice and experience, people develop strate-gies to guide the information-seeking process. These include strategies for choosing information sources and searching these sources. As dis-cussed by Marchionini (1995), information technologies such as the Internet have a dramatic impact on the information-seeking process. For example, instead of using the library and accessing information in hard copy, we now use online databases and access information in elec-tronic form. These technologies require the information seeker to develop specialized knowledge and skills. Specifically, these include domain expertise, system expertise, and information-seeking expertise. Domain expertise involves knowledge and skills related to the problem domain and allows the persons to solve problems and access informa-tion quickly and effectively. Generally, experts in a domain have exten-sive knowledge of the domain and have an organized knowledge base of the general problem area. System expertise refers to knowledge and skills related to the search system and the physical interface to this system. In the case of the Internet, these include the abilities to use a keyboard, mouse, and menus, and to manage windows and screen information. It also means having an understanding of how databases are organized, what information is available, and how documents are structured. Information-seeking expertise refers to knowledge and skills related to the process of information seeking. This includes, for example, knowledge of relevant information sources and how these sources are organized. It also includes knowing where to look for infor-mation and how to request it.

Information seeking is a highly variable process, and individuals develop distinct patterns for searching that involve a variety of strate-gies and tactics. These strategies vary according to the task, context, and setting. Generally, two broad types of strategies can be distinguished: analytic strategies and browsing strategies. Analytic strategies are goal driven, and require planning methods that are precise and systematic. They tend to be methodical and deterministic. Browsing strategies are more data driven and more opportunistic, informal, and interactive. People tend to use a combination of analytic and browsing strategies when searching the WWW. However, novice users or people with limited domain or system expertise tend to adopt browsing as opposed to analytic strategies (Marchionini, 1995). While browsing is often the basis for serendipitous discoveries and incidental learning it can also result in distraction, confusion, frustration, cognitive overload, and general problems associated with being "lost in hyperspace" (Nielsen, 1990). These problems may be exacerbated with the recent proliferation of websites and the lack of consistency among Web designers. Many users may not have the opportunity to develop the expertise needed to use current search systems efficiently.

Essentially, use of the Internet requires learning a new set of skills to locate, access, manipulate, and use information sources. Given that aging is associated with changes in cognitive abilities and that older adults typically have some difficulty acquiring new skills, learning to use the Internet for communication and information seeking may be challenging for older adults.

Older Adults and the Acquisition of Computer Skills

A number of studies have examined the ability of older adults to learn to use computer technology. These studies span a variety of computer applications and also vary with respect to training strategies such as conceptual vs. procedural training (Morrell, Park, Mayhorn, & Echt, 1995) or computer-based or instructor-based vs. manual-based training (Czaja, Hammond, Blascovich, & Swede, 1989). In addition, the influence of variables such as attitude toward computers and computer anxiety on learning have been examined. Overall, the results of these studies indicate that older adults are, in fact, able to use computers for a variety of tasks. However, they often have more difficulty acquiring computer skills than younger people and require more training and more help during training. Also, when compared to younger adults on measures such as speed they often achieve lower levels of performance.

Egan and Gomez (1985) conducted a series of experiments in an attempt to identify individual difference variables that predict ability to learn text editing. They found that age and spatial memory were significant predictors of learning difficulty. Both of these variables contributed to the prediction of first try errors and execution time per successful edit change. In particular, age was associated with difficulty producing the correct sequence of symbols and patterns to accomplish the desired editing change.

Elias, Elias, Robbins, and Gage (1987) conducted a study to examine age differences in the acquisition of text editing skills and to identify sources of difficulty encountered by older adults. The training program included an audiotape and a training manual. The results indicated that all participants were able to learn the fundamentals of word processing, however, the older adults required more time to complete the training program and required more help. The older people also performed more poorly on a review examination. Garfein, Schaie, and Willis (1988) examined the ability of older adults to learn a spreadsheet package. They also attempted to identify component abilities that are predictive for computer novices to acquire computer skills. The results of their study indicated that all participants were able to operate a computer and use the spreadsheet package after only two 90-minute sessions of training. There were no significant age effects for the performance measures. However, this may be because the age range of the participants was restricted and only included people ranging in age from 49 to 67 years of age. In terms of other factors affecting computer proficiency, they found that fluid intelligence was an important predictor of performance. Gist, Rosen, and Schwoerer (1988) also examined the influence of age and training method on the acquisition of a spreadsheet program. The training program consisted of two approaches: tutorial or behavioral modeling. The tutorial approach involved a computer-based, step-by-step, interactive instructional package. The behavioral modeling involved watching a videotape of a middle-aged male demonstrating the use of the software and then practicing the procedure. The results indicated that the modeling approach was superior to the tutorial approach for both younger and older participants. They also found that older adults performed more poorly on a post-training test.

Zandri and Charness (1989) investigated the influence of training method on the ability of older people to use a calendar and notepad system. Specifically, they examined whether providing an advanced organizer would have an impact on the acquisition of computer skills for younger and older adults. They also examined whether learning with a partner would have an influence on learning. The results indicated an age by training method interaction (learning alone or with a peer) by organizer (with or without an organizer) for performance on a final test. For the older adults who received training without a partner, the advanced organizer resulted in better performance. For the other group of older people, there was no performance effect. For the younger subjects, having the advanced organizer resulted in worse performance if they learned alone but it made no difference if they learned in pairs.

These results suggest that the provision of an advanced organizer may be differentially effective for older people under some learning conditions. Furthermore, the older people were about 2.5 times slower than the younger people in the training sessions and they required about three times as much help.

In a follow-up study, Charness, Schumann, and Boritz (1992) examined the impact of training techniques and computer anxiety on the acquisition of word processing skills in a sample of younger and older adults. In the first study, 16 computer novices, ranging in age from 25–81 years, learned word processing skills under a self-paced training program. Half of the participants received the organizer prior to training. Overall, the provision of the organizer did not improve performance. The results also indicated that older adults took about 1.2 times longer than younger adults did to complete training and they required more help. In a second study, the investigator attempted to control the nature of the training session. Thirty computer novices were assigned either to a self-paced learning situation where they were actively involved in the tutorial, or a fixed-paced situation where they passively observed a predetermined sequence of activities. The results indicated that both the younger and older adults performed better in the self-paced training situation relative to fixed-paced condition. Again the older adults took about 1.2 times longer than the younger adults to complete training and required more help.

Czaja, Hammond, Blascovich, and Swede (1989) evaluated three training strategies for novice adults in leaning to use a word processing program. The training strategies were instructor-based, manual-based, and online training. The results indicated that younger adults were more successful learning the word processing program. The older adults were slower and made more errors. The results also indicated that the manual-based and instructor-based training were superior to online training for all participants. The investigators also found that there were age differences in performance on the post-training tasks. The older adults took more time to complete the tasks and made more errors.

In a later study, Czaja, Hammond, and Joyce (1989) attempted to identify a training strategy that would minimize age differences in learning text editing. Two training programs were evaluated: a goal-oriented program and a traditional approach that included a manual and a lecture. The goal-oriented approach introduced the elements of text editing in an incremental fashion, moving from the simpler to the more complex tasks. The training sessions included problem-solving tasks with objectives of discovering and achieving methods for completing the tasks. The manual was written as a series of goal-oriented units. It used simple language, drew similarities between computer and familiar concepts, and minimized the amount of necessary reading. The results indicated that post-training performance was better for participants who were trained using the goal-oriented approach. These participants took less time to complete the tasks and made fewer mistakes. In spite of training manipulation, performance was lower for older than for younger adults. Older adults required more time to complete tasks, completed fewer editing changes, and made more mistakes.

Caplan and Schooler (1990) evaluated whether providing the participants with a conceptual model of the software would improve their ability to learn a painting software program. They provided half of the participants with an analogical model of a painting software program before training. The results indicated that the model was beneficial for younger but detrimental for older adults. Similar results were found in the Morrell, Park, Mayhorn, and Echt (1995) study. They examined the ability of young-old (ages 60–74 years) and old-old (ages 75–89) adults to perform tasks on ELDERCOMM, a bulletin board system. The participants were presented with procedural instructional materials or a combination of conceptual information and procedural instructions. The results indicated that all participants performed better with the procedural instruction material. They also found that the young-old adults had better performance than the old-old adults; the old-old adults made more performance errors. The investigator concluded that conceptual training may not be beneficial for older adults because they need to translate the model into actions, which may increase working memory demands.

More recently, Rogers, Fisk, Mead, Walker, and Cabrera (1996) assessed the efficacy of several instructional methods in teaching older adults to use automatic teller machines. The results indicated that training method did have an influence on performance such that an online tutorial that provided specific practice on the task components was superior to written instructions and written instructions accompanied by graphics. The authors discuss the importance of providing older adults with actual training on technologies such as ATM machines. Sole reliance on instructional materials or self-discovery may not be optimal for this population, especially for more complex technological applications such as the Internet. Identification of efficacious training strategies for older adults is especially important, given that continued development of technology will require lifelong learning for people of all ages. In this regard, Mead and Fisk (1998) examined the impact of the type of information presented during training on the initial and retention performance of younger and older adults learning to use ATM technology. Specifically, they compared two types of training: concept and action. The concept training presented factual information whereas the action training was procedural. The action training was found to be superior for older adults. They showed superior speed and accuracy immediately after training and superior speed following the retention interval. They concluded that presenting procedural information to older adults during training was more important than presenting conceptual information. Mead and colleagues (1997) examined the effects of type of training on efficiency in a World Wide Web search activity. The participants were trained with a hands-on Web navigation tutorial or a verbal description of available navigation tools. The hands-on training was found to be superior, especially for older adults. Older adults who received hands-on training used more efficient navigation tools. These findings suggest that type of training strategy does have an impact on the ability of older people to use complex computer technologies. Generally, the data suggest that procedural hands-on training with an action component is superior for older adults. However, more research is needed to identify training strategies that facilitate the ability of older people to acquire computer-based skills. A recent study (Charness, Kelly, Bosman, & Mottram, 2001) found that prior experience with computer software applications has a significant impact on the ability to learn new software applications. Specifically, the data from this study presented strong evidence that prior experience with software applications can compensate for age-related performance differences. These findings indicate that older people can effectively interact with new information technologies if they are provided with adequate training.

Generally, the literature indicates that older adults are able to use computers for routine tasks and that they are able to learn a wide variety of computer applications. However, they are typically slower to acquire computer skills than younger adults and generally require more help and hands-on practice. Furthermore, they typically need training on basic computer concepts, such as mouse and windows management, in addition to training on the application area of interest. They may also require information on the types of technologies that are available, the potential benefits associated with using these technologies, and where and how to access them. Finally, greater attention needs to be given to the design of training and instructional materials to accommodate age-related changes in perceptual and cognitive abilities.

Older Adults and Electronic Information Seeking

As discussed, information seeking is a complex process and places demands on cognitive abilities such as working memory, spatial memory, reasoning, and problem solving. Information seeking within electronic environment also requires special skills such as knowledge related to the search system. Given that older adults typically experience declines in cognitive abilities such as working memory and are less likely than younger people to have knowledge of the structure and organization of search systems, a relevant question is the degree to which they will experience difficulty searching for information in electronic environments. Although the topic of electronic information search and retrieval has received considerable attention within the human-computer interaction literature as shown in Table 3.1, the available data on this topic for older people is limited.

Westerman, Davies, Glendon, Stammers, and Matthews (1995) examined the relationships among spatial ability, spatial memory, vocabulary skills, and age, and the ability to retrieve information from a computer database that varied according to how the database was structured (e.g., hierarchical vs. linear). In general, they found that the older subjects were slower in retrieving the information than the younger adults; however, there were no age-related differences in accuracy. The learning rates also differed for the two groups such that the older people were slower than the younger people. They found that the slower response on the part of the older adults was more dependent on general processing speed than on other cognitive abilities.

Freudenthal (1997) examined the degree to which latencies on an information retrieval task were predicted by movement speed and other cognitive variables in a group of younger and older adults. The participants were required to search for answers to questions in a hierarchical menu structure. Results indicated that the older subjects were slower than the younger subjects on overall latencies for information retrieval and that this slowing increased with each consecutive step in the menu. Similar to Westerman and colleagues (1995), he also found that movement speed was a significant predictor of overall latency. He also found that other cognitive abilities, such as reasoning speed, spatial ability, and memory, were also predictive of response latencies. However, memory and spatial abilities are only predictors for latency on steps later in the menu structure. Freudenthal suggests that deep menu structures may not be appropriate for older adults as navigation through these types of structures is dependent on spatial skills that tend to decline with age. Vicente, Hayes, and Williges (1987) also found that

TABLE 3.1   Electronic Information Seeking and Older Adults

Investigators	Age Range (Years)	Task	Findings
Westerman, Davies, Glendon, Stammers, & Matthews (1995)	18–27 45–57	Information retrieval/menu search	Older adults performed more slowly, especially in initial blocks; no differences in navigation efficacy
Mead, Sit, Jamieson, Rousseau, & Rogers (1996)	18–33 63–76	Online library catalog search	Older adults were less successful than younger adults; more query errors and less efficient recovery
Mead, Spaulding, Sit, Meyer, & Walker (1997)	19–36 64–81	WWW search activity	Older adults had less "search success"; less search efficiency
Freudenthal (1997)	18–25 60–70	Information search in a hierarchical menu	Older adults were slower and less accurate than younger adults
Czaja & Sharit (1999)	20–75	Information search and retrieval—health insurance database	Older adults completed fewer inquiries; no differences in navigational efficiency

age, spatial ability, and vocabulary were highly predictive of variance in search latency for a computer-based information retrieval task. They postulated that people with low spatial ability tend to "get lost" in the database. Other investigators such as Gomez, Egan, Wheeler, Sharma, and Gruchacz (1983), Sein and Bostrom (1989), and Czaja and Sharit (1998) have also found spatial ability to be predictive of ability to perform computer-interactive tasks.

Mead, Sit, Jamieson, Rousseau, and Rogers (1996) examined the ability of younger and older adults to use an online library database. Overall, the younger adults achieved more success than did the older adults in performing the searches. They also used more efficient search strategies. The older adults made more errors when formulating search queries and had more difficulty recovering from these errors.

Kubeck, Miller-Albrecht, and Murphy (1999) found that older adults had more problems than younger adults using the Web to search for information to answer questions. They also found a trade-off between efficiency and quality such that if older adults were less efficient than younger adults their answers to the queries were comparable. However, when they were as efficient as the younger adults the quality of their answers was not as good. A study conducted by Czaja and Sharit (1999) examined age differences in the performance of a database inquiry task. The task was a simulation of a customer service representative task in the health insurance industry. The participants were required to search through computerized data files to answer customer queries regarding their health insurance coverage. The results indicated that the older adults completed fewer queries and were less effective in documenting their responses. However, when controlling for differences in response speed, there were no age differences in navigational efficiency. In addition, age, cognitive abilities such as working memory and spatial skills, and prior computer experience influenced performance. The data showed that prior experience with computers was an important predictor of performance, as were cognitive abilities such as working memory and processing speed. As expected, the older participants had less prior experience than the younger participants. Czaja and Sharit (1999) suggest that providing older adults with basic training in the use of computers is as important as providing them with training on the particular application. The results also showed that for all participants performance improved with task experience. This finding reinforces the importance of providing people with adequate training and practice.

In their study of the World Wide Web, Mead and colleagues (1997) found that older adults were less successful than younger adults in searching the Web for specific information and that they used less efficient search strategies. The older people tended to have difficulty remembering previously followed links and the information on previously searched pages. The data suggest that history markers may be particularly beneficial for older people.

Generally, the available literature suggests that older adults are able to search and retrieve information within electronic environments. However, they appear to have more difficulty than do younger adults and tend to use less efficient navigation strategies. They also appear to have problems remembering where and what they searched. In order to maximize the ability of older people to successfully interact with electronic information systems such as the WWW and have access to the information highway, we need to understand the source of age-related difficulties. This type of information will allow us to develop interface design and training strategies to accommodate individual differences in performance. Currently, there is very little information on problems experienced by older people when attempting to learn and navigate the Web, especially in real world contexts. This is fertile area for research.

CONCLUSIONS

The explosion of the World Wide Web has dramatically increased opportunities for gaining access to a wide variety of information. For those who are frail, isolated, or have some type of mobility restrictions, such as a significant number of older persons, access to the Web holds the promise of enhancing independence by providing linkages to goods and resources, facilitating communication, and enhancing the ability to perform routine tasks such as banking and shopping. The Web can also help older people access information on health and other topics and manage personal finances. As developments in Web technology continue to emerge users will have faster access to more channels of information in myriad formats.

Unfortunately, because of the rapid and expansive growth in Web technology, there have been limited opportunities to develop and test Web interfaces as compared to other Human-Computer Interaction (HCI) domains. This problem is exacerbated by the fact that many Web developers have limited knowledge with respect to interface concerns (Ratner, Grose, & Forsythe, 1996). In fact, the report by the National Research Council (1997) indicated that current interface structures significantly limit the use of the Web by many users, especially those who have some type of constraint on their abilities, such as older users. To date, there is limited empirical research examining usability issues for the Web, especially for users who are less technically proficient, have physical or cognitive limitations, or are older. To help ensure that the World Wide Web is available to the entire population, research is needed to support effective interface and training for users of all ages and abilities.

Although most older people are receptive to using new technologies they often encounter difficulties when attempting to adopt these systems. Barriers to successful adaptation of technology are largely related to a failure on the part of system designers to perceive older adults as active users of technical systems. Overcoming these barriers depends on training and design solutions that accommodate age-related declines in perceptual, cognitive, and motor abilities. This might involve, for example, software modifications, alternative input devices, or redesign of instructional manuals. The development of these solutions requires an understanding of the needs, preferences, and abilities of older people. In essence, in order to design interfaces for information systems so that they are useful and usable for older people it is important to understand why and when technology is difficult to use, how to design technology for easier and effective use and how to effectively teach people to use and take advantage of available technologies.

REFERENCES

Caplan, L. J., & Schooler, C. (1990). The effects of analogical training models and age on problem-solving in a new domain. *Experimental Aging Research, 16,* 151–154.

Charness, N., Kelly, C. L., Bosman, E. A., & Mottram, M. (2001). Word processing training and retraining: Effects of adult age, experience, and interface. *Psychology and Aging, 16,* 110–127.

Charness, N., Schumann, C. E., & Boritz, G. A. (1992). Training older adults in word processing: Effects of age, training technique and computer anxiety. *International Journal of Aging and Technology, 5,* 79–106.

Czaja, S. J., Guerrier, J., Nair, S., & Laudauer, T. (1993). Computer communication as an aid to independence for older adults. *Behavior and Information Technology, 2,* 97–107.

Czaja, S. J., Hammond, K., Blascovich, J., & Swede, H. (1989). Age-related differences in learning to use a text-editing system. *Behavior and Information Technology, 8,* 309–319.

Czaja, S. J., Hammond, K., & Joyce, J. B. (1989). *Word processing training for older adults.* Final report submitted to the National Institute on Aging (Grant #5 R4 AGO4647-03).

Czaja, S. J., & Rubert, M. (2002) Telecommunications technology as an aid to family caregivers of persons with dementia. *Psychosomatic Medicine, 64,* 469–476.

Czaja, S. J., & Sharit, J. (1998). Ability-performance relationships as a function of age and task experience for a data entry task. *Journal of Experimental Psychology: Applied, 4,* 332–351.

Czaja, S. J., & Sharit, J. (1999, August). *Age differences in a complex information search and retrieval task.* Paper presented at Annual Meeting of American Psychological Association. Boston.

Czaja, S. J., Sharit, J., Charness, N., Fisk, A. D., & Rogers, W. (2001). The center for research and education on aging and technology enhancement (CREATE): A program to enhance technology for older adults, *Gerontechnology, 1,* 50–59.

Egan, D. E., & Gomez, L. M. (1985). Assaying, isolating, and accommodating individual differences in learning a complex skill. *Individual Differences in Cognition, 2,* 174–217.

Elias, P. K., Elias, M. F., Robbins, M. A., & Gage, P. (1987). Acquisition of word-processing skills by younger, middle-aged, and older adults. *Psychology and Aging, 2,* 340–348.

Family Caregiving Alliance. (1997). *Annual report: California's caregiver resource center system fiscal year 1996–1997.* San Francisco: Author.

Freudenthal, D. (1997). *Learning to use interactive devices: Age differences in the reasoning process.* Doctoral thesis, Eindhoven University of Technology, The Netherlands.

Furlong, M. S. (1989). An electronic community for older adults: The SeniorNet network. *Journal of Communication, 39,* 145–153.

Galliene, R. L., Moore, S. M., & Brennan, P. F. (1993). Alzheimer's caregivers: Psychosocial support via computer network. *Journal of Gerontological Nursing, 12,* 1–22.

Garfein, A. J., Schaie, K. W., & Willis, S. L. (1988). Microcomputer proficiency in later-middle-aged adults and older adults: Teaching old dogs new tricks. *Social Behavior, 3,* 131–148.

Georgia Tech Graphic, Visualization and Usability Center. (1996). Available at: http://www.cc.gatech.edu/gvu/user_surveys/survey-04-1995/

Gist, M., Rosen, B., & Schwoerer, C. (1988). The influence of training method and trainee age on the acquisition of computer skills. *Personal Psychology, 41,* 255–265.

Gomez, L. M., Egan, D. E., Wheeler, E. A., Sharma, D. K., & Gruchacz, A. M. (1983). How interface design determines who had difficulty learning to use a text editor. *Proceedings of the CHI '83 Conferences on Human Factors in Computer Systems,* 176–181.

International Telework Association and Council. (2001). Telework in the United States: Telework America Survey 2001. Available online: http://www.telecommute.org/twa/index.htm.

Kubeck, J. E., Miller-Albrecht, S. A., & Murphy, M. D. (1999). Finding information on the World Wide Web: Exploring older adults' exploration. *Educational Gerontology, 25,* 167–183.

Marchionini, G. (1995). *Information seeking in electronic environments.* Cambridge, UK: Cambridge University Press.

Mead, S. E., & Fisk, A. D. (1998). Measuring skill acquisition and retention with an ATM simulator: The need for age-specific training. *Human Factors, 40,* 516–523.

Mead, S. E., Sit, R. A., Jamieson, B. A., Rousseau, G. K., & Rogers, W. A. (1996, August). *Online library catalog: Age-related differences in performance for novice users.* Paper presented at the Annual Meeting of the American Psychological Association, Toronto, Canada.

Mead, S. E., Spaulding, V. A., Sit, R. A., Meyer, B., & Walker, N. (1997). Effects of age and training on World Wide Web navigation strategies. *Proceedings of the Human Factors and Ergonomics Society 41st Annual Meeting,* 152–156.

Morrell, R. W., Dailey, S. R., Feldman, C., Mayhorn, C. B., & Echt, K. V. (2001). *Older adults and information technology: A compendium of scientific research and Web site accessibility guidelines.* Washington, DC: National Institute on Aging.

Morrell, R. W., Mayhorn, C. B., & Bennett, J. (2000). A survey of World Wide Web use in middle-aged and older adults. *Human Factors, 42,* 175–182.

Morrell, R. W., Park, D. C., Mayhorn, C. B., & Echt, K. V. (1995, August). *Older adults and electronic communication networks: Learning to use ELDERCOMM.* Paper presented at the 103 Annual Convention of the American Psychological Association. New York.

National Research Council. (1997). *More than screen deep: Toward every-citizen interfaces to the nation's information infrastructure.* Washington, DC: National Academy Press.

Nickerson, R. S., & Landauer, T. K. (1997). Human-computer interaction: Background and issues. In M. G. Helander, T. K., Landauer, & P. V. Prabhu (Eds.), *Handbook of human-computer interaction* (2nd ed., pp. 3–32). Amsterdam: Elsevier.

Nielsen, J. (1990). *Hypertext and hypermedia.* Boston: Academic Press.

Nua Internet Surveys. (2002, March 19). *Global Internet audience increases.* Retrieved March 21, 2002, from http://www.nua.ie/surveys/index.cgi?f= VS&art_id=905357762&rel=true

Otten, A. (1991, April 22). About 15% of US adults care for ill relatives. *Wall Street Journal,* p. B1.

Pew Internet & American Life (2002, March 3). *Getting serious on line.* Retrieved March 21, 2002, from http://www.pewinternet.org/releases/ release.asp?id=39.

Ratner, J. A., Grose, E., & Forsythe, C. (1996). Traditional vs. Web style guides: How do they differ? *Proceedings of the Human Factors and Ergonomics Society 40th Annual Meeting,* 365–369.

Rogers, W. A., Fisk, A. D., Mead, S. E., Walker, N., & Cabrera, E. F. (1996). Training older adults to use automatic teller machines. *Human Factors, 38,* 425–433.

Sein, M. K., & Bostrom, R. P. (1989). Individual differences in conceptual models in training novice users. *Human-Computer Interaction, 4,* 197–229.

SeniorNet and Charles Schwab & Co. (1998). *Graying of the Internet.* Available online: http://www.headcount.com/globalsource/profile/index.htm? choice=ussenior&id=190.

U. S. Bureau of Census. (2001). *Home computers and Internet use in the United States: August 2000.* Washington, DC: U.S. Government Printing Office.

U. S. Department of Commerce. (2002). *A national online: How Americans are expanding their use of the Internet.* Washington, DC: NTIA and Economics and Statistics Administration.

U. S. Department of Health and Human Services. (2001). *A profile of older Americans: 2001.* Washington, DC: Administration on Aging.

U. S. Government Accounting Office. (2001). *Older workers: Demographic trends pose challenges for employers and workers.* Washington, DC: U.S. Government Printing Office.

Vicente, K. J., Hayes, B. C., & Williges, R. C. (1987). Assaying and isolating individual differences in searching a hierarchical file system. *Human Factors, 29,* 349–359.

Vora, P. R., & Helander, M. G. (1997). Hypertex and its implications for the Internet. In M. G. Helander, T. K. Landauer, & P. V. Prabhu (Eds.), *Handbook of human-computer interaction* (2nd ed., pp. 877–914). Amsterdam: Elsevier.

Westerman, S. J., Davies, D. R., Glendon, A. I., Stammers, R. B., & Matthews, G. (1995). Age and cognitive ability as predictors of computerized information retrieval. *Behavior and Information Technology, 14,* 313–326.

Zandri, E., & Charness, N. (1989). Training older and younger adults to use software. *Educational Gerontology, 15,* 615–631.

Commentary

Applying Research:
The NIHSeniorHealth.gov Project

Roger W. Morrell, Stephanie R. Dailey, and Gabriel K. Rousseau

INTRODUCTION

As Czaja and Lee noted in this volume, it is very likely that computer applications such as the World Wide Web (Web) hold promise of enhancing the independence and quality of life for older people. Therefore, it is important to consider older adults as active users of information technology (computers and the Internet) and other types of electronic devices, and their particular needs in the design of such systems. Primary among these considerations is the necessity to make the Web accessible to them.

With these issues in mind, we propose that there are three basic conditions that must be met in order to make Web sites or individual Web pages generally accessible. The first condition is that the material on Web pages (whether text, graphics, animation, or video) should be able to be seen or read without effort. The second condition is that the content on a website should be able to be readily understood. The third condition is that the website should be relatively easy to navigate.

These requirements appear fairly simple and straightforward. There are numerous sets of general guidelines available for building web pages and websites that meet some part of each of these conditions. Many of these recommendations are available on the Web itself (e.g., www.usability.gov). Moreover, software manufacturers such as Microsoft and Oracle have constructed usability laboratories to develop such directives and have applied their findings in the development of their web-based products (Kanerva, Keeker, Risden, Shuh, & Czerwinski,

1998; Wichansky & Hackman, 1998; respectively). Regardless of these efforts, there remain concerns. Although some of the sets of guidelines have been developed through usability testing (e.g., Borges, Morales, & Rodriguez, 1998), the process of making all of the myriad Web sites on the Web truly accessible is a enormous task and is much more complex than it would initially appear.

Coupled with the enormity of the task is the fact that many of the lists of available recommendations for building accessible Web sites are too general, vague, or difficult to translate into online designs (Czaja & Lee, 2001). Some of the sets of suggestions are more concerned with highly technical aspects of hypermedia rather than usability (Wiebe & Howe, 1998). Others are based on conjecture, anecdotal evidence, unscientific observation, or design principles derived from the graphic arts (Grabinger & Osman-Jouchoux, 1996). Furthermore, many sets are not comprehensive and in most instances, little, if any, of the scientific research that was used to form the basis of the individual suggestions is cited along with the recommendations. Moreover, many Web site designers are simply not applying some of the general guidelines that are available. Therefore, locating information on the Web may be troublesome because most Web sites remain inaccessible at some level. This may be especially true for older adults who are searching for information on the Web because any normal age-related problems in vision, cognition, and/or motor skills they may be experiencing could make the process even more arduous (Holt & Morrell, 2002).

As a rule, the needs of the elderly are not considered in web site design. This is remarkable because there is considerable systematic evidence available to indicate that older adults can learn how to use computers and the Web and retain these abilities over time (National Institute on Aging, 2001a). Furthermore, they are very interested in learning how to use the Web (Morrell, Mayhorn, & Bennett, 2000). Moreover, older adults are currently surfing the Web with increasing confidence and frequency, thus dispelling long-held myths that they are afraid of and reluctant to use new technologies (Adler, 2002; Pew Internet & American Life Project: Online Life Report, 2000; U.S. Department of Commerce, 1999). The number of adults over the age of 60 is also expected to increase substantially over the next several decades (Administration on Aging, 1999). As the baby boomers move into old age, it is likely that they will become a significant presence on the Web.

Most Web sites at present are built to be used by young people. That is, few designers have taken into consideration how age-related declines in vision, cognition, and motor skills might impede accessibility for older adults to their Web sites. Furthermore, until recently there were only a few somewhat comprehensive sets of guidelines available for increasing accessibility to Web sites for older adults (see Holt, 2000; Morrell, 2002). In addition, many other sets of accessibility guidelines for Web use by older adults have fallen somewhat short of their mission because they focused on the issue from only one perspective: either on declines in vision or on providing suggestions from a limited human factors approach (Echt, 2002).

Therefore, the NIHSeniorHealth.gov Project was launched as a joint project between the National Institute on Aging (NIA) and the National Library of Medicine (NLM) to accomplish two goals. The first goal was to develop comprehensive, scientific, research-based guidelines on how to make Web sites more accessible for older adults. The second goal was the implementation of the guidelines in the construction of a Web site that was designed to be used specifically by older adults to gain health information.

THE NIHSeniorHealth.gov PROJECT

The NIHSeniorHealth.gov Project began in the Fall of 1999 and was originally conceived as a series of online short courses based on AgePage health information brochures that had been developed and distributed by the National Institute on Aging over the past three decades. Although AgePages were already online, it was clear that the health information they contained could be expanded if presented on the Web in hypermedia (i.e., text, graphics, illustrations, photographs, video, and animation). The project was then conceptualized as a single Web site containing multiple topics concerning issues on aging and was initially known as the Interactive AgePage Project. The name of the Web site was changed to NIHSeniorHealth.gov in August, 2001 (see Dailey, 2000; Morrell & Dailey, 2001a, 2001b).

Before construction of the Web site began, the development team had to first determine how to meet the three basic conditions for accessibility outlined at the beginning of this chapter. The first condition stated that the material on web pages (whether text, graphics, or video) should be able to be viewed or read easily. Therefore, the team was required to determine how to present information online in a readable form for older persons with normal age-related visual problems. The second condition mandated that the content on a Web site should be comprehensible. Thus, the team had to resolve how to increase the grasp of the material by people who might be experiencing normal age-related declines in cognitive abilities. The third condition required that the Web site should be relatively easy to navigate. Because of this, the team was obligated to judge how to design a Web site that was simple to use in terms of navigational structure and could be easily managed by older adults experiencing normal age-related declines in motor skills. Most important, the methods for meeting all of these conditions would have to be based on the most current scientific research on the topic. By meeting these three conditions, the Web site would be designed to mediate some of the common age-related declines in vision, cognition, and motor skills that are observed as part of the normal aging process (see Morrell, 1997, for a general discussion). The project's early phase predates the federally mandated section 508 accessibility guidelines for persons with disabilities. However, the final product is completely 508 compliant (see Architectural and Transportation Barriers Compliance Board, 2000, for a listing of the 508 standards for persons with disabilities).

Developing the Guidelines

It was important to identify the state-of-the-art basic and applied research in cognition and aging, perception and aging, and human factors and aging in order to determine how best to design a Web site that could mediate declines in vision, cognition, and motor skills. Because a current, well-referenced, comprehensive set of guidelines was not at hand, an extensive literature search was conducted utilizing several online scientific databases (i.e., PsychNet). All of the literature that was uncovered from the search was integrated with articles and book chapters on the topic that were already available to the team and compiled into a position paper.

The position paper focused primarily on three areas: (1) normal age-related changes in vision, (2) normal age-related differences in cognition, and (3) normal age-related effects on motor skills. The guidelines were derived directly or indirectly from the research found in each of these three areas. Each of the guidelines is discussed in the next section of this chapter, as well as how the guidelines were implemented in the construction of the NIHSeniorHealth.gov Web site.

DESIGNING READABLE TEXT
FOR OLDER ADULTS
Age-Related Changes in Vision

Normal age-related declines in vision can render visually conveyed information difficult to comprehend (Charness, 2001). Some of the age-related visual problems that have been documented are caused, in part, by physiological changes within the eye (see Morrell & Echt, 1996, 1997). Because of these physiological changes, and other conditions, there may be a loss of eye function with age that results in a lessening of acuity, contrast sensitivity, depth of visual field and eye movements, and the ability to discern colors (see Echt, 2002; Haegerstrom-Portnoy, Schneck, Brabyn, & Lott, 1999; and the chapters by Schieber and Kline in this volume for more in-depth discussions of these topics).

In addition, there is research available that documents that text on computer screens is more difficult to read and is also read slower than printed text (Gould, Alfaro, Finn, Haupt, & Minuto, 1987; Meyer & Poon, 1997). Therefore, age-related impairments in vision, in tandem with the problems associated with screen presentation, may dramatically affect an older adult's ability to see and read information presented in hypermedia. All of these findings have a direct impact on the typeface, type size, and type weight that are used in web-based materials. Physical spacing and justification of the type, as well as the use of color and backgrounds, are also affected. In order to mediate age-related visual problems, the guidelines outlined in Table 3.2 were developed. Because of the lack of research with online materials, many of these guidelines were derived in part from research conducted with printed materials. Most researchers agree that the generalization of findings from print to the computer screen is an acceptable starting point (Hartley, 1994). A description is also provided on how the guidelines were employed in the creation of the NIHSeniorHealth.gov Web site in Table 3.2.

PRESENTING INFORMATION TO OLDER ADULTS

Age-related Declines in Cognition

There is a large body of evidence available that documents the aspects of cognition that decline with advancing age (see Craik & Salthouse, 2000; Fisk & Rogers, 1997, for extensive reviews) and how these declines might affect functioning in the everyday world (Park, 1992; Rogers & Fisk, 2000). We suggest that there are four basic cognitive processes (among others) that may affect the use of information technology by older adults. The cognitive processes are verbal and spatial working memory, the ability to comprehend text, and perceptual speed (Morrell, 1997).

TABLE 3.2 Mediating Age-Related Declines in Vision: Design Considerations, Guideline Rationales, Guidelines, and Guideline Implementation on the NIHSeniorHealth.gov Web Site

Design Consideration	Rationale for Guidelines from Research Findings	Guidelines*	Method of Implementation on the Web Site
Typeface	Text set with sans serif typeface has been found to be read more easily by older adults, (Grabinger & Osman-Jouchoux, 1996). Sans serif typefaces have also been shown to be preferred by older adults (Ellis & Kurniawan, 2000). Sans serif typefaces include Helvetica, Ariel, and Univers.	Use a sans serif typeface that is not condensed.	All text on the Web site is set in Helvetica.
Type Size	Most findings demonstrate that type size should be increased to maximize text legibility (Hartley, 1994, 1997, 1999). Performance has been shown to increase on paper tasks when a 12–14 point size is employed; many older adults seem to prefer these sizes of type relative to smaller sizes (Ellis & Kurniawan, 2000).	Use 12- or 14-point type size for body text.	All of the text presented on the Web site is set in 12- or 14 point.
Type Weight	Type should be intense enough to be read easily. The use of a medium or bold form of a typeface will meet this qualification (Hartley, 1994, 1999).	Use medium or boldface type.	All of the text is set in either medium or boldface.

(continued)

TABLE 3.2   Mediating Age-Related Declines in Vision: Design Considerations, Guideline Rationales, Guidelines, and Guideline Implementation on the NIHSeniorHealth.gov Web Site *(Continued)*

Design Consideration	Rationale for Guidelines from Research Findings	Guidelines*	Method of Implementation on the Web Site
Capital and Lower-case Letters	Bodies of text set entirely in capital letters are difficult to read (Hartley, 1994). Text set in upper- and lower-case letters forms words that are distinct and increases reading speed (Carter, Day, & Meggs, 1993; Conover, 1985).	Present body text in upper- and lower-case letters. Use all capital letters and italics in headlines only. Reserve underlining for links.	All text on the Web site is set in upper- and lower-case letters. Only links are underlined. No italics are used in the bodies of text.
Justification	There are three ways to justify type: left-justified, right justified, and center justified (Morrell & Echt, 1996). The preferred way to present text to older adults is to increase comprehension is to format it as left-justified (Hartley, 1994, 1999; Hooper & Hannifin, 1986).	Left-justified text is optimal for older adults.	All bodies of text are left-justified on the Web site.

Backgrounds	Contrast between background and text is important for older adults to be able to read the text presented. Patterned backgrounds may interfere with the readability of text. Therefore, the use of solid, light backgrounds with dark text will make the text easier to read by older adults (Echt, 2002).	Use dark type and graphics against a light background, or white lettering on a black or dark-colored background. Avoid patterned backgrounds.	All text is black on the Web site and presented on a white background. All headlines are black, dark purple, or dark blue. No wallpaper is used anywhere on the Web site.
Color	Decreased sensitivity to color, can make distinguishing between certain colors difficult for older adults, particularly for yellow and blue/green combinations (Echt, 2002). Blue and green can be used in decorative graphic elements as long as their use does not require discrimination for the understanding of the graphic. References to colors in text should be avoided because they may not be detectable to all readers, especially individuals who are color blind (Hartley & Harris, 2001).	Avoid yellow and blue and green in close proximity. These colors and juxtapositions are difficult for some older adults to discriminate. Ensure that text and graphics are understandable when viewed on a black and white monitor.	Shades of blue and and green are used in graphic elements on the Web site. However, the graphics are easily distinguishable with or without the color and the colors are not used in close proximity. All blue hyperlinks are presented on white backgrounds throughout the Web site. Colored text or references to colors are not used as directives.

* The guidelines included in this table are modified from those listed in National Institute on Aging, 2001b.

Working memory is the simultaneous storage and processing of verbal or spatial information (Baddeley, 1986). One of the clearest findings from basic cognitive aging research is that older adults perform less well than younger adults on a variety of verbal and spatial working memory tasks, especially as the tasks become more complex (see Craik & Salthouse, 2000). This trend has been documented in the performance of computer tasks with young and old adults (Charness, Kelley, Bosman, & Mottram, 2001; Charness, Schumann, & Boritz, 1992; Czaja & Sharit, 1998) and with young-old (ages 60–74) and old-old adults (ages 75 plus) (Echt, Morrell, & Park, 1998, Morrell, Park, Mayhorn, & Kelley, 2000). Web site navigation often requires maintaining an information search goal while examining potentially numerous Web pages. Therefore, if working memory demands of Web site navigation can be lessened, the site will be more accessible for the elderly.

The ability to comprehend text also decreases as one ages (see Craik & Salthouse, 2000). This is especially evident when inferences are required or links must be made between dissimilar parts of the text (Rogers, Rousseau, & Lamson, 1999). Text comprehension may be improved in older adults by the manner in which the text is written (see Park, 1992). In addition, Hartley (1994) has noted that illustrations and animated sequences can aid recall when combined with text. Therefore, the addition of text-relevant illustrations and/or animations in close proximity to sections of text they explain may increase the reader's ability to understand the text, as well as reduce working memory requirements.

Perceptual speed is the speed at which mental operations are performed (Salthouse, 1993). Many studies on cognition and aging have reliably demonstrated that older adults are slower than younger adults when performing most types of cognitive tasks (see Craik & Salthouse, 2000). This finding has also been consistently documented in the performance of computer tasks and implies that navigation of the Web site needs to be under the manual control of the user. That is, automatically scrolling text should not be used on a Web site unless it can be halted to be read at a slower pace (see Charness & Bosman, 1992; Czaja & Lee, 2001; and National Institute on Aging, 2001a, for a more detailed discussion on all of these topics).

The guidelines for increasing the comprehensibility and memory of the material presented on a Web site are based on these findings and are presented in Table 3.3. A brief description of how the guidelines were implemented on the NIHSeniorHealth.gov website is also conveyed in this table.

TABLE 3.3 Mediating Age-Related Declines in Cognition: Design Considerations, Guideline Rationales, Guidelines, and Guideline Implementation on the NIHSeniorHealth.gov Web Site

Design Considerations	Rationale for Guidelines from Research Findings	Guidelines*	Method of Implementation on the Web Site
Writing the Text			
Style	Writing information in a clear manner is beneficial for readers of all ages, but especially for older people (Morrell, 1997). Findings also have revealed that older people are less able to make inferences from recently presented material and are less able to ignore irrelevant information (Botwinick & Storandt, 1974; Hoyer, Rebok, & Sved, 1979).	Present information in a clear and familiar way to reduce the number of inferences that must be made.	All text presented on the Web site is written in a clear and precise manner to reduce working memory demands. This method of presentation has reduced the number of inferences that must be made when reading the text. Irrelevant information is excluded.
Phrasing	The manner in which a sentence is phrased is important in order to Increase the comprehensibility of the statement. Most researchers agree that phrasing a sentence in the active rather than the passive voice makes it more understandable (Park, 1992).	Use the active voice.	All text on the Web site is written in the active voice.

(*continued*)

TABLE 3.3 Mediating Age-Related Declines in Cognition: Design Considerations, Guideline Rationales, Guidelines, and Guideline Implementation on the NIHSeniorHealth.gov Web Site (*Continued*)

Design Considerations	Rationale for Guidelines from Research Findings	Guidelines*	Method of Implementation on the Web Site
Simplicity	Findings have shown that older adults understand and remember information better when it is presented in simple rather than complex language (Park, 1992).	Write the text in simple language. Provide an online glossary for technical terms.	All items are discussed completely in easy to understand terms before moving along to another topic on the Web site. Technical terms are avoided whenever possible or carefully explained within the text.
Other Issues to Consider			
Organization and Repetition	Precise labeling aids in organizing material to be read (Hartley, 1994). Furthermore, short documents have also been shown to make retrieval of facts easier and to assist users with finding the information that is sought (Morrow & Leirer, 1999). Repeating information has been shown to increase comprehension.	Organize the content in standard format. Break lengthy documents into short segments.	All sections on the Web site are well-labeled. Information is often repeated in different sections (e.g., in the text, animation, videos, quizzes, and Frequently Asked Questions sections). Short documents that appear on one screen are used whenever possible.
Illustrations and Photographs	It is important to use images only if they add to the meaning of the text (Morrell & Echt, 1996, 1997). If Web pages give instructions of any type, adults of all ages perform	Use text-relevant images only.	Only text-relevant illustrations and photographs are on the Web site. Screen captures are used with text to identify the videos in the icons used to open them.

	better with instructions composed of both text and text-relevant illustrations (Morrell & Park, 1993).		Illustrations and photographs are embedded within the segments of the text they further explain.
Animation and Video	Animation and video can be used effectively on Web sites designed for use by older adults if they further explain the material presented in the text (Morrell & Dailey 2001a, 2001b). The addition of these features is assumed to reduce working memory demands (Morrell & Echt, 1996, 1997). However, older computers may not be able to accommodate or may take a long time to download complex or long sequences of graphics and other hypermedia (Holt, 2000).	Use text-relevant video and animation only with text. Use short segments to reduce download time.	Both animation and video are used on the Web site to elaborate on the topics outlined in the text. The animations and videos are embedded within the text at appropriate points. Most of the videos and animations used on the site do not exceed 2 minutes in length, thus reducing download time.
Text Alternatives	If audio or animations are used, they must be accompanied by text alternatives for those users who are unable to view the images due to age-related declines in vision or other causes (Morrell, Mayhorn, & Bennett, 2002).	Provide text alternatives such as open captioning or access to a text alternative for all videos and animations.	All video and animations used on the Web site are accompanied by open captioning. A static text version of the audio is also available. These features have been rated to be the most popular components of the Web site by the older individuals who have participated in the assessments of the Web site.

* The guidelines included in this table are modified from those listed in National Institute on Aging, 2001b.

INCREASING THE EASE OF NAVIGATION

Researchers in human factors and aging have made numerous major contributions to the literature on how older adults use computers and Web sites. These include results from systematic research on the use of input devices and usability studies conducted on specific Web sites. In brief, results from systematic studies on input devices indicate that older adults are slower and less accurate than younger adults when using a mouse (Walker, Millians, & Worden, 1996). In addition, they have more problems in clicking and especially, double-clicking (Smith, Sharit, & Cazja, 1999). Walker and colleagues (1996) also observed that older adults had difficulty hitting very small targets (3 pixels). Their accuracy rate was 75% for the small targets compared to 90% for larger targets (6, 12, or 24 pixels).

In general, most results from usability studies with older adults on specific Web sites have indicated that they also have problems in using the mouse to scroll and are somewhat unable to understand the concept of scrolling, although they sometimes expressed a preference for a Web site with fewer pages that were longer (Ellis & Kurniawan, 2000; Mead et al., 1997). In addition, navigation was found to be particularly difficult for the older participants as they moved through deeper levels of a Web site (Dailey, 2000). Taken together, these findings suggest that navigation should be simplified as much as possible for older adults and the number of levels built into a site should be kept at a minimum. The guidelines developed from these findings are presented in Table 3.4 with an explanation of how the guidelines were applied to the construction of the NIHSeniorHealth.gov website.

ASSESSING THE ACCESSIBILITY OF THE WEB SITE FOR OLDER ADULTS

In order to determine how accessible the NIHSeniorHealth.gov Web site might be to older adults, usability testing was conducted twice: immediately after the prototype was constructed and after revisions were made as directed from the results of the initial usability testing. Results from the second usability testing were used to guide final revisions to the site and are seen as the most valuable for refining the final site that was opened to the public. For this reason, only the results from the second segment of this testing are briefly discussed in the next section of this chapter (for a detailed discussion of the results from both sets of usability testing, see Morrell & Dailey, 2001a, 2001b).

TABLE 3.4   Other Issues to Take into Account in Web Site Design for Older Adults: Design Considerations, Guideline Rationales, Guidelines, Guideline Implementation on the NIHSeniorHealth.gov Web Site

Design Consideration	Rationale for Guidelines from Research Findings	Guidelines*	Method of Implementation on the Web Site
Navigation	The larger the site, the more simple the navigation should be (Rogers & Fisk, 2000). The use of explicit step-by-step procedures whenever possible ensures that users will understand the navigational structure of the site (Morrell & Park, 1993). Carefully labeled links and navigational tools aid in navigation (Holt & Morell, 2002).	Design the navigation system of the website to be simple and straightforward. Explicit step by step navigation procedures should be used. Carefully and clearly label links.	The web site was designed to be easy to navigate. The navigation consists of a top down format from which additional information can be accessed from an initial overarching list of topics. Videos and quizzes are embedded in the text. Instructions on how to use these features are included in close proximity to where they appear. Navigation buttons are consistent throughout the site and are clearly labeled.

(continued)

TABLE 3.4   Other Issues to Take into Account in Web Site Design for Older Adults: Design Considerations, Guideline Rationales, Guidelines, Guideline Implementation on the NIHSeniorHealth.gov Web Site (*Continued*)

Design Consideration	Rationale for Guidelines from Research Findings	Guidelines*	Method of Implementation on the Web Site
The Mouse	It is important to minimize the number of clicks to access information to make the site more accessible to individuals who are experiencing problems in motor skills (Charness, Bosman, & Elliott, 1995; Walker, Millians, & Worden, 1996). Icons on some Web sites have been found to require double clicks for activation.	Use single mouse clicks for icons to access information.	All icons require one click for activation on the Web site.
Backward and Forward Navigation	Older readers have been shown to comprehend text better when they are given the chance to read sections of the text again (Harris, Rogers, & Qualls, 1998). Placing navigational buttons on each page of the Web site reduces reliance on browser features that may not be known to novices (Dailey, 2000).	Incorporate buttons such as "Previous Page" and "Next Page" to allow the user to review the material or move forward or backward within the site easily.	"Previous Page" and "Next Page" buttons are on every page of the Web site where bodies of text are presented.
Consistent Layouts	According to Hartley and Harris (2001) the layout of text may be	Use a standard page design and	All page layouts and location of navigational icons are identical

	just as important as the typeface used. Each page on a Web site should use the same design, the same set of icons, and the same means of navigation (Holt & Morrell, 2002).	the same symbols and icons throughout the Web site. Use the same set of buttons in the same place on each page. Label each page of the site with the name of the Web site.	on all pages of the web site. All information text blocks are presented in the center of each page. All navigational features are positioned either at the top (Help, Index, and Home buttons), at the same place on far left (buttons to access information on overarching topics within a section of the Web site), or at the bottom of the screen ("Next Page" and "Previous Page" icons).
Style and Size of Icons and Buttons	Buttons and icons should be large and conspicuous. This ensures that they will be easy targets for mouse functions and also that the label on the button or icon is easy to identify (Walker et al., 1996). Furthermore, the addition of clip art or other graphics may lead to a better understanding of a button label (King, Boling, Annelli, Bray, Cardenas, & Frick, 1996). Visual feedback is useful to determine if a button or icon has been activated (e.g., buttons or links change color when clicked on; Jones, 1995).	Incorporate text with the icon if possible, and use large buttons that do not require precise mouse movements for activation. Include visual feedback to indicate that a button or link has been activated.	All buttons on the Web site are large enough for direct and easy mouse manipulation. All links set in text are at least 12-point. Screen captures are used with text for all of the videos that are embedded within the text. All buttons and links change color (i.e., buttons change from purple to gold and links change from blue to black) when they are activated.

(continued)

TABLE 3.4 Other Issues to Take into Account in Web Site Design for Older Adults: Design Considerations, Guideline Rationales, Guidelines, Guideline Implementation on the NIHSeniorHealth.gov Web Site (*Continued*)

Design Consideration	Rationale for Guidelines from Research Findings	Guidelines*	Method of Implementation on the Web Site
Pull Down Menus	Pull down menus require precise movements that may be problematic for older users because of age-related declines in motor skills or other conditions such as arthritis (Rogers & Fisk, 2000).	Use pull down menus sparingly.	No pull down menus are used on the Web site.
Site Maps	Site maps are very effective in helping older users to understand where they are on a Web site in relation to other pages and in giving a direct indication of how to navigate to other pages on the site (Holt, 2000; Westerman, Davies, Glendon, Stammers, & Matthews, 1995).	Provide a site map to show how the site is organized.	A highly detailed site map is included on the Web site. It is easily accessed from any Web page.

| Scrolling | Mead, Spaulding, Sit, Meyer, and Walker (1997) reported that while younger adults scroll down pages in order to look for information, older adults are more likely to read the information on each page. This findings suggests that short Web pages, where there is less scrolling required, would facilitate web navigation for older adults. (Stronge, Walker, & Rogers, in press). Morrell and Dailey (2001b) have also consistently demonstrated that scrolling is a particular problem for older adults. Automatically scrolling text does not allow the user to read the text at his or her own pace and may present problems in comprehension for older adults (Holt & Morrell, 2002). | Avoid automatically scrolling text. If manual scrolling is required, incorporate instructions at the end of a screen of text or scrolling icons on each page to indicate that the text is continued below the screen. | Whenever possible all text is broken into short passages that can fit onto one page or screen on the Web site to avoid scrolling. When this is not possible, directions are provided on the page to scroll down to read the remaining text. No automatically scrolling text is used on the Web site. |

* The guidelines included in this table are modified from those listed in National Institute on Aging, 2001b.

Participants

The sample for the usability testing was composed of healthy, diverse older adults. Three males and four females participated individually in the usability testing in order to detect the nature of the problems that users would encounter on the Web site. (It is recognized that this sample is small compared to usual recommendations. Therefore, see Lewis (1994) for a discussion of sample sizes to be employed in usability testing.) They ranged in age from 62 to 86 years old ($M = 72$). One participant had some college education and one person had a college degree. The remaining five individuals had professional education above high school. All participants rated their health as fair to excellent in relation to others their own age. Two of the participants were African Americans and five were Caucasians. English was the first language for all but one.

The participants were asked to rate their computer skills on a Likert Scale from 1–5 (i.e., 1 = Not Skilled, 5 = Highly Skilled). One participant rated at level 1; one at level 2; four at level 3; and one at level 4. These scores indicated a range of skills that could be expected from the projected older users of the site. The Backward Digit Span Test from the Wechsler Adult Intelligence Scale (Wechsler, 1999) was administered as a measure of verbal working memory capacity. All participants reached at least the second level on the test indicating that they were representative of the older population at large.

Testing Procedures

The testing procedure consisted of the following steps:

1. The project was introduced to the individual participants.
2. Participants were given 20–25 minutes of free play on the website to allow them to become familiar with the features.
3. Usability testing on the Alzheimer's disease topic on the Web site was conducted. Participants were required to perform tasks on each of the following components of the Web site: General Information on the Health Topic, Quizzes, Video Clips, Frequently Asked Questions (FAQs), and the Resources Section.
4. A Satisfaction Questionnaire was administered that measured the participants' opinions on different attributes of the Web site. Quantifiable data could be gathered from this instrument.
5. A short questionnaire was completed to gather general demographic, perceived health, and prior computer experience data on the participants.
6. The measure of verbal working memory was administered.

Results from the Satisfaction Questionnaire

The Satisfaction Questionnaire used a five-point Likert scale that ranged from "Strongly Disagree" (1) to "Strongly Agree" (5) on 30 items. A subset of the items taken from the questionnaire related directly to the readability of the text and how well the information was presented on the Web site based on the Elder Accessible Guidelines. If an average score of 4 or higher (80% plus) is considered a passing score, then the findings from this subset of items suggest that most users would be satisfied with the Web site design and that the information presented would be accessible to most older adults as shown in Table 3.5. The average score across all of these items was 4.68.

Results from the Usability Testing

Although the responses to the Satisfaction Questionnaire indicated that the information presented on the Web site was readable and could be easily understood, the navigation of the site was found to be troublesome. In general, when the participants were asked to perform tasks on the upper level of the site (e.g., enter the Web site or open a major health topic section) there were few failures in performance. However, when the participants had to navigate into the lower levels of the Web site, failures became more common on most of the tasks, as indicated in Table 3.6 (Midlevel tasks required participants to transverse one or more additional pages in order to find supplementary information on an overarching topic. Lower-level tasks required the participants to transverse additional pages and also to perform specific manipulations on these pages, such as "click here to find answer" to a quiz question.) A task was considered failed if the participant required assistance from the experimenter to complete a task or did not entirely complete a task.

Clearly, as the tasks became more complex, performance declined, as has been shown in other findings from studies that have focused on determining the optimal training method for teaching older adults how to use information technology (see Czaja & Lee, 2001, for an overview). Interestingly, some of the most common mistakes made involved the application of basic Web skills, such as how to close a window or how to skip pages within a particular section of the site to reach a specific destination. In addition, most of the participants were not able to grasp the concept of scrolling and in many instances scrolling was difficult to perform, possibly due to lack of education on how scrolling is done or declines in motor skills. These observations suggest the need for basic Web skill training for this population before they begin to surf the Web on their own, and for alternative

TABLE 3.5   Average Satisfaction Ratings for Items Related to the Readability of the Text and How Well the Information Was Presented on the Web Site*

Item	Average Rating
I liked the Web site.	4.43
The text was large enough for me to read.	4.86
The pictures and photographs added to my understanding of the materials on the Web site.	4.86
I liked the colors used in the design of the Web site.	4.29
The video clips add variety and interest to the Web site.	4.71
The buttons were easy for me to click on.	4.57
The video clips helped to clarify the information presented.	4.71
The information is well presented on the Web site.	4.43
The repetition of some of the information throughout the Web site helps me to remember it better.	4.57
The information is presented in a way that is easy for me to follow.	4.86
The way the information is organized on the Web site helps me to understand it better.	4.57
It is easy to find the information I am looking for on this Web site.	4.86
Being able to go through the Web site at my own pace will help me understand and remember the information better.	5.00
I like the simplicity of the Web site.	4.71
I find the style of writing to be clear and straightforward.	4.71

* For a listing and summary of the responses to all of the items included in the Satisfaction Questionnaire, see Morrell and Dailey, 2001a, 2001b.

methods for scrolling to be incorporated on web pages containing long documents such as distinct scrolling icons (i.e., Return to Top of Page).

The overall implications of these findings are that the Elder Accessible Guidelines as they stand are somewhat vague on exactly how to make a Web site easy to navigate for older adults. The primary reason for this is that little systematic research has been conducted on how older adults actually navigate Web sites or on how to best design the navigation system of a Web site to make it truly accessible for older adults. As noted in an earlier portion of this chapter, research has been conducted on how older adults conduct searches (see Table 3.4). Although

TABLE 3.6   Percentage of Successful Completions of Tasks on the Web Site*

Item	Percentage of Participants Passing Task
Upper-Level Tasks	
Go into the website.	100.00
Open the section on Alzheimer's disease.	100.00
Open the Frequently Asked Questions section on Alzheimer's disease.	87.71
Open the Further Resources Section on Alzheimer's disease.	100.00
Midlevel Tasks	
Read through this section (as indicated by the experimenter) until you find a video.	87.71
Where would you go to find information about the risk factors of Alzheimer's disease?	100.00
Read until you find the interactive quiz questions in this section (as Indicated by the experimenter).	87.71
Where would you go to find the definition of Alzheimer's disease?	85.71
Lower-Level Tasks	
What is the answer to the sixth question in the Frequently Asked Questions section on the topic of Alzheimer's disease?	42.85
What would you do to watch this video?	42.86
Answer the first question (in the quiz as indicated by the experimenter).	100.00
How would you check your answer (to the quiz question as indicated by the experimenter?	85.71
Now answer the third question and check your answer (in the quiz as indicated by the experimenter)	42.86

* For a detailed discussion of these findings, see Dailey, 2000; Morrell and Dailey, 2001a, 2001b.

this work is important, little if any work has been done on how best to design the navigation system of a Web site that relies heavily on buttons, icons, or links. Thus, the Guidelines will remain incomplete until such research is conducted.

With regard to web design, the usability testing highlights the importance of using a combination of subjective and objective measures to improve Web site navigability. Aesthetic factors are likely to influence an individual's decision to use a Web site, and satisfaction ratings can be used to address questions of this nature. However, satisfaction ratings may mask problems people actually encounter when using a Web site. This was evident in the disparity between satisfaction ratings and the percentage of successful navigations. Satisfaction ratings should not serve as a proxy for actually assessing usability. The best way to determine what problems older users have is for them to try to navigate a Web site.

SUMMARY

In this chapter, it was our intention to provide an example of how to construct a Web site that is accessible for older adults. We have briefly outlined the process of how the NIHSeniorHealth.gov Project was developed. We focused primarily on the development of the accessibility guidelines for designing Web sites for older adults that we constructed. We also described how we applied these guidelines in the construction of the NIHSeniorHealth.gov Web site. Assessment of the Web site indicated that its navigation was troublesome for the older adults who participated in the usability testing. Overall, this discussion and the NIHSeniorHealth.gov Project was intended to serve as a model for the construction of Web sites that are more accessible to older adults. In general, implementing the guidelines as outlined and following the recommendation for more research on the navigational issues that face older Web users will result in making Web sites more accessible to everyone.

ACKNOWLEDGMENTS

The NIHSeniorHealth.gov Project was jointly developed and funded by The National Institute on Aging and The National Library of Medicine. Support for the development of this chapter was provided by the Office of Communications and Public Liaison of the National Institute on Aging to Roger W. Morrell, PhD as a consultant on aging and technology to the NIHSeniorHealth.gov Project. The authors would like to thank Richard J. Hodes, MD, Director of The National Institute on Aging; Jane Shure, Director, and Claudia Feldman, Deputy Director, of the Office of Communications and Public Liaison of the National Institute on Aging; Donald A. B. Lindberg, MD, Director, and Kathleen Gardner Cravedi, Joyce E. B. Backus, J. J. Intoronat, and Susan Anderson of the National

Library of Medicine; and Pat Lynch and members of the staff of the Alzheimer's Disease Education and Referral (ADEAR) Center for their contributions to and continuing support of this project.

Two publications are available on constructing Web sites to meet the needs of older adults as a result of the NIHSeniorHealth.gov project. They are: *Making Your Web Site Senior Friendly: A Checklist,* and a more in-depth document that includes referenced scientific research on how aging affects the use of information technology and a more detailed discussion of the Elder Accessibility Guidelines, *Older Adults and Information Technology: A Compendium of Scientific Research and Web Site Accessibility Guidelines.* A printed version of the *Checklist* and a mini-CD-ROM version of the *Compendium* may be obtained free of charge from the National Institute on Aging by phoning 1-800-222-2225. The *Checklist* may be downloaded also in pdf format from the following Web site: http://www.nlm.nih.gov/pubs/checklist.pdf.

REFERENCES

Adler, R. (2002, June 26). *The age wave meets the technology wave: Broadband and older Americans.* National Press Club Briefing, Washington, DC.

Administration on Aging. (1999). *Profile of older Americans.* Available online: www.aoa.gov/aoa/stats/profile/default.htm.

Architectural and Transportation Barriers Compliance Board. (2000). Electronic and Information Technology Accessibility Standards. Available online: http://www.access-board.gov/sec508/508standards.htm.

Baddeley, A. D. (1986).*Working memory.* Oxdord, UK: Clarendon.

Borges, J. A., Morales, I., & Rodriguez, N. J. (1998). Page design guidelines developed through usability testing. In C. Forsythe, E. Grose, & J. Ratner, (Eds.), *Human factors and web development* (pp. 137–152). Mahwah, NJ: Erlbaum.

Botwinick, H. R., & Storandt, M. (1974).*Memory, relation function and age.* Springfield, IL: Charles C Thomas.

Carter, R., Day, B., & Meggs, P. (1993). *Typographic design: Form and communication.* New York: Van Nostrand.

Charness, N. (2001). Aging and communication: Human factors issues. In N. Charness, D. C. Park, & B. A. Sabel (Eds.), *Communication, technology, and aging: Opportunitites and challenges for the future* (pp. 1–29). New York: Springer.

Charness, N., & Bosman, E. A. (1992). Human factors and aging. In F. I. M. Craik & T. A. Salthouse (Eds.), *Handbook of aging and cognition* (pp. 495–545). Hillsdale, NJ: Erlbaum.

Charness, N., Bosman, E. A., & Elliott, R. G. (1995, August). *Senior-friendly input devices: Is the pen mightier than the mouse?* Paper presented at the 104th

Annual Convention of the American Psychological Association Meeting, New York.

Charness, N., Kelley, C. L., Bosman, E. A., & Mottram, M. (2001). Word processing training and retraining: Effects of adult age, experience, and interface. *Psychology and Aging, 16,* 110–127.

Charness, N., Schumann, C., & Boritz, G. (1992). Training older adults in word processing: Effects of age, training technique, and computer anxiety. *International Journal of Technology and Aging, 5,* 79–105.

Conover, T. E. (1985). *Graphic communications today.* New York: West Publishing.

Craik, F. I. M., & Salthouse, T. A. (2000). *Handbook of aging and cognition.* Mahwah, NJ: Erlbaum.

Czaja, S. J., & Lee, C. C. (2001). The Internet and older adults: Design challenges and opportunities. In N. Charness, D. C. Park, & B. A. Sabel (Eds.), *Communication, technology, and aging: Opportunities and challenges for the future* (pp. 60–78). New York: Springer.

Czaja, S. J., & Sharit, J. (1998). Ability-performance relationships as a function of age and task experience for a data entry task. *Journal of Experimental Psychology: Applied, 4,* 332–351.

Dailey, S. R. (2000, November). *The interactive online AgePage learning project: Results from usability testing.* Paper presented at the 43rd Annual Meeting of the Gerontological Society of America. November, Washington, DC.

Echt, K. V. (2002). Designing web-based health information for older adults: Visual considerations and design directives. In R. W. Morrell (Ed.), *Older adults, health information, and the World Wide Web* (pp. 61–87). Mahwah, NJ: Erlbaum.

Echt, K. W., Morrell, R. W., & Park, D. C. (1998). The effects of age and training formats on basic computer skill acquisition in older adults. *Educational Gerontology, 24,* 3–25.

Ellis, R. D., & Kurniawan, S. H. (2000). Increasing the usability of on-line information for older users: A case study in participatory design. *International Journal of Human–Computer Interaction, 12,* 263–276.

Fisk, A. D., & Rogers, W. A. (1997). *Handbook of human factors and the older adult.* San Diego: Academic Press.

Gould, J. D., Alfaro, L., Finn, R., Haupt, B., & Minuto, A. (1987). Reading from CRT displays can be as fast as reading from paper. *Human Factors, 29,* 497–517.

Grabinger, R. S., & Osman-Jouchoux, R. (1996). Designing screens for learning. In H. van Osterndorp & S. De Mul (Eds.), *Cognitive aspects of electronic text processing: Advances in discourse processes, vol. 58* (pp. 181–212). Norwood, NJ: Ablex.

Haegerstrom-Portnoy, G., Schneck, M., Brabyn, J. A., & Lott, L. A. (1999). Longitudinal changes in spatial vision among the aged. *Investigative Ophthalmology & Visual Science, 40,* S441.

Harris, J. L., Rogers, W. A., & Qualls, C. D. (1998). Written language comprehension in younger and older adults. *Journal of Speech, Language, and Hearing Research, 41,* 603–617.

Hartley, J. (1994). *Designing instructional text.* East Brunswick, NJ: Nichols.

Hartley, J. (1997). Applying psychology to text design: A case history. *International forum on Information and Documentation, 22,* 3–10.

Hartley, J. (1999). What does it say? Text design, medical information, and older readers. In D. C. Park, R. W. Morrell, & K. Shifren (Eds.), *Processing of medical information in aging patients* (pp. 233–248). Mahwah, NJ: Erlbaum.

Hartley, J., & Harris, J. L. (2001). Reading .the typography of text. In J. L. Harris, A. G. Kamhi, & K. E. Pollack (Eds.), *Literacy in African American communities* (pp. 109–125). Mahwah, NJ: Erlbaum.

Holt, B. J. (2000). Creating senior-friendly web sites. *Center for Medicare Education Newsletter, 1,* 1–8.

Holt, B. J., & Morrell, R. W. (2002). Guidelines for web site design for older adults: The ultimate influence of cognitive factors. In R. W. Morrell (Ed.), *Older adults, health information, and the World Wide Web* (pp. 109–132). Mahwah, NJ: Erlbaum.

Hooper, S., & Hannifin, M. J. (1986). Variables affecting the legibility of computer generated text. *Journal of Instructional Development, 9,* 22–28.

Hoyer, W. J., Rebok, G. W., & Sved, D. M. (1979). Effects of varying irrelevant information on adult age differences in problem solving. *Journal of Gerontology, 34,* 553–560.

Jones, M. G. (1995, October). Visuals for information access: A new philosophy for screen and interface design. In A. C. Eric (Ed.), *Imagery and Visual Literacy: Selected readings from the Annual Conference of the International Visual Literacy Association* (pp. 264–272). Tempe, AZ.

Kanerva, A., Keeker, K., Risden, K., Shuh, E., & Czerwinski, F. (1998). Web usability research at Microsoft Corporation. In C. Forsythe, E. Grose, & J. Ratner (Eds.), *Human factors and web development* (pp. 189–198). Mahwah, NJ: Erlbaum.

King, K. S., Boling, E., Annelli, J., Bray, M., Cardenas, D., & Frick, T. (1996). Relative perceptibility of hypercard button using pictorial symbols and text labels. *Journal of Educational Computing Research, 14,* 67–81.

Lewis, J. R. (1994). Sample sizes for usability studies: Additional considerations. *Human Factors, 36,* 368–378.

Mead, S. E., Spaulding, V. A., Sit, R. A., Meyer, B., & Walker, N. (1997). Effects of age and training on World Wide Web navigation strategies. *Proceedings of the Human Factors and Ergonomics Society,* 152–156.

Meyer, B. J. F., & Poon, L. W. (1997). Age differences in efficiency of reading comprehension from printed versus computer-displayed text. *Educational Gerontology, 23,* 789–807.

Morrell, R. W. (1997). The application of cognitive theory in aging research. *Cognitive Technology, 2,* 44–47.

Morrell, R. W. (2002). *Older adults, health information, and the World Wide Web.* Mahwah, NJ: Erlbaum.

Morrell, R. W., & Dailey, S. R. (2001a, February). *The NIHSeniorHealth.gov online learning project.* Paper presented at the Second Biennial Conference: Older Adults, Health Information, and the World Wide Web. Bethesda, MD.

Morrell, R. W., & Dailey, S. R. (2001b, November). *The process of applying scientific research findings in the construction of a web site for older adults.* Pre-conference workshop presented at the Annual Meeting of the Gerontological Association of America, Chicago, IL.

Morrell, R. W., & Echt, K. V. (1996). Instructional design for older computer users: The influence of cognitive factors. In W. A. Rogers, A. D. Fisk, & N. Walker (Eds.), *Aging and skilled performance: Advances in theory and applications* (pp. 241–265). Hillsdale, NJ: Erlbaum.

Morrell, R. W., & Echt, K. V. (1997). Designing instructions for computer use by older adults. In A. D. Fisk & W. A. Rogers (Eds.), *Handbook of human factors and the older adult* (pp. 335–361). New York: Academic Press.

Morrell, R. W., Mayhorn, C. B., & Bennett, J. (2000). A survey of World Wide Web use in middle-aged and older adults. *Human Factors, 42,* 175–182.

Morrell, R. W., Mayhorn, C. B., & Bennett, J. (2002). Older adults online in the Internet century. In R. W. Morrell (Ed.), *Older adults, health information, and the World Wide Web* (pp. 43–60). Mahwah, NJ: Erlbaum

Morrell, R. W., & Park, D. C. (1993). The effects of age, illustrations, and task variables on the performance of procedural assembly tasks. *Psychology and Aging, 8,* 389–399.

Morrell, R. W., Park, D. C., Mayhorn, C. B., & Kelley, C. L. (2000). The effects of age and instructional format on teaching older adults how to use ELDERCOMM: An electronic bulletin board system. *Educational Gerontology, 26,* 221–236.

Morrow, D. G., & Leirer, V. O. (1999). Designing medication instructions for older adults. In D. C. Park, R. W. Morrell, & K. Shifren Eds.), *Processing of medical information in aging patients* (pp. 249–266). Mahwah, NJ: Erlbaum.

National Institute on Aging. (2001a). *Older adults and information technology: A compendium of scientific research and Web site accessibility guidelines.* Washington, DC: Author.

National Institute on Aging. (2001b). *Making your Web site senior friendly: A checklist.* Washington, DC: Author.

Park, D. C. (1992). Applied cognitive aging research. In F. I. M. Craik & T. A. Salthouse (Eds.), *Handbook of cognition and aging* (pp. 449–493). Mahwah, NJ: Erlbaum.

Pew Internet & American Life Project: Online Life Report. (2000). *The online health care revolution: How the Web helps Americans take better care of themselves.* Available online: http://www.pewinternet.org/.

Rogers, W. A., & Fisk, A. D. (2000). Human factors, applied cognition, and aging. In F. I. M. Craik & T. A. Salthouse (Eds.), *The handbook of aging and cognition* (2nd ed., pp. 559–591). Mahwah, NJ: Erlbaum.

Rogers, W. A., Rousseau, G. K., & Lamson, N. (1999). Maximizing the effectiveness of the warning process: Understanding the variables that interact with age. In D. C. Park, R. W. Morrell, & K. Shifren (Eds.), *Processing of medical information in aging patients* (pp. 267–290). Mahwah, NJ: Erlbaum.

Salthouse, T. A. (1993). Speed mediation of adult age differences in cognition. *Developmental Psychology, 29,* 722–738.

Smith, M. W., Sharit, J., & Czaja, S. J. (1999). Aging, motor control, and the performance of computer mouse tasks. *Human Factors, 41,* 389–396.

Stronge, A. J., Walker, N., & Rogers, W. A. (in press). Searching the World Wide Web: Can older adults get what they need? In W. A. Rogers & A. D. Fisk (Eds.), *Human factors interventions for the health care for older adults.* Mahwah, NJ: Erlbaum.

U.S. Department of Commerce. (1999). *Americans in the information age— Falling through the net.* Available at: www.ntia.doc.gov/ntiahome/digitaldivide/.

Walker, N., Millians, J., & Worden, A. (1996). Mouse accelerations and performance of older computer users. *Proceedings of the Human Factors and Ergonomics Society 40th Annual Meeting, 1,* 151–154, Philadelphia.

Wechsler, D. (1999). *Wechsler Adult Intelligence Scale* (3rd ed.). San Antonio, TX: The Psychological Corporation.

Westerman, S. J., Davies, D. R., Glendon, A. I., Stammers, R. B., & Matthews, G. (1995). Age and cognitive ability as predictors of computerized information retrieval. *Behaviour and Information Technology, 14,* 313–326.

Wichansky, A. M., & Hackman, G. (1998). Web user interface development at Oracle Corporation. In C. Forsythe, E. Grose, & J. Ratner (Eds.), *Human factors and web development* (pp. 175–188). Mahwah, NJ: Erlbaum.

Wiebe, E. N., & Howe, J. E. (1998). Graphics design on the web. In C. Forsythe, E. Grose, & J. Ratner (Eds.), *Human factors and web development* (pp. 225–239). Mahway, NJ: Erlbaum.

Commentary

Social Aspects of Gerontechnology

John C. Thomas

THE PROBLEM OF CUMULATING
KNOWLEDGE IN HCI

Human-Computer Interaction (HCI) is an interdisciplinary field whose aim is to ensure that systems that include computers and humans are designed to be effective and efficient and to be good for the people who use them. People in HCI variously have backgrounds in computer science, engineering, psychology, education, documentation, or design. In order to design and build such systems, it is necessary to bring to bear an understanding of how people perceive, learn, think, and behave, as well as how computing technology operates. In most cases, it is also necessary to know how groups and organizations function.

What Is the Value of HCI When Properly Applied?

The value of HCI has been established in many separate studies. Perhaps the most extensive single source is Landauer, *The Trouble with Computers* (1995). The "trouble," of course, is not with computers, but with designing and building systems while only paying attention to the properties of the technological components. Few would be foolish enough to design a human-computer system without any detailed understanding of the computer technology, relying instead on an informal and implicit mental model of computers. Unfortunately, all too often people have designed human-computer systems without any detailed understanding of how people work, relying instead on an implicit mental model of people.

This is to some extent an understandable error. After all, as people, we do interact with other people all the time and it seems reasonable that we would learn how they operate. Unfortunately, this is not true. People interacted with and had to survive in the physical world for many millennia, but until a systematic approach to understanding the physical world was undertaken, people had many fundamental misconceptions. Even today, people who grow up in our culture without formal training in physics and astronomy have extraordinarily inaccurate intuitive models even of some of the most basic properties of the world around them (see, e.g., McCloskey, 1983). Many people believe, for example, that it is warmer in summer because the earth is closer to the sun; that if the earth stopped spinning on its axis, we would fall off because gravity would cease; that if you whirl a stone in a sling around your head in a circular path and then release it, it will fly in a curved path.

People's intuitive models of human behavior are similarly flawed. One case in point is the "fundamental attribution error." Basically, both laboratory and field studies show that behavior is determined primarily by circumstances; however, people believe that their own behavior is primarily determined by internal decision making. Another common adage is that "you can't teach an old dog new tricks" when the picture is actually more complex. Cross-sectional age effects over the range from 20 to 70 years among healthy men were found to be about a quarter the size of individual difference (Fozard, Thomas, & Waugh, 1976; Thomas, Fozard, & Waugh, 1977). Furthermore, the impact of aging on learning depends to a great extent on circumstances and the nature of the learning task. In some cases, older individuals can use knowledge they have gained about "learning how to learn" in order to accelerate learning; in other cases, previous knowledge is mostly a source of proactive interference. Meta-analyses of age and episodic memory suggest a moderate correlation of $r = -.33$ (Verhaeghen & Salthouse, 1997). Another way to assess age-related effects is in terms of SD units. Verhaeghen, Marcoen, and Goossens (1993) found that the old are worse than the young by between .7 and 1.0 SD units for episodic memory tasks. The practical impact of such differences can vary widely depending on circumstances. Differences in learning rate can be exaggerated, for example, by being "tangled" with perceptual problems (print too small to read) or adverse social situations (older adults being put in a competitive situation with people who are not only younger but also have more computer experience). On the other hand, following appropriate guidelines for older adult learning and ensuring that the system itself has been developed with good human factors can help minimize the impact.

The point of the two examples above is that merely "experiencing" the world does not lead to correct models of physics or psychology. What Landauer (1995) documents is that when systems require human-computer interaction, new information technology systems typically result in about a 1%/annum productivity increase. In a score of cases, however, new systems were designed via accepted HCI methodology. In these cases, the average productivity gain was 33%/annum.

What are the HCI Methodologies?

Various methodologies have been developed for designing and building good human-computer interaction systems. Initial designs can be constructed with a scientific understanding of how people operate (from the social sciences) in mind. This knowledge exists in varying degrees of specificity. In some cases, there are known facts. For example, we know the font size required to have a certain percentage of the population be able to read at a certain distance. Keyboards that give auditory and tactile feedback lead to fewer errors and faster typing. People can generally recognize faster than they can generate. On the whole, performance increases with practice according to a fairly predictable power law. This means that if we observe improvements in performance over a short period of time, we can predict asymptotic performance. In a few cases, with very well learned routine behaviors such as typing, reading, and talking, we can make fairly detailed mathematical models that can be used to "test" out proposed, complex, real-world human-computer systems (Gray, John, Stuart, Lawrence, & Atwood, 1990).

Despite a large body of knowledge however, complex new systems exhibit emergent properties. To build good systems, it is generally necessary to prototype and to observe users attempting to use the prototype doing real tasks in situations that mirror as closely as possible real contexts. Thomas and Kellogg (1989) document some of the difficulties in extrapolating from laboratory studies of behavior to the field and give strategies for maximizing valid transfer.

Although empirical studies have been shown to have a high Return On Investment (ROI) relative to most of the other expenditures in development projects (Bias & Mayhew, 1994), it often turns out to be the case that people are reluctant to build and adequately test prototypes. A number of faster methodologies can help. For example, interface inconsistency can be minimized by having developers adhere to a style guide that specifies how certain functions will look and feel. Intelligent architectural design can be employed to make modifications easier, for example, putting error messages in a table and ensuring that each error source leads to a separate error message, at least initially.

Prototypes or designs can be evaluated by heuristic evaluation. Here, a small set (5–10) of HCI experts independently evaluates the design or prototype and points out potential difficulties. This typically results in finding about 50 to 85% of the problems (with 5 evaluators) up to 65 to 85% (with 10 evaluators) (Nielsen & Landauer, 1993). There is some evidence that these numbers might be improved by encouraging evaluators to take sequentially different viewpoints (Desurvire & Thomas, 1993).

Despite various effective HCI methods, numerous applications have not used these (or other) methods and consequently have severe problems in effectiveness and efficiency. These problems continue to plague new hardware and software products. A recently developed web-based system for ordering equipment asks the user to go through ten modules just to learn to navigate! Since this system will be used only a few times a year, requiring so much learning will entail substantial relearning each time the system is used. Users will simply read manuals, ask each other, use help systems, and call support until the problem is solved. The lost productivity to companies is probably enormous but generally unmeasured. The effectiveness of HCI has been demonstrated; yet, the required processes are often not followed. This situation is not unique, however, to Human-Computer Interaction. Fred Brooks (1975) demonstrated (and common sense would verify) that the two most common management responses to a slipped software schedule (adding more people and requiring more frequent progress reports) are both counterproductive. Yet, these practices also continue.

How Broadly Effective Is the Current HCI Methodology?

When applied, the current HCI paradigm seems to work fairly well in individual applications. However, what is not clear is how often appropriate methodologies are applied. An examination of the Web makes it clear that there are many sites that are confusing to navigate. Moreover, it is even clearer that while individual application programs may or may not have good HCI, it is rare that an overall integrated system has good HCI.

AN ALTERNATIVE PROPOSAL: HCI-FRIENDLY MIDDLEWARE

What Are the Factors of Good HCI?

A system with good Human-Computer Interaction is designed, built, implemented, delivered, and supported in such a way that it is based on both a solid understanding of computer science (understanding what computer technologies can do and how best to accomplish those aims) and social science (understanding how people operate individually and in various kinds of groups). In order to reach this goal, system designers should ideally understand the particularities of the computer system that they are building upon. In the early days of computing, it was extremely important for systems analysts and programmers to understand the specifics of the hardware for which they were programming (How many cycles does it take to do a Shift versus an Add?). Later, this became less important, but programmers still needed to focus on the specific operating system that they were using. Now, focus has shifted to building platform independent functionality, for example, in Web Services using common standards such as SOAP (Simple Object Access Protocol), XML (Extensible Markup Language), WSDL (Web Services Description Language), and UDDI (Universal Description, Delivery, and Integration).

Just as the hardware of a PDP-8 and an IBM 360 (although both based on a Von Neumann architecture) are quite different, so too, in order to build a system that is optimal for people, we need to understand who the people are to use the system. People vary in physical capabilities, educational backgrounds, native and secondary languages, motivations, social context, environmental context, abilities to learn and use arbitrary mappings, spatial abilities, visual discriminations, and so on. If cost were no object, every system would be optimized both for the machinery and operating systems that were involved and for the specific human beings who were to use the system. However, cost does matter. As a practical consideration, it is necessary to generalize (intelligently, it is hoped) in the human dimension no less than in the computer science dimension to provide functionality that is widely useful under common sets of circumstances.

HCI—Friendly Middleware

Significant improvements in usability can result from instantiating significant, reusable software components into a middleware layer from which developers can select needed functionality. For example, a social network analysis provides useful input for many office applications. Knowing who communicates with whom can be useful in disambiguating e-mail recipients, in collaborative filtering for Web browsing, in putting together teams, in skills mining, in focusing sales effort on opinion leaders, and so on. But developers of any one application are unlikely to have the time or the knowledge to include a social network analysis in that specific application. Similarly, many applications can provide data to enable a social network analysis. Again, developers of any one application are highly unlikely to provide the monitoring functionality to collect such data. Putting such functionality into a middleware layer will enable developers to invoke, rather than design, build, and debug such functionality. An added benefit for the end user is that any explicit information need only be input once, not once per application.

There are many other potentially useful examples of functionality that could be added to a middleware layer. A partial list might include representing the formal organization, conversational agents, embedded style guides, creativity tools, monitoring and feedback capabilities, accessibility functions, state tables for describing interactions, history traces, and knowledge representations for physical proximity.

Need for a Pattern Language

For this vision of useful and usable application software to be realized, however, the development team must become aware of the existence of such middleware functionality and understand how to use it. We believe we can greatly expand the pool of capable developers via Pattern Languages. Patterns essentially encapsulate, in succinct diagrams, natural language and/or pseudo-code, the essence of a recurring problem, its analysis, and its solution. A Pattern Language is an interrelated set of such Patterns with cross-references that covers a coherent domain.

TOWARD A SOCIOTECHNICAL PATTERN LANGUAGE

Christopher Alexander and Architectural Patterns

Pattern Languages were first introduced by Christopher Alexander (Alexander et. al., 1977). His patterns are named descriptions of recurring architectural problems, analyses of those problems, and suggested solutions. His proposed Pattern Language includes patterns at many different levels, from those describing how to organize large areas of land, to city planning, to neighborhood planning, to patterns relevant to specific dwellings, to low-level details, for example, "Things from your Life" (as a way to decorate your room). Many of his patterns are themselves concerned with the social impact of the way space is organized. For example, in "Pools of Light" he suggests that people want to congregate in pools of light and that uniform lighting is unnatural and disconcerting, giving people no hints about where to interact. Instantiating such a pattern in a real design however, must take into account the users, tasks, and contexts. While the pooling-congregation effect probably occurs for well-intentioned people across the entire age range, the *level* of light needed in and between pools will depend heavily on age, task, and context (see Charness & Dijkstra, 1999).

"Beer Hall" essentially points out that the design of traditional European pubs encourages social interaction and provides space for "legitimate peripheral participation" (cf. Lave & Wenger, 1991). It is beyond the scope of this chapter to review architectural patterns relevant to social interaction, but designers of spaces for older adults (or people of any age) would be well-advised to delve into Alexander's work.

Other Pattern Language Examples

Inspired by Alexander's work in the domain of architectural patterns, other communities of practice have applied the basic ideas of patterns and Pattern Languages to other domains, first and most notably, perhaps, to the domain of object-oriented programming where there are numerous conferences and books that deal with various recurring problems and solutions in object-oriented programming (see, e.g., Coplien and Schmidt, 1995; Gamma et al., 1995; Vlissides, Coplien, & Kerth, 1996). In addition, attempts have been made to build pattern languages in Human-Computer Interaction (Bayle et al., 1997), business process design, change management, organizing software projects, and social change (DIAC-2002).

To reiterate, a Pattern consists of the named solution to a recurring problem. A complete Pattern consists of several parts: a useful, evocative, and mnemonic pattern name, the author (with reviewer and revision dates), synonyms, an abstract (possibly including an evocative picture), a problem statement, the context(s) in which the problem occurs, an analysis of the forces, the solution (possibly including one or more schematics), some examples, the context(s) that results from applying the pattern, the rationale, links to related patterns, reference to some known uses, and a reference section. A Pattern Language is an interrelated set of such patterns that cover a coherent domain.

Pattern Languages have wide utility in providing a way to access and understand the functionality provided by specialists. In particular, one focus of our research group is on providing a Sociotechnical Pattern Language. Increasingly, corporate customers, as well as governmental agencies and communities, are interested in systems that facilitate the productivity of teams and organizations, and even foster communication and cooperation across semipermeable organizational boundaries. Knowledge of the sociotechnical aspects of systems is currently quite fragmentary. The knowledge that does exist has not been codified in ways directly useful for development teams.

A complete Pattern Language for HCI would not only include those Design Patterns that are generally useful, but complementary Pattern Languages that focus on Design Patterns specifically useful in more specific contexts. In particular, we can imagine Design Patterns dealing with specific groups of users, for example, older adults, children in various age groups, nonliterate adults, hearing impaired adults, and so on. In addition, there are Patterns that are appropriate to specific kinds of environmental and social contexts. For example, there may be Patterns that are quite different for combat situations, office work, and entertainment. Finally, different Patterns may also be applicable for specific tasks such as idea generation, vigilance tasks, psychomotor tasks, idea evaluation, idea integration, interpersonal communication, and so on.

Ideally, development teams should always study specific users in specific contexts doing specific tasks. However, we claim that a set of interrelated Pattern Languages offers both a starting point for professionals and some encapsulated design knowledge for the nonexpert. To illustrate the potential value of patterns, consider various ways that one might present a finding about older adults. Older adults, on average, take longer to name an object when presented with a picture of that object (Thomas, Fozard, & Waugh, 1977). Even if designers of a system happen to discover this finding, what are they to make of it? How should this finding influence design?

A standard way of providing help for designers is to present a set of guidelines. A guideline related to the above finding might read, "When designing for older adults, if they need to name an object, provide extra time for them to do so." But this is still problematic for the designer. How much extra time? The meta-analysis of Verhaegen & Meersman, (1998) suggests a quantitative factor of 1.5 to 2.0 for age-related slowing. How does this relate to other guidelines, such as one that might say, "Don't waste the user's time." More deeply, if a designer is designing a Web site, say, with changing graphic images as navigation tools, it begs the question of whether the older adult user actually needs to be able to name an image before knowing to click on it.

In contrast, a pattern typically offers direct, positive suggestions for the designer. In this case, a relevant pattern might include text that says, "People of different generations (as well as different cultures) have different interpretations of the meaning of images. In addition, the speed of reading changes much less with age than the speed of naming pictures. If there is a compelling reason to present sequences of images in the same place as navigation tools, you can minimize any age-related effects by pairing clickable words with each image." The complete pattern might be called, "Provide redundant words for images used for navigation." This might be a special case of a more general pattern that might be called, "Provide information redundantly in various encoding schemes."

THE SOCIAL IMPACTS OF TECHNOLOGY

It is easy for technology to have inadvertent side effects. Social factors may be vital for individuals, groups, and even large organizations. We believe that many of the disappointments in the field of "knowledge management," for instance, come from attempts to address what is essentially and fundamentally a sociotechnical problem (such as knowledge sharing) in a purely technical way (Thomas, Kellogg, & Erickson, 2001). Yet, technology offers great promise to people in general, and to the elderly in particular, for enhancing life in many areas, including the social realm, provided thought is given during design to the interaction of the social and technical factors.

Some Example Patterns

We are developing a sociotechnical pattern language and will be eliciting additional patterns and commentary from others. So far, we have constructed about 75 patterns. A couple of examples may give something of the flavor of these patterns. In this section, we will give an example of a pattern that is currently a suggested social practice, "Who Speaks for Wolf?" (but which certainly could be supported by technology), and a pattern that allows technology to provide clues in an online world that we would get from other sources in face-to-face interaction, namely, "Context-Setting Entrance." The full patterns are not presented; there is only enough material to give the reader a feeling for the basic context, solution, and analysis.

Who Speaks for Wolf?

Problem

Problem solving or design that proceeds down the wrong path can be costly or impossible to correct later. As the inconvenience and cost of a major change in direction mount, cognitive dissonance makes it likely that new information will be ignored or devalued so that continuance along the wrong path is likely.

Context

Complex problems such as the construction of new social institutions or the design of complex interactive systems require that a multitude of viewpoints be brought to bear. Unfortunately, this is all too often not the case. One group builds a "solution" for another group without fully understanding the culture, the user needs, the extreme cases, and so on. The result is often a "system," whether technical or social, that creates as many problems as it solves.

The idea for this pattern comes from a Native American story transcribed by Paula Underwood (1983). In brief, the story goes as follows. The tribe had as one of its members a man who took it upon himself to learn all that he could about wolves. He became such an expert that his fellow tribes people called him "Wolf." While Wolf and several other braves were out on a long hunting expedition, it became clear to the tribe that they would have to move to a new location. After various reconnaissance missions, a new site was selected and the tribe moved.

Shortly thereafter, it became clear that a mistake had been made. The new location was in the middle of the breeding ground of the wolves. The wolves threatened the children and stole drying meat. Now the tribe faced another tough decision. Move again? Post guards day and night? Or should they destroy the wolves? And did they even want to become the sort of people who would destroy another species for their own convenience?

At last they decided to relocate. As was their custom, they also asked themselves, "What did we learn from this? How can we prevent making such mistakes in the future?" Someone said, "Well, if Wolf would have been at our first council meeting, he would have prevented this mistake."

"True enough," they all agreed. "Therefore, from now on, whenever we meet to make a decision, we shall ask ourselves, "Who Speaks for Wolf?" to remind us that someone must be capable and delegated to bring to bear the knowledge and perspective of any missing stakeholders."

Forces

- Gaps in requirements are most cheaply repaired early in development; it is important for this and for reasons of acceptance (as well as ethics!) by all parties that all stakeholders have a say throughout any development or change process.
- Logistical difficulties make the representation of all stakeholder groups at every meeting difficult.
- A new social institution or design will be both better in quality and more easily accepted if all relevant parties have input.
- Once a wrong path is chosen, both social forces and individual cognitive dissonance make it difficult to begin over, change direction or retrace steps.

Solution

Provide automated remindings of stakeholders who are not present. These could be procedural (certain Native Americans always ask, "Who Speaks for Wolf?" to remind them), visual, or auditory with technological support.

Context-Setting Entrance

Context

A group of people has been attempting to accomplish some task as effectively and efficiently as possible. Because human beings function in many different contexts and come from many different backgrounds and cultures, there are a wide variety of behaviors that are considered appropriate in various circumstances. Sometimes we are expected to compete with each other vigorously. Other times we are expected to be highly cooperative. Sometimes the point of a group is to make a lot of noise. At other times we are expected to maintain a respectful silence. When our own expectations are violated, we may feel resentful, angry, or afraid. When we violate what we later find to be the expectations of others, we may feel embarrassed or resentful. A lack of understanding of expectations not only tends to produce negative emotions, it also can directly and negatively impact productivity. We don't want to be the only person at a party to show up in a tuxedo while everyone else is in blue jeans, or vice versa.

Problem

How can people select from the tremendous variety of possible behaviors those that fit in smoothly with an overall group process?

Forces

- People have a drive to learn and practice new skills.
- People have a drive to be as productive as possible in order to acquire things and experiences.
- People have a drive to become defensive if they are blamed for a violation of expectation when they had no idea what that expectation was.
- It is easier to behave in a way that complements the behaviors of others if the expectations of other people are clear.
- Conventions of ritual, architecture, event, and style have been developed that help clue people in about the type of interaction that is expected.
- When it comes to new technologies or systems with which people have little or no experience, people face great uncertainty about how they are supposed to behave.

Solution

When developing a new system, use the appearance of the system to help set expectations by relying on cultural conventions.

Analysis of the Czaja-Lee Paper
From This Perspective

Czaja and Lee (this volume) begin with a short history of the Internet, followed by some demographics concerning older adults and the Internet. Mainly, these sections point to a seeming contradiction: on the one hand, older adults could benefit greatly from the Internet; on the other hand, they use it less than younger people. They then analyze Internet usage and state that it is primarily for the purpose of finding information. They analyze further and distinguish two main strategies: browsing and analytic strategies. However, their analysis seems to consider browsing as just a strategy for what is still viewed as an information-finding task. Certainly, there are occasions when people of any age are using the Internet for a defined and specific purpose; however, people may also wish to "surf" or "browse" with very general goals in mind. The degree of specificity in various situations may differ considerably. A person may be exploring various possible vacation sites, trying to come to a conclusion about back surgery, or trying to find the very best possible price on golf clubs. Both optimal user strategy and the best site would be different in these situations.

Czaja and Lee go on to give a cogent review of relevant literature. A concern is that the information is in a form primarily geared toward gerontologists; it is not clear that typical application developers will seek it or know what to do with such information in terms of actual design. This really is *not* a critique of Czaja and Lee; rather, the suggestion is that in addition to scholarly and well-documented articles, we should consider, as a community, taking the further step of developing a design Pattern Language for people designing for older adults. Such a Pattern Language should be developed jointly with designers. It would presumably be organized hierarchically by the concerns of designers and succinctly state contexts, problems, analyses, and solutions. It could provide a lingua franca for various stakeholders in a development project including users, psychologists, designers, and computer scientists (cf. Erickson, 2000). We need to involve such designers in order to determine the content and format of patterns that would be maximally useful during real design activity. We might also discover important reusable tools and components that could be instantiated in middleware. Otherwise, given the way design generally works (Thomas & Carroll, 1978), it is unlikely that designers will typically find and appropriately interpret information relevant to HCI in general, or designing for the elderly in particular.

Some of the general sociotechnical patterns such as "Who Speaks for Wolf?" and "Context-Setting Entry" are equally applicable across many user groups and contexts. In addition, projecting the knowledge gained by studies such as Czaja and Lee's into a Pattern Language could make designing systems for older adults a more effective and efficient process for the designers and result in a much better experience for the end user.

REFERENCES

Alexander, C., Ishikawa, S., Silverstein, M., Jacobson, M., Fiksdahl-King, I., & Angel, S. (1977). *A pattern language.* New York: Oxford University Press.

Bayle, E., Bellamy, R., Casaday, G., Erickson, T., Fincher, S., Grinter, B., Gross, B., Lehder, D., Marmolin, H., Potts, C., Skousen, G., & Thomas, J. (1997). Putting it all together: Towards a pattern language for interaction design: Summary report of the CHI '97 workshop. *SIGCHI Bulletin, 30*(1), pp. 17–23. New York: ACM.

Bias, R. G., & Mayhew, D. J. (1994). *Cost-justifying usability.* New York: Academic Press.

Brooks, F. J., Jr. (1975). *The mythical man-month. Essays on software engineering.* Reading, MA: Addison-Wesley.

Charness, N., & Dijkstra, K. (1999). Age, luminance, and print legibility in homes, offices, and public places. *Human Factors, 41*(2), 173–193.

Coplien, J. O., & Schmidt, D. C. (Eds.). (1995). *Pattern languages of program design*. Reading, MA: Addison-Wesley.

Desurvire, H., & Thomas, J. C. (1993). Enhancing the performance of interface evaluators using non-empirical usability methods. *Proceedings of the Human Factors and Ergonomics Society 37th annual meeting*, 1132–1136. Santa Clara, CA: HFES.

DIAC-2002. (2002, May 16–19). Shaping the network society: Patterns for participation, action, and change. Available online: http://www.cpsr.org/conferences/diac02/.

Erickson, T. (2000). Lingua francas for design: Sacred places and pattern languages. *Proceedings of DIS 2000*, pp. 357–368. New York: ACM Press.

Fozard, J. L., Thomas, J. C., & Waugh, N. C. (1976). Effects of age and frequency of stimulus repetitions on two-choice reaction time. *Journal of Gerontology, 31*(5), 556–563.

Gamma, E., Helm, R., Johnson, R., & Vlissides, J. (1995). *Design patterns: Elements of reusable object-oriented software*. Reading, MA: Addison-Wesley.

Gray, W. D., John, B. E., Stuart, R., Lawrence, D., & Atwood, M. E. (1995). GOMS meets the phone company: Analytic modeling applied to real-world problems. In R. M. Baecker, J. Grudin, W. A. S. Buxton, & S. Greenberg (Eds.), *Readings in human-computer interaction: Toward the year 2000* (2nd ed., pp. 634–639). San Francisco: Morgan Kaufmann Publishers.

Landauer, T. (1995). *The trouble with computers*. Cambridge, MA: MIT Press.

Lave, J., & Wenger, E. (1991). *Situated learning: Legitimate peripheral participation*. Cambridge, UK: Cambridge University Press.

McCloskey, M. (1983). Naïve theories of motion. (1983). In D. Genter & A. Stevens (Eds.), *Mental models* (pp. 229–324). Hillsdale, NJ: Erlbaum.

Nielsen, J., & Landauer, T. K. (1993, April 24–29). A mathematical model of the finding of usability problems. *Proceedings ACM/IFIP INTERCHI '93 Conference*, pp. 206–213. Amsterdam, The Netherlands.

Thomas, J., & Carroll, J. (1978). The psychological study of design. *Design Studies, 1*(1), 5–11.

Thomas, J. C., Fozard, J. L., & Waugh, N. C. (1977). Age-related differences in naming latency. *American Journal of Psychology, 90*, 499–509.

Thomas, J., & Kellogg, W. (1989, January). Minimizing ecological gaps in interface design. *IEEE Software*, 78–86.

Thomas, J., Kellogg, W. A., & Erickson, T. (2001). The knowledge management puzzle: Human and social factors in knowledge management. *The IBM Systems Journal, 40*, 63–84.

Underwood, P. (1983). *Who speaks for Wolf: A Native American learning story*. Georgetown, TX (now San Anselmo, CA): A Tribe of Two Press.

Verhaeghen, P., Marcoen, A., & Goossens, L. (1993). Facts and fiction about memory aging: A quantitative integration of research findings. *Journal of Gerontology: Psychological Sciences, 48*, 157–171.

Verhaegen, P., & Meersman, L. D. (1998). Aging and the Stroop effect: A meta-analysis. *Psychology and Aging, 13*, 120–126.

Verhaeghen, P., & Salthouse, T. A. (1997). Meta-analyses of age-cognition rela-
    tions in adulthood: Estimates of linear and non-linear age effects and
    structural models. *Psychological Bulletin, 122,* 231–249.
Vlissides, J. M., Coplien, J. O., & Kerth, N. (Eds.). (1996). *Pattern languages of
    program design2.* Reading, MA: Addison-Wesley.

CHAPTER 4

Assistive Technology

William C. Mann

A s we age we face age-related chronic conditions and declines associated with the aging process that can result in impairment and disability. Yet elders do not comprise a homogeneous population, particularly in terms of impairments and disabilities. Impairments in hearing, vision, neuromusculoskeletal system, and cognition vary in severity and mix. About 10% of people in their 60s, and about half of those in their 80s, have significant impairments resulting in the need for assistance with basic activities of daily living. The good news is that there are a wide variety of tools or assistive devices that can help in compensating for the activity limitations caused by impairments.

This chapter will review the evidence for assistive technology (AT) as a cost-effective intervention. It begins with an overview of the research of the Rehabilitation Engineering Research on Aging to develop a framework for introducing assistive technology to older persons with disabilities. The chapter goes on to discuss new computer-based technology for home monitoring and communications that holds promise for older adults with dementia.

Since 1991, the Rehabilitation Engineering Research Center on Aging (RERC-Aging) has studied the needs of older persons with impairments relative to their need for and use of assistive devices, also called assistive technology (AT). Figure 4.1 represents the RERC-Aging line of research relative to the current focus on home monitoring and communications technology:

Oval I in Figure 4.1 reflects the Consumer Assessments Study (CAS) conducted from 1991 to 2001. The CAS was a longitudinal study of the

FIGURE 4.1   Research path of the Rehabilitation Engineering Research Center on Aging.

coping strategies of a sample of 792 elders with disabilities in Western New York (WNY) initiated in 1991, and 312 in North Florida (NFl), initiated in 1999. A comparison of initial interviews of the CAS sample with the 1986 National Health Interview Survey (NHIS) (Prohaska, Mermelstein, Miller, & Jack, 1992; U.S. Department of Commerce, Economics and Statistics Administration, 2002) and the 1987 National Medical Expenditure Survey (NMES) (Leon & Lair, 1990) reported that CAS study participants resembled the approximately 8 to 12% of the elder population who have difficulty with at least one ADL or IADL (Mann, Hurren, Tomita, & Charvat, 1997). Examination of one ADL indicated that 83% of the CAS participants have difficulty with walking, while 4.6% of NHIS participants and 7.7% of NMES participants report difficulty walking. For one IADL, 80.5% of CAS participants have difficulty shopping, while 12.8% of the NHIS participants, and 11.0% of the NMES participants have difficulty with shopping. Although only 5 to 8% of noninstitutionalized elders in the population studies reported difficulty in performing ADLs, IADLs, or both, every subject in the CAS reported difficulty in completing at least one ADL or IADL.

The CAS has proven valuable in guiding the RERC-Aging and others to areas for device development, areas where there are gaps in AT service delivery, and areas where additional research was, and in some cases still is, needed. It has provided a unique longitudinal database on the lives of older persons with disabilities, focusing on how they use assistive technology and other compensatory strategies.

Data from the CAS permitted the Correlation/Matched Pairs Analysis (Oval II: 1993–1995), which provided strong suggestive evidence that use of AT by noninstitutionalized, physically disabled elderly was positively related to functional independence (Mann, Hurren, Tomita, & Charvat, 1995). Predictors of functional independence were determined through correlation analysis on a sample of 364 CAS subjects. These predictors included age, sex, education, mental status, physical disability, and visual impairment. From the sample of 364 elders, 117 pairs of subjects were matched on these predictors and compared for levels of functional independence relative to assistive device use. Two instruments were used for assessing functional independence: the Functional Independence Measure (FIM™) Motor Section for Activities of Daily Living (ADLs), and the Older Americans Research and Service Center Instrument (OARs) for Instrumental Activities of Daily Living (IADLs). For 60 subject pairs, the subject in the matched pair who used more assistive devices was more functionally independent than the subject who used fewer devices on both measures (FIM-Motor and OARs IADLs). For 36 subject pairs the opposite was found. For 21 subject pairs the results were mixed; within most subject pairs, the subject with more devices was more independent in ADLs but less independent in IADLs. Given the limitations of the study design, results suggest that increased use of assistive devices relates to increased functional independence. Results also suggest that for these subjects the devices they were using had more impact on their ADLs than on their IADLs.

Building on the report of the Matched Pairs Analysis in 1996, the RERC-Aging secured additional funding from the AARP Andrus Foundation and the Administration on Aging to support a Randomized Controlled Trial (RCT) titled "Effectiveness of Assistive Technology Devices (AT) and Environmental Interventions (EI) in Maintaining Independence in the Home-Based Elderly" (Oval III). This study represents the first RCT to study outcomes of the use of assistive technology. We demonstrated that by giving older persons with physical and sensory impairments the AT they need, along with training and follow-up and other home modifications, not only did their functional performance exceed that of people receiving more traditional home care, the costs of institution-based health care (nursing home and hospital) were dramatically reduced (Mann, Ottenbacher, Fraas, Tomita, & Granger, 1999). Over the 18-month intervention period the treatment group received a mean of 15.2 AT devices and 1.2 EI, while the control group received 1.4 AT devices and .2 EI. Both groups showed significant decline for FIM™ Total Score, and the FIM™ Motor Score, but there was significantly more decline for the control group. For FIM™ Total Score the treatment group declined a mean of 4.0 points while the control group declined 11.5 points. For FIM™ Motor Score the treatment group declined a mean of 2.5 points, while the control group declined 8.6 points. Pain scores increased significantly more for the control group. In comparing health care costs the treatment group expended more for AT/EI ($\overline{X}_T$ = $2620, $\overline{X}_C$ = $443). The control group required significantly more expenditures for institutional care ($\overline{X}_T$ = $5630, $\overline{X}_C$ = $21,847). There was no significant difference in total in-home personnel costs, although there was a large effect size (d = .56). Total in-home costs included visits by nurses, case managers, occupational and physical therapists, speech-language pathologists, and aides. The control group did have significantly greater expenditures for two of these areas of in-home personnel costs: nurse visits ($\overline{X}_T$ = $426, $\overline{X}_C$ = $842) and case manager visits ($\overline{X}_T$ = $110, $\overline{X}_C$ = $193).

In this study, a larger percentage of participants in the control group declined in functional status than in the intervention group on 7 of 9 measures of functional status. We examined individual items on the FIM instrument, compared them to the type of AT provided, and found that for those items that showed decline for the control group, devices were provided to intervention group subjects that addressed that area. For example, the control group declined significantly on the FIM walking item, while the intervention group participants who received devices and instructions related to walking did not show a significant decline. Similar findings were found for dressing. While the physically frail elders in both groups in this trial experienced functional decline over time, the results indicate that rate of functional decline can be slowed and institutional and certain in-home personnel costs reduced through a systematic approach to providing assistive technology and environmental modifications.

Having demonstrated through an RCT that we could reduce the amount of decline in independence, the amount of pain experienced, and the costs of nursing home and hospitalizations, we proposed and in 1999 received funding for a three-year study to use computers for monitoring self care needs of elders (Oval IV). Titled "The Effectiveness of a Computer-Based Monitoring System to Enhance Self-Care of Older Persons with Disabilities," this 3-year RCT is examining the impact on independence and health-related costs of increased contact and support to elders through computer-based monitoring of their self-care needs and use of AT. Dr. Laura Gitlin, a respondent for this paper presentation, also serves as Co-PI for this trial. We have a control group of 75 elders, and an intervention group of 50. We have installed computers in the homes of those in the intervention group, and we have completed initial training on computer use. While we will not test the primary hypotheses (effectiveness of intervention) until all subjects have received the intervention for one year, we can report some information on training and computer use. All but three study participants had no prior computer experience. We found that an average of 11.75 (range 4–28) hours of computer training, with an average of 6.7 (range 1–16) visits were required, significantly more than we had originally estimated. This need for a relatively high level of training may, at least in part explain the low use of computers by disabled older adults (U.S. Department of Commerce, 2002). However, once trained, elders appear to enthusiastically embrace using the computer as a communication device. Time on the Internet occupied over 90% of the time spent on the computer, and one-third of participants' computer time was spent sending and receiving e-mails (Malcolm et al., 2002).

FUTURE WORK IN THE AREA OF HOME MONITORING AND COMMUNICATIONS TECHNOLOGY

Recently we proposed funding for an RERC with a focus on the National Institute on Disability and Rehabilitation Research (NIDRR) priorities for an RERC on Technology for Successful Aging. The RFP for this center stressed home monitoring and communication technology for elders with disabilities. The concept of home monitoring includes the monitoring of (1) the home environment (e.g., lighting, air, security), (2) the person's movement in the home (e.g., opening doors, using appliances), (3) health status (e.g., blood pressure, weight), and (4) self-care needs (e.g., shopping, managing money, dressing). Communication technology can be as basic as a traditional phone and can be integrated into an overall home monitoring system. Communication technology is used directly as an aid for self-care (shopping, banking), socialization, and calls for help. The next generation of truly "smart" home monitoring systems will integrate such advanced technologies as wireless, sensors, computers, and the World Wide Web into systems that "observe," respond, and communicate with elders themselves, their caregivers, and health providers.

Between 1991 and 1996 the RERC will test currently available home monitoring products and prototype systems and demonstrate their effectiveness in relation to independence, quality of life, and health-related costs. The RERC will also identify needs and barriers to home monitoring and communication technology, and will address needs of special populations, including rural-living elders and people aging with disability. The results of this research will be relevant to health policy makers, device developers, and other investigators. The RERC on Technology for Successful Aging will work with companies on pre-product testing, including Honeywell's very promising Independent LifeStyle Assistant (ILSA). We will advance very new consumer products, such as Motorola's Smart Phone, to provide applications useful for older people with disabilities. We will also study the requirements for, and begin development on, a device/system for elders with cognitive impairment.

ADDITIONAL RESEARCH RELATED
TO THE RERC FOCUS

The RERC focus in home monitoring and communications technology relates to other findings from our earlier work and the work of others. Through the CAS we found that elders did not have current information on the availability of many types of assistive devices, including home monitoring and communications technologies. Within the CAS we asked elders to suggest inventions for new assistive devices. In every case, they listed devices that were already available, sometimes with several different products, suggesting that they do not have current or adequate information on assistive devices in the marketplace (Mann, Hurren, Tomita, Packard, & Creswell, 1994).

In the area of communication devices, phones have been one of the most important and most common technology items in the homes of elders, providing opportunities for socializing, banking, shopping, and calls for help. Even before the widespread use of cell phones, the electronics marketplace offered inexpensive phones with many features useful for older persons with disabilities, such as large buttons, backlit buttons, voice amplification, and hands-free use. We discovered through the CAS that many elders with disabilities are either not taking advantage of these phones, or the features on their phones are not adequate for their needs (Mann, 1997). We found high rates of problems and dissatisfaction with traditional (non-cell) phones (Mann, Hurren, & Tomita, 1993). In a follow-up intervention study focused on phones, we found that most phone-related problems experienced by elders were correctable with readily available products, and once the problems were corrected, phone usage increased by over 50% (Mann, Hurren, Charvat, & Tomita, 1996a). Many elders have difficulty getting up to answer the phone. Providing a cordless phone that could be carried around the house and kept close by easily solved this problem. Other problems related to phones that were old, not working properly, and needed to be replaced. Rearrangement of furniture, adding a table for a phone next to the bed, providing phones with the features mentioned above (large buttons, backlit buttons, etc.) made a significant difference in the ability of the study participants to use a phone.

FOCUS ON ELDERS WITH COGNITIVE IMPAIRMENT

The work of the RERC on Technology for Successful Aging includes a strong focus on elders with cognitive impairment. Dementia is a broad term to describe a decline in intellectual functioning that is not a normal part of the aging process, and that results in cognitive impairment in at least three of these areas: language, memory, visual-spatial skills, personality, and cognition (Cummings, 1984; Glickstein, 1997). Alzheimer's disease is a form of dementia and is the most common cause of dementia in persons over 65 (National Institute on Aging, n.d.). Cognitive impairments resulting from strokes are the second most frequently occurring type of dementia (Butin, 1991).

In investigating the need for assistive devices by home-based elders with impairments, we found that elders with cognitive impairment used the least number of assistive devices among all elders with impairments. Elders with cognitive impairment also had higher levels of dissatisfaction with the devices they owned (Mann, Karuza, Hurren, & Tomita, 1993).

Nochajski, Tomita, and Mann (1996), found that devices for physical disabilities tended to be more readily accepted and used than devices for cognitive impairments by elderly persons with cognitive impairment. Furthermore, this study found that cognitively impaired participants with higher Mini-Mental Status Examination (MMSE) scores (15 to 23 out of 30), and their caregivers, tended to accept devices more than participants with lower MMSE scores (10 to 14). In another CAS analysis we found that over time elders with Alzheimer's disease decreased their use of cognitive devices and used more devices that assisted care providers with tasks like bathing, transfers, and mobility (Mann, Hurren, Charvat, & Tomita, 1996b).

The use of cognitive devices and interventions has been shown to be effective. Bailey (1993) found that switch-controlled assistive devices help some persons with severe physical and cognitive impairments with activities such as exploring their environment and socializing with friends. Other studies have shown that assistive devices such as memory aids can be used to stimulate conversation, enhance socialization, and reinforce accurate memories (Bourgeois, 1993). Reality orientation (Baldelli et al., 1993) and daily routines such as planned walking (Friedman & Tappen, 1991), have also been found to be effective in maintaining and improving environmental awareness and communication skills of persons with cognitive impairments.

An emerging area of research and development is focused on assisting persons with cognitive impairments in their daily activities through the use of computerized devices. Mihailidis, Fernie, and Cleghorn (2000) developed a computerized cueing device to assist with the task of hand washing in elderly persons with dementia. The computerized system consisted of a nine-step verbal prompting device equipped with transducers to monitor step completion, and did not require user input or intervention for effective operation. A pilot study using this device was conducted with an 81-year-old male with alcoholic dementia. Improved performance was demonstrated based on the level of assistance needed for task completion, with fewer caregiver interactions required.

Computerized Task Guidance (C-TG) systems have also been used to aid in completion of complex activities with persons with cognitive impairment. These systems work by providing interactive cues to the user to assist in the completion of complex activities. Kirsch, Lajiness, Levine, and Schnyder (1990) found that by using a C-TG system, as compared to written index cards (IC-TG), two of four subjects with cognitive impairment demonstrated improved performance during a janitorial task. In a second trial, two persons with cognitive impairment performed a cooking task using either C-TG or IC-TG. Both participants had notable improvements in performance following use of IC-TG but improvement with C-TG occurred only after practice.

People with Alzheimer's have been taught to use a simple computer program. They have learned to do a simple task on a computer using a touch screen. The investigators reported that subject acceptance of the training was positive, motivation was high, and there appeared to be a transfer of the trained skills into real situations (Hofmann, Hock, Kuhler, & Muller-Spahn, 1995). Another study looked at behavioral approaches to improving ADLs with nursing home patients with dementia. This study reported that patients improved in independence in dressing, and increased participation in dressing when prompted (Rogers et al., 1999).

By increasing opportunities for independent activity with severely cognitively impaired elders, using more nondirective and directive verbal assists rather than physical assists, independence was increased. This study also found that there were more appropriate requests for help when independence was encouraged (Rogers et al., 2000). A study of nursing home residents found similar results. Certified nursing assistants were trained to use more prompting and praise rather than physical assistance with elders with dementia. Following 20 weeks of implementation, active engagement by the elders almost doubled (Engelman, Altus, & Mathews, 1999).

CONCLUSION

AT has been shown to be effective in reducing functional decline and reducing health-related costs. As underlying technologies are designed into new products and systems, the potential for AT is even greater. We have more powerful computers and sensors, the emergence of new and more flexible wireless technologies, better batteries and other power sources, miniaturization of the underlying technology in our products—all of these will be combined into a new electronic world, already being called "pervasive computing." Pervasive computing offers great promise to help even those who have been helped least by assistive technology—elders with cognitive impairment. The RERC Aging has been actively involved in research and development in the area of AT for older people with disabilities since 1991. Over the next 5 years, in partnership with other research centers and companies working in this field, the RERC will continue to conduct research and develop assistive technology for older people with disabilities, with a focus on home monitoring, communications devices, and the needs of elders with cognitive impairment.

REFERENCES

Bailey, D. H. (1993). Technology for adults with multiple impairments: A trilogy of case reports. *American Journal of Occupational Therapy, 40*(4), 341–345.

Baldelli, M. V., Pirani, A., Motta, M., Abati, E., Mariani, E., & Manzi, V. (1993). Effects of reality orientation on elderly patients in the community. *Archives of Gerontology and Geriatrics, 17,* 211–218.

Bourgeois, M. S. (1993). Using memory aids to stimulate conversation and reinforce accurate memories. *Gerontology Special Interest Section Newsletter, 16*(4), 1–3.

Butin, D. N. (1991). Helping those with dementia to live at home: An educational series for caregivers. *Physical and Occupational Therapy in Geriatrics,* 9(3/4), 69–82.

Cummings, J. (1984). Dementia: Definition, classification, and differential diagnosis. *Psychiatric Annals, 14,* 85–89.

Engelman, K., Altus, D., & Mathews, R. (1999). Increasing engagement in daily activities by older adults with dementia. *Journal of Applied Behavior Analysis, 32,* 107–110.

Friedman, R., & Tappen, R. M. (1991). The effect of planned walking on communication in Alzheimer's disease. *Journal of the American Gerontological Society, 39,* 650–654.

Glickstein, J. (1997). *Therapeutic interventions in Alzheimer's disease: A program of functional skills for activities of daily living and communication.* Gaithersburg, MD: Aspen.

Hofmann, M., Hock, C., Kuhler, A., & Muller-Spahn, F. (1995). Computergestutztes individualisiertes Gedachtnistraining bei Alzheimer-Patienten. [Computer-assisted individualized memory training in Alzheimer patients]. *Nervenarzt, 66,* 703–707.

Kirsch, N., Lajiness, R., Levine, S., & Schnyder, M. (1990). Performance of functional activities with the aid of task guidance systems. *Archives of Physical Medicine and Rehabilitation, 69,* 714.

Leon, J., & Lair, T. (1990). *Functional status of the non-institutionalized elderly: Estimates of ADL and IADL difficulties.* In Public Health Service (Ed.), National Medical Expenditure Survey Research Finding 4, Agency for Health Care Policy and Research. (DHHS publication [PHS] 90-3462). Rockville, MD: Public Health Service

Malcolm, M., Mann, W. C., Tomita, M. R., Fraas, L. F., Stanton, K. M., Gitlan, L. (2002). Computer and Internet use in physically frail elders. *Physical and Occupational Therapy in Geriatrics, 19*(3), 15–31

Mann, W. (1997). An essential communication device: The phone. In R. Lubinski & J. Higginbotham (Eds.), *Communications technologies for the elderly: Hearing, vision, and speech conference* (pp. 323–339). San Diego: Singular Publishing Group.

Mann, W. C., Hurren, D., Charvat, B., & Tomita, M. (1996a). The use of phones by elders with disabilities: Problems, interventions, costs. *Assistive Technology, 8,* 23–33.

Mann, W. C., Hurren, D. M., Charvat, B. A., & Tomita, M. (1996b). Changes over one year in assistive device use and home modifications by home-based older persons with Alzheimer's disease. *Topics in Geriatric Rehabilitation, 12*(2), 9–16.

Mann, W. C., Hurren, D., & Tomita, M. (1993). Dissatisfaction with assistive devices among elderly persons with disabilities. *Proceedings of the 16th Annual RESNA Conference* (pp. 534–536). Las Vegas, Nevada.

Mann, W., Hurren, D., Tomita, M., & Charvat, B. (1995). The relationship of functional independence to assistive device use of elderly persons living at home. *Journal of Applied Gerontology, 14,* 225–247.

Mann, W., Hurren, D., Tomita, M., & Charvat, B. (1997). Comparison of the UB-RERC Aging Consumer Assessment Study with the 1986 NHIS and the 1987 NMES. *Topics in Geriatric Rehabilitation, 13,* 32–41.

Mann, W. C., Hurren, D., Tomita, M., Packard S., & Creswell, C. (1994). The need for information on assistive devices by older persons. *Assistive Technology, 6*(2), 134–139

Mann, W. C., Karuza, J., Hurren, D. M., & Tomita, M. (1993). Needs of home-based older persons for assistive devices: The University at Buffalo rehabilitation engineering center on aging consumer assessment study. *Technology and Disability, 2,* 1–11.

Mann, W. C., Ottenbacher, K. J., Fraas, L., Tomita, M., & Granger, C. V. (1999). Effectiveness of assistive technology and environmental interventions in maintaining independence and reducing home care costs for the frail elderly: A randomized trial. *Archives of Family Medicine, 8*(3), 210–217.

Mihailidis, A., Fernie, G., & Cleghorn, W. (2000). The development of a computerized cueing device to help people with dementia to be more independent. *Technology and Disability, 13,* 23–40.

National Institute on Aging. (n.d.). *2000 Progress report on Alzheimer's disease: Taking the next steps.* Retrieved July 26, 2001, from http://www.alzheimers.org/pubs/pr2000.pdf.

Nochajski, S. M., Tomita, M., & Mann, W. C. (1996). An intervention study of the use and satisfaction with assistive devices by elderly persons with cognitive impairments. *Topics in Geriatric Rehabilitation, 12*(2), 40–53.

Prohaska, T., Mermelstein, R., Miller, B., & Jack, S. (1992). *Functional status and living arrangements.* Vital and Health Statistics, Health Data on Older Americans. Hyattsville, MD: U.S. Department of Health and Human Services.

Rogers, J., Holm, M., Burgio, L., Granieri, E., Hsu, C., Hardin, M., & McDowell, B. (1999). Improving morning care routines of nursing home residents with dementia. *Journal of the American Geriatrics Society, 47,* 1049–1057.

Rogers, J., Holm, M., Burgio, L., Hsu, C., Hardin, J., & McDowell, B. (2000). Excess disability during morning care in nursing home residents with dementia. *International Psychogeriatrics, 12,* 267–282.

U.S. Department of Commerce, Economics and Statistics Administration, National Telecommunications and Information Administration. (2002). *A nation online: How Americans are expanding their use of the Internet.* Retrieved from http://www.ntia.doc.gov/ntiahome/dn/.

Commentary

Next Steps in Home Modification and Assistive Technology Research

Laura N. Gitlin

en years of home modification and assistive technology research underscores the importance of this strategy for improving life quality and enabling older frail elders and their family caregivers to age in place. Regardless of the increased recognition of the potential benefits of home modifications, this approach has not been systematically integrated into health professional practices, long-term home and community-based services and, most important reimbursement mechanisms. Of equal significance is that many research questions that are critical to informing the delivery of home modification services remain unanswered. The purpose of this commentary is thus twofold: to highlight key areas of knowledge obtained from the extant research on home modification and assistive device use, and identify future directions for inquiry in this critical area.

WHY DO WE NEED MORE HOME MODIFICATION RESEARCH?

A central departure point for a discussion on home modification research is the rationale or justification for continuing and expanding systematic inquiry in this area. On an intuitive level, it may seem paradoxical that one must justify the importance of home modification research in view of the aging demographic profile and the high rate of home ownership in the United States. For example, currently, in the

188

United States approximately 83% of older people 65 years of age or older own their own homes compared to only 4% of older persons who reside in nursing home facilities (National Center for Health Statistics, 1997; United States Census Bureau, 2000). Nevertheless, despite the dramatic projected increases in the numbers of older people and the fact that the home will continue to be the primary context for growing old, few federal and foundation funding mechanisms target home modification research. Moreover, only recently has there been an interest among gerontologists in the health-promoting role of this approach. Therefore, providing a strong rationale beyond the demographic argument for centering attention and resources on home modification research is an essential starting point from which to articulate future research directions.

Importance of Aging in Place

A rationale for the continuation and expansion of home modification research is grounded in four societal trends. Chief among these trends is the subjective appraisal by the elderly themselves as to the importance of the home to their own well-being and the consensual preference and demonstrated commitment of informal caregivers to helping aging family members remain in their location of choice. The aspiration of older people to age in place has been consistently documented in the gerontological literature dating back 40 years and continuing to the present, as represented by national surveys (Population Reference Bureau, 2002; American Association Retired Persons, 1990; Population Bulletin, 2000). The vast majority of older people want to remain in their own homes regardless of the condition of their housing or neighborhood. The importance of the home is also highlighted by past and current research on time use, which has consistently shown that the vast majority of time spent by older people occurs inside the home (Evans, 1999; Moss & Lawton, 1982). Consequently, the use of home modifications, including assistive devices, to offset declining competencies that threaten the ability to remain at home resonates with the personal goals and life choices of older people themselves. Moreover, the acceptability of and preference for the use of this type of strategy is also supported by evidence from national representative surveys in the United States. A consistent finding from such surveys is a trend toward increased assistive device and home modification use and a subsequent decline in reliance on personal assistance among functionally impaired older adults (LaPlante, Hendershot, & Moss, 1992; Manton, Corder, & Stallard, 1997; Norburn et al., 1995).

Reparative Role of the Home

A second factor supporting the need for and expansion of home modification research is the growing evidence of the reparative role of staying at home in a supportive environment. For example, research shows that living at home supports personal notions of normalcy and continuity in self-identity in view of the disruptive effects of age-related declines, chronic illness, and multiple personal losses (Rubinstein, 1989). Furthermore, research suggests that the home environment may buttress daily functional abilities and buffer the threat of loss of personal autonomy and control, two important contributors to well-being.

The Home as a Care Setting

A third factor supporting the need for more home modification research is that the home is quickly becoming the context for a wide array of health and human services. This trend is expected to expand as the baby boomer generation ages (Wahl & Gitlin, 2003). Additionally, there has been a dramatic growth in the volume of home care services covered by Medicare in the past 10 years and increased home use of rehabilitation technologies traditionally reserved for inpatient services. Thus, the boundaries between hospital and home are being blended, particularly in the care of the physically frail (Binstock & Cluff, 2000; Mann, 1997).

Related to this point is the fact that the home is the setting for short- and long-term unpaid informal caregiving by families, friends, and/or neighbors. Currently, informal caregivers provide over 80% of care to dependent older persons living at home (Binstock & Cluff, 2000). Recent research also shows that home modifications help the family caregiver cope with the increasing functional dependence of individuals with dementia and using such strategies results in reduced caregiver upset and enhanced self-efficacy (Gitlin et al., 2001; Gitlin et al., in press).

Self-Management of Chronic Conditions

Finally, the rise in the dominance of chronic over acute health conditions is yet another trend underscoring the significance of home modification research. Central to the shift in focus in health care delivery is the search for strategies that promote self-management of conditions that do not resolve but which potentially are complicated by the overlay of age-related decrements with the passage of time. Thus, the use of home modifications and assistive devices for helping people self-manage offers a compelling cost-effective approach that may offset the need for formal and informal care and delay or prevent relocation to residential facilities.

RESEARCH DEVELOPMENTS

Given these societal developments, the significance of home modification research cannot be overstated. It is thus highly commendable that this particular adaptive mechanism is the focal point of this book. What, then, has been gained from the past 10 plus years of research on this important strategy for older people and what future directions should be pursued? The efforts of Dr. Mann and his team, as presented in the previous chapter, as well as by numerous other researchers, demonstrate a logical research progression of inquiry from an initial generation of basic descriptive studies of home modification use and reasons for non-use to explanatory models of factors associated with use of this strategy to, more recently, predictive or experimental design-based knowledge regarding outcomes of home modification interventions.

Descriptive Research on Home Modifications

The first wave of research studies on home modification and assistive device use focused principally on demonstrating that older people are successful users of these strategies. The chief concern was with documenting utilization rates and reasons for non-use. This focus was initially warranted in view of identified barriers to gaining access to modifications and the societal myth that the elderly were unable or resistant to learning new care approaches, particularly if it involved technology (Gitlin, 1995).

Four key points can be gleaned from this early descriptive research, much of which was generated by Dr. Mann and colleagues' consumer assessment surveys, as well as by others using large-scale national representative surveys. Perhaps one of the most elemental but important and consistent finding from these early surveys is that older people are indeed users of a wide range of adaptive strategies including equipment use (principally mobility aids). Also, these surveys showed that older people identify specific home modification needs in addition to those they currently have (Mann et al., 1994). Secondly, older people are selective in their use of devices and choose those that help them accomplish their own identified personal goals (Gitlin, 1998). Third, some devices (e.g., computer technology) require more extensive training than others (e.g., reacher), but more importantly, older adults and family members need instruction to use home modifications effectively. Finally, common devices such as wheelchairs, canes, and hearing aids continue to pose significant challenges for users, highlighting the importance of research that informs device development, improves design elements of existing devices, and identifies needs, acceptability and utilization.

Complementing the findings from survey research are qualitative investigations that provide a rich description of the subjective world of older adult users and the personal significance and impact of adaptive technology (Gitlin, 1998; Gitlin, Luborsky, & Schemm, 1998; Kaufert, Kaufert & Locker, 1987). This research has shown that chief among the benefits described by older users is a renewed sense of normalcy, of being able to participate in valued daily activities. Other life enhancements as reported by older users include opportunities for increased social engagement and participation in discretionary activities (e.g., use of adaptive playing cards or game boards), maintenance of social contact (e.g., use of door adapter, outside elevator, or hand rails to facilitate egress), and reserved energy (e.g., use of a stair glide) to carry out activities of choice. This research has also shown that despite its important benefits, there may be negative consequences to home modification and device use. Foremost is the symbolic meaning of a device such as a wheelchair, which serves as a visible reminder of a change in functioning (from abled to "disabled") and level of independence. Research shows that certain modifications and devices (e.g., mobility aid, out door ramp) may heighten feelings of loss and serve as painful reminders of former competencies. Finally, this research suggests that a fundamental aspect of device use is a process referred to as biographical management (Gitlin et al., 1998). This management process entails evaluating the trade off, or weighing the relative gains and losses of device use in view of cultural notions of normalcy, social stigmata and the profound personal feelings of loss that use may engender. Accordingly, although device use enables older people to continue performing lifelong and valued personal routines, it may simultaneously create feelings of personal disruption and discontinuity. Older people may have to contend with this duality and reconcile feelings of loss with the gains obtained by using a device.

Biographical management may be particularly acute in the case of an abrupt onset of a disabling condition such as a stroke or congestive heart failure.

Correlation Research on Home Modifications

A second wave of research may be characterized as explanatory in nature. This body of research has sought to articulate relationships between user and device characteristics as reflected in Dr. Mann's correlation analyses from his Consumer Assessment Survey described in his chapter and by others seeking to identify predictors of use and differences between users and non-users. Four core findings emerge from this research. One of the most consistent findings is that the use of mobility devices is more prevalent among older people with physical frailty than among younger cohorts (Manton, Corder, & Stallard, 1997). A related point is that device use, and in particular use of mobility aids, is associated with having functional difficulties (Manton et al., 1997). Alternately, older adults with cognitive impairments use fewer devices. Another consistent finding is that devices, rather than assistance from others, tends to be preferred by older people and use of devices is associated with enhanced self-efficacy (Verbrugge, Rennert, & Madans, 1997). Finally, a primary indictor of long-term home use of a device that is issued during hospitalization is the person's psychological readiness to use it at the time of training (Gitlin et al., 1996).

Effectiveness of Home Modification Use

More recent research endeavors can be characterized as predictive or experimental, that is testing the effectiveness of home modification and device use for improving health as well as functional and psychological outcomes. There is relatively little research that systematically documents the range of benefits afforded to older people by using devices using clinical trial methodology. One of the first intervention studies of significance, conducted by Mann and his colleagues, showed that home use of assistive devices lowers long-term care costs and postpones relocation (Mann, Ottenbacher, Fraas, Tomita, & Granger, 1999). Research with family caregivers of individuals with dementia shows that use of adaptive devices and environmental modification strategies have multiple benefits for both dementia caregivers and care recipients

(Gitlin et al., 2001; Gitlin et al., in press). Some of these important benefits include slowing the rate of functional dependence in persons with dementia and reducing upset with care recipient behaviors.

FUTURE RESEARCH DIRECTIONS

Although much research has been conducted, many questions remain unanswered about the characteristics of users and non-users and the specific role and contribution of home modifications in supporting quality of life of older people. Four broad directives for future inquiry in this area are described here. These are the need for theory development and the application of theory to home modification research, measurement issues, the need for using clinical trial methodologies to evaluate outcomes, and the complementary role of health policy research.

Theory-Driven Research

For the most part, home modification research has not been theory-driven. For example, although numerous studies delineate reasons for the use or non-use of assistive devices, an explanation as to why use occurs and by whom has not been clearly articulated. Most studies assume a medical model framework in examining the role and importance of assistive technology. This theoretical framework is limiting in that it views adaptive equipment principally as a compensatory mechanism, to enhance physical performance in persons with functional limitations. However, the potential role of assistive devices in the lives of older people is more far reaching and may include improving everyday competencies and quality in a range of life domains such as psychological well-being and socialization. The lack of attention to theory-driven research in this area continues to pose as a barrier to advancing the field.

Future research needs to either develop new theories or apply existing theoretical frameworks to the study of home modification. One potentially useful framework is personal control and its recent application to physical disability. Briefly, control theory contends that individuals are motivated to maintain control over difficult life situations (Schulz, & Heckhausen, 1999), based on a premise that control is a human imperative. To maintain control, individuals adapt various strategies referred to as primary and secondary mechanisms. Primary mechanisms are behavioral, active attempts to manipulate external forces or modify immediate environments (people, objects) to maximize control. Secondary mechanisms refer to internal cognition, emotions or cognitive reframing techniques that are employed as well to offset loss of control. Secondary mechanisms support or enable the use of primary, active behavioral strategies.

Critical to the concept of personal control is a person's engagement with his or her immediate environment to afford positive outcomes and buffer threats or actual losses to personal abilities. Within this framework, device use reflects a primary adaptive strategy that is supported by selective secondary processes. To use this primary strategy, secondary mechanisms of control, such as the cognitive reformation of personal goals or self-expectations, are important. The biographical management process evident in new device users as discussed earlier may be a reflection of secondary readjustments. An important outcome of enacting strategies and exerting control is enhanced self-efficacy. One prediction based on this framework is that to the extent that a home modification or assistive device is successful in helping older people sustain control over their ability to carry out daily routines and feel efficacious, then negative affective responses to disability, such as anxiety or depression, will be minimized. There is some support for this prediction. Recent research shows that individuals with disability who use assistive devices as a primary source of assistance report enhanced self-efficacy (Verbrugge, Rennert, & Madans, 1997). Family caregivers of persons with dementia also report improved self-efficacy following intervention that provides home modification strategies (Gitlin et al., 2001). Most important, previous research suggests that control is positively linked to both physical and psychological health. The use of devices, then, might have an impact on well-being by enhancing self-efficacy.

Certainly, other theories and models, such as the World Health Organization's International Classification of Function framework, should be applied to the study of home modifications to understand and examine the breadth of issues related to use and outcomes.

Measurement Issues

Related to the use of theory are issues of measurement. Still lacking is an instrument grounded in theory that captures person-environment transactions as a way of describing older people's fit within their homes and identifying appropriate intervention approaches. One new measure, the "Enabler," developed by occupational therapists in Sweden, captures key physical components of a home that may pose as a barrier to accessibility and links these to the specific functional capacity of an individual. By matching particular physical environmental and person characteristics, a measure of person-environment fit is derived from which to identify clinical interventions. Although it is not widely known or used in the United States, preliminary research shows that it is a useful clinical and research tool with adequate inter-rater reliability (Iwarsson & Isacsson, 1996; Iwarsson & Slaug, 2001). Yet another measurement need is for an objective, multidimensional, and standardized battery by which to evaluate the outcomes of home modification and device use.

Randomized Clinical Trial Research

A second directive for future research is the need to apply clinical trial methodology to the systematic evaluation of the relative benefits (and risks) of home modification and assistive device use. Intervention research has much to contribute to the development and refinement of device delivery systems and health policy formulation (Gitlin, 1998). Specifically, intervention research can provide knowledge as to the structure and process of service delivery, including who should deliver technology services, the number of optimal contacts for training, the short- and long-term outcomes for target risk groups, and cost effectiveness. These are specific and significant issues that have an impact on the development and implementation of a wide range of home modification and technology service delivery programs for which we do not have answers. Clinical trial methodology is the most effective way to evaluate the typology of likely benefits of home modification and assistive device use and discern who might benefit and how. Beneficial outcomes might be both immediate and distal. Proximal effects might include positive changes in person-environment transactions (e.g., improved home safety or enhanced efficiency of performance), improved behavioral competence (e.g., increased independence in self-care), and psychological well-being (e.g., improved mastery). More distal outcomes may include enhanced quality of life, satisfaction with staying in place, or delayed relocation to a residential setting.

Clinical trial methodologies need to be applied to the evaluation of new technological approaches such as Mann and colleagues new direction in research on the benefits and outcomes of home monitoring systems. Finally, clinical trial research should also involve the evaluation of multifactorial interventions, that is, multicomponent interventions in which home modification is one aspect. Given the complexity and multiple risk factors associated with living with chronic conditions, home modification in combination with other self-management strategies may be more beneficial than implementing modifications alone. Examining the relative contribution of home modification in combination with other treatment approaches would enhance its translation into health care delivery.

Related Clinical Trial Considerations

Related to the need for more intervention research is the importance of examining the mechanisms by which home modification and assistive device use evince positive outcomes (Gitlin et al., 2000). Questions need to be answered such as: Who benefits and why? Is early introduction of home modification following acute onset of a disabling condition preferable? If so, for whom? What are the barriers to successful device use for specific groups of elders (e.g., impairment groups, gender, race)? These questions reflect issues related to the underlying pathways by which a home modification or device intervention is effective. The answers to such questions are critical to the development and refinement of service delivery and for closing the research-service gap.

The task of developing and testing home modifications and new types of technologies for older people is indeed complex and involves multiple steps. Researchers must not only develop the viable technology or home modification service, but also must substantiate the theoretical base for the effectiveness of the technology or program, demonstrate its acceptability and compliance in use, its utility for older adults, caregivers, or health professionals; the specific anticipated outcomes, the training needs of the user, and its cost and cost-effectiveness.

Associated with the task of testing effectiveness is the need to develop a uniform and meaningful typology of the delivery characteristics of the full range of home modification and assistive technology strategies. Strategies may range in complexity in use (e.g., a simple reacher versus a voice activation system), training requirements, type of interface with the user (e.g., grab bars are placed in the physical environment whereas mobility aids are placed with the user), interface with health professionals (e.g, a computer monitoring system involves ongoing interaction, telephonic support may be intermittent interaction, whereas training in use of a stair glide may be brief and a one-time interaction), and the dimensions of daily life that are targeted (e.g., dressing, ambulating, meal preparation, safety monitoring). A typology of delivery characteristics would facilitate comparisons across strategy-type to obtain a refined understanding as to whether certain modification strategies are intrinsically more acceptable or result in better outcomes than others. Also, such a typology presents as an organizing framework from which to systematically develop intervention protocols that address each dimension.

Health Policy Research

Yet another gap in our knowledge and a necessary research direction is health policy research. Legislation such as the Technology Related Assistance for Individuals with Disabilities Act of 1988 (Tech Act, Public Law 100-407), and its reauthorization in 1994 (Public Law 103-218), represent an important source of funding for assistive technology information and referral services for older people. The Medicaid Waiver program enacted in 1981 as section 2176 of Omnibus Budget Reconciliation Act (OBRA), is an important source of funding for home modification services. Approximately 57% of the 234 waiver programs now include a home modification and device component. Nevertheless, despite legislative gains and the emergence of home modification programs, service delivery remains fragmented, inadequately funded, and unstandardized. Additionally, there is no single source of funding for obtaining modifications or assistive devices. Research that tracks service developments and health policy trends and compares home modification programs nationally can help inform best practices that lead to standardized care.

DEVICE USE IN REAL LIFE: PERSONAL VIGNETTES

I would like to conclude with two recent personal vignettes that occurred as I was writing this commentary and which illustrate enduring themes of device use. My 15-year-old son had a sports-related injury this past year resulting in two stress fractures in his lower back. He had to wear an uncomfortable brace to immobilize his back, upper hip and leg motion for 24 hours a day for 6 weeks. He had to limit stair climbing and walking. Initially, he was advised to not attend school since it did not have an elevator for his second floor classes, nor was he initially permitted to go to his bedroom in the third floor of our house. However, the medical staff adjusted their prescription given the consequences for his learning, social engagement and psychological well-being. Upon removal of the brace, he had six months of physical therapy rehabilitation (6 hours weekly) to strengthen his entire back and abdominal muscles and overcome significant de-conditioning. This injury dramatically changed his immediate world, particularly his self-identify as an athlete and independent teenager. His initial reaction to the diagnosis ("I am not a cripple") and the body brace was concern as to its visibility ("I'll wear the brace as long as no one can see it") despite the temporality of his situation. His cognitive readjustments, re-conceptualization of his identity, his felt sociocultural expectation for independence yet compliance to the medical regimen, and concern with peer evaluations were quite evident. He demonstrated insight, resilience, and adaptability as well as an altered life view ("I asked the school why they discriminate against kids in wheelchairs since they obviously can not attend school here"). Although this represented a very short disjuncture in a "normal" life, even here we see the need for biographical management to fully embrace device use. This may be an essential activity in the initial phase of device use even when the need is short-term (e.g., hip fracture patients).

My second story is about my mother, who had three broken bones in her foot this past year, and whose recovery took close to six months. In her mid-seventies, my mother is an extremely active person, in excellent health, who worked part-time at the time of the injury. To ambulate with her broken foot, she was issued a wheelchair and a walker rather than crutches due to balance concerns. She received four different wheelchairs, each of which was defective. It took over four weeks to receive the wheelchair that was appropriate for her. This meant missed days of work, an inability to continue with a meaningful and active social life, and confinement to her apartment. As a consequence of this abrupt change in capabilities, daily routines, and immediate life goals, my mother began to feel anxious. With this threat of loss to her independence, she developed and implemented immediate solutions including setting up a "control center" near her bed and a chair, rearranging furniture to enable her to cruise the apartment, and purchasing a bar stool to prepare meals at the kitchen counter. As she stated, these strategies offered "at least some sense of control." Despite the temporal nature of her confinement and decreased functionality, it had a profound effect on her well-being in that brief period.

With the arrival of a working wheelchair, new possibilities emerged. My 12-year-old son assisted my mother on her first out doors excursion in the wheelchair. He came home distressed because of the difficulties he encountered: "I almost tipped Grandmom. The streets are slanted; some streets have big curbs; sidewalks are under construction. We couldn't open doors to stores and we had to come home right away. How does anyone do this?"

Thus, regardless of the temporal or chronic nature of the disability or the age group, there are commonalties in the person-environment transactional challenges that present as a consequence of the limitations of the device design, physical environment, psychological profile and societal values. These brief vignettes are a reminder of the daily "small" struggles that cumulatively affect the life quality of older people with functional limitations.

CONCLUSION

In summation, research on home modification use needs to be enhanced through the application of theory, use of innovative and standardized measures, a more comprehensive understanding of its psychosocial benefits and costs, and clinical trial methodology to evaluate the multiple benefits of this approach. There is no doubt that home modification will emerge as a key component of long-term care in the United States. Its use will assume increasing importance as aging population trends advance and as we search for cost-effective strategies to manage functional disability. A continuation and expansion of research in this area is necessary at the descriptive, explanatory, and experimental levels to assure effective application of this intervention approach to a diverse population of older people.

REFERENCES

American Association of Retired Persons (AARP). (1990). *Demographics.* Washington, DC: Author.

Binstock, R. H., & Cluff, L. E. (2000). *Home care advances: Essential research and policy issues.* New York: Springer.

Evans, G. W. (1999). Measurement of the physical environment as stressor. In S. L. Friedman & T. D. Wachs (Eds.), *Measuring environment across the life span* (pp. 249–270). Washington, DC: American Psychological Association.

Gitlin, L. N. (1995). Why older people accept or reject assistive technology. *Generations,* 41–45.

Gitlin, L. N. (1998). From hospital to home: Individual variation in the experience with assistive devices among the elderly. In D. Gray, L. A. Quatrano, & M. L. Lieberman (Eds.), *Designing and using assistive technology: The human perspective* (pp. 117–136). Baltimore: Brookes.

Gitlin, L. N., Corcoran, M., Martindale-Adams, J., Malone, C., Stevens, A. & Winter, L. (2000). Identifying mechanisms of action: Why and how does intervention work? In Schulz (Ed.), *Handbook on dementia caregiving: Evidence-based interventions for family caregivers* (pp. 225–248). New York: Springer.

Gitlin, L. N., Corcoran, M. A., Winter, L., Boyce, A., & Hauck, W. W. (2001). A randomized, controlled trial of a home environmental intervention to enhance self-efficacy and reduce upset in family caregivers of persons with dementia. *The Gerontologist, 41,* 15–30.

Gitlin, L. N., Luborsky, M., & Schemm, R. L. (1998). Emerging concerns of older stroke patients about assistive device use. *The Gerontologist, 3,* 169–180.

Gitlin, L. N., Schemm, R. L., Landsberg, L., & Burgh, D. Y. (1996). Factors predicting assistive device use in the home by older persons following rehabilitation. *Journal of Aging and Health, 8*(4), 554–575.

Gitlin, L. N., Winter, L., Corcoran, M., Dennis, M., Schinfeld, S., & Hauck, W. (in press). Effects of the Home Environmental Skill-building Program on the Caregiver-Care Recipient Dyad: Six-month Outcomes from the Philadelphia REACH Initiative. *The Gerontologist.*

Iwarsson, S. & Isacsson, A. (1996). Development of a novel instrument for occupational therapy of assessment of the physical environment in the home: A methodologic study on "The Enabler." *The Occupational Therapy Journal of Research, 16,* 227–244.

Iwarsson, S., & Slaug, B. (2001). *Housing enabler. An instrument for assessing and analyzing accessibility problems in housing.* Lund, Sweden: Studentlitteratur.

Kaufert, J. M., Kaufert, P. A., & Locker, D. (1987). After the epidemic: The long-term impact of poliomyelitis. In D. Coburn (Eds.), *Health and Canadian Society* (pp. 345–362). Toronto: Fitzhenry.

LaPlante, M. P., Hendershot, G. E., & Moss, A. J. (1992). *Assistive technology devices and home accessibility features: Prevalence, payment and trends.* Hyattsville, MD: U.S. Department of Health and Human Services, 217. Advance Data No. 217.

Mann, K. J. (1997). The home as a framework for health care. *Disability and Rehabilitation, 19,* 128–129.

Mann, W. C. Hurren, D., Tomita, M., Bengali, M., & Steinfeld, E. (1994). Environmental problems in homes of elders with disabilities. *Occupation Therapy Journal of Research 14,* 191–211.

Mann, W. C., Ottenbacher, K. J., Fraas, L., Tomita, M., & Granger, C. V. (1999). Effectiveness of assistive technology and environmental interventions in maintaining independence and reducing home care costs for the frail elderly. *Archives of Family Medicine, 8,* 210–217.

Manton, K., Corder, L., & Stallard, E. (1997). Chronic disability trends in elderly United States populations: 1982–1994. *Proceedings of the National Academy of Sciences, 94,* 2593–2598.

Moss, M., & Lawton, M. P. (1982). Time budgets of older people: A window in four life styles. *Journal of Gerontology, 37,* 115–123.

National Center for Health Statistics. (2000, March 1). *An overview of nursing home facilities: Data from the 1997 National Nursing Home Survey.* Advance Data No. 311.

Norburn, J. E. K., Bernard, S. L., Konrad, T. R., Woomert, A., DeFriese, G. H., Kalsbeek, W. D., Koch, G. G., & Ory, M. G. (1995). Self-care and assistance from others in coping with functional status limitations among a national sample of older adults. *Journal of Gerontology: Social Sciences, 50B,* S101–S109.

Population Reference Bureau, (2002), Bulletin #2, Washington, DC.

Rubinstein, R. L. (1989). The home environments of older people: A description of the psychosocial processes linking person to place. *Journal of Gerontology, 44,* S45–S53.

Schulz, R., & Heckhausen, J. (1999). Aging, culture and control: Setting a new research agenda. *Journal of Gerontology: Psychological Sciences, 54B,* P139–P145.

United States Census Bureau. (1997). *American Housing Survey.* Washington: DC.

United States Census Bureau. (2000). Profiles of General Demographic characteristics: United States 2000, Census of Population and Housing, accessed online at *www.census.gov/prod/cen2000/index.html.*

Wahl, H.-W., & Gitlin, L. N. (2003). Future developments in living environments for older people in the U.S. and Germany: Potential and constraints. In K. W. Schaie, H.-W. Wahl, H. Mollenkopf, & F. Oswald (Eds.), *Aging in the community: Living arrangements and mobility* (pp. 281–301). New York: Springer.

Verbrugge, L. M., Rennert, C., & Madans, J. H. (1997). The great efficacy of personal and equipment assistance in reducing disability. *American Journal of Public Health, 87,* 384–392.

Commentary

Assistive Technology: Potential and Preconditions of Useful Applications

Heidrun Mollenkopf

W illiam Mann's chapter on Assistive Technology (AT, this volume) is examined with respect to three major issues. I begin with some comments on assistive devices that are currently available to address the impairments faced by frail elders and Mann's research in this area. Second, as a result of these observations, I pose several questions with respect to future research and development in this field. And finally, at a more general level, I reflect upon the question of how AT can improve independent living, quality of life, and self-awareness of older persons.

RESEARCH ON ASSISTIVE DEVICES FOR FRAIL ELDERS

It is known from earlier research, from exhibitions, experience, catalogues, and other publications that there are many assistive devices that have been developed to address the impairments faced by handicapped persons and frail elders. Technical aids offer a multitude of positive opportunities for the preservation of independence, mobility, and social participation, as well as for supporting people in need of care.

Assistance with everyday tasks for persons with failing strength is provided first of all by appropriate *household technology*. With the help of technical *communications equipment* such as traditional telephone or cell

203

phones, and with new interactive modes of video communication and e-mail, it is possible to ensure that a connection to the important people in one's life can be maintained at all times over long distances in spite of limited physical mobility. Internet access, multimedia, and information services, which are just beginning to show their potential, can be used to address presumed and real social deprivation in the lives of elders who live alone and can help to protect them from severe isolation. Safety-alarm systems provide the assurance that help can be obtained quickly in an emergency, and, in case of special impairments, electronic devices that perform speech synthesis and speech recognition serve to compensate for seeing and hearing handicaps.

The *mobility* of elderly people is supported by various technical means, such as private cars, buses and trains of the regional mass transport authorities, as well as by mobility aids that were developed for special function losses, such as different types of wheelchairs, stair lifts, and elevators for the handicapped. The private automobile plays an ever-greater role in maintaining mobility. In particular, the elderly individual whose physical strength is waning frequently requires a car to deal with everyday life (Mollenkopf, Marcellini, Ruoppila, & Tacken, 1999). Thanks to new intelligent systems, it will become even easier to traverse both small and great distances quickly and efficiently (Hanowski & Dingus, 2000; Küting, 1999). A multitude of technical aids are available for dealing with various limitations to mobility that range from the vague insecurity some elders feel when walking to the case of total immobility. Various solutions have been developed over the last few years in wheelchair technology. These advances have made it possible to provide an appropriate aid for every type of handicap. *Medical technologies and auxiliary devices,* special bathroom technology, nursing beds, and lifters help provide care for those with health impairments. With regard to *prevention,* medical screening and routine check-ups will become automatic, allowing the medical practitioner to make an early diagnosis without a personal consultation.

Thus, the adequate provision of assistive devices and systems seems to be a financial rather than a technical problem. However, surprisingly little systematic research has been done on the effectiveness and impact of these technologies, despite the general assumption that older people benefit from whatever type of assistive device is made available to them, and despite the obvious changes that the availability and use of technology can bring to their everyday lives (McWilliam, Diehl-Jones, Jutai, & Tadrissi, 2000). Moreover, few researchers have examined the consequences associated with assistive technology, such as changes in social relationships and the societal participation of older people.

Research on assistive technology and aging conducted at the Rehabilitation Engineering Research Center (RERC) on Aging is a notable exception. For the past ten years, the RERC has studied the needs of older persons with disabilities relative to assistive technology (AT) and the effectiveness of those technologies in a consistent, systematic way.

Findings

The findings from the Consumer Assessments Study (CAS) suggest that increased use of assistive devices is related to increased functional independence. Results also provide evidence that the devices used had more impact on the older people's ADLs than on their IADLs. While the first result is immediately apparent, an explanation of the second one is called for: What is it about the older user, or about the nature of assistive devices, that limits their effectiveness to ADLs?

Findings of further research on the "Effectiveness of Assistive Technology Devices (AT) and Environmental Interventions (EI) in Maintaining Independence in the Home-Based Elderly" showed that providing assistive technology and environmental modifications can (a) improve functional performance in older persons with physical and sensory impairments, (b) slow down the rate of decline, and (c) reduce the costs of institution-based health care. In this respect I think we should know more precisely what exactly made the difference between the special services and the technical interventions taken compared with traditional home care services in order to be able to draw conclusions on how these services would have to be improved.

Further research presented by Mann indicated that (a) substantial training is necessary to optimize the use of devices, (b) that older people often have no information on the availability of many types of assistive devices, and (c) that devices or particular features are not adequate for their needs. These are findings we have confirmed through our own research. Based on 100 comprehensive interviews with social experts, with experts in technology and with elderly people, we have investigated how technology—from commonly used everyday appliances to highly complex systems—can contribute to the preservation of an active and qualitatively satisfying lifestyle for the elderly and also for those with health impairments (Mollenkopf, 1994; Mollenkopf & Hampel, 1994).

Training

Older people often view technology with mistrust or they reject technologies that are unknown or unfamiliar to them. Their skepticism is, however, not simply directed against technological innovations and thus cannot be equated with a lack of acceptance of technology. It can definitely be overcome if the person is or can be motivated to use a technological innovation. The prerequisite for such an intervention is the experience or anticipation that a device can significantly contribute to one's quality of life by preserving mobility, assisting with communication, or helping to improve one's bodily well-being and thereby lessening burdens for the person providing care. In addition, ease of use, competent advising, and a supportive training program are decisive factors to device use; they can help to overcome initial cognitive, sensory, and/or motor-related difficulties. Merely providing a technical aid does not suffice; elderly people need encouragement and time to become familiar with the device. Therefore, the introduction of a new technology must always be tied to motivation strategies, with training and support.

Lack of Information

With regard to information on the current availability of assistive devices, we found that information about how to acquire assistive devices is the most important prerequisite for the use of technical aids, in particular if one's own funds do not suffice for the purchase of the device. The lack of information is shared by the potential users and by those who, personally or professionally, are concerned with the well-being of the elderly. In this regard, the institutional differentiation between ambulatory and stationary care as well as between the need for nursing care and the need for medical treatment, is critical (cf. Mayer et al., 1992). In Germany, a person is by definition either healthy, sick, or in need of nursing care, and different support systems are responsible in each case. In an acute emergency, older people are hopelessly overtaxed with the demands that face them, especially those who no longer have relatives or friends who are able to intercede for them. In the end, whether or not elders are able to obtain appropriate technical aids depends heavily on the knowledge and interest of doctors and nurses, the commitment of the people responsible at the health insurance or community offices, and the knowledge and perseverance of the elderly or their relatives. Added to this, access to technical devices is often made difficult by the fact that they are too complicated and difficult to use and that their use may come to symbolize a clear indication of old age and frailty. I will come back to the latter aspect.

The Ease of Use

With respect to the ease of use, problems emerge, especially when habitual behaviors have to be changed—when, for example, the indicators and activating elements of a new car or radio are designed and positioned somewhat differently than previously—or when courses of action are required that are totally new for the elderly, and thus connected with a fear of failure, as is the case with electronic communication aids. Altogether, however, assistive technology has been shown to be effective in reducing functional decline and health-related costs. New electronic products and systems promise an even greater potential for AT.

FUNCTIONAL EFFECTIVENESS IS NOT EVERYTHING

Up to now, the focus of research of the RERC has been limited to functional effectiveness, though, measured in terms of ADL/IADL and cost savings. In the face of changing demographics, this focus is most important. The changing demographics of modern society are well known: increased life expectancy combined with the trend toward living alone, a shrinking of the family network, and hence the family's diminishing potential to care for or otherwise support the elderly individual. There are further trends toward centralization and globalization among businesses today that create greater spatial dispersal of the work force from their home communities. As a consequence, parents and their adult children live further apart, leading in turn to the necessity of expanded care and support services for the vulnerable elderly.

In the European welfare states, too, demographic trends have become an issue, for example in the debate over retirement benefits and over the burden of providing for health services and long-term care. In this regard, technical aids promise to be a possible contribution toward dealing with present and future problems. In the case of failing strength and loss of bodily functions in old age, the technologies are instruments that replace functions or mitigate the loss of capabilities and thus support the independence of older people. Furthermore, technology can be used to compensate for the general lack of support that a family can provide to the chronically ill older individual. In Germany, this topic was taken up as early as the eighties by the Federal Ministry for Research and Technology with the grant concept "Research and Development for an Active Old Age," and in the European Union, the advent of substantial funding programs for joint European projects has led to a definite increase in research and development activity, as well as increased cooperation across national borders (Fagerberg, 2001).

The second issue I wish to address is that functional effectiveness is not everything. To preserve the quality of life in old age, a far wider perspective must be taken. In order to ensure that elderly people who suffer from impairments will use the positive opportunities of technical aids, and thus retain control over their destiny, it is necessary that these devices also fulfill the criteria of *social functionality*. The objectives Mann mentioned in regard to the ongoing and future projects of the RERC on home monitoring and communication technologies for successful aging already seem to bear this in mind. But as they have not been explained in detail in his chapter, I would like to address some aspects that are crucial for future research and development of assistive devices and systems.

QUESTIONS ABOUT FUTURE RESEARCH AND DEVELOPMENT

First, there is a *need for more data on the immediate person–technology interaction*. Dealing with a new PC, for instance, means that there will be a change of patterns of person-environment interchange. What exactly is different compared to the handling of traditional mechanical devices? Other questions are: What can we really expect from *PC use in the home?* What are the *effects* of such interventions? Don't we need further research to find the right measures and efficient ways for intervening and raising the acceptance levl for technology-related intervention? A corollary to this is the question of whether there is a need for a *disability-related approach,* or whether we should strive for a *universal design*. Is designing for old age the same as designing for the disabled? Do the findings gained for some specific assistive devices hold true in the same manner for all devices, for all types of impairments, and for all older people? Or do we have to differentiate between and within all of these groups?

While there are question marks after all of these issues, one statement can be taken for granted: To adapt assistive devices and systems to the needs of older people, a *link back from research to the developers and manufacturers* is a must. The results of objective, evaluative research conducted by neutral institutions should decidedly influence the development of future products. In this respect, the latest project of the RERC is based upon cooperation with relevant firms in the field. Therefore I would like to add to Mann's ovals a field that symbolizes mutual feedback (see Figure 4.2).

A second type of research that I think is needed concerns the *long-term effects and drawbacks* of the increased use of technology. We still do

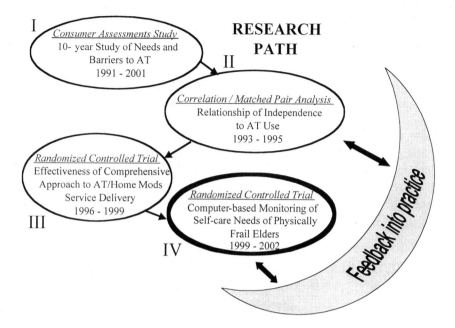

FIGURE 4.2   Link back from research to the developers and manufacturers.

not have a clear picture of what kind of difference the use of technology really makes in the everyday life of older people. Most often, for the sake of economy, only short-term data sets are generated. However, the proven, short-term benefits of technology can easily turn into disadvantages in the long run. For example, ordering services from a home computer may compensate quickly and very effectively for mobility impairment, but over time may lead to feelings of being out of touch with the everyday world. Home monitoring and new communication technologies in a "smart" home may become the ideal solution for solving practical everyday problems of frail elders, but may also stunt their remaining competencies. In most instances, we simply do not know how these technologies affect individuals and their emotional well-being and social connectedness as time goes by.

Even more difficult *ethical questions* must be raised concerning the application of computerized devices for assisting persons with cognitive impairments. Many new systems in the home, such as monitoring devices employed in the interests of improving the supervision of the mentally ill and ensuring their safety, "involve both environmental intrusion (equipment) and personal intrusion (the virtual presence of others) and thus the maintenance of personal control becomes very important" (Severs, 1999, p. 5). To some extent, such measures may lead to unjustified restriction and control, as, for instance, the infringement on the patient's rights of privacy and self-determination.

Thus, *the goal of research should be a broad set of scientific approaches,* revealing what kinds of technology are associated with which kinds of consequences in important life domains. Such consequences should include independence in daily activities and cost savings, but also social interactions, subjective well-being, and feelings of self-efficacy. Within such a holistic approach, it would also be useful to take the *social embeddedness of aging and technology* into account. I would like to briefly draw the attention to some cultural preconditions that are important for both the shaping and use of technical possibilities for preserving the quality of life of elderly people.

CULTURAL PRECONDITIONS FOR SHAPING AND USE OF TECHNOLOGY

With regard to their construction and function, technological constructions are socioculturally shaped artifacts (Bijker & Law, 1992). The question as to which options will be generated, selected, or eliminated is dependent on the societal and cultural context that the crucial actors are tied into. The last assumption becomes particularly salient when a certain technology or technology user is associated with aspects that are societally desirable or undesirable. A combination of different aspects is conceivable in regard to the technology for the elderly that is being discussed here, as both—old age and technology—can be connected with very positive and very negative models and values. Thus, on the one hand, technology is considered to be *the* symbol for progress and modernity. On the other hand, it can be considered as an expression of human inadequacy, as a prosthesis. To attain old age is considered to be something that is societally and individually worth striving for. Being old, on the other hand, is often equated with being no longer young and thus no longer physically and mentally competent. These societal stereotypes influence, on the one hand, the development and design of technologies, and the acceptance or rejection of their potential users, on the other (see Figure 4.3).

The result is a gap between devices that are produced and offered universally for all age groups and those that can be grouped under the term "rehabilitation aids" or assistive technologies. Thus, manufacturers of technology are caught in a double-bind: In the first case, they avoid the social exclusion of the older people. In the second, the direct

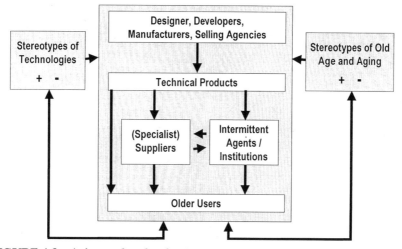

FIGURE 4.3   Aging and technology.

involvement of users in the development and adaptation of the devices, as well as the frequent personal commitment expressed by the producers, has a positive effect on the usability of the technology. At the same time, however, precisely by emphasizing either the "universal" or the "assistive" aspects of the different types of technology, those people who are not able to use the first type but are dependent upon a special technical aid may feel excluded from the rest.

Societal stereotypes of old age and technology manifest themselves also at the level of *individual attitudes* and thus influence the success or failure of their use. Many older people feel technical aids to be a stigma, a personal affront. In contrast to "normal" technology, which is connected with the image of modernity and efficiency, they are an unmistakable reference to increasing weaknesses and failing strength. Unlike people who have had to adjust to a handicap all their lives, or, as is the case with younger people who suffered an injury in an accident and could replace certain bodily functions through technology, the purchase of a device identifies them as handicapped people, and that is something no one wants to be. This outcome may change, however, with the implementation of modern communication technologies that are still associated with being "young" and "hip."

REFLECTIONS AND CONCLUSIONS

Let me conclude with a few thoughts on what AT and systems mean for independent living, quality of life, and the self-awareness of older people. The fact that technical devices can objectively be an assistance for dealing with everyday requirements, that they contribute to expanding mobility and maintaining communication over long distances and thus expand the life space of elderly people, is undisputed. Growing old and frail is not a pleasure, but technical aids could be helpful by compensating for impairments emerging in the aging process. What is missing is a general acceptance of the fact that aging is a totally normal process. Impairments of differing degrees of severity can occur for which there are different possibilities for obtaining relief, so that a convergence of the extremes of the so-called "young technology" and "technology for the handicapped" could be achieved via a multitude of interim solutions. This convergence would allow people of all ages to resort to technical aids at the proper time and without fear of discrimination, as has long been the case for visual aids.

Based upon advances in modern engineering that decrease the size and increase the sensitivity of sensors and that increase the amount of information stored on chips, biotechnology seems destined to lose its prosthetic nature: it will no longer be viewed as a replacement for a missing body part or a means of compensation for a particular deficiency. Rather, sensors can and will be implanted in the human organism and be directly connected to nerve cells, using microelectronic technology. The distinction between *natural and technological* will become blurred, as will the distinctions between *health and illness,* between the *individual* as subject, with his or her own body and identity, and *technology* as an object separate from the individual.

Thanks to those advances in technological development, the distinction between *autonomy and dependency* (or need for support) may be based upon new criteria, but it will still continue to exist. The proliferation of new technologies will require new skills and abilities. The competent use of such technologies can strengthen the self-confidence and self-efficacy of everyone, including the frail and sensory or mobility impaired elderly. But the growing palette of skills necessary to deal with those devices and systems may well create even larger rifts between the technologically competent and rich and the technologically illiterate and poor.

In addition, *technology will not be able to remediate everything,* nor will it be able to compensate for all kinds of deficits. First, there will be certain deficits that technology will be unable to support, and second, technology will not only create new opportunities, but also new fears and feelings of dependency (for instance, when systems crash). Technology has enormous—and hardly foreseeable—potential for improving how people age even under trying circumstances. The application of technology reduces physical hardship, provides practical solutions to the daily grind, and compensates for age-related limitations. New electronic devices and systems offer considerable benefits, especially with regard to aging individuals and to people with physical disabilities, and they might also be capable of improving the quality of life of people with cognitive impairments. At the same time, their application clearly increases a *new reliance—and thus a dependency—upon technology and the dangers of isolation and surveillance in a modern hermitage.*

Technologies have rich potential for directly and tangibly improving one's quality of life, regardless of the impairment in question. But all of the advantages and opportunities afforded us by new technologies will not prevent our growing old and frail, and it would be completely false to assert that a critical life event—such as, for instance, the irreversible loss of visual capacity in advanced age—could be remedied by some form of technology in the foreseeable future. By contrast, the focus on the apparently unlimited possibilities afforded by new technologies and systems might keep all of us who are growing older from the search for meaning in life, from the responsibility of actively shaping our old age (regardless of biological predisposition), and, finally, from preparing for the end of our lives.

REFERENCES

Bijker, W. E., & Law, J. (1992). *Shaping technology/building society: Studies in sociotechnical charge.* Cambridge, MA: MIT Press.

Fagerberg, G. (2001, September). *Technology and older people: Research and development in Europe.* Paper presented at the International Conference on Technology and Aging, Toronto.

Hanowski, R. J., & Dingus, T. A. (2000). Will intelligent transportation systems improve older driver mobility? In K. W. Schaie & M. Pietrucha (Eds.), *Mobility and transportation in the elderly* (pp. 279–298). New York: Springer.

Küting, H. J. (1999). Supporting mobility of the elderly by means of safe and comfortable cars. In M. Tacken, F. Marcellini, H. Mollenkopf, & I. Ruoppila (Eds.), *Keeping the elderly mobile: Outdoor mobility of the elderly: Problems and solutions* (pp. 293–299). Delft, The Netherlands: Delft University Press.

Mayer, K. U., Baltes, P. B., Gerok, W., Hafner, H., Helmchen, H., Kruse, A., Mittelstrass, J., Staudinger, U. M., Steinhagen-Thiessen, E., & Wagner, G. (1992). Gesellschaft, Politik und Altern [Society, politics, and aging]. In P. B. Baltes & J. Mittelstraß (Eds.), *Zukunft des Alterns und gesellschaftliche Entwicklung [The future of aging and societal development]* (pp. 721–757). Berlin/New York: de Gruyter.

McWilliam, C. L., Diehl-Jones, W. L., Jutai, J., & Tadrissi, S. (2000). Care delivery approaches and seniors' independence. *Canadian Journal on Aging/La Revue canadienne du vieillissement, 19*(Suppl. 1), 101–124.

Mollenkopf, H. (1994). Technical aids in old age—Between acceptance and rejection. In C. Wild & A. Kirschner (Eds.), *Technology for the elderly: Safety-alarm systems, technical aids and smart homes* (pp. 81–100). Knegsel, The Netherlands: Akontes.

Mollenkopf, H., & Hampel, J. (1994). *Technik, Alter, Lebensqualität* [Technology, old age, and quality of life]. Schriftenreihe des Bundesministeriums für Familie und Senioren, Band 23. Stuttgart, Germany: Kohlhammer.

Mollenkopf, H., Marcellini, F., Ruoppila, I., & Tacken, M. (1999). A comparative investigation into the mobility of elderly people: The project "Keeping the Elderly Mobile—Technology to Meet Their Outdoor Mobility Needs." In M. Tacken, F. Marcellini, H. Mollenkopf, & I. Ruoppila (Eds.), *Keeping the elderly mobile: Outdoor mobility of the elderly: Problems and solutions* (pp. 33–42). Delft, The Netherlands: Delft University Press.

Severs, M. (1999). Will the information technology revolution improve services to elderly people in the new millennium? *Age and Ageing, 28-SI,* 5–9.

CHAPTER 5

Impact of Everyday Technology in the Home Environment on Older Adults' Quality of Life

Hans-Werner Wahl and Heidrun Mollenkopf

The topic of aging and technology is *en vogue*. This chapter addresses one specific aspect of the relationship of aging and technology, that of its role in the home environment (see also Fisk & Rogers, 1997; Gutman, 1998a; Mollenkopf, Mix, Gäng, & Kwon, 2001). A number of time-budget–oriented studies have shown that the home environment is the setting of primary importance to aging individuals (e.g., M. Baltes, Maas, Wilms, & Borchelt, 1999; M. Baltes, Wahl, & Schmid-Furstoss, 1990; Moss & Lawton, 1982). The "technicalization" (technological retrofitting) of the home environment, a major expression of the cultural development of Western (industrialized) societies (Rybczynski, 1987) has therefore affected the daily lives of older persons, although more slowly than compared with the general population.

We consider primarily the evolution and outcome of what might be called the "rearmament" of the home using *everyday technology* ("Alltagstechnik"; see Mollenkopf et al., 2001) as it affects older persons. Our focus will be on classic household technology (such as washing machines, dishwashers, or central heating) as well as on "old" and "new" information, communication, and entertainment technology (such as the telephone, video cassette recorders, or the personal computer), all of which are able to facilitate activities of daily living within the home as well as enrich the older person's quality of life in general. Not much attention will be given to the latest technological developments, such as intelligent housing or robotics (e.g., Engelhardt & Goughler, 1997; Meyer & Mollenkopf, 2003) since these innovations are unlikely to be typical household amenities of older adults. We also limit this paper to individual home settings and therefore exclude institutional living environments or other variants of sheltered housing (e.g., Gutman, 1998b) or public technologies, such as automatic teller or ticket machines (e.g., Marcellini, Mollenkopf, Spazzafumo, & Ruoppila, 2000; Rogers, Cabrera, Walker, Gilbert, & Fisk, 1996). Neither will we discuss explicitly the role of assistive devices in the home (see Mann, this volume). Hence, our focus is primarily on *normal aging* and less so on aging with chronic conditions and disease.

We have tried to balance empirical and conceptual findings from the perspectives of psychology and sociology (since one of the authors [HWW] is a psychologist and one [HM] a sociologist). With respect to empirical research, we refer to data from an ongoing German panel data set, the so-called "Socio-economic Panel" (Sozio-oekonomisches Panel, SOEP Group, 2001) as well as to data from a survey gathered within the interdisciplinary research project "Everyday Technologies for Senior Households" (German title: "Seniorengerechte Technik im häuslichen Alltag" abbreviated as *sentha;* Mollenkopf, Meyer, Schulze, Wurm, & Friesdorf, 2000). In terms of conceptual issues, we draw upon person-environment approaches located at the micro- (e.g., psychology, design) as well as macro- (e.g., sociology, social policy) levels of analysis (Lesnoff-Caravaglia, 1988; Scheidt & Windley, 1998; Wahl, 2001).

This chapter is organized around four topics: (1) What main historical trajectories can be differentiated in Western (industrialized) countries with respect to everyday technology in the home environment of older persons? (2) What kind of impact has everyday technology in the home environment had on the daily lives of older people in a historical perspective? Or, to put it simply: Has daily life in old age become "better" due to the technological improvements of the home over the years? (3) What is the current state of everyday technology in home environments of older households? What needs of older persons are or are not met by technological advances? And, does technology now available have negative consequences for the well-being of older persons? (4) What kind of conceptual approaches have been used to understand older persons' interactions with everyday technology in their home environment and what are the further challenges for theory and research?

We are well aware that these are broad and complex questions and that our treatment must therefore be selective and tentative in character.

Nonetheless, we hope we will stimulate discussion and help formulate new and alternate approaches (see chapters of Scheidt and Gutman in this volume).

LIVING ENVIRONMENTS OF OLDER PEOPLE AND EVERYDAY TECHNOLOGY IN INDUSTRIALIZED COUNTRIES: MAIN TRAJECTORIES FRAMED WITHIN A HISTORICAL PERSPECTIVE

The relation among society, culture, and technology is a classic issue in the social sciences that frequently draws upon the concept of the human individual as a "Biologisches Mängelwesen" (biological incomplete being), as described by the German anthropologist Arnold Gehlen (1956). Interestingly enough, Paul Baltes and Jaqui Smith (1999) have recently argued that old age, and particularly the condition of the oldest old (beyond age 80 to 85 years), may be interpreted as an extreme form of the human condition of being a "Biologisches Mängelwesen." Hence, human creativity plays a critical role in overcoming human incompleteness, prototypically by use of technology, particularly in the old and very old in terms of "declining the decline" (Baltes & Smith, 1999, p. 159; Lesnoff-Caravaglia, 1988). However, everyday technology in the home has only recently been given attention with respect to older adults, and is currently addressed by the field of "Gerontechnology" (Vercruyssen, Graafmans, Fozard, Bouma, & Rietsema, 1996).

From a historical perspective, household technology has lagged behind the general industrial technological revolution. The latter took place around the middle of the nineteenth century, while widespread use of technology in the individual home setting ("household revolution") occurred only in the second half of the twentieth century in industrialized societies (Sackmann & Weymann, 1994). However, North American treatises on "Planning the Efficient Home," "The New Housekeeping," or "Management in the Home" date back to the early part of the twentieth century, mostly written by what were then called "domestic engineers" or "household engineers" (Rybczynski, 1987). The driving factor behind these developments was the use of low cost electricity after its broad introduction as early as the beginning of the 1880s in sewing machines (1889), vacuum cleaners (1901), electric irons (1909), fans (1910) and not much later in toasters, coffee percolators, hot plates, and cookers (Rybczynski, 1987). Since the early 1980s, digitalization has also entered the home technology domain in devices such as microwave ovens, video cassette recorders, personal computers, and the so-called intelligent control of classic home devices such as cooking stoves, washing machines, and telephones.

Table 5.1 illustrates the historical development of household technology. Today, most of the devices listed may be regarded as essentials to any home. In addition, this table gives tentative data on the current availability of these devices in elderly households in North America and Germany, to provide general background information for this chapter. This information supports the notion that classic household devices such as the telephone, television, washing machine, and dishwasher had already been invented and developed toward serial production by the end of the nineteenth century or during the first two decades of the twentieth century. As can also be seen in Table 5.1, practically all elderly households, both in North America and Germany, currently enjoy basic items of home technology such as radio, television, refrigerator, and telephone. Also, at least half of elderly households are equipped with central heating, a washing machine, and air conditioning in the United States. Items found in fewer than 50% of today's elderly households include dishwashers, microwave ovens, and personal computers. One should also mention here that the households of older people, apart from basic household technology items, tend to have fewer common technology devices than the average population in Germany and America (Sackmann & Weymann, 1994).

Obviously, information of the kind provided in Table 5.1 is very general and does not inform us about the use or non-use of technology, user needs and fears, or life quality aspects related to home technology in later life. Common sense tells us, for instance, that the introduction of technological devices such as a washing machine or a telephone should have had positive impact on the daily lives of people by reducing the burden of several ADL/IADL tasks or by enriching social exchange. One might even argue that such an effect was particularly important for older adults because of the age-related decline in competencies and the concomitant risk of social isolation, role losses (especially professional roles), and critical life events in the social domain (especially the death of a spouse). On the other hand, we know that rational reasons have seldom been the only basis for purchasing technical devices. In Germany, for example, television and the washing machine became available at about the same time in the 1950s. The washing machine would have been most useful for decreasing the work load of women, most of all for working mothers. Nevertheless, it was the TV that was diffused far more rapidly throughout German households. A similar phenomenon occurred about 20 years later when

TABLE 5.1 Prevalence of Selected Items of Everyday Technology in the Home in a Historical Perspective

Kind of technology	Availability for serial production in terms of technology development[a]	Availability in a substantial portion of households in America (A) and Germany (G)[a]	Availability in current elderly households (65+) in America (A) and Germany (G)
Radio	1890s	1940s in A and G	Nearly 100% in A and G
TV	1920s	1950s in A, 1960s in G	Nearly 100% in A and G
Refrigerator	1910s	19650s in A, 1960s in G	Nearly 100% in A and G
Telephone	1870s	1930s in A, 19650s in G	A: around 95%[b] G: around 95%[c]
Central Heating	1880s	1930s in A, 1950s in G	A: around 60%[b] G: around 80%[c]
Air Conditioning	1940s (not fan-based)	1950s (only A)	A: around 70%[b] G: ?
Washing Machine	1910s	1950s in A, 1960 in G	A: around 80%[b] G: around 90%[c]

(continued)

TABLE 5.1   Prevalence of Selected Items of Everyday Technology in the Home in a Historical Perspective (*Continued*)

Kind of technology	Availability for serial production in terms of technology development[a]	Availability in a substantial portion of households in America (A) and Germany (G)[a]	Availability in current elderly households (65+) in America (A) and Germany (G)
Dishwasher	1920s	1970s in A, 1980 in G	A: around 40%[b] G: around 30%[c]
Microwave Oven	1960s	1970s in A, 1980s in G	A: around 40%[b] G: around 30%[c]
Video Cassette Recorder	1960s	1980s in A, 1980s in G	A: around 50%[d] G: around 40%[c]
Personal Computer	1970s	1980s in A, 1990s in G	A: around 24%[e] G: around 10%[c]

Notes:

[a] Based on Rybczynski, 1987; Sackmann & Weymann, 1994; and an according Internet search.

[b] Based on U.S. Bureau of the Census (1996) (housing-related data from survey 1991).

[c] Based on our own calculations from the Socio-economic Panel (data from 1998; SOEP Group, 2001).

[d] We were not able to identify recent percentages for these items; thus, as a very rough estimate, we added 10% to the German percentages based on the assumption that the United States generally tends to be somewhat ahead of Germany in terms of advanced household technology.

[e] Based on data (August 2000) from the U.S. Census Bureau (www.census.gov/prod/2001pubs/p23-207.pdf).

families could choose between the dishwasher and the video cassette recorder (VCR). It was then that the VCR became a popular household appliance (Hampel, Mollenkopf, Weber, & Zapf, 1991; Meyer & Schulze, 1989). Observations like these tell us something about the relative value of entertainment and communication versus work reduction, as well as whose desires tend to be first served in the family. When discussing the advantages technology might provide for the elderly, one must therefore take into account variables such as social structure and individual coping strategies, marital power and personal interests, and individual attitudes and societal trends. Let us consider then whether everyday technology—apart from the obvious complex mix of reasons to buy and use technology—has actually improved the life of older persons.

THE IMPACT OF EVERYDAY TECHNOLOGY IN HOME ENVIRONMENTS ON OLDER PEOPLE'S LIFE QUALITY OR: HAS LIFE IN LATE ADULTHOOD BECOME "BETTER" DUE TO TECHNOLOGY?

Ideally, data on sequential cohorts are needed in order to draw conclusions about the evolutionary trends in home technology in general or the use of a specific device (such as the telephone) to determine how it affects outcomes such as everyday competence, leisure use, social integration, or life satisfaction. Surprisingly or not, such data are hard to find. For example, we were unable to find data on the availability of a telephone in older persons' households since the 1950s, and its influence on social exchange patterns, social isolation, or feelings of social integration. Moreover, there is little data available that would make it possible to address the question of how the use of the telephone by older adults has changed across the years, for example, in terms of arranging leisure time events, ordering goods, gathering all kinds of information, or buying airplane tickets.

The Socio-economic Panel (SOEP Group, 2001), a panel data-set collected in Germany in regular waves since 1984, can be used to tentatively address issues such as the ones mentioned above. We have used this public domain data set in the following way for a secondary data analysis. First, we have taken advantage of the fact that the availability of a set of everyday technology items has been included in the measurement program, albeit with slightly different items and at different measurement points since the beginning of the nineties. We selected two measurement waves for analysis, namely the year 1993, when a question regarding the availability of a personal computer (PC) was first included, and the year 1998, when the availability of a PC was again included and additional "new" household technology items such as a microwave oven, video cassette recorder, and dishwasher were also assessed. Second, we selected three outcomes of home-related life quality as dependent variables that were measured in the SOEP by means of one-item scales: residential satisfaction, a classic indicator of place-related life quality (e.g., Carp & Christensen, 1986); satisfaction with leisure; and general life satisfaction. Third, we controlled in each of the analyses for additional variables with theoretically expected influence on these outcomes, namely age, gender, east-west (that is living in the "old" versus "new" German states), household composition, household income per head, and subjective health. Secondary data analyses always possess some measure of uncontrollability due to the design and collection of these data by others. Furthermore, the relatively large sample size, which in our case is roughly $N = 1,500$ persons over 65 years (1993) and $N = 1,870$ persons over 65 years (1998), depending on the proportion of missing data, capitalizes on random statistical significance. Thus, we decided to follow a rather conservative testing strategy in that an effect must fulfill six criteria in order to be interpretable: it must be significant on the $p < .05$ level in the total weighted data set, in two weighted subsample cross validations as well as in the total unweighted data set and again in two unweighted subsample cross validations.

Results based on General Linear Model analyses (procedure GLM of SAS, SAS Institute Inc., 1993) are presented in Tables 5.2 (1993 data) and 5.3 (1998 data). These analyses examined as well the interaction of household technology items with household composition (living alone vs. living not alone). We also ran analyses taking into account the interaction with gender (not shown). As can be seen in these tables, only one everyday technology item revealed a consistent effect in both 1993 and 1998 and only with respect to residential satisfaction, namely the availability of central heating. No consistent effects were found for all remaining main effects including interactions; this was also true for the interactions with gender. Of the additional control variables, only subjective health had a consistent effect across measurement time and all three outcomes. Moreover, income had a consistent effect on general life satisfaction in 1993 and 1998, while an effect on residential satisfaction was observed only in the 1998 data set.

We interpret these results to mean that among the everyday technology items chosen for analysis, only central heating showed a significant effect on at least one of the three outcomes, namely residential

TABLE 5.2 Effects of Selected Everyday Technology Items on Residential Satisfaction (RS), Satisfaction with Leisure (SL), and General Life Satisfaction (GLS) in 1993

	RS	SL	GLS
Telephone (T)	A		A B
Personal Computer (PC)		E	
Washing Machine (WM)			
Television (TV)	B	F	
Freezer Cabinet (FC)	A C D F		
Central Heating (CH)	A B C D E F		A B
T X Househ. Comp. (HC)	A B		
PC X HC			
WM X HC			
TV X HC	A B D E		A C D F
FC X HC	A D E		
CH X HC	A B D E		

Notes:

Data set of the Socio-economic Panel (SOEP Group, 2001); included are only persons 65 and older; $N \approx 1,500$, depending on missing values.

A: Significant effect ($p < .05$) in total sample (weighted)

B: Significant effect ($p < .05$) in cross validation subsample 1 (weighted)

C: Significant effect ($p < .05$) in cross validation subsample 2 (weighted)

D: Significant effect ($p < .05$) in total sample (unweighted)

E: Significant effect ($p < .05$) in cross validation subsample 1 (unweighted)

F: Significant effect ($p < .05$) in cross validation subsample 2 (unweighted)

TABLE 5.3   Effects of Selected Everyday Technology Items on Residential Satisfaction (RS), Satisfaction with Leisure (SL), and General Life Satisfaction (GLS) in 1998

	RS	SL	GLS
Telephone (T)	A B D		A B D E
Personal Computer (PC)			C
Washing Machine (WM)			C
Television (TV)	A		C
Central Heating (CH)	A B C D E F	B C E	
Microwave Oven (MW)	B C		
Video Cassette Recorder (VCR)	C D E	A C	F
Dishwasher (DW)	A C E	A B C	A C D E
T X Househ. Comp. (HC)		A B E	A
PC X HC	A C	A B C	A C
WM X HC			
TV X HC			
CH X HC	A	A	E
MW X HC		B D E	
VCR X HC	B	A B	C
DW X HC		A B	

Notes:

Data set of the Socio-economic Panel (SOEP Group, 2001); included are only persons 65 and older; $N \approx 1{,}870$, depending on missing values. The item "Freezer Cabinet" was not included in the 1998 data set.

A: Significant effect ($p < .05$) in total sample (weighted)
B: Significant effect ($p < .05$) in cross validation subsample 1 (weighted)
C: Significant effect ($p < .05$) in cross validation subsample 2 (weighted)
D: Significant effect ($p < .05$) in total sample (unweighted)
E: Significant effect ($p < .05$) in cross validation subsample 1 (unweighted)
F: Significant effect ($p < .05$) in cross validation subsample 2 (unweighted)

satisfaction (with the availability of central heating associated with higher residential satisfaction), after adjusting for additional control variables. Second, three new variables in the 1998 measurement wave—the availability of a microwave, video cassette recorder, and dishwasher—did not consistently help explain any of the three outcomes. Third, neither the interaction of everyday technology with household composition nor with gender revealed a consistent empirical impact. Fourth, additional control variables showed a rather consistent influence in accordance with the literature on these three outcomes, while the geographic region (East versus West Germany) did not play a role. The latter finding is remarkable because differences to the disadvantage of elders from East Germany have been reported in earlier work, but usually were limited to univariate analyses (BMFSFJ, 1998). In sum, by taking advantage of the SOEP as one of the rare data sets that allow tests of the relations between everyday technology devices at different occasions in time in conjunction with home-related outcomes, it can be shown that a significant impact of everyday technology on satisfaction with different life domains of older adults does not seem to exist (with the exception of central heating). However, such a relationship might still be found with respect to behavioral outcomes of life quality such as fine-tuned ADL or IADL performance measures. These variables are hard to measure in large data-sets, such as the one presently employed, but can be approached in in-depth studies (e.g., Mollenkopf, 1994; see also below).

EVERYDAY TECHNOLOGY IN THE HOMES OF OLDER PEOPLE: POTENTIAL, FULFILLED AND UNMET NEEDS, FEARS, AND USER FRIENDLINESS

Empirical literature addressing the role of technology in older persons' households has accumulated over the past 20 years. In historical perspective, human factors approaches were among the first research efforts that explicitly addressed the interactions of older adults with their technological home environments (see, for example, Charness & Bosman, 1990; Faletti, 1984). Meanwhile, the body of available knowledge targeting the normal aging process and everyday technology has been substantial. To provide an overview of this rapidly growing literature it may be helpful to differentiate between older adults' attitudes toward technology, the role of technology in the classic ADL/IADL domains, and issues related to the use and potential of "new" technologies such as the personal computer and/or the Internet.

Attitudes Toward Technology

There is converging evidence that older adults are neither "ene-mies" of technology nor uncritical users of technological innova-tions. For example, data from the interdisciplinary research project entitled "Everyday Technologies for Senior Households" (*sentha;* Mollenkopf et al., 2000) present a multifaceted picture. The repre-sentative survey, conceived by the social sciences team of *sentha* and conducted in 1999, included a sample of 1,417 men and women aged 55 years and older, stratified by age (55–64 years, 65–74 years, and 75 years and older) and gender, and living in private households in eastern and western Germany. The questionnaire included different domains of housing, housework, information and entertainment, communication and social relations, health care, safety, and mobili-ty in the home.

Demographic aspects, psychological scales, and attitudes toward technology were also assessed. Factor analysis based on a set of items representing various aspects of the general acceptance of technology suggested two dimensions of attitudes: the first included cognitive-rational aspects of technology (e.g., "Technological progress is neces-sary and therefore one has to accept some inevitable disadvantages.") while the second one included emotional-affective aspects of technol-ogy (e.g., "Technology is more a threat than a benefit to people."). The combination of these two dimensions of acceptance resulted in four types of older people's relation to technology, namely (1) the positive advocates of technology, (2) the rationally adapting, (3) the skeptical and ambivalent, and (4) those critical and reserved with respect to tech-nology. As can be seen in Figure 5.1, these four types were distributed roughly equally across the *sentha*-sample with the most positively accept-ing respondents constituting the largest group (28.5%). Within the four types there were no significant gender differences. Age differences were not found in the two mixed types ("rationally adapting" and "skep-tical/ambivalent"), but among the positive advocates the share of the "younger old" is significantly greater (55–64 years old: 42.5%) than the share of the older and old-old (65–74 years old: 40.9%; 75 and older: 16.6%; $p < .01$). The critical consist mainly of men and women aged 65 to 74 (55–64 years old: 27.1%; 65–74 years old: 45.6%; 75 and older: 27.3%; $p < .01$). Persons of higher education can be found significantly more often among the positive advocates of technology (44.7%) and persons of lower education most often are rationally adapting (25.5%) and critical (25.9%).

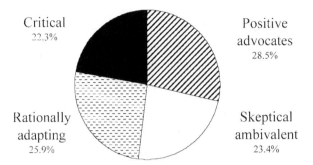

FIGURE 5.1   **Types of technology acceptance (database:** *sentha* **survey 1999,** *N* = **1,417).**

Everyday Technology in the Home Environment and Day-to-Day Competence

Psychological studies and human factors research have probably contributed most to understanding ongoing person-environment dynamics within the home and to the interactions of older adults' behavioral competence in the ADL/IADL domain with existing technological environmental features (for reviews, see Charness & Bosman, 1990; Fisk & Rogers, 1997). Focus group analysis, survey research, and experimental studies all indicate a rather complex picture: Age-related motor, visual, auditory, and cognitive limitations influence the use of technological devices in old age (Fisk & Rogers, 1997). However their influence is probably weaker in the home setting, where, compared to out-of-home environments, adaptations developed across many years have usually led to a variety of efficient compensations (Wahl, Oswald, & Zimprich, 1999). Furthermore, the individual home setting offers training opportunities and socially favorable conditions including no fear of crime or time pressure (see Rogers, Meyer, Walker, & Fisk, 1998). On the other hand, some technological devices frequently used in the home seem to challenge older adults more than younger adults. An example in this regard would be the telephone menus widely used in the United States and increasingly in other industrialized countries as well.

Another aspect of the person-environment and person-technology dynamics of older adults at home is the substantial amount of time (about one third of waking time) allocated to ADL and IADL performance, with correspondingly more time devoted to these tasks by old-old individuals (M. Baltes et al., 1990, 1999; Moss & Lawton, 1982).

The role of home technology in supporting such activities is obvious, especially in regard to bathing, cleaning, cooking, and medication (Park & Jones, 1997). Television is extensively used by older persons throughout the day as a major source of leisure time activity and as compensation for reduced social interactions (almost four hours a day, on average). It is critical, therefore, to enhance the optimal use of television (including the remote control) through efficient design for elders at all levels of competence (Czaja, 1997).

New communication technologies that rely on the personal computer, e-mail software, and many other Internet services might really lead to a "secondary household revolution" for persons of all ages. For older persons, the blurred distinction between the communication potential of the "inside" and "outside" world (be it for social purposes or for obligatory ADL and IADL arrangements) will change the meaning of home in dramatic ways. For example, staying at home will no longer imply sociophysical isolation because many types of information exchange are possible via the Internet. However, most of this information is still based primarily on auditory and visual "text," and tactile communication is not yet available in most applications. This is unfortunate because access to and use of "text" is particularly prone to sensory and cognitive limitations (Charness, 2001). However, training seems to hold promise for improving the competence of older adults with regard to their use of the Internet and personal computers (see also Czaja & Lee, 2001).

Experiences, Fears, User Needs, and Predictors of Technology's Availability

There are additional findings from *sentha* that may be relevant to these issues. Our objective is twofold: First, we present findings as reported by older adults that describe the nature of experiences, fears, and desire for simplification of the handling of technological devices. Second, we address the question of what best predicts the availability of technological items in the households of older adults.

As illustrated in Table 5.4, bad experiences with household appliances were reported by a maximum of about 13% of persons aged 55 and older, particularly by the owners of pressure cookers, microwave ovens, stoves, irons, ladders, and washing machines. Fears were found primarily among owners of pressure cookers (13.5%) and ladders (12.3%). The need for simplification of use was expressed most often with regard to the pressure cooker (10.9%), the microwave (10.3%), and the washing machine (10.7%).

TABLE 5.4   Household Technology: Availability, Experiences, Fears, and Need for Simplification of Use Reported by Older Persons

Device	Availability (%)	Bad experiences (%)	Fears (%)	Need for simplification of use (%)
Stove	100.0	10.1	6.0	4.6
Oven	97.2	9.3	3.7	4.0
Microwave Oven	51.7	12.7	8.0	10.3
Pressure Cooker	56.9	13.2	13.5	10.9
Dishwasher	39.9	5.9	1.9	2.4
Freezer	93.4	1.8	0.6	0.7
Electric Mixing Spoon	81.6	3.1	1.7	1.7
Food Processor	63.4	4.7	4.0	9.3
Coffee Machine	94.5	4.6	1.3	1.3
Washing Machine	98.0	9.3	7.5	10.7
Dryer	31.0	3.9	2.1	4.1
Vacuum Cleaner	99.7	3.3	0.3	1.5
Iron	99.7	9.8	5.8	2.4
Ladder	93.1	9.5	12.3	1.6

Note: Database: *sentha* survey 1999; N (total) = 1,417; all relative frequencies are weighted due to the three age groups (55–64, 65–74, 75+) used in the *sentha* sample as stratification criteria. Percentages with respect to bad experiences, fears, and need for simplification of use refer only to those who own the device in question.

Compared to the relatively infrequent problems related to household technology, electronic communication and entertainment devices raise many more problems for their users (Table 5.5). Nevertheless, of the 15 appliances examined, few devices yielded bad experiences for more than 10% of their users; the exceptions were the video cassette recorder (15.8%) and the TV set (12%). New technologies such as the computer, modem, and video cassette recorder are perceived as daunting for nearly every fifth older owner of such a device, and in nine out of 15 technological devices assessed, 10% or more of the respondents indicated the need to simplify use. The most difficult device to handle seemed to be the video cassette recorder (35.8% need for simplification)

TABLE 5.5   Communication and Entertainment Technology: Availability, Experiences, Fears, and Need for Simplification of Use Reported by Older Persons

Device	Availability (%)	Bad experiences (%)	Fears (%)	Need for simplification of use (%)
TV Set	99.3	12.0	6.9	10.6
Cable Connection	90.4	6.1	4.3	4.6
Video Cassette Recorder	57.7	15.8	17.5	35.8
Teletext	63.7	6.2	5.7	11.4
Video Camera/Camcorder	14.2	3.3	10.1	16.6
Radio	99.4	1.7	0.5	0.8
Stereo System	65.8	5.6	5.7	9.8
CD Player	50.0	3.8	3.6	6.3
Personal Computer	12.6	3.4	17.6	26.6
Modem/Internet Access	5.6	1.4	17.9	20.3
Telephone with Cord	77.9	3.9	1.5	1.1
Cordless Phone	34.4	4.5	5.6	6.9
Mobile Phone	9.1	2.2	10.1	21.1
Answering Machine	20.7	3.8	5.9	10.1
Fax Machine	7.5	1.3	7.9	10.4

Note: Database: *sentha* survey 1999; N (total) = 1,417; all relative frequencies are weighted due to the three age groups (55–64, 65–74, 75+) used in the *sentha* sample as stratification criteria. Percentages with respect to bad experiences, fears, and need for simplification of use refer only to those who own the device in question.

followed by the personal computer (26.6% need for simplification). These data clearly show that much still has to be done to redesign even widespread technologies such as the washing machine or the video recorder in a more user-friendly manner.

We next tried to answer the question of what best predicts the availability of domestic, communication, and entertainment appliances in the households of older adults. We carried out regression analyses including sociodemographic variables like age, gender, parenthood, household composition, education, and income, as well as items representing subjective attitudes toward both technology in general (e.g.,

"Technology has brought predominantly good things for mankind.") and domain-specific technologies (e.g., "Household technology means to me a major support of independence."). (See Tables 5.6 and 5.7).

With respect to household technologies, the included predictor variables explained 27% in the variance of equipment (Table 5.6). Both objective sociodemographic and subjective variables contributed to this explanation. Among the objective variables, age was relatively most important (being older was negatively related to the availability of household items), followed by gender (being female was positively related to the availability of household items), household composition (being single was negatively related to the availability of household items), income (having more money was positively related to the availability of household technology), and parenthood (having no children was negatively related to the availability of household technology). Domain-specific attitudes, both negative and positive, were significant predictors, too. Persons who during their life course always enjoyed using household technologies were more likely to possess them in old age than those who preferred to minimize the use of such devices. Similarly, having avoided technology in general during one's life course explained why some older persons rarely own domestic technologies. Perceived obsolescence, again both the domain-specific attitude and the general feelings of obsolescence, was also negatively associated with owning household technology.

Differences and similarities were found with regard to the prediction of ownership of communication and entertainment technologies (Table 5.7). Similarities include the relevance of domain-specific and general obsolescence, which showed even higher significance in the domain of communication and entertainment than in the domain of domestic technologies. The impact of age, household composition, and income, and the domain-specific attitude toward communication and entertainment technologies was also similar between domains. However, gender and parenthood had no impact on ownership of communication and entertainment devices. Instead, level of education and experience with technology ("During all of my life I always had a lot to do with technology.") turned out to be significant predictor variables in this domain. In summary, this means that aspects of social structure, as well as individual attitudes and lifelong habits, constitute important preconditions that influence one's access to and ownership of electronic devices, both in the domestic domain and with respect to communication and entertainment technologies. An interesting additional question in this context is how much answers of elders on statements such as "During all of my life I always had a lot to do with technology"

TABLE 5.6 Predictors of the Availability of Household Technology (HT) in Old Age

	p	Standardized beta	Semi-partial r^2 (%)	Partial r^2 (%)
Sociodemographic variables:				
Age	***	−0.2	3.7	4.9
Gender (male = 0)	***	0.18	2.2	3.0
Parenthood (no children = 0)	***	0.12	1.3	1.7
Household composition (single = 0)	***	0.15	1.4	1.9
Net income per person	***	0.15	1.8	2.4
Completed 10. class		−0.02	<0.1	<0.1
Completed 12. class		0.02	<0.1	<0.1
Attitudes toward household technology:				
Use I: "Always liked to use HT"	***	0.25	3.2	4.2
Use II: "Prefer to minimize the use of HT"	**	−0.08	0.4	0.6
Acceptance I: "HT is a major support"		−0.03	<0.1	<0.1
Acceptance II: "HT is a risk"		0.01	<0.1	<0.1
Technology-related obsolescence: "It's not worth buying new HT anymore"	*	−0.07	0.3	0.4
General technology related attitudes and experiences:				
Acceptance of technology I: "Use"		0.01	<0.1	0.1
Acceptance of technology II: "Threat"		<0.01	<0.1	0.1
Experience I: "Had much to do with technology"		−0.03	<0.01	<0.01
Experience II: "Always avoided using technology"	*	0.09	0.4	0.5
Perceived obsolescence	**	−0.09	0.6	0.8

Note: r^2 = .28; adjusted $r2$ = .27; * $p < .05$; ** $p < .01$; *** $p < .001$; calculations were done with unweighted data.

TABLE 5.7 Predictors of the Availability of Communication and Entertainment Technology (CET) in Old Age

	p	Standardized beta	Semi-partial r^2 (%)	Partial r^2 (%)
Sociodemographic variables:				
Age	***	−0.21	3.3	5.6
Gender (male = 0)		−0.04	<0.1	0.2
Parenthood (no children = 0)		0.04	0.2	0.3
Household composition (single = 0)	***	0.28	5.2	8.5
Net income per person	***	0.24	4.3	7.1
Completed 10. class	***	0.09	0.8	1.3
Completed 12. class	***	0.08	0.6	1.0
Attitudes toward communication and entertainmant technology:				
Use I: "Always liked to use CET"	*	0.08	0.3	0.5
Use II: "Prefer to minimize the use of CET"	**	−0.08	0.5	0.8
Acceptance of CET I: "CET is a major support"		0.02	<0.1	<0.1
Acceptance of CET II: "CET is a risk"		0.04	0.2	0.3
Technology-related obsolescence:				
"It's not worth buying new CET anymore"	***	−0.14	1.2	2.1
General technology related attitudes and experiences:				
Acceptance of technology I: "Use"		0.03	<0.1	0.1
Acceptance of technology II: "Threat"		−0.03	<0.1	0.1
Experience I: "Had much to do with technology"	***	0.10	0.5	0.9
Experience II: "Always avoided using technology"		0.04	<0.01	0.2
Perceived obsolescence	***	−0.09	0.6	1.0

Note: r^2 = .44; adjusted r^2 = .43; * $p < .05$; ** $p < .01$; *** $p < .001$; calculations were done with unweighted data.

are influenced by the lifelong experience with technology per se as compared to the potential influence of personality traits such as "openness to experience" (Costa & McCrae, 1980). Questions of this kind were, however, not answerable on an empirical basis with the measures available in *sentha*.

THEORETICAL ISSUES CONCERNING THE RELATIONSHIP BETWEEN AGING AND EVERYDAY TECHNOLOGY IN THE HOME AND SOME CONCLUSIONS

There is general consensus that the impact of technology on the quality of older adults' lives should be approached by use of an interactional conception of aging and human development, placing the person and his or her environment (including technological devices) in a dynamic and reciprocal interchange system. However, there are many ways to apply a person-environment view to aging and technology. In the following, we suggest a simple scheme to systematize these conceptions. We also apply this scheme to support our notion that a major theoretical challenge lies in counteracting the widely met tendency to reduce the issue of person-environment dynamics to one single discipline (e.g., psychology or, even more narrowly, an information-processing view of the older person interacting with technology); instead, we opt for a broader and multidisciplinary view.

Figure 5.2 depicts a four-cell scheme based on a cross-classification of two dimensions: level of analysis (micro- vs. macro-perspective) and kind of knowledge creation and action approach (strong research vs. strong application orientation). Within the first cell of this scheme, combining the micro-perspective with the strong research orientation, three models have been used in the recent literature on aging and technology. First, human factors models draw from the in-depth knowledge of man-machine interactions. Charness and Bosman (1990) have shown already how much empirically based quantitative material is available with respect to light and auditory environments and their interaction with aging individuals (see also Fisk & Rogers, 1997). Secondly, the information-processing view on age and technology interactions has substantial overlap with the human factors approach; both place strong emphasis on the role of age-related decrements in perception, attention, memory, and (fluid) intelligence (Howard & Howard, 1997). A third family of models, abbreviated in our scheme as ecological models, focuses on the aging-technology relation at the

		Level of analysis	
		Micro-Perspective	Macro-Perspective
Kind of knowledge creation and action approach taken	Strong research orientation	• Research based on human factors models • Research based on information processing models • Research based on ecological models	• Research concerned with historical relativity and cohort dynamics • Research concerned with social-structural aspects
	Strong application orientation	• Design directives and planning processes • Home adaptation and retrofitting	• Social policy agenda • Legislative regulations

FIGURE 5.2   Meta-theoretical view on research on aging and technology: Level of analysis and kind of knowledge creation and action approach taken.

micro-level and points to age-related changes in the role of the environment (Scheidt & Windley, 1998; Wahl, 2001).

According to these models, the aging organism and its adaptational capacity are vulnerable to environmental overdemands ("press") as well as underdemands; misfits between behavioral competence, personal needs, and environmental conditions might undermine life quality (Carp & Carp, 1984; Lawton & Nahemow, 1973). The data presented in this chapter on the impact of household technology and selected outcomes would probably best fit within the latter approach. They support the notion that (at least in German elders) the lack of central heating is an important form of "environmental press" for older people that has a measurable negative effect on their residential satisfaction. Furthermore, *sentha* data on user problems and fears of technology increase our understanding of risks as misfits between the competencies/personal needs of older people and their home environment. Such knowledge can be of great benefit for the planning of preventive or training strategies that reduce these risks.

A major limitation of all of these models is, however, their tendency to neglect the macro-conditions of the aging-technology relationship (see cell in Figure 5.2 combining the strong research orientation with the macro-perspective). For instance, current cohorts of older technology users have their special "technology biography," which is quite different from that of earlier and later cohorts, and human factors considerations must always be framed within historical contexts (Docampo Rama, de Ridder, & Bouma, 2001). Take the example of menu control: An older person today might need one hour to learn the menu control of a simple e-mail device. Future older persons will be acquainted with menus due to previous extensive socialization experiences with this kind of control surface. But if control devices of this kind become more cognitive resource demanding, future elders could possibly be even more disadvantaged than those of today. A second example: Today, the behavioral competence of older people in the realm of activities of daily living is strongly dependent on physical conditions; in the future, the most influential factor may become the availability and creative use of a scope of household and information technology devices. A third example: During the seventies and eighties of the last century, a discussion in Germany began on the role of domestic technology in absorbing women's tasks in reproduction versus easing household burdens. Many studies have shown meanwhile that neither view was realistic because mechanization gave rise to a whole range of new tasks and demands (Bose, Bereano, & Malloy, 1984; Cowan, 1976, 1983). Similarly, new technologies, although less physically demanding, may raise expectations toward older men and women about their performances, activities, and independence from social support. Furthermore, we should not forget that social and structural forces determine access to education and income—and thus to technology-relevant competencies and devices—and the divide between the "haves" and the "have nots" will probably persist into the future.

We are still far from constructing models that are capable of acknowledging the complex interchange processes between the micro- and macro-levels, but both deserve a more integrative view in forthcoming theory building. As alluded to in earlier sections of this chapter, cross-sequential data across long observation intervals do not seem to be available for testing model-based predictions; major current longitudinal data sets simply do not address technology issues. More generally, empirical research has been mainly driven by the micro-model approach described above. Findings from *sentha,* which address the attitudes of older adults toward technology, contribute to this research need and support the notion that very focused as well as general attitudes (both of which probably are subject to historical-societal influences) play a role for the "rearmament" of current senior households.

The remaining two cells of our scheme underscore that the literature on aging and technology is full of strong application-oriented strategies as well. Besides the pursuit of basic research knowledge, there is also a very broad "database" of design directives and home adaptation guidelines based on practical planning experience and intervention (see Regnier & Pynoos, 1987, for a classic volume in this regard). However, this knowledge base needs to be more strongly integrated into ongoing research at the micro- and macro-levels to stimulate empirical research and to profit from existing but ignored evidence-based research findings. There is a macro-perspective with respect to application when it comes to the planning of social policy and legislative regulations, having a direct impact on the other cells of the scheme. Finally, it should also be emphasized that all four cells of the model operate in complex interaction processes, influencing each other in one or the other direction.

In sum, there is a strong need to counteract the existing tendency in research to attend predominantly to the micro-level, and to neglect other levels of analysis or available knowledge and action bases when targeting the relation of aging and (household) technology. At the practical research level, better integration of micro- and macro-approaches would imply stronger collaboration among psychologists, human factors researchers, designers, and architects, as well as among sociologists, anthropologists, and social policy researchers. As one means to promote this kind of approach, major funding agencies involved in fostering research on aging and technology might stipulate that following such a multidisciplinary research track should be one critical prerequisite for a positive funding decision.

ACKNOWLEDGMENTS

We would like to thank Roman Kaspar and Oliver Schilling for their valuable support with data analyses. David Burmedi has helped to improve the writing style of the chapter.

The data of the Socio-economic Panel (SOEP) used in this work have been provided by the Deutsches Institut für Wirtschaftsforschung (DIW), Berlin.

The project "Everyday Technologies for Senior Households" (*sentha*) is funded by the German Research Council (Deutsche Forschungsgemeinschaft) at the Technical University of Berlin, and is conducted in cooperation with experts from the natural sciences, engineering, design, and social sciences.

REFERENCES

Baltes, M. M., Maas, I., Wilms, H.-U., & Borchelt, M. (1999). Everyday competence in old and very old age: Theoretical considerations and empirical findings. In P. B. Baltes & K. U. Mayer (Eds.), *The Berlin aging study* (pp. 384–402). Cambridge, UK: Cambridge University Press.

Baltes, M. M., Wahl, H.-W., & Schmid-Furstoss, U. (1990). The daily life of elderly Germans: Activity patterns, personal control, and functional health. *Journal of Gerontology: Psychological Sciences, 45,* 173–179.

Baltes, P. B., & Smith, J. (1999). Multilevel and systemic analyses of old age: Theoretical and empirical evidence for a fourth age. In V. L. Bengtson & K. W. Schaie (Eds.), *Handbook of theories of aging* (pp. 153–173). New York: Springer.

BMFSFJ (Federal Ministry for Family, Senior Citizens, Women and Youth). (1998). *Second report on older people.* Bonn: German Federal Government. Available from: Carp, F. & Christensen, D. L. *Research on Aging.*.

Bose, C., Bereano, P., & Malloy, M. (1984). Household technology and the social construction of housework. *Technology and Culture, 25,* 53–82.

Carp, R., & Carp, A. (1984). A complementary/congruence model of well-being or mental health for the community elderly.*Human Behavior and Environment: Advances in Theory and Research, 7,* 279–336.

Carp, F., & Christensen, D. L. (1986). Technical environmental assessment predictors of residential satisfaction: A study of elderly women living alone. *Research on Ageing, 8,* 269–287.

Charness, N. (2001). Aging and communication: Human factors issues. In N. Charness, D. C. Park, & B. A. Sabel (Eds.), *Communication, technology and aging: Opportunities and challenges for the future* (pp. 1–29). New York: Springer.

Charness, N., & Bosman, E. A. (1990). Human factors and design for older people. In J. E. Birren & K. W. Schaie (Eds.), *Handbook of the psychology of aging* (3rd ed., pp. 446–464). San Diego: Academic Press.

Costa, P. T., & McCrae, R. R. (1980). Still stable after all these years: Personality as a key to some issues in adulthood and old age. In P. B. Baltes & O. G. Brim (Eds.), *Life-span development and behavior* (pp. 65–102). New York: Academic Press.

Cowan, R. S. (1976). The "Industrial Revolution" in the home: Household technology and social change in the 20th century. *Technology and Culture, 17,* 1–23.

Cowan, R. S. (1983). *More work for mother: The ironies of household technology from the open hearth to the microwave.* New York: Basic Books.

Czaja, S. J. (1997). Using technologies to aid the performance of home tasks. In A. D. Fisk & W. A. Rogers (Eds.), *Handbook of human factors and the older adult* (pp. 311–334). San Diego: Academic Press.

Czaja, S. J., & Lee, C. C. (2001). The Internet and older adults: Design challenges and opportunities. In N. Charness, D. C. Park, & B. A. Sabel (Eds.), *Communication, technology and aging: Opportunities and challenges for the future* (pp. 60–80). New York: Springer.

Docampo Rama, M., de Ridder, H., & Bouma, H. (2001). Technology generation and age in using layered user interfaces. *Gerontechnology, 1,* 25–40.

Engelhardt, K. G., & Goughler, D. H. (1997). Robotic technologies and the older adult. In A. D. Fisk & W. A. Rogers (Eds.), *Handbook of human factors and the older adult* (pp. 395–413). San Diego: Academic Press.

Faletti, M. V. (1984). Human factors research and functional environments for the aged. In I. Altman, M. P. Lawton, & J. F. Wohlwill (Eds.), *Elderly people and the environment* (pp. 191–237). New York: Plenum.

Fisk, A. D., & Rogers, W. A. (Eds.). (1997). *Handbook of human factors and the older adult.* San Diego: Academic Press.

Gehlen, A. (1956). *Urmensch und Spätkultur [Early man and late culture].* Bonn: Athenäum.

Gutman, G. (Ed.). (1998a). *Technology innovation for an aging society: Blending research, public and private sectors.* Vancouver, Canada: Simon Fraser University.

Gutman, G. (1998b). Technological approaches to management of "problem" behaviors in home and institutional settings. In G. Gutman (Ed.), *Technology innovation for an aging society: Blending research, public, and private sectors* (pp. 51–68). Vancouver, Canada: Simon Fraser University.

Hampel, J., Mollenkopf, H., Weber, U., & Zapf, W. (1991). *Alltagsmaschinen [Everyday machines].* Berlin: edition sigma.

Howard, J. H., Jr., & Howard, D. V. (1997). Learning and memory. In A. D. Fisk & W. A. Rogers (Eds.), *Handbook of human factors and the older adult* (pp. 7–26). San Diego: Academic Press.

Lawton, M. P., & Nahemow, L. (1973). Ecology and the aging process. In C. Eisdorfer & M. P. Lawton (Eds.), *The psychology of adult development and aging.* Oxford, UK: American Psychological Association.

Lesnoff-Caravaglia, G. (1988). Aging in a technological society. In G. Lesnoff-Caravaglia (Ed.), *Aging in a technological society* (pp. 271–283). New York: Human Sciences.

Marcellini, F., Mollenkopf, H., Spazzafumo, L., & Ruoppila, I. (2000). Acceptance and use of technological solutions by the elderly in the outdoor environment: Findings from a European survey. *Zeitschrift für Gerontologie und Geriatrie, 33,* 169–177.

Meyer, S., & Mollenkopf, H. (2003). Home technology, smart homes, and the aging user. In K. W. Schaie, H.-W. Wahl, H. Mollenkopf, & F. Oswald (Eds.), *Aging independently: Living arrangements and mobility* (pp. 148–161). New York: Springer.

Meyer, S., & Schulze, E. (1989). Fernseher contra Waschmaschine—Wie Familienstrukturen auf Technik wirken [TV against the washing machine—How family structures impact on technology]. In G. Wagner et al. (Eds.), *Familienbildung und Erwerbstätigkeit im demographischen Wandel [Family formation and involvement in the labor force in demographic transition]* (pp. 251–262). Berlin/Heidelberg/New York: Springer.

Mollenkopf, H. (1994). Technical aids in old age—Between acceptance and rejection. In C. Wild & A. Kirschner (Eds.), *Technology for the elderly: Safety-alarm systems, technical aids and smart homes* (pp. 81–100). Knegsel, The Netherlands: Akontes.

Mollenkopf, H., Meyer, S., Schulze, E., Wurm, S., & Friesdorf, W. (2000). Technik im Haushalt zur Unterstützung einer selbstbestimmten Lebensführung im Alter. Das Forschungsprojekt "sentha" und erste Ergebnisse des sozialwissenschaftlichen Teilprojekts [Everyday technologies for senior households: The project "sentha" and first results of its social science part]. *Zeitschrift für Gerontologie und Geriatrie, 33,* 155-168.

Mollenkopf, H., Mix, S., Gäng, K., & Kwon, S. (2001). Alter und Technik [Age and technology]. In Deutsches Zentrum für Altersfragen (Ed.), *Personale, gesundheitliche und Umweltressourcen im Alter [Personal, health-related and environment-related resources in old age] (Vol. 1—Expertisen zum Dritten Altenbericht der Bundesregierung,* [Expert's reports to the third Report on Aging of the German Federal Government], pp. 253–438). Opladen, Germany: Leske + Budrich.

Moss, M., & Lawton, M. P. (1982). Time budgets of older people: A window on four life styles. *Journal of Gerontology, 37,* 115–123.

Park, D. C., & Jones, T. R. (1997). Medication adherence and aging. In A. D. Fisk & W. A. Rogers (Eds.), *Handbook of human factors and the older adult* (pp. 257–288). San Diego: Academic Press.

Regnier, V., & Pynoos, J. (Eds.). (1987). *Housing the aged: Design directions and policy considerations.* New York: Elsevier.

Rogers, W. A., Cabrera, E. F., Walker, N. Gilbert, D. K., & Fisk, A. D. (1996). A survey of automatic teller machine usage across the adult life span. *Human Factors, 38,* 156–166.

Rogers, W. A., Meyer, B., Walker, N., & Fisk, A. D. (1998). Functional limitations to daily living tasks in the aged: A focus group analysis. *Human Factors, 40,* 111–125.

Rybczynski, W. (1987). *Home: A short story of an idea.* New York: Penguin.

Sackmann, A., & Weymann, A. (1994). *Die Technisierung des Alltags. Generationen und technische Innovationen [The technicalization of everyday life: Generations and technical innovations].* Frankfurt: Campus.

SAS Institute. (1993). *Companion for the Microsoft Windows Environment* (6th Version, 1st ed.). Cary, NC: Author.

Scheidt, R. J., & Windley, P. G. (Eds.). (1998). *Environment and aging theory. A focus on housing.* Westport, CT: Greenwood.

SOEP Group. (2001). The German Socio-Economic Panel (GSOEP) after more than 15 years—Overview. In E. Holst, D. R. Lillard, & T. A. DiPrete

(Eds.), *Proceedings of the 2000 Fourth International Conference of German Socio-Economic Panel Study Users (GSOEP2000). Vierteljahreshefte zur Wirtschaftsforschung, 70*(1), 7–14.

U.S. Bureau of the Census. (1996). *Current population reports, special studies, 65+ in the United States.* Washington, DC: U.S. Government Printing Office.

Vercruyssen, M., Graafmans, J., Fozard, J. L., Bouma, H., & Rietsema, J. (1996). Gerontechnology. In J. E. Birren (Ed.), *Encyclopedia of gerontology: Age, aging and the aged, vol.1* (pp. 593–603). San Diego: Academic Press.

Wahl, H.-W. (2001). Environmental influences on aging and behavior. In J. E. Birren & K. W. Schaie (Eds.), *Handbook of the psychology of aging* (5th ed., pp. 215–237). San Diego: Academic Press.

Wahl, H.-W., Oswald, F., & Zimprich, D. (1999). Everyday competence in visually impaired older adults: A case for person-environment perspectives. *The Gerontologist, 39,* 140–149.

Commentary

The Nested Context of Technology: A Response to Wahl and Mollenkopf

Rick J. Scheidt

Wahl and Mollenkopf (this volume) consider technological changes occurring within private home settings and the possible impact these may have on older residents. They issue three invitations that I am pleased to accept: first, that we view their work as a catalyst for discussion; second, that we utilize interdisciplinary models and methods to improve our thinking and research here; and third, that we focus on multilevel contexts, especially macro-context, when examining classic technology in home settings.

Before I consider salient issues in their work, I will describe my own reference point. I am a psychological social psychologist and a field researcher. I have spent 25 years working with behavioral ecologists/architects studying environment-behavior relations among rural elders during both better and worse economic times. A large part of our recent work has focused on the well-being of older residents of small ghost towns. Our early work utilized data from large interview surveys (Scheidt, 1986; Scheidt & Windley, 1985; Windley & Scheidt, 1987), but our recent work is ethnographic—anthropological psychology, actually (Scheidt, 2001; Scheidt & Norris-Baker, 1999). So I offer reactions as one who does more macro-level environment-behavior research on elders living in rural contexts.

In my view, the research that Wahl and Mollenkopf are sharing becomes more interesting as it progresses from the historical trajectory work to the consideration of conceptual models, so I will comment about each of these phases and indicate why their last phase—the call to frame technological research within a sociohistorical context—holds particular interest for me.

HISTORICAL TRAJECTORIES

The historical trajectories for classic household technology items are primarily useful as rough norms for tracking their adoption in elderly households in Germany and America. They may have other potential uses as well. These trajectories reveal the *historical event impact density* of technology (Schaie, 1984). Some environmental (especially cultural) trends have greater impact on behavioral development than others. Several years ago, Warner Schaie (1984) suggested that developmentalists would be wise to taxonomize and track the more "development-relevant events" in order to examine their range of competitive influence on research-targeted populations. He argued that this would certainly be more useful to developmentalists than the practice of indexing these "period effects" solely with discrete dates. Schaie illustrated his prescient argument using rates of adoption of technology over time.

Though not constructed for developmental purposes, the Wahl and Mollenkopf trajectories do have some theoretical value when used to reveal historical lags between older and younger cohorts and highlight differences between the have's and have nots within older cohorts. It is important to know that there are a number of older subpopulations that still do not have access to technological tools that form the basic infrastructure of households. Many rural elders are among them. I think the usefulness of the technology trajectories would be greatly enriched if examined along side trajectories for other event domains, particularly trajectories that map changes in local culture that directly affect the viability of the household technological infrastructure. I return to this point in my concluding statement.

Wahl notes that in Germany, TV diffused much more rapidly than washing machines, VCRs, and dishwashers, and suggests that we can gain a rational understanding of this seemingly irrational behavior if we take into account, "in principle," the social-structural and individual mediators. In survey research,"in principle" often means representing these contextual variables with global indices of limited meaning. On the whole, the Wahl and Mollenkopf research is refreshing because it actualizes this ideal rather than treating such mediators as noise and controlling them out of the data.

It was not their purpose, really, but I found myself wondering about cohort-related projections for technology use in the near future, given what we know about cohorts that are already here. In this country, the "echo boomers"—those born since 1977—are projected to number 137 million or 46% of the population by 2010. When they start buying homes, they will expect technology to enhance living. Ownership rates of household technology items will likely increase dramatically, particularly those items related to information technology (Adler, 1999).

THE SOCIOECONOMIC PANEL STUDY

The second phase of the work mined the socioeconomic panel data drawn from a German population in 1993 and 1998. It assessed the predictive links between availability of household tech items and three home-related life quality (or satisfaction) factors and examined sociodemographic covariates. Theoretically, we move a step up here, linking ownership to outcomes. However, it was a low-yield assay, and only one tech predictor, central heating, survived the six criteria for consistency. I wonder, however, if it is valid to conclude that household technology has "no clear and empirically measurable impact" on the "emotional-evaluative level of life quality," and whether secondary data analysis provides a fair test here. Wahl and Mollenkopf note the general constrictions of secondary data analysis. Oftentimes, it is an effort in psychological archeology. The data are laid down earlier and the fragments or variables of interest do not exist in whole states. In this data set, the three satisfaction domains—resident satisfaction, leisure satisfaction, and general life satisfaction—are second-order constructs assessed via single-item scales. Within these broad second-order domains, a number of first-order constructs remain unarticulated. These first-order constructs probably bristle with their own positive and negative evaluative features. The constraints of this method put us in the position of those who drop a coin in the dark but look for it under the street lamp.

The clearest understanding of phenomena that are on the ground, like the coin, is gained by *getting on the ground,* using holistic strategies that allow the meaning of constructs to be carefully derived from the total context in which they are embedded, rather than in isolation or in a fashion that presumes their meaning a priori (Scheidt, 2001). Wahl and Mollenkopf acknowledge "that the impact of technology on the quality of older adults' lives should be approached" with conceptions that place the older person and his or her environment—including tech items—in a "dynamic and reciprocal interchange system." For example, it is possible that any of the three components of satisfaction might influence ownership of household tech items, rather than the other way around. Grounded research strategies may put us in a better position to understand this dialectic, revealing which individual variables should be included in prospective survey analyses. I am thinking here of the case of a 70-year-old rural Kansas man I met a few years ago who was recovering from a recent stroke. He took me on a tour of his home to show me the renovations he made to accommodate his partial paralysis. In his workshop, I noticed a long string of firecrackers hanging from a nail in the ceiling. "What's that?" I asked. He grinned at me and said, "That's my fire alarm." As I talked more with him, I learned that he held a number of anti-tech attitudes that outlined who he was, an amateur inventor struggling to hold on to his pre-stroke identity.

THE *SENTHA* PROJECT: EVERYDAY TECHNOLOGIES FOR SENIOR HOUSEHOLDS

With the *sentha* data, we see a more fully fleshed approach, a more interesting strategy for understanding the meaning of tech item availability and experience. The factor analysis typology illustrates nicely and but not surprisingly the diversity that exists in acceptance of household tech by older people. What I find most interesting here are the possibilities the data offer for educational intervention. Among the profiles, the "positive advocates" and "skeptics" are less interesting to me than the "rationally adapting"—those of all ages with lower educational levels who seemed resigned and have learned to bite the bullet.

Some older individuals will hold the attitudes they do toward technology because of highly specific, tech-related experiences or features. Many attitudes are formed and maintained for mundane reasons, including bad experiences with telephone menus. Other attitudinal clusters may distinguish tech biographies in a more psychological sense. I am not suggesting that we go Freudian, putting older people on the couch and asking them to reflect on their first encounter with that nasty microwave oven. But neofunctionalist theories of attitude change might be nicely folded in here to allow us to identify why older adults hold the attitudes they do and, if desired, to tailor interventions targeting the psychological functions they serve, such as ego-defensive functions in the case of my older inventor.

The nice aspect of the Sentha data is that they include a richer array of personal variables, including reports of bad experiences and tech-related fears. The predictor domain for availability of domestic, communication, and entertainment appliances includes sociodemographic dimensions and subjective attitudes toward both general and domain-specific technology. As I look over results connected to item ownership and related fears and bad experiences, I wonder if the data are purely normative or whether they have wider value. For example, it makes logical sense to me that at baseline—on a population level—anywhere from 3% to 14% of older tech owners, depending on the item, will have "fears" related to using these items and that 5% to 12% will report having "bad experiences." We can use these data to guide ways to make devices more user friendly, but what relative standards, numerical or otherwise, should we use to judge the seriousness of the complaints and the success of the efforts? I am thinking here of the trait-related personality research showing that "happy are they who are happy" (McCrae & Costa, 1999; Stones & Kozma, 1986) One is less likely to pose this question for the entertainment and communication complaints and fears. The levels here are high enough to cross a threshold of concern in almost anyone's book, for example, where one out of five reports fears of using personal computers and 18% report bad experiences with them.

With regard to the prediction models, the lion's share of the variance in tech item availability is predicted by a half-dozen sociodemographic index variables. Again, this presents a fairly good case for the need to "unpack" and elaborate the *meanings* of these variables if we are to understand more precisely what they index and why and how they afford prediction (Scheidt, 2001). I have a "cut and paste" curiosity to see how well the independent variables used in these *sentha* prediction models would do using evaluative outcome variables like those used in the Socioeconomic Panel Study—that is, more direct indicators of quality of life. It would be of value, I would think, to develop some a priori theory that could host such prediction, using micro-to-macro or near-to-far outcomes like housing satisfaction, neighborhood satisfaction, community satisfaction, and global measures of psychological well-being.

THE NEED FOR BRIDGING MODELS

At a personal level, I found the last section of the work to be the most exciting, particularly the call for increased contextualism. The four-cell conceptual model not only sorts out action approaches to tech-aging research but invites us to find models that bridge micro-to-macro environments and strong research-to-strong application efforts.

I am familiar with models of life span human development and models of environment-behavior relations. I am always struck by the their mutual ignorance of one another. Most environment-behavior or ecological theories focus on immediate person-environment congruence issues. Contextual developmental models are faced with the enormous challenge of developing more complete conceptions of Person X Environment interactions at multiple levels over considerable periods of time.

There are a couple of developmental approaches that I would like to see applied within an ecological perspective. Baltes' *S.O.C.* (Selection, Optimization, Compensation) *model* focuses on adaptation as it occurs in the face of an increasingly negative ratio of gains and losses in old age (Baltes, 1997; Baltes, Lindenberger, & Staudinger, 1998). It is light on the "E" end of the P x E equation, but this feature gives it a more flexible application across a wide range of social and physical environments. It may have immediate application in the Wahl and Mollenkopf work, for example, the observation that the household tech items may have lower assistive value in the ADL/IADL domains because of long-term compensatory adaptations older folks have made to their home environments. I believe that Lerner's *Applied Developmental Science* model is attractive for taking researchers to problems in situ in local ecologies (Lerner, Fisher, & Weinberg, 2000). This outreach approach urges applied developmentalists to conduct "research that engages public policy" and to work directly with "communities in collaborative actions that merge research and service in support of civil society" (Lerner et al., 2000, p. 15). It has genuine potential for guiding field-located technology research that might inform public policy on community sustainability.

A RURAL ILLUSTRATION

I would like to close with an example that illustrates why it is essential to take context into account when studying technology at any level.

Successful aging in many rural areas means creating or adapting resources to sustain the local community. The "Heartland of America" (as defined by the Federal Reserve Board) includes 12 states and stretches from North Dakota to New Mexico and from Colorado to Minnesota. It includes my own state of Kansas. Within this region, over half of the counties have lost population and over half of the towns less than 2,500 in size are dying. The most seriously affected are those in remote rural counties. They are among the losers of the economic boom of the 1990s that lifted the growth of about one-third of the heartland counties but left the remainder behind (Drabenstott, 1999)

I have conducted many interviews with older, lifelong residents in several of these ghost towns or "geriatric ghettos" (Scheidt, 1998). They are the endangered, shrinking middle-class—many quite old—living in modest but comfortable homes (Stauber, 2001). They own many of the classic household tech items discussed by Wahl and Mollenkopf and, in fact, may be more dependent upon them, given the changing context of the wider community. (A recent U.S. Bureau of Census [September, 2001] survey shows that compared to other adult [18 + years] age groups, older Americans are far less likely to report home computer access [28.4%] and Internet use [12.8%]. Though the survey indicates nearly half of rural Americans [47.1%] report home computer access and 29% report Internet use, current access or use data are not configured for older adults residing in more remote rural counties where most small, declining communities are located.)

With allowances for rural and age-related lags evidenced by Wahl and Mollenkopf, the personal tech biographies of these rural elders probably mirror the recent historical tech trajectories for these items. However, when you step outside the front doors of the residents, you stare down streets lined with vacant lots and empty and decaying buildings—former churches, schools, businesses and homes—abandoned over the years due to a chronic spiral of economic decline, evidence of an entirely different historical trajectory for the immediately adjacent geophysical environment.

The economic infrastructure of the prototypical dying town is virtually missing. The original covenant of many of these towns was agriculture (Norris-Baker & Scheidt, 1992). Now many search for new identities and resources to stay alive. I raise this scenario simply to underscore the need to examine the *nested* context of household technology and to stress that tech trajectories must be examined in conjunction with both micro- and macro-economic trajectories, as well as trajectories of culture change, often marked by decline and degradation, that surround those seeking to age in place.

As Drs. Wahl and Mollenkopf have stressed, communication technology is changing the "inside" and "outside" permeability of home environments. Nowhere is this more apparent than in the variety of technological projects that are now directed toward serving residents, rebuilding infrastructures, and resurrecting the economies of some of these villages. I will not review these options here, except to note that some of the most novel applications of communication technology, in terms of delivery modes as well as programs, are being explored to bridge the digital divide in rural areas (Malecki, 2001).

In conclusion, it is clear that overcoming "human incompleteness" in old age may often necessitate the use of technology to rectify the incompleteness of wider native environments—environments that may have far shorter life spans than those who occupy them.

REFERENCES

Adler, D. (1999, September 30). *Changing demographics roundtable.* National Association of Home Builders Research Center. Retrieved March 2, 2002 at http://www.nahbrc.org/tertiaryR.asp?TrackID=&DocumentID=2308& CategoryID=1496

Baltes, P. (1997). On the incomplete architecture of human ontogeny: Selection, optimization, and compensation as foundation of developmental theory. American Psychologist, 52, 366–380.

Baltes, P., Lindenberger, U., & Staudinger, U. (1998). Life-span theory in developmental psychology. In W. Damon & R. Lerner, *Handbook of child psychology: vol 1. Theoretical models of human development* (5th ed., pp. 1029–1144). New York: Wiley.

Drabenstott, M. (1999, October). Rural America in a new century. *The Main Street Economist.* Center for the Study of Rural America, Kansas City, MO: Federal Reserve Bank of Kansas City.

Lerner, R., Fisher, C., & Weinberg, R. (2000). Toward a science for and of the people: Promoting civil society through the application of developmental science. *Child Development, 71*(1), 11–20.

Malecki, E. J. (2001, September). Going digital in rural America. In *Exploring policy options for a new rural America: The Center for Rural America* (pp. 49–68). Kansas City, MO: Federal Reserve Bank of Kansas City. Also available at: http://www.kc.frb.org

McCrae, R., & Costa, P. (1999). A five-factor theory of personality. In L. Pervin & J. Oliver (Eds.), *Handbook of personality: Theory and research* (2nd ed., pp. 139–153). New York: Guilford.

Norris-Baker, C., & Scheidt, R. (1992). Community covenants: An indicator of sustainable small-town habitats? In E. Arias & M. Gross (Eds.), *Equitable and sustainable habitats* (pp. 30–41). Oklahoma City, OK: Environmental Design Research Association.

Schaie, K. W. (1984). Historical time and cohort effects. In K. McCluskey & H. Reese (Eds.), *Life-span developmental psychology : Historical and generational effects* (pp. 1–15). Orlando, FL: Academic Press.

Scheidt, R. (1986). The mental health of small-town Kansas elderly: A report from the Great Plains. *American Journal of Community Psychology, 14,* 541–554.

Scheidt, R. (1998). The mental health of elderly in rural environments. In R. Coward & J. Krout (Eds.), *Rural elders: An exploration of the life circumstances and distinctive features of aging in rural America* (pp. 85–104). New York: Springer.

Scheidt, R. (2001). Individual-cultural transactions: Implications for the mental health of rural elders. *Journal of Applied Gerontology, 20,* 195–213.

Scheidt, R., & Norris-Baker, L. (1999). Place therapies for older adults: Conceptual and interventive approaches. *International Journal of Aging and Human Development, 48,* 1–15.

Scheidt, R., & Windley, P. (1985). The ecology of aging. In J. Birren & K. W. Schaie (Eds.), *Handbook of the psychology of aging* (2nd ed., pp. 245–258). New York: Van Nostrand Reinhold.

Stauber, K. (2001). Why invest in rural america—and how? A critical public policy question for the 21st century. *Economic Review* (Second Quarter), 33–63.

Stones, M., & Kozma, A. (1986). "Happy are they who are happy . . . ": A test between two causal models of relationships between happiness and its correlates. *Experimental Aging Research, 12*(1), 23–29.

Windley, P., & Scheidt, R. (1987). Rural small towns: An environmental context for aging. *Journal of Rural Studies, 4,* 151–158.

Commentary

Gerontechnology and the Home Environment

Gloria M. Gutman

In the introduction to their chapter, Wahl and Mollenkopf (this volume) make a number of key points. The first is that the issue of aging and technology is *en vogue*. To be sure, gerontological researchers have had an interest in the area dating back to the late 1980s. As Graafmans and Taipale (1998) note, the first formal aging and technology program was established at the Eindhoven University of Technology in the Netherlands in 1989. The First International Congress on Gerontechnology was held in 1991. What is new, however, is the popularization that has taken place. In North America, one has only to look at recent publications and conferences held by such consumer and practitioner-oriented organizations as the American Association for Retired Persons (AARP) (2001), the American Society on Aging (1999), and Canada's National Advisory Council on Aging (1995, 1999, 2001) to see that application of technology in service of the elderly has become a rallying call for these groups. Further, interest in gerontechnology, defined by Bouma (1992) as the study of technology for the improvement of the daily functioning of the elderly and encompassing research, design, manufacture, and marketing, has moved far beyond the small group of academic researchers who originally coined the term.

A second key point is that the home is the primary location in which aging takes place. Although Wahl and Mollenkopf state that their emphasis is on normal aging rather than on chronic conditions and disease, it should be emphasized that as people age they experience chronic disease and disabilities, and that as a result, their "home range" contracts. When they were younger and able to drive a car or use public transportation, they could venture out for social and recreational activities, to shop, or to visit the doctor whenever they wished. But when people develop chronic disease and/or disability, arrangements need to be made in advance for others to provide transportation and to assist. Arranging for a family member or volunteer to drive, or for special transport, requires planning and consumes energy. Eventually, venturing out, even with the aid of others, becomes more than the person can cope with. In the final stages of life, commonly, one room becomes the person's home.

A third key point that Wahl and Mollenkopf make in the introduction to their chapter, and that I will return to later, is that "technicalization" of the home environment of older persons tends to be delayed relative to younger age groups.

Wahl and Mollenkopf also note in the introduction that the focus is on "rearmament" of the home in terms of everyday technology, including classic household technology (such as washing machines, dishwashers, or central heating) as well as "old" and "new" communication and entertainment technology (such as the telephone, video cassette recorder, or personal computer).

When I first read the chapter (the draft is dated September 9, 2001), I thought that the choice of the word *rearmament* was interesting because it conveyed the image of a war being fought against aging and the ravages of old age. The word *rearmament* of course takes on added significance in light of September 11, 2001, and the events currently taking place on the world stage. With the advent of armed conflict there is a loss of social support. The energies of younger generations become diverted to the war effort; quite literally, old people get left behind when young men and women take up arms and engage in warfare. Even in times of peace—that is, if the events of September 11 and their aftermath had not happened—with the drop in fertility rates and more and more women in the paid labor force, there are fewer wives and daughters to provide the everyday care needed by frail elders.

But the word *rearmament* also has a positive connotation, one of empowerment, the idea that technologies in the context of the home environment can be used as weapons in the fight to remain independent in performing ADLs and IADLs and in maintaining contact with the outside world.

Returning to the image of the person with a highly restricted home range: on the one hand, the individual may be socially isolated with the view from the window of the one room to which he or she has become confined being the sole link to the outside world. Alternatively, that room can become a "control center" (a term coined by the late Powell Lawton). Technology can enable the person to have control over the entire home. Even with severely compromised mobility, with the aid of remote control technology people can open and close doors and windows, draw drapes, turn lights on and off, and so forth. Additionally, modern communication and information technologies can function as lifelines, enabling shut-ins to maintain contact and interact actively with the outside world.

FOUR IMPORTANT QUESTIONS

In the main body of the chapter, Wahl and Mollenkopf address four questions. The first concerns the historical trajectory of household technology. They refer to the concept of *"Mangelwesen Mensch"*—the incompleteness of the individual and the role that technology can play as a prosthesis or replacement for lost functions. While they reference Paul Baltes, it is interesting that they do not speak of his conception of the fourth age—the period from age 85 onward—when we no longer can count on the plasticity of the nervous system and the ability of mental and physical fitness and other types of training to "decline the decline" (see Baltes, 1997). Rather, they draw our attention to the importance of the availability of low-cost electricity and its introduction into the home environment toward the end of the nineteenth century, which enabled us to have vacuum cleaners, electric irons, toasters, coffee percolators, hot plates, and cookers. This was followed, as shown in their first table, by the introduction of the radio, television, refrigerator, and telephone—all of which are now commonplace in most elderly persons' households. They note, however, that such items as dishwashers, microwave ovens, video cassette recorders, and personal computers are far from ubiquitous among the elderly. They also note the generally slower diffusion of such potentially labor-saving devices as dishwashers compared with entertainment items such as television sets and video cassette recorders. We might add to this latter list electronic games, cellular telephones, Palm Pilots and other electronic and wireless "boy toys." In looking for reasons for the generally slow development of technological solutions to problems of the elderly in maintaining independent function, Brink (1991) notes that technology is often considered as an aid in the prosthetic sense rather than as a market venture. As she points out:

> The potential market for products supporting independent living for aging populations is widely recognized. Most developed nations have embraced the principles of independent living in the community for their elderly citizens. . . . [but] there exists what has come to be known as a technology gap with respect to products in the market that support independent living. Commercial exploitation of the possibilities has simply not kept pace. . . . [p. 211]

Brink goes on to ask whether such gaps appear because the process of "technology flow" is itself a problem or whether the technology gap has occurred because the products apply to a relatively small proportion of the population. She answers both questions with a resounding "no." Technology flow to products serving other sectors has not been hindered to the same extent. For example, technology serves the information sector very well, whether it is for the management or for the dissemination of information. With respect to the argument that seniors only constitute 10%–20% of the population and that large numbers live in poverty or on fixed incomes, Brink notes that this scenario could be applied equally well to preschoolers. However, technology flow has not been affected to the same extent by small numbers and small income in the case of preschoolers.

A second question Wahl and Mollenkopf address is whether the lives of older people have become "better" with the application of everyday technology in the home environment. They cite data from the 1993 and 1998 waves of the German Socio-economic Panel (SOEP). Somewhat surprisingly, after adjusting for control variables, only one household technology item—central heating—had a measurable effect and then only on one of their three outcome variables deemed to measure quality of life, namely, residential satisfaction. It is unfortunate, indeed, that the dataset did not contain measures of the impact of common household technologies on performance of ADLs or IADLs because that is where I would expect the effect to be maximal.

The third question addressed concerns fulfilled and unmet needs, fears, and user friendliness issues. Using data from the "Everyday Technologies for Seniors Households" study, conducted with a sample of 1,417 German men and women aged 55+, Wahl and Mollenkopf identify four approximately equally distributed types of people in terms of attitudes to technology: (1) positive advocates, (2) rational adaptors, (3) skeptics and ambivalents, (4) critics.

It is noteworthy that while there were no significant age differences for types 2 and 3, the "younger old" were significantly more strongly represented among the positive advocates while the "oldest old" were more often found to be critics. Higher education was also significantly associated with positive advocacy while lower education was associated with rationally adapting. Given that in virtually all countries for which data are available, succeeding generations reaching age 65 are better educated than their predecessors, these findings bode well for the uptake of technology by future cohorts of elders. They should be prominently drawn to the attention of potential product developers and manufacturers. Manufacturers of existing household technology should also be made aware of those products identified in the study as being most problematic. Although I do not see much hope of a reduction in the prevalence of telephone menus, there may be ways that they and VCRs can be made more user friendly to older (and younger) consumers.

The fourth and final question Wahl and Mollenkopf address concerns theoretical and research approaches that might capture the dynamic interaction between the individual and technology. They consider the efficacy of human factors models, information-processing models, and ecological models, and conclude that a major limitation of each of these approaches is that they neglect macro-conditions. To be sure it is important to consider the "big" picture, namely the societal conditions and historical era that the current or potential technology user has lived through. Virtually all social gerontology introductory textbooks and textbooks on research methods for gerontologists urge sensitivity to the potential confounding elements of period and cohort effects when analyzing cross-sectional data comparing age groups. Service providers need to be equally sensitive to considering a person's "techno-generation" (Docampo Rama, de Ridder, & Bouma, 2001) when deciding how much or how little training might be required by new users of assistive technology. The same applies to families with respect to selecting gifts of household technology for elderly relatives. Having to call one's son or grandson to come to the house to reprogram a flashing clock on the VCR or to reset the clock radio may be seen by some as a way of promoting family interaction, but after the nth such call for help, may provoke irritation instead.

Wahl and Mollenkopf also draw attention to the existence of a large number of design directives, home adaptation guides, and catalogues of products.

Some Examples of Design Directives, Home Adaptation Guides, and Product Catalogues

Since they do not provide them, I have taken the liberty of listing several guides and catalogues below as an aid to readers. These include both print and web-based resources. While some may think the print materials are outdated, in fact they are not. Many of the devices described in these volumes, especially those of the low-tech variety, still have currency for older adults. The volumes themselves constitute a primary resource for those seniors (and practitioners) who are not computer literate. Print resources include the following:

D. La Buda (Ed.). (1985). *The Gadget Book—Ingenious Devices for Easier Living*. Glenville, IL: Scott, Foresman: This volume lists 325 items divided into seven sections addressing the following activities: personal care, home environment, home maintenance, communications, mobility, health care, and leisure and recreation. The introduction states that the book was conceived and created to broaden awareness of numerous new "low-technology" products that can make everyday tasks easier and help eliminate frustration and struggle with daily activities.

M. W. Selvidge, M. A. Wylde, and M. Rummage. (1990). *Enabling Products: A Sourcebook*. Oxford, MS: Institute for Technology Development: This book was commissioned in order to suggest ideas about elderly housing products to architects, developers, builders, planners, service providers, and product manufacturers. Readers will want to give special attention to the initial chapter that contains a number of very useful product review criteria. Several examples, grouped by function, are shown below (Selvidge, Wylde, & Rummage, 1990, pp. 2–6).

Cognition
- Is the function of the product and its components self-explanatory?
- Are controls arranged sequentially?
- Does the arrangement of controls follow a logical pattern?
- Does the operation of controls require more than a maximum of two steps per function?
- Are graphics and symbols simple to comprehend?

Vision
- Do surfaces have a matte or semi-matte finish to reduce glare?
- Are instructions presented in high contrast graphics and lettering?
- Are graphics and lettering presented in preferred combinations of light on dark?

Upper Body Dexterity and Mobility
- Do controls allow activation by persons with low grip strength?
- Are control knobs a minimum of 1" in diameter?
- Are touch pad activators a minimum of ½" square?
- Are C- or U-shaped handles installed when straightforward pulling movements are required?

Another good source of information on home technology, particularly with respect to Universal Design Home Modifications, is found on the AARP Web site (http://www.aarp.org/universalhome/home.html). The first page of this section of the website provides interactive home tours, followed by suggestions concerning, respectively, the kitchen, the bathroom, doors and doorways, storage and closets, the outside of the home, electrical concerns, and lighting. There is also a section on finding solutions to particular individual needs and a checklist designed to ascertain whether one's home meets one's needs.

For design guidelines on application of smart home technology to meet the needs of persons with visual, hearing, mobility, or cognitive impairments, the reader is referred to the Web site of the European Domotics project (http://www.stakes.fi/cost219/smarthousing.htm). Particularly interesting are the "best-practice" examples from Norway, Belgium, and the Netherlands, although at the time the guidelines were written, most were not fully operational.

THE DEARTH OF BEHAVIOR RESEARCH IN ECOLOGICALLY VALID SETTINGS

While the information in the above documents and Web sites, and others like them, is useful, it is important to note that much of it is anecdotal rather than evidence based. With a few notable exceptions (e.g., Czaja, Weber, & Nair, 1993), generally, there is a dearth of information from research that goes beyond focus groups and self-report surveys to actually observe and systematically analyze problems older persons experience as they interact with the built environment or perform everyday living tasks using assistive technology. The situation should change dramatically in the future however, with the development of research facilities able to manipulate physical space and unobtrusively measure the impact of different environmental designs on performance of ADLs and IADLs. The Dr. Tong Louie Living Laboratory in Vancouver, Canada, is one such facility (http://www.sfu.ca/livinglab). A joint project of the Simon Fraser University Gerontology Research Centre and the Technology Centre at the British Columbia Institute of Technology, the "Living Lab" was established to test products and environments designed for older persons and adults with disabilities. The objective is to ensure that these meet the intended end users' needs in a way that is cost effective, efficient, and that enhances their independence and quality of life. The "Living Lab" is composed of three spaces. The experimental studio, which resembles a movie set, is a 1,000 square foot open area that contains a movable wall system that can be configured to represent, in full scale, a variety of living and work spaces (e.g. one-bedroom apartment, nursing home unit, several different kitchen or bathroom designs). A data center processes the information captured by the video and audio recording equipment, remote sensors, force plate, and other equipment that is used in the experimental studio. The third part consists of an interactive viewing area. When combined, the three components provide a powerful tool for behavioral observation, ergonomic analysis, physiological monitoring, and product evaluation.

Like the SFU-BCIT Living Lab, The Smart Medical Home Research Laboratory at the University of Rochester, in Rochester, New York (http://www.futurehealth.rochester.edu/smart_home/index.html) is also experimenting with home automation technology in service of the physically frail elderly and persons with dementia. The setting is a five-room "house," outfitted with infrared sensors, computers, biosensors, and video cameras.

Four other laboratories are contained in free-standing buildings resembling conventional housing. Premiere among them is the Aware Home located on the campus of the Georgia Institute of Technology in Atlanta, Georgia (http://www.cc.gatech.edu/fce/ahri/projects/index.html). This purpose-built three-story, 5,000 square foot facility, described in chapter 1 of this volume, was designed to accommodate two to four residents and also has living quarters for the researchers. An array of smart equipment (microphones, cameras), as well as smart sensors embedded in the walls, ceiling, and floors, have the potential to gather vast amounts of long-term data about lifestyles that can be correlated with information about disease.

The Gloucester Smart House (http://www.dementia-voice .org.uk/Projects_GloucesterProject.htm), located in Gloucester, UK, consists of a three-bedroom house that has been retrofitted by Housing 21, the Bath Institute of Medical Engineering, and Dementia Voice, a dementia services development center, to include technology to assist older persons with dementia to remain independent. Devices include a stove monitor, bath/basin monitor, picture phone, and item locator. In addition to serving as a research laboratory, the functions of the Gloucester Smart House are to serve as a show home and demonstrator for technical equipment and systems and to provide accommodation for people with dementia and their caregivers on a short-term basis.

The MavHome (http://www-cse.uta.edu/smarthome/), a multidisciplinary research project at the University of Texas at Arlington, views the smart home as an intelligent agent that perceives its environment through the use of sensors, and can act upon the environment through the use of actuators. Among the overall goals of the home are to minimize the cost of maintaining the home and to maximize the comfort of its inhabitants.

The Adaptive House (a.k.a The Neural Network House) at the University of Colorado in Boulder, Colorado (http://www.cs.Colorado.edu/~mozer/house/) uses artificial intelligence algorithms to automatically adjust basic residential comfort systems (heating, ventilation, and air conditioning), water heater, and interior lighting based on the living patterns of the inhabitants. Objectives are to free the occupants from manual control of the house and promote energy conservation.

SUMMARY AND CONCLUSION

The Wahl and Mollenkopf chapter is provocative and evocative. Beyond the very useful data it provides from these researchers' analysis of several large data sets, it draws attention to a number of important research questions and issues. These include how to better assess whether introduction of household technology has made life "better" and, if so, for whom. Clearly, the type of data they had to work with, drawn from a larger survey designed for a different purpose, does not provide the raw material to answer the question in a fully satisfactory manner.

Issues of unmet need and user friendliness similarly needed to be approached in a different or at least more comprehensive manner. Existing theoretical and research approaches do not, in this writer's opinion, capture the dynamic interaction between person and technology generally, and between older person and technology in particular, especially if used in isolation. The clarion call in the technology and aging area, as in many other areas of gerontology, is for triangulation of methodology—combination or supplementation, of large-scale surveys with in-depth substudies using other methodologies including "smart," full-scale simulated residence laboratories.

There is also a need for renewed interest and emphasis in theory development. As Wahl and Weisman (2001), Golant (2001), and Gitlin (2001) have recently argued, after great enthusiasm and productivity in the 1970s and 1980s there has been a hiatus with respect to theory in the environment and aging area.

The "gray wave" of aging baby boomers and the market they represent are beginning to capture not only media but also commercial attention. Residential, recreational, and health care environments, assistive technology, and other products for each of these environments

CHAPTER 6

Technology and the Promise of Independent Living for Adults: A Cognitive Perspective

Linda L. Liu and Denise C. Park

INTRODUCTION

The availability of powerful new technologies presents a wealth of opportunities for enhancing independent living in older adults. With a growing number of seniors continuing to lead active lives well into their 80s and 90s, it is important to recognize that the demographic composition of technology users is changing and to acknowledge that senior adults are becoming increasingly avid consumers of technology that can enhance their ability to lead independent lives. Seniors' consumption of valuable new technologies such as telemedicine services and wireless technology, however, occurs against a backdrop of age-related changes in cognition and information processing. Furthermore, as these technologies undergo almost constant revision and development, seniors are faced not only with the challenge of learning new technologies but also with the challenge of keeping up with the constant stream of technological upgrades and improvements.

In this chapter, we discuss how the promise of technology can fundamentally change how senior adults approach and perform everyday tasks, such as the Instrumental Activities of Daily Living (IADL) (Lawton & Brody, 1969). These activities include using the telephone, preparing meals, maintaining a household, shopping, using transportation, managing medications, and managing finances. We begin by *will* be developed and marketed to them. Using the environmental gerontology venacular of "P-E fit," reflected in the theories of Lawton and Nahemow (1973), Kahana (1982), and Carp and Carp (1984), which were developed to elucidate person-environment transactions as they relate to older people, one might hazard a guess that whether these items meet the needs of baby boomers and whether they sell (i.e., are profitable), will depend, in large measure, on how well product developers understand Baby Boomer-Environment (BB-E) fit and Baby Boomer-Technology (BB-T) fit. There are tremendous opportunities ahead, as well as challenges, for those gerontological theorists and researchers who can capture the dynamics and translate and transmit them to the marketplace.

REFERENCES

American Association for Retired Persons. (2001). *Global aging: Achieving its potential.* Washington, DC: Author.

American Society on Aging. (1999, December). *Promoting independence and quality of life for older persons: An international conference on aging.* Crystal City, VA.

Baltes, P. (1997). On the incomplete architecture of human ontogeny— Selection, optimization, and compensation as foundation of developmental theory. *American Psychologist, 52*(4), 366–380.

Bouma, H. (1992). Gerontechnology. In H. Bouma & J. A. M. Graafmans (Eds.), *Gerontechnology, studies in health technology and informatics, Vol. 3* (pp. 1–5). Amsterdam: IOS.

Brink, S. (1991). Bridging the technology gap: The links between research, development, production and policy for products supporting independent living. In G. M. Gutman & A. Wister (Eds.), *Progressive accommodation for seniors: Interfacing shelter and services* (pp. 211–222). Vancouver, Canada: The Gerontology Research Centre, Simon Fraser University.

Carp, F. M., & Carp, A. (1984). A complementary/congruence model of well-being or mental health for the community elderly. In I. Altman, M. P. Lawton, & J. Wohlwill (Eds.), *Elderly people and the environment* (pp. 279–336). New York: Plenum.

Czaja, S. J., Weber, R. A., & Nair, S. N. (1993). A human factors analysis of ADL activities: A capability-demand approach. *The Journals of Gerontology, 48*(Special Issue), 44–48.

Docampo Rama, M., de Ridder, H., & Bouma, H. (2001). Technology generation and age in using layered user interfaces. *Gerontechnology, 1*(1), 25–40.

Gitlin, L. N. (2001). Methods in home environmental research: Lessons learned and new directions for research. *Gerontology, 47*(Suppl. 1), 429.

Golant, S. (2001). Theory in environmental gerontology: Challenges and promising new pathways. *Gerontology, 47*(Suppl. 1), 430.

Graafmans, J., & Taipale, V. (1998). Gerontechnology—A sustainable invest-ment in the future. In J. Graafmans, V. Taipale, & N. Charness (Eds.), *Gerontechnology—A sustainable investment in the future* (pp. 3–6). Amsterdam: IOS.

Kahana, E. (1982). A congruence model of person-environment interaction. In M. P. Lawton, P. G. Windley, & T. O. Byerts & (Eds.), *Aging and the envi-ronment: Theoretical approaches* (pp. 97–121). New York: Springer.

La Buda, D. (Ed.). (1985). *The gadget book—Ingenious devices for easier living.* Glenville, IL: Scott, Foresman.

Lawton, M. P. & Nahemow, L. (1973). Ecology and the aging process. In C. Eisdorfer & M. P. Lawton (Eds.), *The psychology of adult development and aging* (pp. 619–674). Washington, DC: American Psychological Association.

National Advisory Council on Aging. (1995). *The NACA position on health care technology and aging.* Ottawa, Canada: Author.

National Advisory Council on Aging. (1999, Spring). *Expression, 12*(3).

National Advisory Council on Aging. (2001). Seniors and technology. *Writings in Gerontology,* No. 17, Ottawa, Canada: Author.

Selvidge, M. W., Wylde, M. A., & Rummage, M. (1990). *Enabling products: A sourcebook.* Oxford, MS: Institute for Technology Development.

Wahl, H-W., & Weisman, G. (2001). Environmental gerontology at the begin-ning of the new millennium: Major achievements and some concerns. *Gerontology, 47*(Suppl. 1), 429.

proposing that new technologies have the potential to play a role in more than just compensating for age-related deficits in sensory, motor, and cognitive abilities, but additionally may serve to expand the world of senior adults due to the availability of a broad array of information services, instrumental services, and communication partners. We believe that the standard IADLs are all important markers of independence. We propose, however, that these IADLs should be supplemented by including the ability to seek and manage information via contemporary communication systems that will allow for continued independence and even expansion of life experiences for even the frailest elderly.

The chapter is organized so that we briefly review the importance of communication technologies for tasks of everyday living and evaluate the changing demographics of technology consumers. We follow this review with a discussion of how the cognitive decline associated with aging may limit technology use but also how the role of experience may buttress some of these limitations. Subsequently, we consider in detail how information and communication-seeking behaviors interface with the performance of traditional IADLs and, in a final discussion, address how cognitive factors may impact web design and use by older adults.

COMMUNICATION: A NEW IADL FOR THE 21ST CENTURY

As technology evolves, its use provides extraordinary benefits in the form of external compensatory mechanisms for older adults, such as speech synthesizers that can compensate for visual declines and elaborate personal medical devices capable of summoning help quickly if an older adult falls or requires medical assistance. However, it is also important to recognize that technology is no longer limited to compensatory devices for fading sensory function or the limited mobility that occurs with age. Rather, technology gives older adults access to services and information that can provide them with a higher quality of life and allow them to maintain their independence in the face of multiple frailties. Internet technology provides seniors with the capability of checking medical information, the weather, or even stock report information, and wireless devices provide access to these services from any location. As medical technology continues to improve and people continue to lead longer and healthier lives, people are also becoming more critical consumers of technological services. Consequently, technology developers may need to revise their strategies for creating products for senior adults, particularly as seniors become increasingly reliant on these technologies to execute the activities of daily life. Perhaps the IADL of being able to communicate via the Internet should be added to the list of IADLs for the twenty-first century, as this is rapidly becoming fundamental to function in contemporary society. Not only does the Internet provide access to a wide range of goods and services, it provides an important measure of control to physically frail older adults who can manage their assets and acquire what they need without being hindered by their limited mobility. In addition to assisting seniors with their IADL, communication via the Internet also has changed how people interact with one another. Online social networks can provide a chance for older individuals to communicate with others with the same disorder or on the same medication. In fact, older adults may be particularly enthusiastic to share their experiences in online chatrooms and message boards where their identities and appearance are hidden and they are less likely to be judged based on a stereotype (Henke, 1999). Furthermore, for homebound older adults, social interaction becomes rare because of their limited mobility. Although many seniors do eventually move into some type of long-term care facility, some choose to live alone. Consequently, older adults have the potential to become isolated and lonely. The Internet links individuals around the world and has the potential to increase social interactions they might have with people outside their immediate area.

We should note that nearly all elderly have access, at present, to telephones (which is the only technological device included in the original list of IADLs), but many older adults do not have access to current forms of information technology, even if they are desirous of using it. Increasingly, these services are available in public libraries and senior centers, but homebound elderly, who would perhaps profit most dramatically from this technology, may have the least access to it due to socioeconomic disadvantages. Considering how to make technologies and associated training to use them available to poor and frail elderly is an important national priority.

THE DEMOGRAPHICS OF TECHNOLITERACY

The increasingly widespread use and availability of the Internet has increased the technoliteracy of seniors, expanding the range of options for older adults in reading the news, shopping, or collecting information about their personal health issues (see Czaja & Lee, this volume, for a full discussion). Senior adults represent the fastest growing segment of the United States population. In the next 20 years, the population aged 65 to 74 years in the United States is expected to increase by as much as 74%, compared to only a 24% expected increase in the population under age 65 (U.S. Bureau of the Census, 1997). This increase in the senior population has important implications for the direction of technological advances for several reasons. As the baby boomers join the ranks of senior adults, they bring with them a number of years of experience using the Internet and enjoying the widespread availability of wireless phones and electronic devices. Consequently, the population of senior adults in coming years is likely to be technology-literate and well-grounded in the use of computers and the Internet.

Currently, senior adults fall into two groups: those who are skilled in using technology and those who are less skilled. Although the Internet became widely available in the mid-1990s and has become a technological mainstay in a majority of households, a recent study estimated that as many as 75% of adults aged 50 and over who do not use the Internet have no interest in learning to use it (Vastag, 2001). Seniors who do use the Internet, however, report using it in sophisticated ways: to research health information, to communicate via electronic mail, and to plan their travel arrangements (Morrell, Mayhorn, & Bennett, 2000).

Among technologically inexperienced older adults, the primary reason for low technology use seems to be lack of exposure. Hence, this may be the first obstacle to getting this subgroup of older adults to use new technologies. Non-use of technology typically is associated with negative attitudes toward the technology (Smither & Braun, 1994). Research suggests, however, that individuals who have at least a single experience using a new technology such as an ATM or who receive a brief training session on a new technology demonstrate significantly more positive attitudes toward this technology (Czaja & Sharit, 1998; Kelley, Morrell, Park, & Mayhorn, 1999; Smither & Braun, 1994). Thus, the goal of increasing technology use among senior adults requires a twofold strategy: Among older adults who are already technology-literate, it may be more important to focus on making new technologies easier to learn and use; on the other hand, older adults who have negative attitudes toward learning new technologies will benefit greatly simply from being exposed to new tools and being trained to use them.

AGING, COGNITION, AND TECHNOLOGY

The declines in both sensory and cognitive functions that occur with age may limit technology use among seniors. At the same time, however, tasks that are rehearsed repeatedly and executed frequently become cognitively less demanding over time (Park, 2000). A good case in point is that of medication adherence. It would appear that managing medications poses a multitude of cognitive requirements. These include the working memory task of integrating a schedule in which several different medications must be taken in different dosages at different times of day, and the long-term memory task of remembering what needs to be done once the schedule has been integrated. Other cognitive aspects of adherence include remembering prospectively when to take a particular medication, computing the time since the last dose, calculating when the next dose should be taken, and remembering retrospectively which medications have been taken already (Park & Jones, 1996; Park & Mayhorn, 1996). Despite demonstrable age-related declines in component cognitive processes of working memory and long-term memory of old compared to middle-aged adults, a number of studies have paradoxically demonstrated that older adults remember to take medications more accurately than do younger adults (Morrell, Park, Kidder, & Martin, 1997; Park et al., 1999).

The case of medication adherence illustrates how years of practice and familiarity in a task domain can support seniors' performance of even difficult and challenging tasks. Park (2000) argues that if a behavior is exercised with great regularity, an everyday task has the potential to become automatized over time and eventually requires little cognitive effort to sustain its performance. Older adults lead more routine lives than do younger adults and are also less busy (Martin & Park, in press). Park and colleagues (1999) reported that busyness and routineness of lifestyle were better predictors of medication adherence than cognitive variables such as working memory and processing speed. Thus it is important to recognize that everyday behaviors occur in a context, and if these behaviors are performed with high frequency and in the same context, their performance may require little cognitive capacity, even if on the surface the behaviors seem largely cognitive.

AGE-RELATED DECLINE IN COGNITION

There is evidence that the speed of information processing and the amount of information that can be processed decline with age, and that these processes limit the rate at which older adults can acquire and learn new information. Speed of processing is measured by the rate at which individuals perform simple perceptual matching tasks. For example, in the Letter Comparison Task (Salthouse, 1996), subjects receive two strings of letters side by side and must determine if the two letter strings are the same. The number of items that can be completed within a specific time frame (typically a minute or two) is a highly accurate measure of the rate at which information is processed. How much information can be stored and manipulated on one's mental desktop is a measure of working memory. Air traffic control, for example, is a job with high working memory demands, as controllers must be considering new information (airplanes entering into the air space) while simultaneously coordinating the positions of the planes currently in the air and bringing down still other planes for landing. In a recent study, we collected multiple measures of cognition, including speed of processing, working memory capacity in the visuospatial and verbal domain, verbal knowledge, and recall of words and abstract visual shapes in 350 individuals, aged 20 to 90 (Park et al., 2003). The results of this research are presented in Figure 6.1, in which there are several striking features worth noting. The first is the equivalence in decline that occurs across age in all of the measures that involved effortful processing (speed, working memory, and long-term memory), regardless of the modality. Second is the increase in age in the measures of verbal knowledge (which were assessed using multiple-choice problems that required merely the recognition of knowledge, and thus required less self-initiated processing). Third is the evidence that declines across the life span are steady and regular. Aging appears to be more of a slippery slope than a cliff. The graph illustrates that cognitive aging is a continuous process that begins in the 20s and continues at a steady, gradual rate across the entire life span.

Structural equation modeling has shown that the most fundamental mediators of age-related decline in long-term memory are speed of processing and working memory (Park et al., 1996; Park et al., 2002), so it is declines in these two mechanisms that are critically important in understanding the role of cognitive decline in acquisition and use of technology. Very seldom do activities in daily life occur in isolation and allow us to attend to tasks one at a time. Similarly, it is rare that we are given an unlimited amount of time to complete an activity; rather most tasks must be completed under time constraints and some decisions (e.g., during driving) must be made quickly based on a limited amount of information. Consequently, speed and working memory are the building blocks of ability to acquire new technologies. Technologies that target older adults must take into consideration how these building blocks change with age, as these changes affect the ease with which new technologies are learned and accepted into regular use.

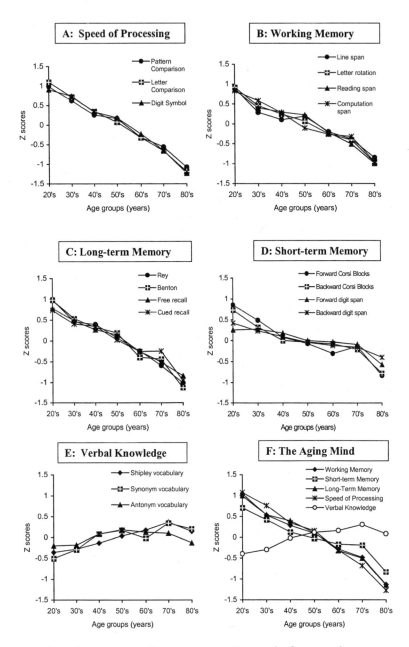

FIGURE 6.1 **Life span performance on (A) speed of processing measures, (B) working memory measures (visuospatial and verbal), (C) long-term memory measures (visuospatial and verbal), (D) short-term memory measures (visuospatial and verbal), (E) knowledge-based verbal ability measures, and (F) a composite view of the above measures.**

Composite scores for each construct represent the z score of the average of all measures for that construct. From Park et al. (2002).

It is extraordinarily important that as individuals age, they continue to adapt to learning new technologies. Learning a new skill requires fewer processing resources when one has learned similar skills in the past. For example, it would be considerably easier to learn how to use an updated version of a spreadsheet or word-processing program than it would be to start at the beginning in late adulthood and learn how to use a computer and several new programs. The extent that individuals "keep up" and engage in lifelong learning of technology will play a critical role in their ability to utilize the many opportunities to maintain independence and intellectual health that technology is certain to bring into the lives of older adults.

COGNITION, TASKS OF DAILY LIVING, AND TECHNOLOGY

Just as declines in sensory ability can be offset by enlarging a display window or increasing the volume of sounds on a medical device, cognitive aging research suggests that age-related changes in cognition can be offset to some extent by providing contextual and environmental support for older adults. Support in the form of external memory aids can compensate for cognitive deficits by reducing the demands on older adults to self-initiate processes that they find difficult to remember (Craik & Byrd, 1982; Craik & Jennings, 1992).

To illustrate this point, Park, Morrell, Frieske, and Kincaid (1992) provided senior adults with very basic cognitive supports—medication charts and medication organizers—to help them organize their medication schedules. The organizational charts showed their daily medications on a grid that displayed a timetable for each day and allowed medications to be checked off as they were taken. The medication organizers were commonly available in drugstores and consisted of compartments corresponding to four medication dosage times for each day of the week. Older adults loaded their own organizers and an experimenter corrected any errors before they left the laboratory. Park and colleagues found that when used together these very basic cognitive supports were extremely successful at reducing the number of missed pills. The efficacy of this relatively simple and inexpensive intervention suggests, perhaps, that the comprehension and memory demands of medication adherence benefit greatly from a small boost. For instance, the medication organizers directly addressed the perceptual demands associated with confusing similar-looking pills and vials, while checking off each medication on the chart relieved the retrospective memory demands of remembering whether the last dose was taken or not. Together, these findings provide strong evidence that seniors stand to gain a great deal from even very low-tech external support.

Because technology can provide an important means of cognitive support for the special needs of older adults, it is important to consider how age-related changes in cognition intersect with specific demands of independent living. Here, we will return to an analysis set forth by Park (1997) that evaluated the cognitive, sensory, and motor demands of the IADLs (Lawton & Brody, 1969). The IADLs consist of managing medications, using the telephone, preparing meals, maintaining a household, shopping, using transportation, and managing finances. Each of these activities presents a unique constellation of demands, and it is important to evaluate the type of support available from technological devices to meet these demands. Park (1997) evaluated the cognitive demands of these tasks (Table 6.1) and suggested ways in which the technology of 1997 might address those demands. We wish to update this discussion by focusing on the cognitive component of these IADLs, by bringing current technologies into the discussion, and by evaluating the role of communication in facilitating the IADLs.

Managing Health and Medications

Although the IADLs focus on the aspect of independent living that involves managing medications (Morrell, Park, Kidder, & Martin, 1997), we believe that it is appropriate to construe this more broadly as the act of managing one's health, which includes medication management. Park and colleagues (1999) have done extensive research on the cognitive aspects of managing medications. Interestingly, they reported that older adults make fewer errors in medication adherence than do younger adults, and that middle-aged adults are significantly more at risk for committing medication errors. Structural equation modeling indicated that self-report of leading a busy life style was the strongest predictor of nonadherence, as opposed to cognitive or personality variables. We focus now on technology that is assistive of medication adherence for those adults who are experiencing adherence problems due to cognitive frailty.

Simple high-tech devices may improve upon some of the low-tech supports studied by Park and colleagues (1992) in important ways. Although the medication charts and organizers they used provided external support for the working memory demands associated with maintaining several medication regimens concurrently, these supports did not assist with the prospective memory task of remembering to take

TABLE 6.1   The Physical, Sensory, and Cognitive Demands of the Instrumental Activities of Daily Living (IADLs) with and without Cognitive Supports

IADL	Requirements without support			Requirements with support		
	Sensory	Cognitive	Physical	Sensory	Cognitive	Physical
Using telephone	High	Medium	Low	Medium	Low	Low
Meal preparation	Medium	High	Medium	Medium	Low	Low
Maintaining household	Medium	Low	High	Low	Low	Low
Shopping	Medium	Medium	High	Low	Medium	Low
Using transportation*	High	Medium	Low	*	*	*
Managing medications	Medium	Medium	Low	Low	Medium	Low
Managing finances**	Medium	High	Low	**	**	**

* Training intervention rather than environmental support is recommended.
** Specific supports are not recommended, pending further research.

Note: Adapted from park, D. C. (1997). Psychological issues related to competence: cognitive aging and instrumental activities of daily living. In W. Schaie & S. Willis (Eds.), *Social structures and aging*. Mahwah, NJ: Erlbaum. Appears as Table 2.1, page 73 in the original source. Used with permission.

the medications. Environmental supports in the form of alarms programmed to sound at dosage times would address this problem directly. Hertzog, Park, Morrell, & Martin (2000) used microelectronic caps that recorded medication events for all medications for a 4-week period. Although these devices were used to assess adherence behaviors, there are modified versions available that beep and remind patients to take their medications. A device could be worn, such as a HealthWatch (Bakker, 1999), which is similar to a digital wristwatch but also stores medication information and beeps with appropriate instructions on which medication should be taken at a given time.

Automatic medication dispensers are another example of high-tech support technology that can eliminate the cognitive demand associated with selecting the appropriate medicines that should be taken at a given time. Park (1997) cited two main sources of cognitive difficulty: the working memory demands of assimilating different sets of instructions for multiple medications, and the onerous task of generating a plan that ensures that each medication is taken properly and on time. A dispenser could be programmed to beep when it is time for a pill to be taken, and could reduce the demands of selecting the appropriate pill by storing the different medications in separate compartments and then dispensing only the pill that needs to be taken at the appropriate time. Other features currently in development include dispensers that are computerized and that automatically contact emergency personnel when an important medication is not taken (Bakker, 1999).

With an increasing number of elderly using the Internet, we suggest that another means to improving medication adherence is simply to empower seniors to manage their own medication schedules. The growing volume of medical information on the Internet may be a particularly important resource in helping older adults to learn more about their medication regimens. Rather than simply receiving reminders to take their medications, seniors can learn about drug interactions and *why* some drugs must be taken on an empty stomach and others must be taken with food. The availability of medical information on the Internet may be especially helpful in highlighting contraindications for certain medicines. For example, a sticker on a medication vial may include a brief warning to "avoid sunlight while taking this medication." Additional elaboration of this warning on the Internet may include a more detailed explanation of why the medication increases the skin's sensitivity to sunlight, and could include pictures showing what can occur if precautions are not taken, both of which could improve an individual's memory for the warning. Such an outcome would be consistent with Park and Mayhorn's (1996) observation that patients' beliefs about their illness and their medications often have direct effects on their behavior. Finally, using websites such as American Health Networks (AHN.com), seniors can also read a variety of health reports about different medical technologies and procedures to improve their decisions about their own care.

Although typically not discussed in relation to medication adherence, the act of acquiring medications and remembering to have prescriptions filled before the last prescription runs out is another important component to medication adherence. All of the mobility factors that have an impact on shopping have similar consequences for the acquisition of medications. Having to plan ahead for when a prescription runs out adds a prospective memory component to the task as well. Sites for organizations such as the American Association for Retired Persons (AARP) offer prescription drug services, and dedicated online pharmacies such as Drugstore.com will fill prescriptions online and deliver them. In addition, the increased availability of screen-phones and video-conferencing services may some day allow seniors to have virtual face-to-face medical consultations from home with nurse practitioners or pharmacists. Central to this latter set of high-tech devices is the emphasis on communication. These devices do not perform the desired actions themselves; rather, they allow seniors to access the services used by everyone else and, in that way, allow them to remain plugged in to mainstream society.

Using the Telephone

Park (1997) identified a number of potential difficulties associated with using a telephone. These difficulties have only increased in recent years, as the range of choices in communication devices and telecommunication providers has increased. By the same token, the rapid improvements in communication technology can prove a boon for older adults if the devices are adapted appropriately. For example, one of the authors was able to use mobile phone technology to maintain independence and mobility for her elderly mother (Mrs. X), who became legally blind.

The author purchased a cell phone and printed out the names of friends, family, and a cab service in large, high-contrast type and taped it on the back of the phone with a large, single-digit number next to the name. The phone was programmed so that if that digit were pressed, it would connect her mother with the named individual. Mrs. X retained limited vision and was able to see the names and, by touch, learned which keys on the phone she should press to connect with a given number. She was able to summon cabs and get around independently, as well as reliably call friends and family without searching for or misdialing phone numbers. Additionally, because all relevant information was taped to the telephone, if she ever became lost or confused, she could simply ask for assistance in a store and be connected with a family member. Finally, the cab company kept a running tab for Mrs. X, so she never had to fumble with money or pay drivers. Recent advances in voice recognition technology should allow mobile phones to become even more widely used among the elderly. Voice-activated calling and message retrieval systems virtually eliminate human factors problems due to keypad size, and greatly reduce the cognitive demands required to execute a series of key presses to navigate a phone menu in order to call up a phone number stored in the memory bank.

In the previous example of the mobile phone, at least two other IADLs—transportation and managing medications—were addressed directly with a single piece of technology. The feasibility of performing other IADLs, such as shopping and managing finances, were facilitated indirectly. Increases in the availability of screen phones also may expand the utility of telephones for these other IADLs in the future, making it possible for nurses to provide detailed training procedures or for computer staff to provide technical support over the phone. The ability to see the person on the other end of the phone provides an added measure of cognitive support for older adults by allowing them both to see and hear the person providing the instruction.

Technology in Transportation

Although driving typically is regarded as a cognitively demanding activity, it is a necessary skill for many older adults who wish to live independently. In fact, the mobility of older adults is thought to be a central component of their well-being (Carp, 1988). Furthermore, the cognitive demands of negotiating other means of transportation such as public transit may exceed those of driving, which is at least a relatively familiar procedure to older adults (Park, 1997).

Considerable research on older adults' driving behaviors supports the fact that they are at greater risk of having an accident while driving than younger adults (Owsley, Ball, Sloane, Roenker, & Bruni, 1991; Sixsmith & Sixsmith, 1993). It is important to note, however, that older adults also take steps to curb this risk to themselves and to others. First, most older adults recognize their limitations as drivers and modify their driving behavior in ways to minimize these risks (Park, 1994). Because they recognize that they may take more time to react to unexpected situations, they often drive slower and during the day when visibility is better (Sixsmith & Sixsmith, 1993). Furthermore, older adults report curtailing their driving to avoid challenging driving situations such as driving during rain, heavy traffic, or rush hour (Ball et al., 1998). Overall, older adults drive less frequently than do younger adults, so the absolute number of accidents in which they are involved is still relatively small (Park, 1997).

Driving poses a combination of sensory and perceptual demands, such as reacting to road signs and changes in traffic patterns that may require both multitasking and making speeded judgments. Although driving ability would seem to be most obviously affected by age-related sensory declines in the visual system, Owsley and colleagues (1991) report that early visual attention is a far more important predictor of driving behavior (as measured by number of accidents) than is visual acuity. Visual attention is typically assessed using a visual search task, in which one must detect a target amidst a background of distractors. Early visual attention is particularly relevant to the discussion of driving, since the ability to be captured quickly by visual targets and to direct attention to them immediately are key components of skilled driving behavior, as when one must detect the presence of pedestrians in one's peripheral vision and take immediate action to avoid hitting them (Owsley et al., 1991).

One particularly sensitive measure of visual attention is the measure of Useful Field of View (UFOV). The UFOV is a measure that combines information about the size of a person's perceptual window and the rate at which that person can interpret visual information presented in the surrounding area. In their laboratory, Ball and colleagues have explored the relationship between UFOV and driving measures, including performance on road tests (Myers, Ball, Kalina, Roth, & Goode, 2000) and measures of drivers' risk for crashes (Ball, 1997). Not only is UFOV highly correlated with a number of measures of driving performance (Ball & Owsley, 1993; Myers et al., 2000), it is a much better predictor of motor vehicle crash risk than performance on a test of visual acuity, which is typically administered as part of driving tests (Owsley et al., 1998).

The focus on the relationship between UFOV and driving ability is particularly important for another reason. Recent work by Ball, Owsley, and colleagues suggests that the relationship between UFOV and driving behavior is not fixed but, instead, is plastic and amenable to training (Ball, 1997; Ball & Owsley, 1993). In fact, an individual's UFOV can be increased and even raised to normal levels with training. These improvements in visual attention translate into improvements in driving (Ball,

1997). Thus, although there is a relationship between poor visual attention and poor driving performance, the effect appears to be reversible, and older adults who undergo visual attention training can show markedly improved driving behavior.

Aside from declines in processing speed, senior adults may find that cognitive changes in working memory may also affect their ability to drive. Common complaints among seniors center on problems with navigation and wayfinding, rather than the act of driving itself (Burns, 1999). Driving a familiar route does not present a problem to most older adults, since the act of driving itself is extremely well practiced and becomes automatized over time. When driving new routes, however, seniors' errors in navigation and wayfinding may be dangerous to other drivers (Burns, 1998). The process of navigation involves planning a series of steps required to get to a destination. The secondary process of wayfinding entails the execution of each of these steps and the identification and use of landmarks and signs in real time to decide when a particular step in the navigation process has been reached.

The task of navigation poses problems for drivers because the series of turns given in a set of driving directions is sequentially linked, such that missing a single step or repeating a step can throw off the entire route. Wayfinding presents an additional set of cognitive demands in that older adults may have difficulty performing the multitasking that is necessary to continue driving while reading and following unfamiliar street signs and traffic signals. Burns (1998) reported that the most frequent errors in wayfinding cited by older drivers were spotting a road sign too late or missing a turn, both of which may result from slowed processing speed. Likewise, research using driving simulators has demonstrated that when older adults are presented with cognitively taxing situations while they are driving, their driving performance worsens considerably (Ponds, Brouwer, & Van Wolffelaar, 1988).

Technological supports for driving are termed Road Transportation Informatics (RTI) and fall into two categories: early warning devices and information devices (Burns, 1999). Early warning devices also address the fact that older drivers have more restricted UFOV and, as a result, tend to react more slowly than younger drivers do. These devices provide advance visual or audio warnings of objects present in the vicinity. Because older drivers are prone to miss objects in their periphery, these object detection devices, in a sense, increase their sensitivity to objects they otherwise might not see. The advance warning system increases the time given to react to a potentially problematic situation and may compensate for older drivers who may be slower to process potential hazards.

Other information devices that may warrant future study include those that provide computerized route planning. New automotive technologies such as General Motors' OnStar provide real-time assistance with navigation. Although the availability of real-time assistance is tempting (anyone who has used an Internet navigational device such as Mapquest knows that there is a difference between planning a route to a destination and successfully executing it), the usefulness of these high-tech supports for older adults in the future will depend greatly on whether seniors increase their facility with computers and other forms of technology. If the transportation technology is relatively new and unfamiliar to older adults, these devices have the potential to divert their already limited cognitive resources and increase the risk of accidents and crashes. With sufficient training and practice, however, these devices have the potential to be extremely helpful for older adults, providing support should older adults be required to drive to a new destination (if their favored grocery store relocates) or to traverse a new path between two frequently traveled destinations (making an unplanned trip from the doctor's office directly to the grocery store without going home first). Technologies like OnStar not only put together a sequence of turns required to move from the origin to the destination, they provide guidance as the route is executed, giving updates on road conditions and changes in traffic patterns. Because wayfinding appears to be the dominant problem among elderly drivers who have particular difficulty processing information in real time, these computerized navigational systems have the potential to become an especially important contributor to maintaining seniors' mobility and independence.

Shopping and Preparing Meals

Research on the elderly suggests that these IADLs present the most difficulty among seniors with visual decline (Branch, Horowitz, & Carr, 1989). In addition to the physical demands of getting to the store itself, navigating a grocery store and making decisions about the appropriate products to purchase require both planning and a significant amount of online processing (Park, 1997). Older adults may seek out familiar labels and familiar packaging, only to find that the logos or colors have changed. Research conducted with a wide range of age groups has demonstrated that the similarities of labels can be confusing for adults of all ages (Rafiq & Collins, 1996).

Furthermore, the emergence of weekly sales and specials changes the relative value of products, and determining affordability of different brands can prove to be challenging when comparing different prices for different sizes. For example, if one usually purchases Brand A coffee for $8.99/pound, one may find that Brand B is on sale for $5.99/bag. If Brand B is packaged in 12-ounce bags, however, a series of mathematical operations requiring both online storage and processing must be performed to determine which brand is the better buy. In this example, figuring out which brand is the better buy requires the individual to remember that a one pound bag translates into 16 ounces before mentally calculating the unit price of Brand A ($8.99 / 16 = .56/oz.). Then, he or she must store that result while the unit price of Brand B is determined ($5.99 / 12 = .50/oz.) and then retrieve Brand A's price to make the unit price comparison and decide that Brand B is the better buy. The process of storing and manipulating figures places some demands on working memory. When one considers also the noise and traffic present in a typical grocery store, this becomes a divided-attention task, where attentional resources are diverted due to other shoppers trying to get by or reaching for merchandise nearby. Taken together with the evidence that older adults typically perform worse under conditions of cognitive load or divided attention, these factors suggest that traditional grocery stores do not provide an environment for optimal decision making.

Recent advances in online commerce have increased the usability of online supermarkets, which directly address at least two of the issues described above. Aside from the obvious advantage of being able to conduct shopping trips from home, online grocery services allow shoppers to view more extensive product descriptions and make available unit pricing information that facilitates price comparisons such as the one described above. A popular online grocer, Peapod.com, presents per unit prices that facilitate both within-product and cross-product comparisons. For example, a 24-count bottle of back pain medication is priced at $2.70 while a 20-count bottle of the extra-strength formula of the same medication is $3.50. The Peapod.com interface converted both products to the same scale and provided a price per 10 count for each ($1.13 for the first and $1.75 for the second). Thus, the interface allows an individual who is deciding whether to spend the money for the extra-strength formula to weigh the increased cost against a perceived increase in benefit and to make a better decision.

Although there is enormous potential for benefit associated with learning to use the Web to shop, make travel plans, and fill prescriptions, the success of executing these activities is heavily dependent on an individual's level of Web literacy. Furthermore, visual and motor aspects of the Web may present additional obstacles that keep senior adults from fully enjoying its services.

Maintaining a Household and Managing Finances

In this area, we believe that computer and Internet technology have great potential for improving seniors' lifestyles, but stimulating widespread use of this technology will likely require that seniors receive a great deal of training. As seniors today have diverse spending behaviors and may have a variety of investments as well as a traditional savings account, the act of managing the finances of a household amounts to more than simply writing checks. It encompasses housekeeping tasks such as cleaning and doing laundry, and a variety of financial tasks including paying bills, balancing a checkbook, and checking the performance of stocks and investments.

Although there is currently no technological device available that directly addresses housekeeping issues such as taking out the garbage, the development of computer technology to support the infrastructure of a household has become sophisticated and could prove valuable to older adults juggling multiple bills during the month. A typical household will receive bills for electricity, water, gas, and phone service. Many other households also receive bills for car insurance, credit cards, cellular phone service, and cable television. Each bill requires a separate check that must be stamped and mailed by the due date. Because bills often vary in their arrival times and due dates, it may be difficult to consolidate the task of paying bills into a single event. Consequently, individuals must juggle multiple due dates and remember to pay each bill on an individual basis. This increases the demands on both working memory and prospective memory and thus increases the likelihood that a bill will be forgotten.

The introduction of online billing is a potentially convenient means for older adults to consolidate their financial transactions (Henke, 1999). Many utility companies, insurance providers, and credit card companies offer online billing services now in which bills are sent via electronic mail and can be paid by entering a checking account code, eliminating the memory demand of finding the paper billing statement in the house. If the bill is paid online immediately, when the electronic announcement is received, the prospective memory demand of remembering to pay the bill later can be eliminated as well.

Similarly, the websites of most major credit cards allow users to access their accounts, track their credit card purchases, and obtain copies of previous statements. This relieves credit card holders of the burden of remembering how much was purchased on a given credit card and where the transactions took place. This also provides an important way for seniors to track their expenditures for purposes of keeping a budget. Whereas phone menu systems in the past allowed credit card users to access their account balances and sometimes a partial report of the amounts of the most recent transactions, online menus today provide instant access to a user's account and can generate a complete summary statement of card activity that can be viewed online any time of the month.

Banking is becoming similarly streamlined. Nearly all national bank chains have a Web-based interface that allows many lobby transactions to be conducted from home. The act of going to the bank and depositing a check either via an ATM or a teller involves a rather long, coordinated sequence of steps, including endorsing the checks, obtaining deposit envelopes, copying the amount of each check onto the envelope, remembering (or copying) the appropriate account number onto the envelope, and summing the numbers to calculate the total amount being deposited. The process requires juggling multiple documents (e.g., account number, banking card, and envelope) and multiple procedures. If there is a long line at either the bank or at the ATM, there is the added pressure of performing multiple tasks under a time constraint. All of these factors have the potential to increase the likelihood of committing errors in which deposits are made in incorrect amounts or are transferred to the wrong account.

To circumvent these problems, older adults can now request to have their social security checks deposited directly into their bank accounts and can check their account balances online to ensure that the transactions were carried out properly. Additional advances in computer technology have made possible the centralization of an individual's financial transactions. Software packages such as Microsoft Money coordinate a variety of financial activities and allow users to their pay bills online, obtain their checking or savings account balance, and even check the status of their investments.

The fact that a wealth of financial management technologies are now available certainly does not guarantee that they will be used by senior adults, even though they may stand to gain a great deal from technological support for this IADL. It is important at this point to note that all of the financial technologies described in this section thus far a shift in from "physical" transactions—those conducted in person or by receiving a paper bill and mailing in a paper check—to electronic transactions in which money is transferred online or over the phone without the physical transfer of paper checks or paper money. The ubiquitous presence of credit and debit card readers at gas stations, grocery stores, and the post office, and the burgeoning amount of commerce that is conducted over the Internet have further served to deemphasize the role of cash and check writing on the whole.

Consequently, a key issue in the successful integration of older adults into electronic commerce and online finance simply may hinge on their willingness to rely less on cash and to embrace other forms of payment.

Even something as basic as using an ATM, which younger adults use with relative regularity and without extensive training, can be daunting to older adults. Research on older adults' patronage of ATMs suggests that a common reason they give for non-usage is that they prefer to interact with a human teller (Rogers, Cabrera, Walker, Gilbert, & Fisk, 1996). Thus, it is important to note that older adults' habitual reliance on cash and years of practice in conducting business with cash and in person may be at least as responsible as other reasons we have discussed (e.g., simply never having used the technology before) for older adults' reluctance to use many of the other potentially useful technologies described in this section. Consequently, interventions that attempt to increase older adults' use of technology must work not just to increase their familiarity with these services but also should encourage older adults to practice conducting "cashless" transactions so that this process becomes more familiar and automatic. Rogers, Cabrera, and colleagues (1996) found that the availability of training would increase older adults' willingness to use these machines, and Rogers, Fisk, Mead, Walker, and Cabrera (1996) reported that older adults who received an online tutorial became significantly more adept at conducting ATM transactions they previously considered to be difficult, such as making payments or depositing checks.

In a few cases, training may not be sufficient to improve seniors' use of financial technologies. Unlike routine tasks that senior adults have considerable practice in performing in conjunction with maintaining a household, the act of managing finances is a particularly cognitively taxing task. Barberger-Gateau and colleagues (1992) have reported significant correlations between indicators of cognitive impairment and the inability to manage finances and perform other IADLs, such as using the telephone and transportation. Thus, it is important to consider that many of the high-tech advances that are available to assist with the management of finances may have a limited audience and simply may not be practical for the frail elderly. The development of online "virtual companions," which could provide senior adults with a "human" interface to guide them through execution of many financial tasks, may not be far in the future. Furthermore, some of the research that is being conducted to explore the relationship between cognitive variables and the performance of everyday tasks (Allaire & Marsiske, 1999) may bring up the possibility of using cognitive training in older adults to improve their performance of everyday functions.

Making the Web Senior-friendly:
A Key to Managing the IADLs

Accompanying technology's enormous potential for improving seniors' lives is the equally substantial task of ensuring that seniors update their knowledge to keep pace with changes in technology. This task is especially important, given that seniors' abilities to adapt to changes may be more limited due to declines in cognition. Striking a balance between training seniors to use existing technology and helping them maintain the cognitive flexibility to update their knowledge is a theme that will guide the remainder of the discussion in this chapter.

Technology that addresses the needs of independent functioning must not only acknowledge that declines in cognition are evident, it must work in conjunction both with the compensatory processes and supports that are already in place. The age-related declines in cognition point to areas in which support may be particularly important. To develop skills that may be new or unfamiliar to older adults, it might be worthwhile to provide training and practice that encourages the automatization of particularly valuable behaviors such as using a cellular phone or surfing the Internet. To develop the flexibility to update newly learned skills, seniors should be encouraged to stay mentally active.

There are also a number of sensory and physiological issues at stake when designing websites for senior adults (Hartley, 1999; Morrell & Echt, 1997; Morrell, Mayhorn, & Bennett, 2000; Rogers & Fisk, 2000). From an information-processing standpoint, the highly visual presentation of web information makes it a potentially powerful influence. The sheer amount of information available on a single screen, coupled with the decreases in processing capacity that occur with age, make Internet mainstays such as pop-up windows a particularly insidious problem for seniors. Pop-ups are not only distracting, they potentially can lead older adults down garden paths and into dead-end Web sites. Viewing a number of screen changes in a serial manner functions, essentially, like a working memory span task to integrate information across screens, and backtracking is not always possible when web searches hit a dead end. Even if seniors successfully leave a website they did not intend to visit, the use of Web "cookies" may increase the incidence of future pop-ups.

Apart from the sensory issues, there are also a number of cognitive issues at stake when designing web access for senior adults. Not only are seniors dealing with decreases in *quantity*—declines in sensory, physiological, and cognitive capacity—specific *qualitative* differences in the how older adults process and remember information relative to younger adults are important to consider as older adults' Internet use increases in the next twenty years. Specifically, changes in how older adults process information and, perhaps more important, how they process false information, may make older adults more vulnerable to the types of deception that are present on the internet.

False Information Gains an "Illusion of Truth"

A story from the March 31, 1999 *New York Times* warns against the "Health Hazards of Point-and-click Medicine." The increasing availability of a wide variety of health information has led to a concomitant increase in the number of false claims about diseases and remedies published on websites. Work in our laboratory suggests that age differences figure in how these claims are retained and recalled later. Skurnik, Park, and Schwarz (2000) found, in fact, that when older adults recall information, they display a bias to remember it as being "true" and that this bias increases with the number of times the information is viewed, the "familiarity" of the information. In other words, information loses its valence over time and, as a result, both true and false information tend to be remembered as being true, particularly if the information is presented repeatedly and feels familiar. Because the elderly have particularly poor episodic and explicit memory systems, they are likely to be more susceptible to the illusion of truth. In addition, the illusion of truth seems to be particularly strong for situations in which cognitive load is high and processing resources are occupied.

Skurnik, Park, and Schwarz (2000) developed a series of medical statements that were technically accurate but were both uncertain in truth value and unfamiliar to both younger and older adults. For example, participants read statements such as

- DHEA supplements can lead to liver damage, even when taken briefly.
- Most cold medications cause the eye's pupil to dilate.
- Corn chips have twice as many calories per cup as potato chips.

During the study phase, they presented participants with 36 claims (*study* claims) and randomly assigned each claim a truth value (true or false). The experimenters also varied the repetition of the presentation: Half of the claims were presented once and the other half were presented three times. During the test phase, participants viewed sequentially a mixed list of claims composed of *study* claims and *new* claims. Participants were reminded that half of the claims were true and half were false; for each claim they saw in the test phase they were asked to decide whether that claim was "true," "false," or "new."

When participants were tested three days after the study phase, younger adults displayed a tendency to claim that "false" statements were "true" after studying the statements once. If the "false" statements were studied three times, however, the younger adults were able to identify these statements as "false." In other words, viewing "false" statements three times reinforced to young people the falsehood of the statements and enhanced their ability to remember that they were false. In contrast, for older adults the increased viewing time appeared to have the opposite effect. When older adults studied "false" claims three times, they were even more certain that "false" statements were "true" compared to when they studied them only once. Thus, increasing the repetition of false medical claims paradoxically *increased* the truth value of those claims to older adults over time, despite their having understood the claims to be false in their initial encounter with them. These results have important implications for how seniors use information from questionable sources in the media or on the Web. Elderly adults can be misled easily if they are frequent visitors to a particular Web site and are exposed repeatedly to false information. Of particular concern is that repeatedly warning seniors that a piece of information is false will backfire and that over time this information will gain an illusion of truth.

Age Increases in Gullibility

Senior adults also may be disproportionately likely to be duped by untrustworthy people. A series of studies by Ybarra, Chan, and Park (2001) explored age differences in adults' sensitivity to information about the morality and competence of other individuals. This research tested the hypothesis that age-related changes in cognition may make older adults less capable of being skeptical and socially vigilant when dealing with individuals they have just met. In these studies, older and younger adults performed a lexical-decision task in which they were presented serially with lists of letter strings and were asked to respond quickly whether or not the strings formed words. In a lexical-decision task, the ability to identify certain words more quickly than others relative to the non-words indicates an increased cognitive sensitivity to those words. The results suggested that all people, regardless of age, value personality traits that will allow them to make judgments of whether another individual is moral or immoral. When participants were presented with morality-related personality cues in a lexical decision task, results indicated that there were no age differences in sensitivity: both older and younger adults were sensitive to morality cues. Ybarra, Chan, and Park suggested that an attention to morality cues (versus cues to a person's competence) is adaptive in the social perception domain in that it allows people to assess the potential threat posed by an individual.

In a later study, however, Ybarra and Park (2002) found that despite the age invariance in sensitivity to morality cues, older adults are still less skeptical when they are forming impressions of other individuals. Since social vigilance is cognitively taxing, they suggested that older adults are less able than younger adults to be socially vigilant and to undertake the processes of revising their impressions of people once they are formed. In the second study, older and younger adults were asked to form an initial impression of a person but were subsequently given either confirming (impression-consistent) or disconfirming (impression-inconsistent) information about that person. When participants were given an unlimited amount of time to form their impressions, both older and younger adults utilized the disconfirming information to revise their initial impressions. Under cognitively taxing conditions, however, older adults tended to retain a more positive impression of the individual, indicating that they were less able to be cognitively skeptical.

Older adults' increased gullibility and increased sensitivity to the "illusion of truth" under conditions of cognitive load are important to note, given that older adults may experience some cognitive stress when using new technologies on the Web or when learning about new technologies from a doctor or a salesperson. In particular, those who interact with older adults should be advised to phrase their directives in terms of positives rather than warning against negative results (e.g., "Take this medication with food" rather than "Don't take this medication on an empty stomach"). Furthermore, elderly people should be warned against making speeded judgments when they encounter salespeople or vendors on the Web.

Potential to Make Instant Decisions

The coupling of age-related increases in gullibility with the ability to perform a variety of transactions instantly over the Internet is another area of concern for older adults. Research on e-commerce cautions against allowing the Internet to take over all purchasing decisions, citing evidence that e-commerce encourages irresponsible spending (LaRose, 2001). This is a serious issue in regard to older adults, who seem to be more susceptible than younger adults to believing false claims and may be easily led to make ill-advised purchases on the Internet. Particularly troublesome is the difficulty in warning against this type of behavior. Many well-meaning news programs spotlight scams and urge consumers to be wary of false claims. Because of age-related increases in the "illusion of truth," these warnings potentially can do more harm than good. Clearly, the dissemination of information via technology brings a host of new issues to the study of aging and it is important to keep in mind that Internet technology is not a panacea for accomplishing all of the IADLs.

CONCLUSIONS

We have discussed within a cognitive aging framework the processes by which new technologies can support the demands of daily living. We proposed that new technologies are focused on improving older adults' ability to communicate and engage in mainstream activities. The IADLs should be updated and expanded both to reflect the changing demands on senior adults and to utilize the changing array of technologies that are available. Our goal was to illustrate how the innovative use of technology can provide an important means of external support for older adults and can offset the age-related changes in cognition that might otherwise stand in the way of an independent lifestyle.

REFERENCES

Allaire, J. C., & Marsiske, M. (1999). Everyday cognition: Age and intellectual ability correlates. *Psychology and Aging, 14,* 627–644.

Bakker, R. (1999). Elderdesign: Home modifications for enhanced safety and self-care. *Care Management Journals, 1,* 47–54.

Ball, K. (1997). Enhancing mobility in the elderly: Attentional interventions for driving. In S. M. Clancy Dollinger & L. F. DiLalla (Eds.), *Assessment and intervention issues across the life span* (pp. 267–292). Mahwah, NJ: Erlbaum.

Ball, K., & Owsley, C. (1993). The useful field of view test: A new technique for evaluating age-related declines in visual function. *Journal of the American Optometric Association, 64,* 71–79.

Ball, K., Owsley, C., Stalvey, B., Roenker, D. L., Sloane, M. E., & Graves, M. (1998). Driving avoidance and functional impairment in older drivers. *Accident Analysis and Prevention, 30,* 313–322.

Barberger-Gateau, P., Commenges, D., Gagnon, M., Letenneur, L., Sauvel, C., & Dartigues, J. P. (1992). Instrumental activities of daily living as a screening tool for cognitive impairment and dementia in elderly community dwellers. *Journal of the American Geriatrics Society, 40,* 1129–1134.

Branch, L. G., Horowitz, A., & Carr, C. (1989). The implications for everyday life of incident self-reported visual decline among people over age 65 living in the community. *The Gerontologist, 29,* 359–365.

Brody, J. E. (1999). The health hazards of point-and-click medicine. *New York Times,* August 31, 1999: F1 (col. 3).

Burns, P. C. (1998). Wayfinding errors while driving. *Journal of Environmental Psychology, 18,* 209–217.

Burns, P. C. (1999). Navigation and the mobility of older drivers. *Journal of Gerontology: Social Sciences, 54B,* S49–S55.

Carp, F. M. (1988). Significance of mobility for the well-being of the elderly. (Special Report No. 218). In Committee for the study on improving mobility and safety for older persons (Ed.), *Transportation in an aging society: Improving mobility and safety for older persons* (pp. 1–20). Washington, DC: National Research Council, Transportation Research Board.

Craik, F. I. M., & Byrd, M. (1982). Aging and cognitive deficits: The role of attentional resources. In F. I. M. Craik & S. Trehub (Eds.), *Aging and cognitive processes* (pp. 191–211). New York: Plenum.

Craik, F. I. M., & Jennings, J. M. (1992). Human memory. In F. I. M. Craik & T. A. Salthouse (Eds.), *The handbook of aging and cognition* (pp. 51–110). Hillsdale, NJ: Erlbaum.

Czaja, S. J., & Sharit, J. (1998). Age differences in attitudes toward computers. *Journal of Gerontology: Psychological Sciences, 53B,* 329–340.

Hartley, J. (1999). What does it say? Text design, medical information, and older readers. In D. C. Park, R. W. Morrell, & K. Shifren (Eds.), *Processing of medical information in aging patients* (pp. 233–248). Mahwah, NJ: Erlbaum.

Henke, M. (1999). Promoting independence in older persons through the Internet. *CyberPsychology and Behavior, 2,* 521–527.

Hertzog, C., Park, D. C., Morrell, R. W., & Martin, M. (2000). Ask and ye shall receive: Behavioral specificity in the accuracy of subjective memory complaints. *Applied Cognitive Psychology, 14,* 257–275.

Kelley, C. L., Morrell, R. W., Park, D. C., & Mayhorn, C. B. (1999). Predictors of electronic bulletin board system use in older adults. *Educational Gerontology, 25,* 19–35.

LaRose, R. (2001). On the negative effects of e-commerce: A sociocognitive exploration of unregulated on-line buying. *Journal of Computer-Mediated Communication, 6*(3). Available online: http://www.ascusc.org/jcmc/vol6/issue3/larose.html.

Lawton, M. P., & Brody, E. M. (1969). Assessment of older people: Self-maintaining and instrumental activities of daily living. *The Gerontologist, 9,* 179–186.

Martin, M., & Park, D. C. *The Martin and Park Environmental Demands Questionnaire (MPED): Psychometric of properties of a newly developed questionnaire to measure environmental demands. Aging: Clinical and Experimental Research.*

Morrell, R. W., & Echt, K. V. (1997). Designing written instructions for older adults: Learning to use computers. In A. D. Fisk (Ed.), *Handbook of human factors and the older adult* (pp. 335–361). San Diego: Academic Press.

Morrell, R. W., Mayhorn, C. B., & Bennett, J. (2000). A survey of World Wide Web use in middle-aged and older adults. *Human Factors, 42,* 175–182.

Morrell, R. W., Park, D. C., Kidder, D. P., & Martin, M. (1997). Adherence to antihypertensive medications across the lifespan. *The Gerontologist, 37,* 609–619.

Myers, R. S., Ball, K. K., Kalina, T. D., Roth, D. L., & Goode, K. T. (2000). Relation of useful field of view and other screening tests to on-road driving performance. *Perceptual and Motor Skills, 91,* 279–290.

Owsley, C., Ball, K., McGwin, G., Sloane, M. E., Roenker, D. L., White, M. F., & Overley, E. T. (1998). Visual processing impairment and risk of motor vehicle crash among older adults. *Journal of the American Medical Association, 279,* 1083–1088.

Owsley, C., Ball, K., Sloane, M., Roenker, D., & Bruni, J. (1991). Visual/cognitive correlates of vehicle accidents in older drivers. *Psychology and Aging, 6,* 403–415.

Park, D. C. (1994). *Aging, cognition, and driving.* Arlington, VA: Scientex.

Park, D. C. (1997). Psychological issues related to competence: Cognitive aging and instrumental activities of daily living. In W. Schaie & S. Willis (Eds.), *Social structures and aging* (pp. 66–82). Mahwah, NJ: Erlbaum.

Park, D. C. (2000). The basic mechanisms accounting for age-related decline in cognitive function. In D. C. Park & N. Schwarz (Eds.), *Cognitive aging: A primer* (pp. 3–21). Philadelphia: Psychology Press.

Park, D. C., Hertzog, C., Leventhal, H., Morrell, R. W., Leventhal, E., Birchmore, D., Martin, M., & Bennett, J. (1999). Medication adherence in rheumatoid arthritis patients: Older is wiser. *Journal of American Geriatrics Society, 47,* 172–183.

Park, D. C., & Jones, T. R. (1996). Medication adherence and aging. In A. D. Fisk & W. A. Rogers (Eds.), *Handbook of human factors and the older adult* (pp. 257–288). San Diego: Academic Press.

Park, D. C., Lautenschlager, G., Hedden, T., Davidson, N., Smith, A. D., & Smith, P. (2002). Models of visuospatial and verbal memory across the adult lifespan. *Psychology and Aging, 17,* 299–320.

Park, D. C., & Mayhorn, C. B. (1996). Remembering to take medications: The importance of nonmemory variables. In D. Hermann, M. Johnson, C. McEvoy, C. Hertzog, & P. Hertel (Eds.), *Research on practical aspects of memory, vol. 2* (pp. 95–110). Mahwah, NJ: Erlbaum.

Park, D. C., Morrell, R. W., Frieske, D., & Kincaid, D. (1992). Medication adherence behaviors in older adults: Effects of external cognitive supports. *Psychology and Aging, 7,* 252–256.

Park, D. C., Smith, A. D., Lautenschlager, G., Earles, J., Frieske, D., Zwahr, M., & Gaines, C. (1996). Mediators of long-term memory performance across the lifespan. *Psychology and Aging, 11,* 621–637.

Ponds, R. W., Brouwer, W. H., & Van Wolffelaar, P. C. (1988). Age differences in divided attention in a simulated driving task. *Journals of Gerontology, 43,* P151–P156.

Rafiq, M., & Collins, R. (1996). Lookalikes and customer confusion in the grocery sector: An exploratory survey. *International Review of Retail, Distribution and Consumer Research, 6*, 329–371.

Rogers, W. A., Cabrera, E. F., Walker, N., Gilbert, D. K., & Fisk, A. D. (1996). A survey of automatic teller machine usage across the adult life span. *Human Factors, 38*, 156–166.

Rogers, W. A., & Fisk, A. D. (2000). Human factors, applied cognition, and aging. In F. I. M. Crak & T. A. Salthouse (Eds.), *The handbook of aging and cognition* (2nd ed., pp. 559–591). Mahwah, NJ: Erlbaum.

Rogers, W. A., Fisk, A. D., Mead, S. E., Walker, N., & Cabrera, E. F. (1996). Training older adults to use automatic teller machines. *Human Factors, 38*, 425–433.

Salthouse, T. A. (1996). The processing-speed theory of adult age differences in cognition. *Psychological Review, 103*, 403–428.

Sixsmith, J., & Sixsmith, A. (1993). Older people, driving and new technology. *Applied Ergonomics, 24*, 40–43.

Skurnik, I. W., Park, D. C., & Schwarz, N. (2000, April). *Repeated warnings about false medical information can make it seem true: A paradoxical age difference.* Paper presented at the Cognitive Aging Conference, Atlanta, GA.

Smither, J. A., & Braun, C. C. (1994). Technology and older adults: Factors affecting the adoption of automatic teller machines. *The Journal of General Psychology, 121*, 381–389.

U. S. Bureau of the Census. (1997). *Aging in the United States: Past, present, and future.* Aging Studies Branch, International Programs Center, Washington, DC: Author.

Vastag, B. (2001). Easing the elderly online in search of health information. *Journal of the American Medical Association, 285*, 1563–1564.

Ybarra, O., Chan, E., & Park, D. C. (2001). Young and old adults' concerns about morality and competence. *Motivation and Emotion, 25*, 85–100.

Ybarra, O., & Park, D. C. (2002). Disconfirmation of person expectations by older and younger adults: Implications for social vigilance. *Journals of Gerontology B: Psychological Sciences, 57*, P435–P443.

Commentary

Technology as Environmental Support for Older Adults' Daily Activities

Daniel Morrow

Linda Liu and Denise Park argue persuasively for the relevance of cognitive aging theory to designing technology for older adults. Rather than address all of the points raised in their chapter, I will elaborate on a few issues relating to aging and technology design. First, they emphasize the need to adapt technology to older adults' abilities and interests, rather than vice versa. Second, they show that cognitive aging theory provides an important context for meeting this challenge. More specifically, they focus on two cognitive aging constructs for understanding how technology promotes effective functioning by elders: (1) older adults' "cognitive profiles" (description of age-related changes in cognitive resources) and (2) environmental support. I will expand on the notion of environmental support as it relates to cognitive profiles. In doing so, I emphasize a third point that is more implicit than explicit in Liu and Park's chapter: Effective introduction of new technology requires considering how older adults already accomplish the tasks targeted by this technology. For example, to identify problems that older adults may encounter with cell phones or other wireless technology, it helps to first understand how older adults already use conventional telephones. These points will be illustrated by examples from my research on aging and communication.

OLDER ADULTS' COGNITIVE PROFILES

Liu and Park review evidence that several types of cognitive resources are vulnerable to aging. Older adults often experience gradual declines in visual acuity, hearing sensitivity, and other aspects of sensorimotor function (Schneider & Pichora-Fuller, 2000). "Mental mechanics" such as working memory and processing speed also decline with age (Baltes & Baltes, 1990; Park et al., 1996; Salthouse, 1991). These sensory and cognitive declines become increasingly coupled (Lindenberger & Baltes, 1994). As a consequence, elders' performance becomes both more data-limited and resource-limited. These declines may be compounded by age differences in literacy, reflecting cohort differences in education as well as cognitive declines (Baker, Gazmararian, Sudano, & Patterson, 2000). Age-related changes in other resources may interact with these cognitive declines. For example, self-efficacy beliefs, which may mediate the impact of technology on daily performance, tend to decline with age, in part because of perceived declines in cognitive function (Willis, Jay, Diehl, & Marsiske, 1992).

Balancing these declines are strengths or resources that tend to be stable or even increase with age, including general and domain-specific knowledge (Salthouse, 1991). Another age-related strength is daily expertise about tasks such as managing health, finances, and other instrumental activities of daily living (IADLs). This includes task-specific knowledge such as schemas related to medication taking (Morrow, Carver, Leirer, & Tanke, 2000) and appointment keeping (Morrow & Leirer, 2001), task-specific beliefs (e.g., illness or treatment representations for medication adherence; Leventhal, Leventhal, Robitaile, & Brownlee, 1999), and strategies for using external cognitive aids such as calendars, notes, and organizers (Diehl, 1998; Hultsch, Hertzog, & Dixon, 1987).

The concept of everyday expertise relates to theories of everyday functioning such as selective optimization with compensation (Baltes & Baltes, 1990), everyday competence (Diehl, 1998; Willis, 1996), and the compensation framework of Dixon and Backman (1995), all of which focus on elders' strategies for maintaining daily function in the face of declining cognitive resources. It also relates to contextual theories of expertise that emphasize the role of skilled interaction with the environment, such that experts rely on perceptual supports for performing complex tasks (Hutchins, 1991; Kirlik, 1995).

Because daily expertise is rooted in experience with everyday tasks, there is a danger that this age-related strength will become outmoded or even become a source of interference if these tasks change with technological "advances." Cell phone design may conflict with elders' mental models of conventional phones (Laux, 2001), or medical devices may use symbols that conflict with general conventions in our culture (Gardner-Bonneau, 2001). New technology may also fail to support external aid strategies. For example, older adults often keep paper by the telephone in order to write down phone messages (Lawton, 1990). This strategy may not easily translate to more portable communication technology. Thus, technology may sometimes undermine rather than support elders' existing strengths even as they provide new capabilities.

ENVIRONMENTAL SUPPORT

As Liu and Park point out, the concept of environmental support is helpful for analyzing how technology relates to elders' cognitive profiles. This concept can be refined in order to further analyze links between technology and elders' strengths and limitations. As Figure 6.2 shows, there are two general ways that environmental support maintains elders' performance in the face of cognitive declines. First, it can reduce task demands on vulnerable resources such as sensory function or working memory, thus minimizing age-related bottlenecks in processing. Demands are reduced by improving input to sensory systems or providing substitutes (prosthetics) for sensorimotor systems, both of which minimize data limitations on performance. Demands are also reduced by externalizing mental functions, a process that addresses central resource limitations. This function is similar to Craik's original formulation of environmental support as external support for age-related declines in self-initiated mental processing (Craik & Jennings, 1992).

Second, environmental support can also maintain performance by building on elders' strengths, or preserved resources (see Figure 6.2). For example, technology, tasks, or information can be designed to be compatible with users' knowledge or preferences (Bostrom, Fischoff, & Morgan, 1992; Morrow, Leirer, Carver, & Tanke, 1998; Morrow et al., 2000) or with existing strategies and procedures (Laux, 2001). Technology that is compatible with elders' knowledge and experience may promote positive transfer and decrease negative transfer during learning. Issues related to transfer of learning have a long history in psychology (for a review see Swezey & Llaneras, 1997). These issues are also relevant for designing technology for older adults, especially because there is evidence for an age-related increase in reliance on past knowledge (Hess, 1990) and decrease in the ability to inhibit responses that are no longer relevant to current goals (Hasher, Quig, & May, 1997).

Technology should be more effective to the extent that it both reduces demands on older adults' vulnerable resources and supports reliance on strengths in order to accomplish daily tasks. This prediction is similar to the concept of communication enhancement (Ryan,

- **Reduce demands on vulnerable resources**
  - Improve input
  - Sensory prosthetic
  - Externalize mental functions
- **Build on strengths**
  - Compatibility with
    - Knowledge
    - Daily expertise

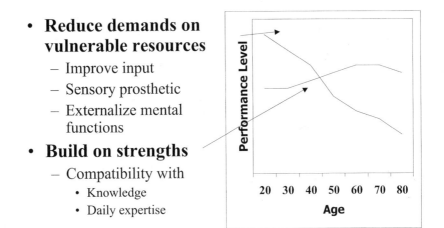

FIGURE 6.2   **Environmental support for daily tasks. The graph depicts ideal- ized age-related decline in cognitive resources and preservation of knowledge.** Adapted from Liu and Park, this volume.

Meredith, MacLean, & Orange, 1995). Communication enhancement strategies require assessing and building on older adults' strengths or competencies as well as avoiding strategies that tax age-related limita- tions. Speakers will overaccommodate to older listeners to the extent that they underestimate elders' strengths, and underaccommodate to the extent that they underestimate limitations (Kemper, 2001). Similarly, designing age-sensitive technology requires assessing older adults' gen- eral and task-specific limitations and strengths. This involves task analy- sis, observation, focus groups, experiments, and other human factors techniques that identify requirements of everyday tasks and analyze how these requirements change with new technology (Clark, Czaja, & Weber, 1990; Rogers & Fisk, 2000). These techniques also help identi- fy daily expertise relevant to these tasks.

The following two studies demonstrate the importance of one facet of daily expertise: external aids that support comprehension and mem- ory related to home and work tasks. These findings have implications for designing technology that builds on elders' daily expertise.

THE CASE OF NOTE TAKING

Appointment Communication

Appointment no-show rates range from 5 to 80%, reducing benefits of preventative and treatment health services and costing billions of dollars a year (Macharia, Leon, Rowe, Stephenson, & Haynes, 1992). Although there is little consistent evidence that older adults have higher no-show rates than younger adults do, even similar rates for older adults would translate into greater health costs because they are more likely to use health services and require more appointments. Thus, it is important to identify successful appointment adherence strategies for older as well as younger adults.

Our analysis of appointment adherence requirements is based on a multifactor model similar to that proposed by Park and Jones (1997) for medication adherence. Attending appointments requires creating an adherence plan, which involves understanding and integrating information about date/time, location, pr-appointment procedures (e.g., fasting), and other categories. The plan must then be implemented, which involves prospective memory (memory for intended actions) as well as logistical issues such as transportation. Creating and implementing effective plans depends on cognitive factors such as comprehension and memory, as shown by the fact that nonadherence is related to misunderstanding and forgetting. Attendance also depends on patients' acceptance of the health service as personally relevant and important, since nonadherence also relates to health beliefs (for a review see Morrow & Leirer, 2001).

Older adults may fail to attend appointments because comprehension, integration, and prospective memory demands tax vulnerable cognitive resources such as working memory. On the other hand, attendance may be supported by age-related strengths such as knowledge about appointments that facilitates comprehension and integration (Morrow & Leirer, 2001), external strategies that support prospective memory (Maylor, 1990), and adherence-compatible beliefs that support task acceptance (Park et al., 1999).

We investigated whether note taking supports comprehension of and memory for spoken appointment information. Note taking has been found to improve comprehension by reducing working memory limitations and encouraging elaboration (Einstein, Morris, & Smith, 1985; Intons-Peterson & Fournier, 1986). It may also improve memory because effort is required to produce the written notes, just as memory is improved when words are generated rather than simply read (on the generation effect, see Slamecka & Graf, 1978). Older as well as younger adults have been found to benefit from the generation effect (McDaniel, Ryan, & Cunningham, 1989; Rabinowitz, 1989). Notes support prospective memory as well as comprehension by serving as external aids (Maylor, 1990). To the extent that note taking prompts rehearsal of the planned action, it may also support prospective memory by activating intentions (Chasteen, Park, & Schwartz, 2001). Finally, note taking may support collaborative cognition and joint problem solving by providing external referents for partners to coordinate their joint activities, since collaboration may be enhanced by a shared external reference frame (Endsley, 1995). Thus, note taking may be an important environmental support that both reduces demands on vulnerable resources such as working memory and supports strengths such as knowledge and collaboration. Not surprisingly, there is evidence that older adults often rely on such external strategies in support of everyday tasks (Hultsch et al., 1987; Maylor, 1990).

We examined note-taking benefits in the context of automated voice messaging (AVM), a technology routinely used to deliver health care information to clients by telephone. While AVM has been shown to increase appointment attendance (for a review see Morrow & Leirer, 2001), our work suggests that long or fast automated phone messages about appointments can tax older adults' comprehension by increasing working memory demands. For example, older adults in one study remembered on average 45% of the automated message while younger adults remembered 64%; this difference was largely explained by age differences on a working memory measure (Morrow et al., 1998). In contrast, participants in a later study were allowed to take notes while listening to the same messages because older adults in our studies reported that they often take notes from important telephone messages. Although there were still age differences in recalling the message because notes were unavailable at test in this later study (Mean recall: O = 60%, Y = 69%), age differences in the accuracy of the notes themselves were small, although significant (O = 89% correct, Y = 93%; Morrow, Leirer, Carver, Tanke, & McNally, 1999). Age differences were eliminated for notes from messages organized in terms of participants' schemas for appointment information, even though these messages were long, containing nine statements. Thus, note taking was effective in part because it reduced working memory limitations, but was most effective when combined with other facets of daily expertise such as messages that were compatible with elders' prior knowledge.

This study suggests that communication technology (AVM) may be more effective when older adults can rely on daily expertise strategies such as note taking. The challenge is to design technology that effectively supports these age-related strengths when possible. Before addressing this challenge, I describe a study showing that note taking supports comprehension in the workplace as well as at home.

Pilot Communication

An ongoing project is investigating benefits of external aids for pilots. As with health-related telephone communication, pilot communication over the radio is heavily dependent on age-vulnerable cognitive resources. Pilots must hear, understand, and respond to Air Traffic Control (ATC) instructions to change aircraft heading, altitude, speed, or other flight parameters in a complex, multitask environment. Comprehension involves processes such as word recognition, identifying propositions, and updating a mental model of the flight by integrating information from the ATC message with information from other sources such as flight displays. Prospective memory is also a factor because there may be a delay before pilots can respond to ATC instructions. Because these processes are dependent on working memory, age-related declines in working memory capacity may reduce pilot communication accuracy (Morrow, Menard, Stine-Morrow, Teller, & Bryant, 2001).

On the other hand, older pilots can draw on several strengths, such as knowledge of ATC messages and use of external cognitive aids. Airline pilots often rely on external aids rather than memory, so that their expertise is as much skilled interaction with their environment as it is knowledge in the head (Hutchins, 1991). Pilots in our studies report frequently taking notes when listening to ATC messages during flight, and older pilots report using this strategy more frequently than younger pilots do (Morrow, Ridolfo, Menard, Sanborn, Stine-Morrow, Magnor, Herman, Teller, & Bryant, 2002). Thus, note taking appears to support older adults' comprehension and memory in the workplace. It may be especially useful for pilots because of continual training and experience related to taking notes.

Younger (20–40 years), middle-aged (50–59 years), and older (60–75 years) pilots were compared to nonpilots from the same age groups (Morrow, Ridolfo, et al., 2002). Pilots as well as nonpilots showed typical age declines on measures of working memory, processing speed, and age stability in verbal knowledge. Thus, the two groups had similar general cognitive profiles. Pilots had an advantage in terms of domain knowledge relevant to the task, including experience with taking notes from spoken messages. Participants listened to and read back (repeated) recorded ATC messages that described a route through an airspace, while referring to a chart of the airspace. For half of the routes, they could take notes while listening to and reading back the messages. When note taking was unavailable, pilots' readbacks were more accurate than nonpilots', presumably because of their knowledge of ATC and navigational concepts. However, they experienced similar age declines in accuracy, reflecting age-related constraints in working memory for both groups (see Figure 6.3). Most important, age differences in pilots' accuracy were eliminated in the note taking condition. While note-taking also improved nonpilots' comprehension, age declines still occurred for this group. Thus, unlike older nonpilots, older pilots could keep up with their younger counterparts when taking notes, perhaps because of their experience in using this external aid (Morrow, Ridolfo, et al., 2002).

IMPLICATIONS OF NOTE TAKING FOR TECHNOLOGY DESIGN

Both studies show that note taking, which older adults often use to support everyday functioning at home and at work, improves comprehension and memory. This strategy may be most effective when combined with other facets of daily expertise such as schema-compatible communication (Morrow et al., 1999) and domain-specific training and experience (Morrow, Ridolfo, et al., 2002). Of course, older adults use many other strategies to support their performance of daily activities, such as linking appointments or other prospective memory tasks to daily schedules (Maylor, 1990), modifying their environment (placing important devices within easy reach of a "command center" at home; Lawton, 1990), or using flight displays or other aspects of the pilot's cockpit environment as external memory aids (Hutchins, 1991).

New technologies may be more effective if they incorporate functions served by daily expertise strategies. Our studies suggest that note taking serves several functions. First, it improves comprehension by reducing working memory constraints associated with the transitory auditory modality, so that comprehension is less likely to tax elders' vulnerable cognitive resources. New technology could similarly support comprehension by providing visual rather than spoken messages. Visual messages about appointments or other health services can be provided by computer (e-mail) or by pager and other wireless technology. Lower-tech solutions, such as answering machines, also reduce the role of working memory in understanding telephone messages. For piloting, radio communication may soon be supplemented by computer data link between air and ground, so that ATC messages are delivered visually as well as aurally. Communication accuracy is generally improved when ATC messages are presented by visual data link compared to voice alone (Kerns, 1999).

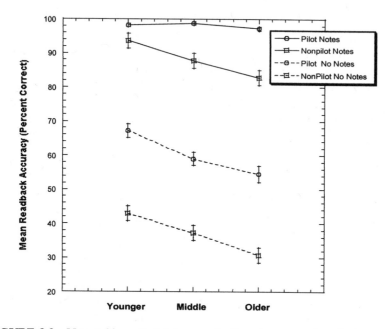

FIGURE 6.3 Note-taking eliminates age declines in comprehension accuracy for pilots (from Morrow, Ridolfo, Menard, Sanborn, Stine-Morrow et al., 2002). Copyright © 2002 by the American Psychological Association. Reprinted with permission.

Second, note taking supports elders' strengths in addition to reducing reliance on vulnerable resources. For example, it promotes elaboration of knowledge-based comprehension. It is possible that technology that provides visual messages will not serve this function because simply reading a message may not encourage elaboration, compared to reading and taking notes. Similarly, reading is unlikely to encourage the generation effect, which has been found to improve memory (Slamecka & Graf, 1978). Computers may promote more active processing and elaboration by enabling note taking. Applications such as "stickies" or other electronic note pads encourage people to take notes about and elaborate on e-mail or Web documents (Wright, Likorish, & Milroy, 2000). However, these benefits may only occur if it is easy to use "e-notes" or to shift between reading documents and writing notes.

Third, note taking can improve prospective memory by providing an external reminder (Maylor, 1990). Technologies that only substitute visual for spoken messages could potentially reduce prospective memory in complex tasks such as piloting because the visual modality can be less salient than the auditory modality (Stanton, 1994). Presenting messages in both modalities may both help capture attention and support prospective memory (auditory modality) and reduce working memory limits and support comprehension (visual modality). More generally, bimodal presentation may help mitigate literacy problems among less educated older adults in a variety of contexts. A potential drawback of bimodal presentation is that requiring listeners to divide attention between modalities will increase age differences in memory, although evidence for this is mixed (Stine, Wingfield, & Myers, 1990; cf. Frieske & Park, 1999). For appointment keeping and other health care tasks, bimodal messages can be delivered by pager and other wireless devices or by screen telephones (Czaja, 2001). For piloting, data link messages can be delivered bimodally and auditory signals can support prospective memory (Kerns, 1999).

Finally, technology can incorporate note taking's collaborative functions. Patient/provider collaboration is essential to patient care (Roter, 2000). E-mail or Web-based sharing of patient information has been found to support patient/provider collaboration (Wasson et al., 1999). Collaboration between members of an aircraft crew is also essential to commercial piloting. There is a concern that new data link technology may hamper collaboration because while all crew members can hear voice ATC messages, only the pilot handling visual data link communication is likely to read ATC messages, so that information is less likely to be shared. Procedures that promote collaboration by having both pilots read data link messages have been proposed (Kerns, 1999).

CONCLUSION

Liu and Park point out that it is essential to adapt new technology to elders' cognitive profiles so that the technology provides environmental support for elders' everyday tasks. In the present chapter, I expanded on the concept of technology as environmental support. Similar to Ryan and colleagues (1995) analysis of communication enhancement strategies, I argued that technology (or other forms of environmental support) is most effective when it both reduces demands on elders' vulnerable cognitive resources (e.g., working memory) and supports strengths such as daily expertise strategies. Such technology should be easier to learn and use and may be more acceptable to older adults (and thus more likely to be used) because its relevance to their goals is more obvious (Melenhorst, Rogers, & Caylor, 2001). This general claim raises several issues, and I conclude by briefly considering two.

First, elders' cognitive profiles are highly variable. At any age there are likely to be substantial individual differences in abilities, and aging tends to amplify these differences. Technology must accommodate this variability both in terms of elders' limitations and strengths. The tools of human factors are critical for meeting this challenge. Observation and focus group techniques help identify dimensions of variability in the resources that elders bring to bear in accomplishing daily tasks. Thus, older adults are themselves an important source of information about daily expertise and should participate with researchers and designers in the process of adapting new technologies to their needs.

Recent microtechnology advances are critical for assessing elders' variable needs and abilities and for delivering services tailored to these individual cognitive profiles. For example, the ability to sense and integrate large amounts of data about users allows systems to rapidly build models of users and to adjust system behavior based on these models (Fisher, 2000). The Internet is also increasingly used to tailor health information to individuals' needs and goals (Kreuter & Holt, 2001).

Second, relating new technology to elders' knowledge and expertise will only be effective if the latter are in fact adaptive. For example, implicit memory or memory based on familiarity rather than explicit recollection is relatively preserved with age. In their chapter, Liu and Park provide a compelling example of how reliance on this strength may backfire, with older adults more likely than younger adults to mis-remember as true information that has been repeatedly presented as false. Thus, elders are more susceptible to the "illusion of truth" effect, which may undermine their ability to function as discerning consumers of health information. These examples underline the importance of human factors techniques not only for identifying how older adults accomplish everyday tasks, but for establishing whether these strategies are adaptive and how they can be improved.

A related point is the need to recognize that integrating new technologies with existing expertise, or combining new and old functions, is not always straightforward. Older adults tend to overrely on knowledge, so that they distort memory for new information to fit their schemas (Hess, 1990). Thus, elders' memory for information can be distorted by prior beliefs (Rice & Okun, 1994). Connecting new information to knowledge through analogy can also impair elders' ability to learn computer applications, perhaps because they have trouble integrating the new information with knowledge (Caplan & Schooler, 1990).

Finally, Liu and Park, as well as other authors in this volume, argue that rapid changes in technology may change elders' everyday life so thoroughly that it is not always possible to relate new technology to elders' everyday expertise. For example, the Internet may dramatically change the way older adults perform daily tasks such as finding information, purchasing services, or communicating with others. Older adults may also encounter novel technology when confronted with new health care tasks such as glucose monitoring. As Liu and Park point out, it is important to train elders to stay abreast of technological advances in order to remain fully functioning members of society. Meeting these challenges may also provide opportunities for growth, because remaining engaged in challenging tasks may yield benefits for maintaining cognitive function with age (Hultsch, Hertzog, Small, & Dixon, 1999). Still, it is essential to consider how new technology or new tasks relate to elders' existing conceptions and strategies for accomplishing similar tasks, so that elders' everyday expertise remains a source of strength rather than becoming a liability.

ACKNOWLEDGMENT

Support for this research was provided by NIA grant R01 AG13936.

REFERENCES

Baker, D. W., Gazmararian, J. A., Sudano, J., & Patterson, M. (2000). The association between age and health literacy among elderly persons. *Journal of Gerontology: Social Sciences, 55B,* S368–S374.

Baltes, P. B., & Baltes, M. M. (1990). Psychological perspectives on successful aging: The model of selective optimization with compensation. In P. B. Baltes & M. M. Baltes (Eds.), *Successful aging: Perspectives from the behavioral sciences* (pp. 1–34). New York: Cambridge University Press.

Bostrom, A., Fischoff, B., & Morgan, M. (1992). Characterizing mental models of hazardous processes: A methodology and an application to radon. *Journal of Social Issues, 48,* 85–100.

Caplan, L. J., & Schooler, C. (1990). The effects of analogical training models and age on problem-solving in a new domain. *Experimental Aging Research, 16,* 151–154.

Chasteen, A. L., Park, D. C., & Schwartz, N. (2001). Implementation intentions and facilitation of prospective memory. *Psychological Science, 12,* 457–461.

Clark, M. C., Czaja, S. J., & Weber, R. A. (1990). Older adults and daily living task profiles. *Human Factors, 32,* 537–550.

Craik, F. I. M., & Jennings, J. M. (1992). Human memory. In F. I. M. Craik & T. A. Salthouse (Eds.), *The handbook of aging and cognition* (pp. 51–110). Hillsdale, NJ: Erlbaum.

Czaja, S. J. (2001). Telecommunication technology as an aid to family caregivers. In W. A. Rogers & A. D. Fisk (Eds.), *Human factors interventions for the health care of older adults* (pp. 165–178). Mahwah, NJ: Erlbaum.

Diehl, M. (1998). Everyday competence in later life: Current status and future directions. *The Gerontologist, 38,* 422–433.

Dixon, R. A., & Backman, L. (1995). *Compensating for psychological deficits and declines: Managing loses and promoting gains.* Mahwah, NJ: Erlbaum.

Einstein, G. O., Morris, J., & Smith, S. (1985). Note-taking individual differences and memory for lecture information. *Journal of Educational Psychology, 77,* 522–532.

Endsley, M. R. (1995). Toward a theory of situation awareness in dynamic systems. *Human Factors, 37,* 32–64.

Fisher, D. L. (2000). Cognitive aging and adaptive technologies. In N. R. Council (Ed.), *The aging mind: Opportunities in cognitive research* (pp. 166–188). Washington, DC: National Academy Press.

Frieske, D. A., & Park, D. C. (1999). Memory for news in young and old adults. *Psychology and Aging, 14,* 90–98.

Gardner-Bonneau, D. (2001). Designing medical devices for older adults. In W. A. Rogers & A. D. Fisk (Eds.), *Human factors interventions for the health care of older adults* (pp. 221–238). Mahwah, NJ: Erlbaum.

Hasher, L., Quig, M. B., & May, C. P. (1997). Inhibitory control over no-longer relevant information: Adult age differences. *Memory and Cognition, 25,* 286–295.

Hess, T. (1990). Aging and semantic influences on memory. In T. M. Hess (Ed.), *Aging and cognition: Knowledge organization and utilization* (pp. 93–160). Amsterdam: North-Holland.

Hultsch, D. F., Hertzog, C., & Dixon, R. A. (1987). Age differences in metamemory: Resolving the inconsistencies. *Canadian Journal of Psychology, 41,* 193–208.

Hultsch, D. F., Hertzog, C., Small, B. J., & Dixon, R. A. (1999). Use it or lose it: Engaged lifestyle as a buffer of cognitive decline in aging? *Psychology and Aging, 14,* 245–263.

Hutchins, E. (1991). *How a cockpit remembers its speed.* Technical report. University of California at San Diego, distributed by Cognition Laboratory.

Intons-Peterson, M. J., & Fournier, J. (1986). External and internal memory aids: When and how often do we use them? *Journal of Experimental Psychology: General, 115,* 267–280.

Kemper, S. (2001). Over-accommodations and under-accommodations to aging. In N. Charness, D. C. Park, & B. A. Sabel (Eds.), *Communication, technology, and aging: Opportunities and challenges for the future* (pp. 30–46). New York: Springer.

Kerns, K. (1999). Human factors in air traffic control/flight deck integration: Implications of data-link simulation research. In D. J. Garland, J. A. Wise, & V. D. Hopkin (Eds.), *Handbook of aviation human factors* (pp. 519–546). Mahwah, NJ: Erlbaum.

Kirlik, A. (1995). Requirements for psychological models to support design: Towards ecological task analysis. In J. M. Flach, P. A. Hancock, J. K. Caird, & K. J. Vicente (Eds.), *An ecological approach to human–machine systems I: A global perspective* (pp. 68–120). Hillsdale, NJ: Erlbaum.

Kreuter, M. W., & Holt, C. L. (2001). How do people process health information? Applications in an age of individualized communication. *Current Directions in Psychological Science, 10,* 206–209.

Laux, L. F. (2001). Aging, communication, and interface design. In N. Charness, D. C. Park, & B. A. Sabel (Eds.), *Communication, technology, and aging* (pp. 153–168). New York: Springer.

Lawton, M. P. (1990). Aging and performance of home tasks. *Human Factors, 32,* 527–536.

Leventhal, E. A., Leventhal, H., Robitaile, C., & Brownlee, S. (1999). Psychosocial factors in the medication: A model of the modeler. In D. C. Park, R. W. Morrell, & K. Shifren (Eds.), *Processing of medical information in aging patients* (pp. 145–166). Mahwah, NJ: Erlbaum.

Lindenberger, U., & Baltes, P. B. (1994). Sensory functioning and intelligence in old age: A strong connection. *Psychology and Aging, 9,* 339–355.

Macharia, W. M., Leon, G., Rowe, B. H., Stephenson, B. J., & Haynes, B. (1992). An overview of interventions to improve compliance with appointment keeping for medical services. *Journal of the American Medical Association, 267,* 1813–1817.

Maylor, E. A. (1990). Age and prospective memory. *Quarterly Journal of Experimental Psychology, 42A,* 471–493.

McDaniel, M. A., Ryan, E. B., & Cunningham, C. J. (1989). Encoding difficulty and memory enhancement for young and older readers. *Psychology and Aging, 4,* 333–338.

Melenhorst, A., Rogers, W. A., & Caylor, E. C. (2001, October). *The use of communication technologies by older adults: Exploring the benefits from the user's perspective.* Paper presented at the Human Factors and Ergonomics Society 45th Annual Meeting, Minneapolis/St. Paul, MN.

Morrow, D., Carver, L., Leirer, V. O., & Tanke, E. D. (2000). Medication schemas and memory for automated telephone messages. *Human Factors, 42,* 523–540.

Morrow, D. G., & Leirer, V. O. (2001). A patient-centered approach to automated telephone health communication for older adults. In W. A. Rogers & A. D. Fisk (Eds.), *Human factors interventions for the health care of older adults* (pp. 179–202). Mahwah, NJ: Erlbaum.

Morrow, D., Leirer, V. O., Carver, L., & Tanke, E. D. (1998). Older and younger adult memory for health appointment information: Implications for automated telephone messaging design. *Journal of Experimental Psychology: Applied, 4,* 352–374.

Morrow, D. G., Leirer, V. O., Carver, L. M., Tanke, E. D., & McNally, A. (1999). Effects of aging, message repetition, and note-taking on memory for health information. *Journal of Gerontology: Psychological Sciences, 54B,* 369–379.

Morrow, D. G., Menard, W. E., Stine-Morrow, E. A. L., Teller, T., & Bryant, D. (2001). The influence of expertise and task factors on age differences in pilot communication. *Psychology and Aging, 16,* 31–46.

Morrow, D. G., Ridolfo, H. E., Menard, W. E., Sanborn, A., Stine-Morrow, E. A. L., Magnor, C., Herman, L., Teller, T., & Bryant, D. (2002). Environmental support promotes expertise-based mitigation of age differences on pilot communication tasks. *Psychology and Aging, 17,* 299–320.

Park, D. C., Hertzog, C., Leventhal, H., Morrell, R. W., Leventhal, E., Birchmore, D., Martin, M., & Bennett, J. (1999). Medication adherence in rheumatoid arthritis patients: Older is wiser. *Journal of the American Geriatrics Society, 47,* 172–183.

Park, D. C., & Jones, T. R. (1997). Medication adherence and aging. In A. D. Fisk & W. A. Rogers (Eds.), *Handbook of human factors and the older adult* (pp. 257–287). San Diego: Academic Press.

Park, D. C., Smith, A. D., Lautenschlager, G., Earles, J. L., Frieske, D., Zwahr, M., & Gaines, C. L. (1996). Mediators of long-term memory performance across the life span. *Psychology and Aging, 11,* 621–637.

Rabinowitz, J. C. (1989). Judgments of origin and generation effects: Comparisons between young and elderly adults. *Psychology and Aging, 4,* 259–268.

Rice, G. E., & Okun, M. A. (1994). Older readers' processing of medical information that contradicts their beliefs. *Journal of Gerontology: Psychological Sciences, 49,* 119–128.

Rogers, W. A., & Fisk, A. D. (2000). Human factors, applied cognition, and aging. In F. I. M. Craik & T. A. Salthouse (Eds.), *The handbook of aging and cognition* (pp. 559–592). Mahwah, NJ: Erlbaum.

Roter, D. L. (2000). The outpatient medical encounter and elderly patients. *Clinics in Geriatric Medicine, 16,* 95–107.

Ryan, E. B., Meridith, S. D., MacLean, M. J., & Orange, J. B. (1995). Changing the way we talk with elders: Promotion of health using the communication enhancement model. *International Journal of Aging and Human Development, 41,* 89–107.

Salthouse, T. A. (1991). *Theoretical perspectives on cognitive aging.* Hillsdale, NJ: Erlbaum.

Schneider, B. A., & Pichora-Fuller, M. K. (2000). Implications of perceptual deterioriation for cognitive aging research. In F. I. M. Craik & T. A. Salthouse (Eds.), *The Handbook of Aging and Cognition* (pp. 155–220). Mahwah, NJ: Erlbaum.

Slamecka, N. J., & Graf, P. (1978). The generation effect: Delineation of a phenomenon. *Journal of Experimental Psychology: Human Learning and Memory, 4,* 592–604.

Stanton, N. (1994). *Human factors of alarm design.* London: Taylor and Francis.

Stine, E. A. L., Wingfield, A., & Myers, S. D. (1990). Age differences in processing information from television news: The effects of bisensory augmentation. *Journal of Gerontology, 45,* 1–8.

Swezey, R. W., & Llaneras, R. E. (1997). Models in training and instruction. In G. Salvendy (Ed.), *Handbook of human factors and ergonomics* (pp. 514–577). New York: Wiley.

Wasson, J. H., Stukel, T. A., Weiss, J. A., Hays, R. A., Jette, A. M., & Nelson, E. C. (1999). A randomized trial of the use of patient self-assessment data to improve community practices. *Effective Clinical Practice, 2,* 1–10.

Willis, S. L. (1996). Everyday cognitive competence in elderly persons: Conceptual issues and empirical findings. *The Gerontologist, 36,* 595–601.

Willis, S. L., Jay, G. M., Diehl, M., & Marsiske, M. (1992). Longitudinal change and prediction of everyday task competence in the elderly. *Research on Aging, 14,* 68–91.

Wright, P., Likorish, A., & Milroy, R. (2000). Route choices, anticipated forgetting, and interface design for on-line reference documents. *Journal of Experimental Psychology: Applied, 6,* 158–167.

Commentary

Using Technology to Foster Engagement and Improve Health in Elderly Persons

Sarah Hall Gueldner and Susan J. Loeb

INTRODUCTION

The purpose of this chapter is to offer commentary on the discussion by Liu and Park, in terms of the relevance it holds for today's older adults, and for those who will shape the quality of life for future generations of elders. The passionate argument of Liu and Park regarding the promise of collective technologies to extend independence for elders is indeed convincing. Their visionary recommendations remind the reader that elders are at serious risk for being left out or behind on access to technology at a time when it is becoming a mainstay for the rest of the world.

The authors are to be commended for the remarkable scope of technology-based topics that they address, including using the telephone, arranging transportation, managing health and medications, shopping and preparing meals, maintaining a household, and managing finances. Their observations about the complex problems that elders face when trying to arrange for transportation were especially detailed and enlightening, given how crucial transportation is to the achievement of many of the Instrumental Activities of Daily Living (IADL) (Lawton & Brody, 1969). The array of problems elders encounter when trying to manage their finances, using even relatively simple technologies such as the ATM, was also particularly germane.

Throughout their discussion, the authors stress the importance of training and adaptation of technology to better accommodate the cognitive changes (such as declines in processing speed and memory) associated with aging. Their imperative for instituting widespread opportunities for training and practice with technology for older persons is well supported by the extant literature on resilience and reserve capacity (Staudinger, Marsiske, and Baltes, 1995). This literature provides evidence that resilience (the ability to maintain, regain, and achieve new levels of functioning) continues to be possible throughout adulthood and old age, and that it can be enhanced by interventions and age-friendly environments (Baltes and Baltes, 1990). In fact, some investigators have found that loss in the ability to function under hurried, changing, or unfamiliar circumstances may not even be noticeable except under demanding performance settings that require additional reserves (Baltes, 1987; Kliegl & Baltes, 1987). A growing body of cognitive intervention research suggests that older adults perform better on tasks that are self-selected and that have personal relevance and high familiarity (Baltes & Baltes, 1990), attributes that can be built through carefully orchestrated cognitive training opportunities. Longitudinal studies have shown that the benefit of such training and practice may be maintained for a year or longer (Verhaeghen, Morcoen, & Goosens, 1992; Willis and Schaie, 1986).

The authors also called attention to a number of less obvious ethical issues associated with Internet use, including the increased gullibility of elders to the "illusion of truth" and their tendency to make ill-advised purchases under the pressure of Web-based vendors. Liu and Park warn of these and other potentially harmful new threats that may accompany technoliteracy in older Web users.

The remainder of this commentary focuses on studies that evaluate the Internet as a medium for education, with particular attention to health applications for older adults. Included also are applications that promote connectedness, entertainment, and engagement, ending with a discourse on the as yet unfulfilled potential of not-so-high-tech applications such as the telephone.

EDUCATIONAL APPLICATIONS OF TECHNOLOGY

The discussion of Liu and Park underscores computer-assisted instruction as an effective way to provide educational opportunities for elders. Lamdin and Fugate (1997) noted that the ready availability of computers and computer information in society today has launched a technology that "serves as both a resource and a motivation for learning new skills" (p. 121). In essence, computer technology gives libraries and other educational entities the potential to assume a more prominent role in elder learning, particularly if access can be provided for elders who do not own computers. In spite of a general notion that computers are for the young, the literature tells us that learning to use the computer is one of the most common learning tasks undertaken by elders. The Elderlearning Survey (ES) of 860 persons aged 55 to 96 from all 50 states revealed that one third of the respondents would like to learn about computers and new technology (Lamdin & Fugate, 1997). While most (74.7%) of the elders in the study still preferred to learn by reading printed materials, 13.6% (19.5% of the males) listed the computer as a preferred learning style and 5.2% listed the Internet as a preference. The interest in learning to use computers held steady across all ages above 55 years and was not markedly influenced by either previous education or income (Hendrix, 2000). The Pew Internet and American Life Project, from September 2000, found that 27% of persons 60 years of age or older in the United States had access to a computer either at home or at work (*SeniorNet*, 2001).

For more than a decade, Park's research team has been on the cutting edge in the study of the best ways to teach older adults to use computers (Morrell, Park, Mayhorn, & Kelley, 2000). In one study, the research team taught 37 community dwelling older adults (aged 58–91) to use computers to access ELDERCOMM, an electronic bulletin board system designed for older adults. Upon completion of the two-week training and retraining sessions, participants were invited to use the four computers at the local council on aging office without charge, and their use of the computers was measured over the next two months (Kelley, Morrell, Park, & Mayhorn, 1999). The findings revealed that prior experience using a computer and success of initial training were the best predictors of continued computer use. A study (Echt, Morrell, & Park, 1998) of 92 community-dwelling older adults confirmed that young-old adults (60–74 years) made fewer errors, required less assistance, and took less time for training than did old-old adults (75–89 years). The investigators concluded, however, that some of the initial training problems, such as managing mouse movements (also found by Hendrix & Sakauye, 2001, to be a major difficulty for elders), may disappear with practice, as the older adults become more familiar and therefore more comfortable with both the hardware and software. Overall, Echt and colleagues (1998) interpreted their findings to suggest that older adults are capable of acquiring computer skills when instructions are designed to take into consideration changes in cognition associated with aging. An age-sensitive instructional format would seem to be of utmost importance, given that success of original training is the best predictor of continued use of the computer.

APPLICATIONS OF TECHNOLOGY
TO IMPROVE HEALTH

Electronic technologies hold particular potential as a medium for disseminating health information to the older segment of the population. More than a third (35.7%) of the respondents in the Elderlearning Survey expressed an interest in learning about health and nutrition, and there is growing empirical evidence that educational programming based on computer technology has the potential to actually improve the health status of older persons (Lamdin & Fugate, 1997). Use of the computer-based Comprehensive Health Enhancement Support System, designed to help elders 65–85 years of age monitor their health status and make health decisions, resulted in a significant reduction in probability of hospital admission and length of stay (Gustafson, Gustafson, & Wackerbarth, 1997). Computer-assisted programs for seniors also have been used to disseminate information about stroke (McNeely, 1991) and to reduce the deleterious effects of providing care for persons with Alzheimer's disease (Brennan, Moore, & Smyth, 1991). Hendrix and Sakauye (2001) suggest that having access to health-related Web documents may promote empowerment and an enhanced sense of control in older adults. However, such positive reports of the actual and potential benefits of Web-based health information for older adults must be tempered with the reality that 73% of Americans 60 and older do not have access to a computer either at home or at work (*SeniorNet*, 2001). While some may utilize the computer resources available at local public libraries, others may face barriers imposed by limited mobility or transportation difficulties, which prohibit their access. Therefore, while widespread dissemination of health information to elders via the Internet may not be feasible at this time, the Web seems certain to increase in its importance as a health information source to future cohorts of older adults.

Park's extensive work utilizing technology to measure adherence and assist elderly persons in taking their medications correctly represents one of the most clearly focused applications of technology to the promotion of health and prevention of complications among elders. Using sensitive and highly reliable measures of adherence such as medication containers with microchips in the caps and credit card sized bar code scanners, Park's team has documented that older adults take their medications much more accurately than is generally believed. In fact, they found that perfect adherence was more common among older than younger adults, with nearly half (47%) of those over 55 years making *no* medication errors in the month-long study period (Morrell,

Park, Kidder, & Martin, 1997; Park et al., 1999). The authors of both studies attributed the high number of errors among younger adults to their busier lifestyles. It is also important to bring forward Park's earlier findings that adherence can be significantly improved by using non-high technology assists such as pictorial labels, carefully adapted instructional techniques, and medication organizers that provide a day by day, hour by hour plan for taking medications (Morrell, Park, & Poon, 1989, 1990; Park & Mayhorn, 1996).

The assist with medications and health regimens is also among the most important applications of technology in terms of extending the years of actual or perceived independence. Challenges related to getting accustomed to and competent with medication taking and daily treatment regimens dominated focus group discussions with 37 community-dwelling elders living with multiple chronic health conditions (Poon, Gueldner, Penrod, Loeb, & Falkenstern, 2001). While Park's work has confirmed that most elders take their medications correctly, the vigilance required sometimes appears to consume a disproportionate amount of their time and energy. Furthermore, the abundance of medicine containers that sit on their breakfast tables is a constant reminder to them and to others that they are no longer healthy; instead they are now "on medications."

APPLICATIONS OF TECHNOLOGY
THAT FOSTER FUN AND ENGAGEMENT

For almost two decades researchers have commented on the value of computer use as an avenue of fun and mental stimulation for elders (Weisman, 1983; Zemke, 1986). Examples of such activities include playing games such as bingo and solitaire; designing and transmitting greeting cards; e-mailing communications; and accessing of information about art collections, history, and genealogy at home. Institutional settings such as nursing homes and adult day care centers are beginning to incorporate computer-assisted activities into the daily routine of their residents as a relatively inexpensive way of enriching and expanding their living environment (Post, 1996; Purnell & Sullivan-Schroyer, 1997; Weisman, 1983; Zemke, 1986).

An area that appears to have been relatively slow in developing is the use of technology to sustain and extend, rather than replace, traditional systems of social support as individuals grow older (McKay, Feil, Glasgow, & Brown, 1998). This gap is particularly noteworthy, given the documented importance of social support in cushioning the challenges that elderly persons meet in their everyday lives (Beckerman & Northrop, 1996). The future holds potential for filling this gap, since in recent years increasing numbers of older adults are using e-mail communication to stay in touch with their family members and friends. Computers provide a unique opportunity for elders to establish a special link with younger family members, helping the older person achieve and/or maintain Erikson's developmental task of generativity, which is focused on guiding future generations (Erikson, 1987). While the authors acknowledge that generativity is not an expectation of all older adults (Erikson, 1997), it certainly can remain a relevant task for some. Also, Erikson's task of integrity can be facilitated through electronic mail communications whereby elders are able to share their wisdom and an integrated heritage with younger generations (Erikson, 1987).

Although Park's team has been unable to confirm psychological benefits from computer use by elders, some research findings have reported that older persons who use computers enjoy increased self-esteem (Kautzmann, 1990; Lustbader, 1997; Purnell & Sullivan-Schroyer, 1997) and life satisfaction (Sherer, 1996), and have less depression (Lustbader, 1997). Others report that they have observed a heightened sense of productivity and accomplishment (Purnell & Sullivan-Schroyer, 1997), increased social interaction and pride (Kautzmann, 1990), and increased feelings of autonomy (McConatha, McConatha, & Dermigny, 1994). A study by Purnell and Sullivan-Schroyer (1997) reported a more upright and alert physical appearance among those who learned to use the computer. Given the extraordinary merit of such benefits to aging adults, it is important that emphasis continue to be directed toward research that tests the effect of computer applications on these variables.

In the climate of increasingly sophisticated technology, a close association must be maintained between high tech and high touch. An example demonstrating negative effects of Internet use is the HomeNet study of the social and psychological impact of the Internet on 93 families over a one- to two-year period of time. The findings of this longitudinal study revealed an association between greater Internet use and the following: waning family communication within the household, lessening size of social circles, and increased depression and loneliness (Kraut et al., 1998). The authors acknowledge that these findings may not be generalizable to elders. For instance, it is possible that elders may feel more socially isolated, and therefore may experience enhanced social interaction and psychological well-being, rather than the declines described by the adolescents and working-age adults in this study.

NOT-SO-NEW TECHNOLOGY

It is important that we not become so taken with *new* technology that we lose sight of the value of *not-so-new* technology for improving the life of older persons. A case in point is the telephone. In his eighties, the first author's father lost interest in reading the newspaper, along with other of his earlier interests. But he kept the telephone on the arm of his recliner, and he continued to be able to recall and dial *one* number without looking it up. It was the number of his somewhat younger friend Jim—"Big Jim" he called him. The two of them had been a dynamic team of lumberjacks over the years, taking pride in being able to fell a tree so accurately that they had never even crushed a nearby tomato growing on the vine. He no longer called anyone else, but he called Jim at least once a day, dialing it himself with stroke-weakened fingers, without having to ask anyone to tell him the number. His persistent and strong link to his telephone for just one call a day served as a catalyst for launching a program of inquiry into telephone use among the oldest old. Secondary analysis of data from two of our earlier studies confirmed that cognitively intact nursing home residents talked on the phone less often ($p < .005$) than their community-dwelling counterparts of similar age and health status (Gueldner, Clayton, Schroeder, Butler, & Ray, 1992; Gueldner & Spradley, 1988). Onsite follow-up revealed that *none* of the 70 nursing home residents (from five nursing homes in two states) had a telephone in their room, even through they were all capable of managing them. These data were collected before the widespread use of cell phones, but a follow-up survey of five nursing homes in the area conducted in 2001 revealed that only 12% of the residents had telephones in their rooms (Gueldner et al., 2001). Given these findings, we would take issue with Liu and Park's assertion that nearly all elders have access to telephones.

An electronic search of the literature from 1990–2000 using the primary search field of "telephone" in combination with the secondary field of "nursing home," located 29 citations. However, almost all (27) of the 29 citations reported use of the telephone as a way to access the staff to screen subjects or collect data, rather than as an intervention to enhance feelings of connectedness between residents and the outside world. Extending the search fields to include "elderly" and "social support" generated 14 additional citations, but only two of these additional studies featured the telephone as an intervention to provide social support for elders.

A study by Roberts and colleagues (1995) tested a telephone intervention as a way to provide problem-solving support for outpatients

($n = 293$) with chronic illness. Participants receiving phone calls from nurses experienced less distress than those in the control group who did not speak with a nurse. In the second study (Berkman, Heinik, Rosenthal, & Burke, 1999) a telephone outreach intervention was implemented to support 93 elderly adults living in Israel during the crisis imposed by the Gulf War. Findings demonstrated the feasibility of the telephone support intervention, and revealed that calls placed by professionals were more effective than calls placed by nonprofessionals. An early study by a team from the discipline of social work (Evans, Smith, Werkhoven, Fox, & Pritzel, 1986) implemented a cognitive therapy intervention using telephone or other electronic group conferencing in a sample of 43 community-dwelling older adults (mean age 62.4) with severe disabilities. The group who participated in the telephone intervention reported significantly decreased loneliness, as measured by the UCLA Loneliness Scale.

Czaja and Rubert (2002) conducted an intervention study where caregivers of persons with dementia ($n = 44$) were provided with a computer-integrated telephone system designed to help them access formal and informal support services, as well as information. Participants reported that the system was easy to use, valuable, and facilitated communication with other caregivers, family members, and therapists. Further, the online discussion groups and resource guide were viewed favorably. Although this study did not focus exclusively on older adult caregivers, the average age of study participants was 67.5 years, indicating that many were in fact older adults.

Inspired by our early findings and the glaring gap in the literature, our research team initiated a study to evaluate the potential of telephone communications as a relatively untapped means of social support for nursing home residents (Gueldner et al., 2001). Using a recording device that was activated each time the receiver was picked up, the research team listened in for one week on all telephone conversations of three mentally alert female nursing home residents (aged 76, 79, and 92) who had telephones at their bedsides. Two of the women lived a hundred miles or more from any family member, and one lived in the same town as her daughter.

The three women had a total of 56 minutes of actual conversation during the week (10, 21, and 25 minutes, respectively), most often with family or longtime friends who lived out of town. Conversations were transcribed verbatim from the audiotape recordings. The content of the conversations revealed that the telephone provided an irreplaceable link with family and lifelong friends the residents had known for years, in one case since childhood. Their conversations brought them glimpses into other people's lives and provided them with rich details about life beyond the walls of their facility. They spoke of everyday life, including food, weather, upcoming events and holidays, ailments and health problems. Collectively, the residents and their telephone companions reflected on the day their mutual friend died, they worried about relatives who seemed headed for unfortunate circumstances, and they "watched" children they cared about grow up. Expressions of encouragement went in both directions.

The telephone conversations also provided a rare opportunity for the residents to engage in gentle joking and laughing at their own foibles as can only occur between people who have known each other for a long time. Each resident laughed aloud at least one time during each minute they talked on the phone—a social support bargain by any measure. Perhaps as important as the 13 people they spoke with were the 44 *other* individuals mentioned during the not quite one hour of telephone conversations. No amount of contrived social support could equal the authentic, two-way support that flowed between these three residents and their tried and true friends and family members. Programmable telephones with large photo buttons, whereby the individual merely has to choose the picture of the person s/he wishes to speak with and push that button, as well as mechanisms to enhance hearing have made independent use of the telephone even easier for older adults.

DISCUSSION

The work of Liu and Park and others have made it clear that computer use can promote older people's abilities and enhance their opportunity to actualize their human potential even into their latest years. Emerging technologies hold promise for widespread improvement in elderly people's interaction with the world beyond their immediate living circumstances. Computers provide elders with a unique way to remain connected to their world. Although separated by distance, they, like their younger counterparts, are beginning to form virtual electronic communities using a medium that did not exist for the first half of their lives. Working on the computer doesn't require leaving one's home in bad weather, night driving, or parking. Also, the virtual environment allows them to leave behind visual images that make others perceive them as weak, old, or disabled (Lamdin & Fugate, 1997). In many instances, they can access the information even if they do not own a computer linking the telephone and the Internet. During the focus group study with community-dwelling elders mentioned earlier, one older gentleman, upon being asked how he obtained his health information replied, with a twinkle in his eye, "[I] call my daughter and ask her to look it up on the Internet" (Poon et al., 2001). This anecdote serves as an example of a fairly common and important information-seeking technique used by elders, that of asking others to help them access online information.

We wholeheartedly agree with Liu and Park's recommendation that teaching and training of elders in the use of technology be designated as a national priority. Otherwise, a generation of elders will be compromised by their inability to access and use Internet-based information. Their point is also well made that coming generations of elders will bring with them a number of years of experience using and enjoying the Internet and other technologies, and therefore will probably not need such concentrated training programs. This point helps the reader to see that the cost of such training would not necessarily become an ongoing budgetary strain for society. The authors' visionary suggestion that ability to communicate via the Internet be added to the list of IADLs for the twenty-first century at first may seem unrealistic, but becomes more reasonable when the reader is reminded that the telephone is the only technological device included on the original list of IADLs.

Beyond individual gains, there are important policy implications as well. Given the benefits that computer technology offers to all segments of the population, it is imperative that policies be introduced that will offset and overcome the potential inequities that presently surround access to computers by elders (Hendrix, 2000). Those who do not have access—at any age—are placed at great risk of losing their place in the mainstream. Use of computer technology has particular value for elderly persons who experience limitations in physical abilities and mobility (Kautzmann, 1990). Without access to computers, persons with such limitations cannot participate fully as members of the community. As a society, we must continue to look for ways to ensure that elderly people are given the opportunity to access computers and to learn the specific skills needed for Internet use. We also must be sure that older adults have the help they need to use all technology that is available to others, including both the new and not-so-new. In fact, Bickson and Bickson (2001) indicate that it is time to consider a public funding measure to assure Internet access for all. While the financial factor is a consideration for elders on fixed or limited incomes, the actual cost of purchasing a computer is decreasing. However, the cost of broadband Internet service continues to be substantially more expensive than traditional dial-up Internet access, and remains a substantive financial issue for elders with limited resources (U.S. Department of Commerce, 2002). It is also important that attention be directed to the point made by Park and Liu that the focus needs to shift from getting older persons to be *receptive* to technology to making technology *easier* for them to use. Training programs should also alert elders to potentially harmful "illusion of truth" issues such as those described by Liu and Park.

The health care system of Western culture has traditionally been more focused on cure and restorative measures associated with disease than on the preservation of health. However, once the disease process appears, it may be too late to make the most effective use of technology to regain or retain health. Therefore, as health applications of technology develop, the repertoire should be expanded to increase the capacity of elders for maintaining their health, including the preservation of function, rather than on disease management and restorative processes.

In closing, we would add our support to the recurring reservation that has been expressed by other colleagues, that we must be careful not to *overrely* on contemporary and evolving technology to achieve the "promise of independent living." Not every limitation imposed by the aging process can be corrected by technology. Therefore, we should not count so heavily on technology that we abandon, or underestimate, the innate resilience of the human spirit to retain independence—and to help others to achieve it—sometimes when it seems impossible. It is also important that we continue to respect the power of words and stories, and of music, art, wonder, beauty, and other expressions that have unique meaning for humans. And whatever else we may do, we must continue to apply the computer and future technologies to enhance human communications.

REFERENCES

Baltes, P. B. (1987). Theoretical propositions of life-span developmental psychology: On the dynamics between growth and decline. *Developmental Psychology, 23,* 611–626.

Baltes, P. B., & Baltes, M. M. (Eds.). (1990). *Successful aging: Perspectives from the behavioral sciences.* New York: Cambridge University Press.

Beckerman, A., & Northrop, C. (1996). Hope, chronic illness and the elderly. *Journal of Gerontological Nursing, 22*(5), 19–25.

Berkman, P., Heinik, J., Rosenthal, M., & Burke, M. (1999). Supportive telephone outreach as an interventional strategy for elderly patients in a period of crisis. *Social Work in Health Care, 28*(4), 63–76.

Bickson, K. L., & Bickson, T. K. (2001). The impact of internet use over time on older adults: A field experiment. In N. Charness, D. C. Parks, & B. A. Sabel (Eds.), *Communication, technology and aging: Opportunities and challenges for the future.* New York: Springer.

Brennan, P. F., Moore, S. M., & Smyth, K. A. (1991). ComputerLink: Electronic support for the home caregiver. *Advances in Nursing Science, 13*(4), 14–27.

Czaja, S. J., & Rubert, M. P. (2002). Telecommunications technology as an aid to family caregivers of persons with dementia. *Psychosomatic Medicine, 64,* 469–476.

Echt, K. V., Morrell, R. W., & Park, D. C. (1998). Effects of age and training formats on basic computer skill acquisition in older adults. *Educational Gerontology, 24,* 3–25.

Erikson, E. H. (1987). *A way of looking at things: Selected papers from 1930 to 1980.* New York: Norton.

Erikson, J. M. (1997). *The life cycle completed: Extended version.* New York: Norton.

Evans, R. L., Smith, K. M., Werkhoven, W. S., Fox, H. R., & Pritzel, D. O. (1986). Cognitive telephone group therapy with physically disabled elderly persons. *The Gerontologist, 26*(1), 8–11.

Gueldner, S. H., Bramlett, M. H., Dye, M., Hertzog, L., Neal, M., Penrod, J., Ryder, J., & Smith, C. A. (2001). Patterns of telephone use among nursing home residents. *Journal of Gerontological Nursing, 27,* 35–41.

Gueldner, S., Clayton, G., Schroeder, M. A., Butler, S., & Ray, J. (1992). Environmental interaction patterns among institutionalized and non-institutionalized older adults. *Physical and Occupational Therapy in Geriatrics, 11*(1), 37–53.

Gueldner, S. H., & Spradley, J. (1988). Outdoor walking lowers fatigue. *Journal of Gerontological Nursing, 14*(10), 6–12.

Gustafson, D. H., Gustafson, R. C., & Wackerbarth, S. (1997). CHESS: Health information and decision support for patients and families. *Generations, 21*(3), 56–58.

Hendrix, C. C. (2000). Computer use among elderly people. *Computers in Nursing, 18*(2), 62–71.

Hendrix, C. C., & Sakauye, K. M. (2001). Teaching elderly individuals on computer use. *Journal of Gerontological Nursing, 27*(6), 47–56.

Kautzmann, L. N. (1990). Introducing computers to the elderly. *Physical and Occupational Therapy in Geriatrics, 9*(1), 27–36.

Kelley, C. L., Morrell, R. W., Park, D. C., & Mayhorn, C. B. (1999). Predictors of electronic bulletin board system use in older adults. *Educational Gerontology, 25,* 19–35.

Kliegl, R., & Baltes, P. B. (1987). Theory-guided analysis of mechanisms of development and aging mechanisms through testing-the-limits and research on expertise. In C. Schooler & K. W. Schaie (Eds.), *Cognitive functioning and social structure over the life course* (pp. 95–119). Norwood, NJ: Ablex.

Kraut, R., Patterson, M., Lundmark, V., Kiesler, S., Mukopadhyay, T., & Scherlis, W. (1998). Internet paradox: A social technology that reduces social involvement and psychological well-being. *American Psychologist, 53,* 1017–1031.

Lamdin, L., & Fugate, M. (1997). *Elderlearning: New frontier in an aging society.* Phoenix, AZ: Oryx.

Lawton, M. P., & Brody, E. M. (1969). Assessment of older people: Self-maintaining and instrumental activities of daily living. *The Gerontologist, 9,* 179–186.

Lustbader, W. (1997). On bringing older people into the computer age. *Generations, 21*(3), 30–32.

McConatha, D., McConatha, J. T., & Dermigny, R. (1994). The use of interactive computer services to enhance the quality of life for long-term care residents. *The Gerontologist, 34,* 553–556.

McKay, H. G., Feil, E. G., Glasgow, R. E., & Brown, J. E. (1998). Feasibility and use of an Internet support service for diabetes management. *The Diabetes Educator, 24,* 174–179.

McNeely, E. (1991). Computer assisted instruction and the older-adult learner. *Educational Gerontology, 17,* 229–237.

Morrell, R. W., Park, D. C., Kidder, D. P., & Martin, M. (1997). Adherence to antihypertensive medications across the life span. *The Gerontologist, 37,* 609–619.

Morrell, R. W., Park, D. C., Mayhorn, C. B., & Kelley, C. L. (2000). Effects of age and instructions on teaching older adults to use ELDERCOMM, an electronic bulletin board system. *Educational Gerontology, 26,* 221–235.

Morrell, R. W., Park, D. C., & Poon, L. W. (1989). Effects of the quality of instructions on memory and comprehension of prescription information in young and old adults. *The Gerontologist, 29,* 345–353.

Morrell, R. W., Park, D. C., & Poon, L. W. (1990). Effects of labeling techniques on memory and comprehension of prescription information in young and old adults. *Journal of Gerontology: Psychological Sciences, 45,* 166–172.

Park, D. C. (2001, October). *Enhancing independent functioning through technology.* Paper presented at the meeting of the Penn State Social Structure Conference, University Park, PA.

Park, D. C., Hertzog, C., Leventhal, H., Morrell, R. W., Leventhal, E., Birchmore, D., et al. (1999). Medication adherence in rheumatoid arthritis patients: Older is wiser. *Journal of the American Geriatrics Society, 47,* 172–183.

Park, D. C., & Mayhorn, C. B. (1996). Remembering to take medications: The importance of nonmemory variables. In D. Herrmann, C. McEvoy, C. Hertzog, P. Hertel, & M. K. Johnson (Eds.), *Basic and applied memory research: Practical applications, vol. 2* (pp. 95–110). Mahwah, NJ: Erlbaum.

Poon, L. W., Gueldner, S. H., Penrod, J., Loeb, S. J., & Falkenstern, S. (2001). *Living with multiple chronic health conditions phase II: Managing consequences in everyday life.* Washington, DC: American Society of Retired Persons Andrus Foundation.

Post, J. A. (1996). Internet resources on aging: Seniors on the net. *The Gerontologist, 36,* 565–569.

Purnell, M., & Sullivan-Schroyer, P. (1997). Nursing home residents using computers: The Winchester house experience. *Generations, 21*(3), 61–62.

Roberts, J., Browne, G. B., Streiner, D., Gafni, A., Pallister, R., Hoxby, H., et al. (1995). Problem-solving counseling or phone-call support for outpatients with chronic illness: Effective for whom? *Canadian Journal of Nursing Research, 27*(3), 111–137.

SeniorNet Market Information and Trends. (2001, September, 4). Retrieved January 28, 2002, from http://www.seniornet.org/php/default.php?PageID=6040&Version=0&Font=0.

Sherer, M. (1996). The impact of using personal computers on the lives of nursing residents. *Physical and Occupational Therapy in Geriatrics, 14*, 13–31.

Staudinger, U., Marsiske, M., & Baltes, P. B. (1995). Resilience and reserve capacity in later adulthood: Potentials and limits of development across the life span. In D. Cicchetti & C. Cohen (Eds.), *Developmental psychopathology, vol. II: Risk, disorder and adaption* (pp. 801–847). New York: Wiley.

U.S. Department of Commerce. (2002, February). *A nation online: How Americans are expanding their use of the Internet.* Retrieved July 1, 2002, from http://www.ntia.doc.gov/ntiahome/dn/nationonline020502.pd.

Verhaeghen, P., Morcoen, A., & Goosens, L. (1992). Improving memory performance in the aged through mnemonic training: A meta-analytic study. *Psychology and Aging, 7*, 242–251.

Weisman, S. (1983). Computer games for the frail elderly. *The Gerontologist, 23*, 361–363.

Willis, S. L., & Schaie, K. W. (1986). Training the elderly on the ability factors of spatial orientation and inductive reasoning. *Psychology and Aging, 1*, 7–12.

Zemke, R. (1986). Taking a byte of the Apple: Computer activities in a senior day care center. *Physical and Occupational Therapy in Geriatrics, 4*(2), 39–48.

Author Index

Subject Index